KORESH

Dear Brethren in the Seventh-day Adventist Church:

I Am the Son of [...] My name. I ha[...] north and My travels are from the rising of the sun.

All the prophets of the Bible speak of Me. I Am The Branch, Isaiah 4:2; The Serpent, Isaiah 5:26; The Immanuel, Isaiah 7:14; The Root, Isaiah 11:10; The Holy One, Isaiah 12:6; The Voice, Isaiah 13:2; The Fiery Flying Serpent, Isaiah 14:29; The Lamb, Isaiah 16:1; The Stammerer, Isaiah 28:11; The King, Isaiah 32:1; The Righteous Man from the East, Isaiah 41:2; The Elect, Isaiah 42:1; The Ravenous Bird, Isaiah 46:11; The Loved One, Isaiah 48:14; The Sharp Sword, Isaiah 49:2; The Learned, Isaiah 50:4; The Arm, Isaiah Ravenous Bird, Isaiah 46:11; The Loved One, Isaiah 48:14; The Sharp Sword, Isaiah 49:2; The Learned, Isaiah 50:4; The Arm, Isaiah 51:9; The Isaiah 55:3,

I have been rejected in the person of My prophets over and over. I have seven eyes and seven horns. My Name is the Word of God and I ride on a white horse (Rev. 19:11). I Am here on earth to give you the Seventh Angel's Message (Rev. 10:7).

of David is in My hand. I only can open the prophecies of David and Solomon. I have ascended from the east with the seal of the living God. My Name is Cyrus and I Am here to destroy Babylon (Rev. 9:14). I have come in a way that is contrary to your preconceived ideas. I will reprove you for your world loving. I will scold your daughters for their nakedness and pride that they parade in My Father's house and by My angels will strip them naked before all eyes because of their foolish pride. Read Isaiah 3:13-26.

The young men will abuse My kindness. They will take My life, but I will arise and take theirs forever more.

You ministers will lam[ent] Your lost flock will tear [...]

I Am the Word and you do not know Me. I ride on a white horse and My Name is secret. Psalm 45 is My invitation to you for extended mercy. I will visit you at your unholy feast. Isaiah 3:13; 12:6; Daniel 2:44; Hosea 2:21...

Am The Branch, Isaiah 4:2; The Serp[ent], Isaiah 5:26; The Immanuel, Isaiah 7:14; Root, Isaiah 11:10; The Holy One, Is[aiah] The Fiery Fl[ying] [La]mb, Isaiah 1[6:1]; The K[ing] Isaiah 32:1; The Righteous Man from East, Isaiah 41:2; The Elect, Isaiah 42:1; Ravenous Bird, Isaiah 46:11; The Loved [One] Isaiah 48:14; The Sharp Sword, Isaiah 4[9:2] The Learned, Isaiah 50:4; The Arm, Is[aiah] 51:9; The Servant, Isaiah 52:13; Da[vid] Isaiah 55:3, 4.

I have been rejected in the person of [My] prophets over and over. I have seven e[yes] and seven horns. My Name is the Wor[d of] God and I ride on a white horse (Rev. 19:[11]). I Am here on earth to give you the Sev[enth]

I have been rejected in the person [of My] prophets over and over. I have seven [eyes] and seven horns. My Name is the We[rd of] God and I ride on a white horse (Rev. 1[9:11]). [give y]ou the Se[venth]

I Am the prophets; all of them. I want to [...]

The young men will abuse My kindness. T[hey] will take My life, but I will arise and [take] theirs forever more.

You ministers will lament your foolishne[ss] Your lost flock will tear you to pieces.

I Am the Word and you do not know Me. I r[ide] on a white horse and My Name is sec[ret]. Psalm 45 is My invitation to you for exten[ded] mercy. I will visit you at your unholy fe[ast]. Isaiah 3:13; 12:6; Daniel 2:44; Hosea 2:[...] 2:5; 4:6; Joel 3:16, 17; Amos 1:2; [...]

Your lost flock will tear you to piec[es]

I Am the Word and you do not kno[w Me] on a white horse and My Name [...] Psalm 45 is My invitation to you f[or] mercy. I will visit you at your u[nholy] Isaiah 3:13; 12:6; Daniel 2:44; H[...] 3:16, 17; Amos[...] [Hab]akkuk 3:13; Zep[...] Malachi 1:11; 4:[...] nies, vol. 2, p. 190, 191.

PREPARE TO MEET THY GOD.

KORESH

The True Story of

DAVID KORESH

and the

TRAGEDY AT WACO

Stephan Talty

MARINER BOOKS | New York | Boston

All photos courtesy of the author unless otherwise noted.

KORESH. Copyright © 2023 by Stephan Talty. All rights reserved. Printed in the United States of America. No part of this book may be used or reproduced in any manner whatsoever without written permission except in the case of brief quotations embodied in critical articles and reviews. For information, address HarperCollins Publishers, 195 Broadway, New York, NY 10007.

HarperCollins books may be purchased for educational, business, or sales promotional use. For information, please email the Special Markets Department at SPsales@harpercollins.com.

FIRST EDITION

Designed by Chloe Foster

Title page art courtesy of Texas State University.

Library of Congress Cataloging-in-Publication Data has been applied for.

ISBN 978-0-358-58128-4

23 24 25 26 27 LBC 5 4 3 2 1

For Delphine,
my darling girl

"Immense sadness everywhere; immense power."

—JOHN JAY CHAPMAN

CONTENTS

PART VI: MY STRANGE WORK

AUTHOR'S NOTE

This is a work of nonfiction, based on interviews, FBI and 911 transcripts, television and radio transcripts, taped sermons, and published sources. No characters or scenes have been invented. All the dialogue is as recorded or reported to me by people who heard it directly firsthand.

This book contains scenes of sexual assault and other forms of violence.

PROLOGUE

O N SUNDAY AFTERNOON, March 28, 1993, David Koresh was in a bitter mood. Dressed in a white wifebeater and jeans, he lay on the second floor of the Branch Davidian compound, his back propped against a wall, on the phone with the FBI. They had cut off the electricity, so the dark interior of the building was lit by candles, and quite cold.

The phone line snaked out of the compound, across land where FBI snipers studied the compound windows, and connected to a phone at a temporary headquarters a few miles away. There, a team of five negotiators—primary, secondary, technical adviser; note taker; and team leader—sat in a minimally furnished room, listening and talking.

It was exactly one month into the siege at Waco, and Koresh felt the FBI was messing with his manhood. They'd invaded his home, scoffed at his Bible teachings, and rutted the land around his home with their tanks. Agents had given him the finger and even pulled down their pants to moon his followers. He was fed up.

"You boys are murderers," he said. "You boys are killers. My country has dealt with me and people I love in a way that's not right . . . What you've done about it is you've disrespected my personage . . . You've disrespected my religion."

The primary tried to calm him. David's mood could turn easily, the FBI had found. At times, he seemed to want to befriend the negotiators, guys mostly in their thirties and forties. In his drawling voice, he even told them he loved them. David had an old-boy charm about him that could work on your mind. He wished he could meet up one day with the

FBI agents, he said, have a beer or two. Maybe they'd ride their motorcycles around Lake Waco.

There were times when their talks seemed more like therapy than negotiations. David's mind roamed back to his childhood in the small towns of North Texas, his family life, schooldays. He talked about what things might have been like if he'd done something differently here or there. Maybe he could have been a true-blue American hero, like the FBI's own Eliot Ness.

DAVID: "If the president of the United States had come to me one day and says, you know, 'Mr. Howell, I want you to work with the United States of America, you've been a good citizen. I've seen your report cards . . . You've been a good citizen and I want you to work on a tactical force with the FBI and I want you to help deal with, with bad guys and everything and I'd like to give you this position . . .'"

Across the staticky phone line, his voice was warm.

"I would have been so honored and so proud . . . ," he went on, "that somebody would have overlooked my apparent bad English and bad history. You know what I mean?"

It was moving, in a way. The negotiators knew that David lied about things and made up stories about himself, but there were times when he seemed to lose his defenses and then he was remarkably human.

The negotiators encouraged him. *Who knows,* they said, *you might beat the charges. Stranger things have happened. Just come on out, David, and you'll see your life isn't over.* More than thirty Davidians and their children had left the compound during the siege, with the last departing five days before. Loud music blared day and night, high-powered spotlights lit up the building's façade, and the engines of Bradley vehicles growled and rumbled through the night.

Inevitably, the conversation would turn. Sometimes, the old memories called back old resentments. "Let me explain something to you," David railed one night. "You are taking me as a fool."

"Absolutely untrue," the negotiator replied. But David went on in the same vein. He was certain the agents were lying to him. They were like IBM computers, each repeating the same words from the same script in remarkably similar voices. Inhuman men. David hinted that he'd dealt with a long line of older dudes just like them that stretched back to his infancy. It was as if the voices of all the hard-asses that had tried to whip him into submission for three decades had been put on a tape that was being played back to him on a loop, over and over and over again.

"You know, you're gonna be punished," he said to the agent. "Your reasoning, your controlled oration, you know, your . . . unconcernment for the situation. You're a cold heart. You're just a freezer, you know what I'm saying? Like I said, you know, you remind me of, like my dad, my stepdad . . ."

"You didn't say he was such a bad guy, though," the negotiator replied.

"Oh, I told you," David said. "I said we never really knew him . . . Oh, yeah, he was bad. He was a gangster."

Part I

CHILD OF THE LONE STAR

1

BONNIE

EARLY IN THE morning of August 17, 1959, Bonnie Clark got out of bed and hurried down to the bathroom of her parents' house in Houston. Her stomach was giving her trouble.

She was just fourteen years old and nine months pregnant, her swollen belly on her slim frame noticeable enough to draw stares on the street. A pregnant teenager was still a topic of gossip in small-town Texas in the late fifties. Throughout her pregnancy, Bonnie had felt the judging eyes of others.

That night, the pain wouldn't let up. Bonnie went back and forth between her bed and the bathroom. Her mother called out to her from her bedroom.

"Let me see what's wrong," she said.

Bonnie told her it was just a stomachache.

Her mother spoke from the dark room. "You're going to have that baby."

The two of them tried to wake Bonnie's daddy, Vernon, to drive them to the hospital, but he was half-drunk from the night before and didn't want to go. Finally, they dragged him outside to the truck and got on the road to the hospital.

It might have been Vernon Clark's hangover that made him reluctant to leave his bed, but it might have been the baby, too. Bonnie's family had been deeply hurt when she turned up pregnant. An already fractious relationship with her father had turned to acid.

For as long as she'd been alive, Bonnie's father had been a menacing presence in her life. The family never learned the origins of Clark's rage, but they had their suspicions. He'd endured a rough childhood. His father had passed away when he was eight, and his mother had taken up with a series of boyfriends, none of which seemed to have made any emotional connection with the young boy.

Clark had made it through high school and, in the wake of Pearl Harbor, joined the Army. After the war, he married Erline, who came from a more well-off family than his own, then led his growing clan through years of wandering East Texas in search of better prospects. He tried his hand at different jobs that rarely lasted long and sent the family shuffling through a series of rented houses all across the state—Atascosa, Houston, Little Elm.

Clark even tried farming. But he battled stiff headwinds as he tried to make a living for his family, which would eventually grow to seven children. In 1949, when Bonnie was just four, a severe drought struck Texas, cutting the amount of rainfall the state received by as much as half. Rivers dried up, topsoil turned to dust, and crop yields plummeted. Fifty percent of the state's farming industry was wiped out, with a ripple effect on the remainder of the economy. Clark struggled to find stable financial footing.

There was, though, always money for alcohol. Over the years Clark turned into a snake-mean blackout drunk who beat Erline and tormented his children. Bonnie's brother Gary ran away when he was twelve, on account of her father whipping on him. Another son joined the Navy at fifteen. For the Clark kids, home was nothing to brag on.

Clark finally did eventually find a decent job—as a carpenter who framed houses—and stuck on that. But they never had any real money. Later on, the Clarks were able to afford a car, but when Bonnie was young, if you wanted to get somewhere, you walked.

For her schooling, Bonnie's parents sent her to a Seventh-day Adventist school in Houston. Both her parents were devoted followers of the church. The Clarks were too poor to pay the tuition, so when lunchtime came, Bonnie had to work in the kitchen, cutting potatoes and doing scut work. After school, she turned into a janitor and cleaned the bathrooms, scrubbing the toilets and replacing the toilet paper. It didn't do much for her self-image.

Bonnie was shy at school and found it hard to make friends. She had red hair that made her feel weird. "What is wrong with me?" she thought to herself. Even her name, Bonnie Sue, seemed to stick in her mouth when she said it.

At school, Bonnie learned about God, the multiplication tables, the correct Sabbath day—Saturday, not Sunday—and about sex. Namely, that it was bad. The Seventh-day Adventists were a socially conservative church, and that was especially true when it came to relations between men and women. Its pastors had long taught that people have a finite amount of "vital force," given to them by God, and that discharging fluids during sex depletes that force. This attitude had withered somewhat by the 1950s, but premarital sex was still considered shameful and wrong.

By the time Bonnie reached her teenage years, she'd overcome her bashfulness. Rebelling against her parents' strict Adventist mores, she grew wild. Her parents tried to keep her home, but Bonnie wanted to wear makeup, meet boys, party, and live her life. If they grounded her, she'd just run away.

When she was thirteen, she met Bobby Wayne Howell. He was eighteen and almost as hot-blooded as she was. Bobby drove fast and did what he wanted. Bonnie thought he was a catch.

One day, Bobby drove her to school in his pickup. Just as she was getting ready to open the door, he leaned over and kissed her right on the mouth. And who spotted him doing it but the school principal. He marched Bonnie into his office and expelled her on the spot. Low morals and all.

Much to her parent's chagrin, Bonnie was forced to enroll in public school. But that didn't turn her off Bobby. A relationship—tumultuous and marked by frequent blowups—began.

When she reached eighth grade, Bonnie asked her mother and father if she could marry Bobby. In Texas, there was no minimum age when it came to marriage; if a judge approved, a child of any age could wed. But the Clarks said no. A thirteen-year-old bride might be technically legal, and it wasn't that uncommon in their part of East Texas, especially in poor and working-class families. But her Adventist parents, spurred on by their faith, wanted no part of it.

A few months later, Bonnie was pregnant.

Vernon and Erline were distraught. The Clarks might be rednecks, but a pregnant young girl was a blot on the family name. Unwed mothers, especially teens, were regarded as "morally corrupt" in Texas in the 1950s. Often, they were forced to leave school and hide away with aunts or uncles in other states until they had their babies. Later, Texas introduced a "homebound" program where teachers visited young mothers in their houses, so they didn't have to appear in public.

Another option was institutions for wayward girls. There, the young mothers' mail was opened and censored, visits were forbidden, and the girls were forced to wear fake wedding rings when they ventured outside. Psychologists of that era even theorized that unwed moms were not only sinful, but unable to raise a well-adjusted child.

Abortion, if Bonnie considered it, was risky. The procedure was illegal in Texas—as it remains today, the moment a fetal heartbeat is detected—and doctors who performed it could go to prison for two to five years. The Adventists were strongly against it, too. Even today, the church considers abortion "out of harmony with God's plan for human life."

Bonnie very much wanted to marry Bobby and dodge the stigma she knew would fall on herself and her family. The couple talked about it, but as Bonnie's belly grew, the ceremony never happened. Bobby's version of things went like this: He and Bonnie went to have their blood tests, which many states had mandated since the 1930s in order to fight syphilis and other STDs. They got those done and headed to the clerk to get a marriage license. But Bonnie hadn't brought her birth certificate, and you needed one to obtain a license. Her parents didn't have a copy, so Bonnie sent away for one.

While they were waiting, Bonnie's friend told her about this nightclub in downtown Houston and they went one night without Bobby. They were there until nearly the break of dawn. When Bonnie got home, Bobby was waiting for her, spitting mad. They got into it right there on the sidewalk. It was a bad fight, and they both said things that wounded the other. The marriage was called off.

Bonnie told it differently. In her version, the couple did get the marriage license and even set a date for the wedding. But on the day of,

Bobby got cold feet and left her at the altar. Bonnie could have written a whole diary on the bad influences of men in her life, and Bobby would have been Exhibit #2, after her dad. Bobby even had a girlfriend the whole time she was pregnant, one he would marry soon after Bonnie gave birth.

Bonnie dropped out of school and waited out her term at home. As she grew more visibly pregnant, her shame was there for everyone to see. Bobby never even came to the hospital.

On August 17, at 8:49 a.m., Bonnie had the baby. The nurses laid the infant on her lap while they got ready to cut the cord. He was crying and making a fuss. Bonnie looked at the squirming little boy and realized that she, Bonnie Sue Clark, had a child now. It was a big, warm feeling; she felt close to the little thing, and hopeful for better things to come.

Bonnie decided to christen the baby Vernon Wayne Howell. The first name came from his grandfather, who had never come to terms with Bonnie having a child. The middle and last name came from Bobby, who would play almost no part in his life. It was an inauspicious start.

2

VERNON

LATER IN LIFE, Vernon would tell people he was always able to sense the circumstances of his birth. Somehow, he said, he knew he wasn't the product of a love match. A hothead named Bobby Howell got a rod for Bonnie Clark and she was ready and willing. Like two animals mating. For many years, Vernon felt that lack of love like a cold spot in his chest.

Soon after the delivery, Bonnie left Vernon with her mom, Erline, in Little Elm while she went out looking for a job, visiting her young son when she had time. She worked at a nursing home, then moved on to waitressing at a Howard Johnson restaurant.

From birth until he was about two, Vernon shuttled between his two grandmothers' houses while Bonnie worked to support him. Bobby and his family took care of the baby when they could. Though he and Bonnie still weren't getting along, Bobby at least attempted to do his part.

Erline was quiet-spoken and kindly. She lavished love on the boy, and he responded in kind. As he grew, Vernon came to think of Erline as his mother, and Bonnie as his aunt. He even called Erline "Mama." No one told Vernon the truth or bothered to explain who was who in his life.

But Bonnie's dad continued to hate the very idea of the boy. When he saw Vernon, he called him "that little bastard." He never accepted the boy at all. Perhaps Bonnie had named Vernon out of simple tradition. But if she'd done it in the hope it would reconcile her father to the baby, or engender a stray spark of affection, she was mistaken. Having this fatherless child carry his name only seemed to increase Clark's enmity toward the boy. For him, Bonnie's shame covered Vernon's face like a veil.

The Clarks' house in Little Elm sat on four acres. There wasn't much to the town, just a gas station and a bunch of blue-collar people scraping by. The national economy was booming in the early sixties, and oil-rich Texas was urbanizing and growing richer along with it. But little of the money seemed to seep into the corner of East Texas where the Clarks lived.

Erline kept house, while her husband worked and drank. The elder Vernon was tetchy enough when he was sober but once he had a gutful of whiskey, he lashed out. He beat Erline with his fists, leaving bruises and other wounds on her face and body. He whipped his kids until they cowered in front of him. Vernon got his share, too.

Vernon Clark's rages seemed to shake the walls of their humble frame house. They tinged Vernon's earliest memories with anxiety. As much as he loved Erline, he lived in fear of his grandfather, the primary male figure in his life.

Later on, Vernon would tell his followers that he stuttered as a boy. Bonnie and the others remembered the opposite. If they went camping and were sitting around the fire, it was Vernon who would start telling stories about ghosts and haunted woods and the rest of it.

But, looking back, Vernon swore that he had a stammer. Maybe he felt he couldn't really say what he thought, or he felt throttled by the heavy mood inside the Little Elm house, and this stayed in his memory as a speech impediment. It was as if he had to keep quiet, to conceal parts of himself in order to survive.

Once Vernon was old enough to walk, he liked zigzagging around his mother's house at supersonic speed. The boy was hyper; his family began calling him Sputnik, after the Soviet satellite, because he wouldn't stop moving. Once, he put a water hose in the gas tank of the family car and filled it up. He was trying to be helpful, but at times it was like he tried too hard to please.

Erline enrolled Vernon in Seventh-day Adventist Sabbath school when he was four or five. He was excited to go.

The SDA church had originated in upstate New York in the 1840s, where William Miller, a Baptist lay preacher, began an intensive reading of the Bible with the sense that deep prophecies were hidden within its words. He focused on the Book of Revelation and its tales of the End Times.

Miller preached that once the Antichrist arrived on earth, the drama of the last days would begin. Pestilence, anarchy, war. Then Jesus would come to establish New Jerusalem and reign over his kingdom. His followers would rise into heaven and begin their eternal lives.

Miller finally settled on a date for the Second Coming: October 22, 1844. He called his followers to await the messiah's arrival. Thousands of Americans sold their homes and belongings, sure that they would soon be fighting as soldiers in Christ's army. But when the day arrived, nothing happened. Miller's followers sobbed, tore their hair out, and returned in despair to their shattered lives.

Out of the shards of the Great Disappointment, as Miller's fiasco was named, several churches arose. One was the Seventh-day Adventists. The church was still focused on Jesus's return, though, stung by the memory of Miller's prophecies, its founders never set a date for the Second Coming.

The church taught things that you'd find in other Protestant congregations: the Trinity, the need for salvation, the supreme authority of the Bible. But it also believed in things that went against the Christian mainstream. It taught that the true Sabbath was Saturday, not Sunday. And it promoted the teachings of its great prophet, Ellen White, as being the products of divine visions. White served as a conduit for God to correct mistakes in Christian doctrines and to assure the faithful of the essential truth of their beliefs. She interpreted the Scripture's more obscure symbols and showed how different passages in the Bible chimed with one another, revealing deeper truths. Like Joseph Smith of the Mormons, another sect that was rising in the mid-nineteenth century, White pioneered a new, American-born faith.

The Adventists believed that men and women were judged by their creator while still alive, not after death. And it stressed a proper diet, a

Kosher one inherited from Judaism. (Adventists believed that they, not the Jews, were the true chosen people.)

The SDA was a church steeped in prophecy. It believed that one day the earth would be scraped clean with fire and the righteous would march with Jesus. It was all there in the Book of Revelation.

Vernon soaked in these teachings every Saturday when Erline took him to church, and then again in Sabbath school. After his first day there, he came home brimming with excitement. "I'll never forget," he told Bonnie. "I remember the room and walking up the stairs." They called the room "cradle row." It was a kindergarten. "Oh! That room was so pretty . . . It had flowers in it and all kinds of toys. It was just beautiful."

At home, Vernon considered himself a real country boy. He loved to take his dog, his bike, and his fishing rod and pedal like crazy to a nearby pond. Fishing offered an escape from his grandfather's fury. As did shooting. There were always guns around the Clark home. Vernon had an old Marlin .22, and a single-shot 410 shotgun. He'd go out and hunt quail with one or the other.

When he wasn't out roaming the woods, Vernon loved to watch TV. He was lucky in this regard; many SDA families forbid televisions in their homes, as the church frowned upon secular entertainment. But Erline and her husband had a thirteen-inch black-and-white set that got the three main channels.

Westerns ruled the airwaves. *Wagon Train, Daniel Boone, Gunsmoke*— the number one show in America the year Vernon was born—and other cowboy stories were all the rage. Every night of the week featured a different show, each with a theme woven into the story: good vs. evil, law vs. anarchy. Reruns of *The Rifleman*, starring Chuck Connors as a New Mexico rancher battling villains along with his son, were a favorite in the Clark home.

Vernon drank in the stories of cowboys on long cattle drives, women in prairie skirts and gingham dresses trying to bring a small touch of civilization to a frontier town, preachers comforting broken souls, sheriffs hunting for black-hatted vigilantes. There was one image he saw again and again on those nights in front of the black-and-white TV. A lone man racing across a raw, empty landscape on horseback. He was often headed toward some confrontation, or a new prospect in the next town, his rifle jostling in its holster.

It was a big country; the shows told their audience. If you could make it to the next settlement, you could reinvent yourself. Though it was true, according to many of the Westerns, that your past always followed you no matter where you went.

When Vernon was around two, Bonnie met a guy named Joe Golden, an ex-con, and with her usual rashness she decided to accept his offer of marriage. Once she'd established herself in her new home, Bonnie went to pick up Vernon from her parents' house. Vernon didn't want to stay with Bonnie and Joe. Their home lacked the warmth that Erline had been able to provide at Little Elm. If Joe and Vernon Clark were equals in their hatred of him, Erline had at least been able to provide a loving refuge that Bonnie couldn't match.

It didn't take Bonnie long to realize she'd made a mistake with Joe Golden. Once she was living with him, he started flying off the handle. He liked to beat on women, just like her father. And he had plenty to spare for Vernon, too. He'd take the boy and whip him so hard that his butt would look like a bruised plum.

One time, Vernon was playing with a toy truck. It rolled across the floor and trundled onto a heating grate set into the floor. The hot metal began to melt the wheels.

Joe spotted the truck. What ran through his mind was anyone's guess. Perhaps he saw an ungrateful stepson being careless with his things, or maybe his free-floating rage just landed on Vernon at that particular moment on that particular day. Either way, he went apeshit.

Joe grabbed Vernon and got him down on the grate, singeing his knees against the hot metal. Vernon screamed but Joe didn't let up. The scars were there for the rest of Vernon's life.

It was a pattern. All the women in Vernon's life—his grandmothers, Bonnie, her friends—fell in love with Vernon the first time they saw him. Vernon had golden hair and dimples. He was smart as a whip and he could talk a blue streak. Whatever Bonnie asked him to do, he did it. He wanted to please her, to please everyone.

He was cute as a button and sweet to go along with it. And he had his manners, too. The use of *yes, sir* and *no, ma'am* were drilled into him, as they were with most Texas children. But the men in Vernon's life took one look at Vernon and wanted nothing to do with him. First his grandfather, and then his stepfather, but there would be many others. It was as if he gave off a noxious chemical that only the male of the species could smell.

Bonnie's marriage with Joe lasted a year before he got sent back to prison on a parole violation. Before he left, he told a guy he knew named Danny to keep an eye on his wife while he was doing his time. Bonnie didn't appreciate the gesture. She wasn't a rental house to be watched over. She filed for divorce, left Vernon with her mom, and headed to Dallas for yet another fresh start.

One thing you could say about the Clarks, about their particular class of people, descendants of the famously contentious Scotch-Irish settlers who swarmed into Texas in the nineteenth century, was that they didn't let divorce or bankruptcy or even a policeman standing in their living room asking about certain matters or anything that reeked of middle-class shame hold them down too long. You might call them rednecks, but you weren't going to bully them into anything.

DALLAS

BONNIE WAS WORKING in Dallas when she met an ex-merchant Marine named Roy Haldeman. Roy was cut from the same cloth as Bobby and her dad: blue collar, drinker, rough and ready. A "macho man," Erline said after meeting him, "country-type Texan." Whether that was what Bonnie liked or whether that was all that North Texas was producing in the mid-1960s was a question that never got answered.

She met Roy in a bar that he owned, Jade Lounge. She went there to meet a friend and Roy's partner spotted her. "We've got a pretty little girl here who just came in," the partner told Roy over the phone.

"Well, put her to work," Roy said.

Bonnie picked up some shifts waitressing at the lounge, and she and Roy became friendly. Danny, the guy her ex-husband had gotten to watch over her, came into the lounge one night and tried to take her away with him. Roy told Danny to leave, then took Bonnie to another place. Danny followed. Roy opened a window in the back of the club and lifted Bonnie through it, then went around and picked her up in his car.

She thought, *my knight in shining armor*. Roy was a big, handsome dude and she loved big, handsome dudes. Soon they were hanging out.

Roy proposed marriage and Bonnie accepted. Roy was thirty-four and Bonnie was eighteen when they got married. The couple decided to move to Dallas and to take four-year-old Vernon with them. Bonnie went to her mother's house to pick Vernon up.

The boy was stunned. He'd had no idea that Bonnie was his real mother and Erline a kind of imposter. "Don't take me from my mama," he cried. "I don't want you to be my mama!" He wailed as Bonnie walked him out to the car.

Bonnie had neither the time nor the inclination to explain in a soft voice what was happening to Vernon. She just grabbed him and left. Later, she wondered, with some guilt, if Vernon ever got over the shock of it.

When she left for Dallas, Bonnie neglected to tell Bobby. She wasn't speaking much with him at the time. Bobby had no idea where she or Vernon had got to. Hoping to find out where his boy was living, Bobby went to Bonnie's brother's house in Houston. He rang the doorbell. The brother came out and gave him a message: "If you ever come back here," he said, "I'll shoot you."

That was enough for Bobby. He didn't try to track Bonnie down, and he lost touch with Vernon.

Bonnie and Roy found a place out in Richardson, north of Dallas. They moved into a green stucco house with a big barn attached, and a long white gravel driveway that led out to the main road. Vernon made the move with them. Soon after the move, Bonnie enrolled Vernon in first grade. A new baby arrived. His name was Roger, Vernon's little half brother.

Dallas was big and modern, but beneath the long shadows of the bank towers and the bright neon-red Pegasus that rotated atop the Magnolia Building, the city fed on Texas groundwater. "It was the state's feverish headquarters of anti-Communism," the historian Stephen Harrigan wrote, "anti-Catholicism, anti-Semitism, anti-fluoride, anti-federal overreach, anti-school milk programs, prosegregation activism, and pro-American militancy."

The metropolis was a mecca for hard-right conspiracists who vied to outdo one another in their prophecies. When one proclaimed that even President Dwight Eisenhower was "a conscious, dedicated agent of the Communist conspiracy," it was nothing out of the ordinary. The city's mood in the mid-sixties was increasingly wild-eyed, with ex-generals, millionaire oilmen, religious leaders, and congressmen gathering in the city's oak-paneled conference rooms to talk about how America was being led into ruin and how it might possibly be saved.

You could hear these men—they always seemed to be men—on shows beamed out from Dallas radio towers. The conservative program *Life Lines* was especially popular. Ten million Americans tuned in to AM 1090 at 6:15 p.m. every night to hear it. "The American founding fathers knew . . . ," the show's founder, Texas oil tycoon H. L. Hunt, once said, "that a democracy is the most evil kind of government possible . . . the handiwork of the devil himself . . ."

The common thread among the theories was that the federal government was in league with darkness. America's politicians wanted to destroy the republic and deliver its citizens to Satan.

Vernon likely heard these ideas early and often. If he tuned in to the radio while driving home from school with Bonnie, or if he glanced at the ultraconservative *Dallas Morning News*, or if he listened to his older relatives and family friends arguing at family gatherings, he would have grown familiar with these theories, expressed with almost violent conviction. In Dallas, paranoia was in the air. Plenty of white working-class Texans felt that Satanic powers had the country under their sway.

Grandma Erline and her family came to visit Vernon at his new home. When he saw their car pull up, he cried out in happiness. He and Erline's kids, Sharon and Kenneth—Vernon's aunt and uncle, both younger than him—ran off to play and were gone the whole day.

When evening came and it was time to leave, Sharon jumped into the back seat of their car and turned and looked out the window as the family got in. Vernon ran to his bike and came whipping up the gravel driveway, pushing the pedals for all he was worth.

His grandfather pressed the accelerator and Vernon grew smaller and smaller in the back window. As the car rolled off, he called out, "Take me with you, take me with you!" But the car didn't stop. This happened every time they visited Bonnie and Roy.

There were other outbursts. One time he visited Erline's and he and Sharon were out in back. He put some baby chicks in a little hollow underneath a board, then he got on top and started jumping on the board, up and down. When he was done, the chicks were dead. Sharon went and told on him, and Vernon was furious.

Perhaps Vernon thought he was too light to hurt the chicks. Or perhaps he was venting the terrible anger he felt at being taken away from his rightful home, the only one where, despite everything, he felt loved.

Vernon attended the local public schools in Richardson. From the beginning, going to class was a chore. The first big stumbling block was reading. Vernon couldn't do it. Other kids in his class were plowing through *When We Were Very Young* and *The Tales of Peter Rabbit*, but Vernon would pick up a book and the words would swim in front of his eyes. It was the same with the letters of the alphabet. He just couldn't see what everyone else saw.

Bonnie took him for tests and Vernon was diagnosed with a language disability, which caused problems with his reading comprehension. You would think having a name for it would make it better for Vernon, but it didn't. In class, unable to follow along in the books or with the writing on the chalkboard, his mind drifted. He found himself looking out the window, over the hedges. "What kind of bird is that?" he thought. "What kind of bee is that?"

Sometimes, when Vernon was young, Roy would take pity on him and try to teach him the alphabet. He'd go through it real slow: "A, B, C, D." Then it would be Vernon's turn.

Vernon couldn't master the first part at all. The only section he could count on getting right was "L, M, N, O, P." And that was only because he'd developed a little trick. When he came to that part, he thought of the word "minnow," because he loved fishing. So he'd say "L, Minnow, P." If he said it fast enough, it sounded like the real thing and Roy wouldn't notice and he wouldn't get angry.

One part of his brain that did work was his memory. If he watched someone fix an engine, he'd remember how to do it. The same thing happened when he looked at, say, a picture of a motorbike. Once he scanned it, he could close his eyes and re-create the thing in his mind down to the last screw. But you'd much rather be able to read and write than to remember some old picture.

When Vernon showed up at school for third grade, he was in a small class, just a handful of other kids. The teachers were nice. "Well now, class, you're special students and we have more teachers to be able to help you," one of them said. Vernon thought that was just great.

When it was time for recess, he and the others went zooming out into the schoolyard, making a beeline for the swings. The other kids in the schoolyard saw them and started laughing: "Here come the retards!" they shouted.

Vernon stopped dead. He hadn't realized he was in a class with "the specials." It was like his world had gone dark.

He staggered through the day. After school, Bonnie came to get him, her car idling at the curb. He walked toward it and got in. As soon as the door closed, he burst into sobs. "I'm in retarded class," he said.

Bonnie tried her best. "You're not in retarded class," she said. "You just have a learning disability." But that was just sugarcoating it.

The school bullies homed in on Vernon almost from day one. Not only was he in the slow class, but he was shy. The large, metal-rimmed glasses he began wearing to correct his vision didn't help, either.

Whenever he'd try to play basketball or climb on the swings in the schoolyard, the kids would gather around him. They chanted "Retard, retard," or "Four eyes." After third grade, they switched to "Mr. Retardo," which stuck for years.

Vernon worked hard to get decent grades, but the learning disability messed everything up. One class he excelled in, however, was civics. It was the only period he did well in, earning an A+.

He loved everything about civics. He loved saluting the flag and reciting the Pledge of Allegiance. He loved learning about being a good citizen and how Congress worked and all that. In his heart, he knew he was the truest, bluest American there was. Something in him yearned to be part of something bigger than himself, something glorious on its own terms.

In fourth grade, when Vernon was nine or ten, he took the required class on Texas history (with another coming in seventh grade). There he learned about the Anglos who'd settled the territory in the 1800s, many of them Scotch-Irish men and women famous for their individualism and irascible, feuding natures.

Vernon didn't know much about his family's past. Bonnie did talk about how her mother came from an English clan called the Tillmans, who had money. Her father's people were Scotch-Irish, originally from Kentucky, rough-and-ready men who wore guns and drank harder than they should have. Folks Bonnie's generation might call hillbillies. But that's about all she knew. Of the Howell side of his family, Vernon was told almost nothing.

Texas history provided him with a myth of who his people were. One of the textbooks used during those years, *The Texas Story*, described the Anglos who arrived in the territory: "Careless and prejudiced writers have pictured early Texas as a paradise for murderers, thieves, embezzlers, ruffians, gamblers and other undesirables," the author wrote. "These statements are not based in fact." The Anglos who came to settle the territory were in fact good people, "able, aggressive and friendly." Among the settlers, there was an emphasis on toughness and self-reliance, producing "men with the bark on," who were left alone to live their lives as they saw fit, unless they violated the community's moral code.

The centerpiece of Texas history as Vernon learned it was the 1836 siege of the Alamo. His textbooks spent page after page detailing the blood-stirring, fight-to-the-death exploits of Stephen Austin, Davy Crockett, and their band of outnumbered Anglos. The famous letter William B. Travis sent from the fort, according to *The Texas Story*, was "the most heroic document in American history." It quoted the letter in full.

"I am besieged, by a thousand or more of the Mexicans under Santa Anna," Travis wrote. "I have sustained a continual Bombardment & cannonade for 24 hours & have not lost a man . . . The enemy has demanded a surrender at discretion, otherwise, the garrison are to be put to the sword . . . I have answered the demand with a cannon shot, & our flag still waves proudly from the walls—*I shall never surrender or retreat . . .*

"P.S. The Lord is on our side . . ."

Much of what Vernon and his classmates were taught was wrong. The Texans didn't fight to the last man, Davy Crockett surrendered to the Mexicans and was executed, and no one drew a line in the sand and asked volunteers to step over it. But the Heroic Anglo Narrative, as it was known, went largely unchallenged when Vernon was in school.

He must have thrilled to the stories, as most Texas children did. *The Alamo*, the 1960 John Wayne movie about the siege, played regularly on his family's thirteen-inch black-and-white TV. It's highly likely Vernon went on a school field trip to the sacred "shrine," where a plaque warned visitors, *Be silent, friend. Here heroes died to blaze a trail for other men.* And he probably acted in a school play about the siege, as many Texan schoolkids do to this day. At the very least, he sat in the audience and watched.

The Alamo was the narrative of who Texans were. Vernon marinated in it for most of his childhood.

At school, he had few friends to play along with his heroic fantasies. Vernon was a loner. But he did have at least one admirer watching him from afar. Teresa Beem was a second grader when Vernon was in fifth.

"I just fell madly in love with him," Teresa said. "He had such a cute face and this gorgeous, curly hair. And I just remember he was very quiet, but he smiled at you." Vernon made a point of being kind to Teresa. He liked to feel he was a protector, someone who treated little kids the way he never was.

It made Teresa wonder just how lonely he was. "He wasn't one of the cool kids," she remembered. "He seemed vulnerable, you know. He was alone a lot."

As his isolation deepened, music became a refuge. Vernon grew up to the sounds of sixties pop and country and western on the family radio, Ray Charles singing "I Can't Stop Loving You" and Little Eva doing "The Loco-Motion." When he wasn't plunked in front of the TV watching Westerns, Vernon tuned in to the country variety show *Hee Haw* and especially *The Buck Owens Show*, a nationally syndicated half-hour variety show that featured the latest hit musicians. Vernon was entranced. One day, he wanted to be Elvis, the next Johnny Cash.

When he was about eight or nine, Vernon started begging his parents for a guitar. Bonnie finally gave in and got him a box model with six strings. There wasn't any money for lessons, so Vernon learned to play without it ever being tuned. He didn't even know what "tuned" was.

By the time he reached sixth grade, Vernon could play a few songs.

That year, his class had a weekly show-and-tell for music, for the students to bring a musical instrument or a favorite album and play it for the class. Vernon was excited to showcase his newfound abilities. He started bragging on himself at school. "Wait till you hear me play," he told his classmates. It made him feel good to be ahead of the other kids at this one thing.

When the day came, Vernon arrived at school with his guitar case. He had a friend, Brent Christiansen, who also played. Brent heard Vernon practicing before the show-and-tell and said, "That guitar's out of tune, let me fix it for you." Vernon handed it over and Brent started turning the keys, bending his head to listen.

The time came and Vernon got up in front of the class. But when he hit the strings with his fingertips, the guitar let out this weird sound. Vernon looked down at his hands, not understanding. He hit the strings again, and the same garbled notes drifted out into the classroom.

He could feel himself starting to panic. *What is wrong with this thing,* he thought. He could hear kids snickering.

Brent had tuned the guitar but now Vernon didn't know how to play it. His big moment had come and it was a bust. He went home that day feeling like a liar and an idiot.

Vernon didn't abandon the guitar; he loved music too much. But the incident was a blow to him. It seemed to him there was nothing in his life that he could count on all the way, except maybe for Jesus.

When Vernon was about nine, Bonnie found religion again after falling off for a few years. Now she started reading the Bible and going to church, taking Vernon with her.

Vernon loved the Bible. They had a radio in the house and Bonnie would tune it to one of the preachers that were all over the dial. Vernon would get in bed with the radio still playing and fall asleep to the sound of the evangelists' voices.

The twang of the Texas preachers cut though the static, their voices rising as they talked about threats to Godly Americans. One thing that distinguished Texas radio preachers from their brethren across the South was their homegrown fusion of politics and religion. Satan wasn't just coming to pluck out individual sinners, he was coming to smash the republic. His methods were legion: Communism, the creeping scourge of homosexuality, drugs, even psychology.

The dominant style was paranoid. In his sermon "Steps in the Degeneration of Our Nation," the Baptist preacher Lester Roloff compared America to the Roman Empire as it tipped into anarchy. "This message," he said, "gives the picture of this sad and Satanic and degenerated generation of ours . . . Getting away from the Bible has led us to the end of the trail as a great nation." It was dark stuff. "America either faces revival or no survival," Roloff told his listeners in a pleasing tenor voice. "Now we just got to make up our minds. And we don't have long to wait, either."

Vernon heard it all through his youth: The end is coming, and America damn well deserves it.

Later, Vernon watched some of the same preachers on TV, their hair fried, dyed, and laid to the side. He tuned in for hours, soaking in the sonorous rhythms. Reading was torture for Vernon but listening to radio sermons was heavenly. The family had a neighbor who was a Baptist minister, and Vernon would sometimes go to his church and listen to his sermons live.

Then on Saturday, the family went to church. Vernon never understood why the other kids in the pews hated being there. They'd squirm and mutter and get cuffed through the whole service. But Vernon loved it. It was like he went into a trance.

Religion was all around him. In the 1960s, Dallas was home to the world's largest Methodist church, the world's largest Presbyterian church, and the world's largest Baptist church. The SDA was tiny compared to these giants, with only eight thousand members in the entire state. But they were strong in the faith and growing. Between 1959, when Vernon was born, and when he turned seven, thirty-eight new SDA churches were built from Dallas to Amarillo. Back in the 1880s, success for the Adventists had been measured in how large a tent they ordered for their traveling evangelists. A sixty-footer was a good sign. Now it was the square feet of the SDA's brick-and-mortar churches.

Vernon took to reading the Bible and through sheer tenacity managed to memorize entire sections. It was like he took pictures of them with his brain instead of reading them. But he wanted to do more. He went on to the SDA classics that his mom had lying around, the Bible studies of William Miller and the lectures of Ellen G. White.

Vernon wore out books and pamphlets like he was studying treasure maps. He was looking for something, but what it was he couldn't exactly say.

He didn't get out of the Bible what some others did. Because of his learning problems, he literally did not see the same words on the pages that his parents and friends saw. When the words eluded him, he had to fill in what he couldn't understand, make up something on the spot, what felt right to him. From early on, Vernon created his own world out of what he saw around him, something he would do for the rest of his life.

As Vernon's obsession with the Bible grew, he started spending a lot of time out in the barn. He'd stay there until dinnertime some nights, with the hay smell and the furtive sounds of mice and animals, praying. Vernon's half brother Roger found this bizarre. Sometimes he'd leave Vernon kneeling by the side of his bed, his hands folded, and come back eight or ten hours later and find him still there in the exact same position. It was like a magic trick. Had he even gotten up to pee?

For Vernon, God loved him like no one else did.

4

VERNON AND ROY

ONEY WAS TIGHT and life was stressful for the Haldemans, who didn't believe in sparing the rod. Sometimes Bonnie would get mad and she'd pick Vernon up and whale on him, a habit she'd learned early and often from her father and her ex-lovers. And she hollered at him just about nonstop. It was heat-of-the-moment type stuff, but the fact that the boy could turn her into her own father, rage-wise, did nothing to endear him to Bonnie.

The boy had ocean depths. He'd charm you until you stood in his way. Then you felt the anchor chain going down to something harder, darker maybe.

His badgering got on Roy and Bonnie's nerves. He couldn't help himself. He wanted to know things; it was one reason the pronouncements of the church struck him so hard. And he was smart enough to know the answers that grown-ups gave kids were often nonsense.

Exhausted by his insatiable curiosity, Bonnie and Roy told him that he was an oddball. "You'd argue with Jesus Christ!" Bonnie exclaimed once. It was like he'd just landed from Planet Weirdo and he was the only one of his kind.

Bonnie told him he didn't even act like her son. Or, if she was really steamed, she'd go a little further, saying, "I don't even know if you're my kid or not." After Grandpa calling him a bastard, and his real dad giving him the slip, Bonnie's words cut into Vernon. *How can she not know if I'm her son,* he thought.

Erline had never said anything like that. It only reinforced his feeling that he'd been stolen away from his true home.

The circle turned downward. The more curious he was about things, the more he pissed off Bonnie and Roy, which made him even more insecure, setting off another round of questions.

In Richardson, it quickly became clear that Roy Haldeman had his own unique problems with Vernon. Vernon cried frequently, setting off Roy's hair-trigger temper. "Be a man!" Roy would shout at him.

Roy hardly ever had real conversations with Bonnie and the boys. He couldn't stand men who blabbed for no reason. Roy called that "watermelon talk." Vernon would think, *He's been around the world a bunch of times but he hasn't got any stories to tell?*

The only time Roy would really loosen up was when he had a few beers in him. It was a big deal—the Sphinx speaks! Vernon hung on every word.

One of Roy's favorite things to talk about was his younger days. He told Roger and Vernon how he'd spend his nights cruising the bars and pool halls. Eventually, he bought one called the Jade Lounge. It was where he'd met Bonnie.

This was the era when bars could still have slot machines, which attracted a certain clientele, guys who could get you whatever you wanted—cocaine or bennies or yellow jackets, which were amphetamines. Or whores.

This one guy, Ed, would come into the lounge every day after work. He'd sit there and look at the girls and smoke and not talk. He wore a nice black suit, drove a brand-new Cadillac, a high roller for sure. Roy sat down beside him one day and they became friends. Not that they spoke much; instead, they spent a lot of time in companionable silence.

They hung out for months, and finally Roy said to Ed, "You want to have some fun?" Ed said "Sure," and Roy told him to stay on after closing time. That's when the real action started. Guys came in and shot pool for $500 a game and strippers arrived and got naked for dollar bills and prostitutes walked in and it was whatever you wanted, nothing off the menu. Drugs and money changing hands. And Roy and Ed were right in the middle of it all.

Weeks later, a car pulled up to Roy's house and Ed stepped out. Roy opened the door ready to say "Come on in," but Ed reached into his lapel pocket and pulled out a badge. FBI. Ed had been a G-man all along.

Roy was in deep trouble, but Ed had taken to him. He liked him so much he arranged a plea bargain. Roy had to forfeit some of the cash he'd made at the Jade Lounge, but in the end the feds let him walk.

Vernon loved that story, loved thinking that his stepdad was a tough guy. It just went to show you how much a real man could get away with in this world. He wished Roy would tell him more tales like that one, show his personable side. But those moments were few and far between.

Vernon yearned for Roy to like him. He'd tell himself to follow all of Roy's rules, to be quiet when entering a room where Roy was sitting with some other adults. That was one of Roy's commandments: Wait until someone asks you a question before opening your mouth. But it was hard when Vernon had so many questions. And if you tried arguing with Roy, you might find yourself on the wrong end of a beating.

But most of all, Vernon wanted Roy to think he was smart. A lot of people thought kids like him were dumb as fence posts. It bothered Vernon. He knew he wasn't stupid. To have your own stepdad think you were a moron, that was tough to think about.

So Vernon collected little factoids. He'd pick them up at school or by listening to his friends, then save them for the right moment. One time, he heard a real zinger and rushed home with it.

He found Roy. "When earth is closest to the sun," he told him, "it's wintertime. And when we're farthest from the sun, it's summertime!" It sounded nuts but it was actually true.

Roy stared at him. "You goofball," he roared. "Where in the hell did you learn that? If I was to light a fire under your ass right now, would it be hotter on your ass or hotter five feet away?"

On summer mornings when he was ten or eleven, his stepfather would leave for work and give his stepson a job to do. "Now Vernon, I want you to clean up this front yard and I want to get home this afternoon and I want it cleaner than a Safeway chicken. You hear me?"

"Yes, sir," Vernon would say.

And he'd have every intention of getting it done, too. But he'd start watching *Tom and Jerry* and that morphed into the Three Stooges and that morphed into other shows, and from seven in the morning till noon the day passed so slowly in the summer doldrums heat, and he'd have his eye on the clock, thinking, *still plenty of time.* But from noon to four or five the clock would just zip right along like it'd saved up all its energy for the late afternoon, and all of a sudden, he'd hear Roy's car pull into the driveway and he hasn't cleared as much as a single leaf off the front yard. And he knew what was coming.

Two minutes later Vernon would be flying from one end of the living room to the other. Roy would beat him with anything handy. Baling wire. Belts. Whatever he saw.

And it wasn't just Roy. Later on, at one of his birthday parties, Bonnie got ticked off by something he said and beat him black and blue in front of all the other kids. Vernon was mortified.

He tried to be good, walk the straight and narrow, but something about him set off a trigger in people. Vernon couldn't figure out what it was.

But the most excruciating moments came in private. Right around the time of the family's move to Dallas, one of Bonnie's relatives started touching Vernon sexually. He was terribly frightened and disturbed by the abuse. "I was five years old," he told a follower later, "a little innocent boy who didn't know anything."

The touching got worse, until the man raped him. It went on for four years. He refused to give the abuser's name; he felt it might get back to Bonnie and hurt her. "It's terrible that people do that to little children," he said.

And it wasn't just this man. When he was six, an older girl started messing with Vernon. Then a bunch of older boys cornered him one day after school. Vernon and his friend were playing in front of the house and these guys grabbed them and dragged them through the fields until they got to a spot where no one could see them. They held the two boys down and violated them.

Vernon kicked, he screamed, but the boys were older and he wasn't strong enough to get away. He hated that feeling, being held down, unable to move, while the pain tore at him.

Of the two boys, Roger was the favorite, probably because he was Roy's real son. Vernon was always getting his ass kicked, while his little brother would skate. The funny thing was that Vernon was a model child, praying and trying to help around the house, if talking too much. Roger was doing all kinds of bad shit, a real knucklehead, but when the belt came off, 90 percent of the time it was for Vernon.

Or maybe Roy secretly wanted Vernon to be bad, to raise a little hell like his little brother, stop being such a pansy.

Roy had a cold heart, that's what Vernon came to believe. An icebox in his chest. Vernon wondered why men didn't seem to like him. It was always the same story. They'd see him and be like, "Hi, how are you, get the fuck out of my way."

Alcohol made things worse. When Roy got to drinking, just about anything could happen. He would shout at Bonnie, and he would beat her, too, leaving dark bruises on her skin. Sometimes, when he was deep in the bottle, he would even hit on her teenaged sisters and try to get them into bed with him.

When Roy was into his whiskey, Bonnie felt she could see the devil shining out of his eyes.

Overwhelmed by self-doubt, Vernon sometimes prayed to God to help him. He got down on his knees and closed his eyes. The prayer went like this:

"Dear God, dear Father, I don't understand why I'm this way . . . I know I'm stupid, but please talk to me because I want to serve you." He didn't think everybody in the world was bad, despite what names they called him. He wanted to save them.

"People tell me to read the Bible. And I look at it and I see what it's saying and then the people say it says something else. And when I ask them, they won't talk to me, but they tell me I'm always wrong."

He was talking about his language disability, but he could have been talking about his life in general. He asked God to please help him to know what to do.

One night, lying in bed, Vernon looked out his window and watched the sky. He saw a very beautiful, soft explosion way, way out into the universe. And he heard a voice. It said one word: "Vernon."

He got so excited that he jumped out of his bed and ran to his parents' bedroom. He told his mother what had just happened. Bonnie said, "Go to sleep and it will go away."

Vernon was confused. Why would he want it to go away? God had spoken to him!

He went back to his bed and tried to sleep. The voice made Vernon feel special and good. God picked Vernon to speak to, out of millions and millions of people.

There was nothing to be ashamed of. In North Texas, as one local writer said, saying God talked to you was like saying the Avon lady rang your doorbell that morning. It happened to someone every day.

But for Adventists, it wasn't so simple. Their great prophet, Ellen White, had dreams in which God sent her messages and instructions. The church believed it was possible for others to receive His divine messages, as well. But White herself warned her followers that many visions arose from everyday causes and had nothing do with God. Sometimes they were Satan pretending to be God.

Every dream had to be studied, White said, to make sure that it corresponded to the Lord's word. If not, danger lay ahead. "Beware that you be not ensnared," White wrote. "Take heed . . . for delusions and deceptions will come . . . as we near the end."

Vernon didn't take heed. He was convinced God was speaking to him.

5

THE CLUBHOUSE

NINETEEN-SEVENTY ARRIVED AND with it a new fitness craze. That year, the twenty-three-year-old Arnold Schwarzenegger became the youngest Mr. Olympia, paving the way for the era of the muscle-bound superstar. Gleaming new gyms sprang up in Dallas, advertising yoga classes, newfangled exercise bikes, even something called Jazzercise. The nation wanted to shake itself out of the sloppy drug funk of the sixties.

Vernon, now eleven, started working out. He'd always been a small kid. It was as if his hyperactive mind burned the calories before they could fuel a growth spurt. He joked that he was so short he could parachute off a dime. His slight frame—and his loner status—attracted the local bullies. At eleven years old, he decided he didn't want to be a target anymore.

To bulk up, he started working out, going at it with his usual intensity: pull-ups, sit-ups, shuttle runs. He even joined the track and field team to build up his legs.

One day at a track meet, his teacher entered Vernon in a race. Vernon didn't think much of himself as a runner. He and Roger used to do sprints at home, flying over the broken-up ground to see who was fastest, but that was all the experience he had. The way he saw it, country boys like him couldn't compete with the city kids who had tracks and nice level streets to run on.

But it turned out the tough terrain had built up his leg muscles. By the finish line, he was ahead of the city boys.

He entered more races and won them. Between events, Vernon skipped around the track, like he had shock absorbers for legs. He could run for hours without getting winded. He even started watching his diet, checking labels to make sure that what he was putting in his body was healthy. The Seventh-day Adventists had always stressed eating right, banning most meat, alcohol, and caffeine. But Vernon took it a step further.

Vernon went on long runs through the neighborhood. He measured out a course from his street to the local shooting range, about six and a half miles, round trip. Just before dusk, he'd slip out of his house and go. On the trip back, when he was about fifty or seventy-five yards from the street sign at the end of his street, he'd lift himself out of his exhaustion and gun it. His whole body would lock into this rhythm. It was like he'd just done the world's best drug, he felt so good.

As Vernon extended his run of number-one finishes, something odd happened. The other kids began cheering him on. Students who'd never spoken to him in his life now came up to him at the meets and said hey. They called him "Vernon," not "four eyes" or "spaz."

It felt weird. Vernon had been a nobody for so long he'd thought it was permanent. Now he was a budding track star.

Suddenly everybody acted like they'd known him for years. *Well, they don't know me*, Vernon thought. They didn't understand him. They just saw a version of Vernon they couldn't laugh at.

By the time he was thirteen, Vernon looked like a superkid. His biceps popped out from under his short-sleeve shirts. His legs were lean and ripped. He was a stud, if he had to say so himself.

With his confidence growing, he thought he'd try out for the football team. There was nothing bigger in North Texas than Friday-night football. Being a good runner was one thing, but being a star on the varsity squad was another galaxy. It would earn him instant respect.

He signed up and spent that summer in long, withering practices under the Texas sun. Vernon didn't mind the calisthenics or the sweating; he thrived on hard work. The problem came when the season started.

When fall arrived, Vernon got an eye-opener. It seemed to him that his coaches, who'd always been gung ho, now transformed themselves into complete lunatics. They screamed at their own players, "Get out there and kill 'em!" The players roared back, psyching themselves up. Even the guys on the sidelines and the people in the stands shouted and stomped. It was as if they'd die if the other team scored.

Vernon hated it. The coaches sounded like they were sergeants on a battlefield. Bloodthirsty. Maybe they reminded him a little too much of Roy.

Plus, the coaches cursed up a storm, taking the Lord's name in vain, which turned Vernon off immediately. It didn't feel right to him, all that yelling and screaming and crazy emotion. He dropped out and went back to track and field.

Sports had afforded him a little group of friends. They weren't jocks and they weren't stoners; they weren't grinds either. Just loners hanging out with other loners.

They often had parents who gave them walking around money so they could go into a store and buy a soda pop or some candy, just for taking out the garbage and doing their chores. Vernon didn't get a dime for taking out the garbage.

One time his granddad had some work to do at the farm. He'd torn down an old barn on the property and he wanted to use the lumber for other projects. So he pointed to this big pile of planks and told Vernon to get to it.

For five or six hours a day, Vernon bent over the lumber, pulling out nails. It took him two weeks before the last plank was done. At the end of it, his granddad put $10 into his hand. Which averaged out to maybe 25 cents per hour.

Vernon took it. He refused to turn bitter. He said to himself, *What appears to be my hardship will be my blessing.*

After music and exercise, there were new obsessions. Vernon was in his early teens when car fever struck. One of his uncles was a regular entrant in local drag races, and that got Vernon working on engines. High-performance stuff. He learned how to install Merlin heads on a motor for low-end power. He and his friends talked Ford carburetor jets vs. Holley jets. He spent as much time under the hoods of cars as he did working out.

But Vernon found a familiar disappointment. Among the car crowd, there were plenty of posers. All the guys in his high school talked about engines and muscle cars, but after a while Vernon realized they were just repeating stuff out of hot-rod magazines. They'd be going on about some super boss engine they were going to put in their Camaro, and then you'd look at the specs and it was just really an old regular 350 with a couple of power pack ends on them and a big fancy intake. Maybe some loud mufflers.

A lot of guys were all talk. It offended him.

Vernon felt God was showing him the falsity in people. He noticed this more and more. Take food: He had cut junk food from his diet, but people around him loved the stuff. One time he came across one of his relatives eating a store-bought lemon pie. She kept going on about how good it was. Vernon, health nut that he was, picked up the box and looked at the list of ingredients. It was names of chemicals fifteen letters long.

His aunt was sitting there eating a lemon pie that was imitation lemon, imitation meringue, imitation crust. Even its smell was fake, made in a lab. But his aunt couldn't see it. She'd say, "Good Lord, this is the best thing I've ever tasted" and fork more of it into her mouth.

Another time, he and his cousin walked into Vernon's house and there was another aunt sitting at the kitchen table. She was on the telephone crying, distraught. Someone had died.

Vernon and his cousin went still, because they didn't know whom in their family it was. But after a few minutes, they realized that the woman was talking about a character on a soap opera. It was too silly even to speak of.

As Vernon grew into a lanky teenager, home remained largely un-friendly territory. It seemed to Bonnie and Roy that their son was questioning everything. In 1972, when he was thirteen, he even demanded to go to an SDA school, the Dallas Junior Academy. He never explained the reason to his parents, but apparently, he wanted more of a Godly education than he was getting at the public school.

It drove Roy up a tree. They'd just bought their first home in a town called Sachse, about twenty-five miles from Dallas, and there were public schools all over the place. But his prima donna stepson wanted the Academy, tuition and all.

Bonnie ignored her husband's hissy fit and enrolled her two boys at the Academy. Now they took a long bus ride every day to reach the school. Vernon would stay there for a couple years before transferring to Garland High, because they had a driver's ed program and the Academy didn't.

At school, Vernon could be ornery. Sometimes he'd ask a question and the teacher, unable to answer it, would try to brush him off with a bunch of nonsense. He thought this was rude. He asked questions because he needed to hear the truth. He couldn't stand when teachers patronized him with a half-assed response.

One time, it was a teacher who'd recently arrived from California. The guy mentioned that Texas had no coyotes.

What? Vernon thought. The state was crawling with coyotes! The other kids rolled their eyes and let it pass. Not Vernon. He wasn't going to let this bullcrap stand. He and the teacher went back and forth. It got heated and the teacher threw him out of the class.

Vernon lasted at Garland High until eleventh grade. He didn't return for his senior year and left high school without his diploma.

Dropping out increased the pressure. It seemed to him that Bonnie and Roy were on his back night and day. If they weren't angry about leaving school, they were angry about his general appearance. "Get a haircut, you dirty son of a bitch" was the general vibe.

Long hair was in, but Roy hated it. He told Vernon it made him look like a woman. To his parents, long hair was everything wrong with the world.

Then there was the music. By the time he left school, Vernon's old obsession from sixth grade had returned. He still exercised, but the high he'd once got from lifting weights and running now came to him through the strings of his guitar. He'd bought an electric model and a wah pedal and an amp and he blasted that sucker so loud the neighbors called Bonnie and Roy to complain. Finally, Bonnie told Vernon to move the stuff into the barn.

When he was fourteen, his parents found that even the barn was too close for them. They shipped him off to Grandma Erline's. Vernon was fine with it.

At Erline's, he was offered his cousin's room. But Vernon spotted a shed in the backyard that he wanted instead. It was full of odds and ends, abandoned junk. Vernon got to work on it. He took out his hammer and nails and fixed the place right up, cleaned it, too. He built a bed out of some two by fours and scrap lumber, found a long extension cord, ran it from the house out to his room, and hooked it up to a black light bulb. He bought rock posters for the walls.

By the time he finished, he had a sweet little clubhouse he could escape to. It was so much better than living with Bonnie and Roy. He didn't have to tiptoe around anymore.

He formed a couple of bands with guys from the neighborhood. They played medium-heavy kind of stuff. No Sabbath, more like Uriah Heep and Foghat.

Once Vernon could play some nice riffs on his guitars, girls seemed to materialize out of thin air. His bandmates were excited. Meeting girls was half the reason they were in the band. They just wanted to smoke weed and have sex.

It was another turnoff for Vernon. He was way into the music, but these guys were faking it. When Vernon told them he was playing for different reasons, they didn't get it. "What different reasons?" they said. "What the hell are you talkin' about, Vernon?"

Vernon thought to himself, *I need something to deliver me, but all these guys want to talk about were how big the tits on some girl are.*

On weekend nights, the clubhouse was full of girls, stacked up against the walls like sheaves of wheat. They watched the band jam and made eyes at the musicians. His aunt Sharon let him know that the girls thought he was dreamy, with his long hair, his biceps, and his guitar.

Here was his chance. He could be a lover boy, Option F, a way into the in crowd. But Vernon shied away. In all honesty, he was scared. He felt like it was his first day in a new school, and the hottest chick in the class had asked him out. He felt awkward about it.

He did like talking to girls. He and his little group of loner buddies would go to a Dallas roller rink and while the others were still lacing up their skates, Vernon would already be out on the wooden rink, sliding up between the girls, chatting them up.

But anything else was too weird. Girls had looked at him like a stain on the sidewalk for most of his life, and suddenly they were acting all coy and breathless. It threw him for a loop. *Man, what hypocrites*, he thought to himself.

A similar thing happened with drugs. Vernon hated them. The feeling of being out of control of his own body and mind was frightening to him.

It caused a good deal of grief with his bandmates. They offered him tokes on their joints and when he refused, they shook their heads. Vernon was a downer. He couldn't loosen up.

One night Vernon got tired of the other guys ragging on him and said, fine, I'll do it. He was riding in the back seat of someone's car when they started passing around some. Hawaiian marijuana. Vernon took a couple of drags and waited. He started getting this feeling, a creeping feeling, all over his body. He felt like two hands were coming up his back, then reaching his neck and going up. His eyes started puffing up.

"What's going on?" he said.

His friends cracked up.

"Well, Vernie, it's your first time, so it's gonna hit you hard."

The music in the car was blasting through his skull. Vernon started to feel a little panicked. He imagined the driver spinning the car into a signpost, flipping it.

Vernon smoked weed a couple more times after that, but it wasn't for him. He didn't want anyone or anything having power over him except God. Plus, he was still keeping himself in shape. If he wanted to feel his heart pounding out of his chest, he'd go for a long run.

His bandmates kept at him. He'd be rehearsing with the band or just hanging out at the local roller rink and they'd be like, "Hey, man, you want to try this?" Holding out a joint.

"No thanks."

"So what, man, aren't you cool?"

"You know I'm cool. I mean, whose jams are you listening to?"

"Well, man, if you, if you smoked some of this, you'd really play good guitar."

Now he needed to smoke to play guitar? Vernon thought that was some BS. "Man, there's gotta be something else," he thought. "I'm just not like these dudes."

He just couldn't fit in all the way. He wasn't rough and tough enough to be a jock. He had small hands with short little fingers, not a football player's mitts. They made him fast on a guitar, but, even in that world, he wasn't druggy enough to become a real rocker. And he sure wasn't smart enough to pull good grades.

It was a lonely feeling, but sometimes it was a good feeling, too. He wasn't going to be just another North Texas redneck.

Two years after arriving at Erline's, his grandmother told him he had to leave. His grandfather, Vernon Clark, didn't want him around anymore.

It could hardly have been a surprise. Grandpa Clark had never relented on his distaste for his grandson. But the fact that his own kin didn't want him around hurt Vernon terribly.

He took down the rock posters and unplugged the black light. His little group of friends dispersed.

Vernon was seventeen now, almost ready to set out on his own. Before he did, he decided it was time to meet his real dad, Bobby Howell. He didn't know anything about the man. He couldn't recall a single memory from his childhood. Vernon couldn't even tell you what the guy looked like.

He drove to Houston and found a phone book of the city. He turned to the H's and started calling every Howell in the directory. After a few "No's," someone got on the line that knew his dad. They told Vernon where to find him.

Vernon called ahead, then drove to the house. The family had been told he was coming and had arranged for all Bobby's children to be there to meet their long-lost half brother.

Vernon pulled up in his pickup truck. He got out of the car and there was this dark-haired man standing a few yards away. It was Bobby Howell. Vernon walked toward him and Bobby held his arms open and Vernon walked into a hug. Bobby's mother, Jean Holub, who'd sang to Vernon when he was a baby, hugged him, too.

He and Bobby went inside the house. People were buzzing around them, cousins angling to get a look at his face. But Vernon just wanted to talk to Bobby.

He asked his father what he did for a living and Bobby said he did carpentry and was a mechanic. Vernon was struck by that. "I know how to do carpenter work. It was just natural. And I am a mechanic, and that came natural, too. Now I know that I got it from you."

Bobby said sure, that sounds right.

The only off moment came when Vernon started talking about God. Bobby nixed that. "I don't want to talk religion," he said. Vernon might have gotten his woodworking skills from his father, but the Jesus thing was his and his alone.

By the time he pulled away in his truck, he was filled with feelings of kinship and belonging. It had been a wonderful day.

The bond didn't take, however. Vernon rarely saw his father again after that.

6

VERNON AND LINDA

I N 1976, SEVENTEEN-YEAR-OLD Vernon landed a construction job. He'd moved back in with his parents after Erline kicked him out and relations between Vernon and his parents had improved enough for Bonnie to buy him a brand-new pickup, a black Silverado with red velour interior. Vernon stocked it with cassettes—Van Halen, Aerosmith, Nugent.

The good vibes didn't last. One afternoon, Vernon was off work. He decided to take a nap in the house. While he was asleep, the mailman came with a letter. It was from the school district. Vernon's little brother Roger was failing his classes, not for the first time.

Roy, who'd been drinking heavily, read the letter and flew into a rage. He found Roger in the garage, whipped off his leather belt, and began beating his son with it. Vernon woke up to his brother's screams. He dashed out to the garage and saw Roy tearing into Roger.

Vernon had seen abuse almost since he was born, a long line of "country type" men beating on him and his loved ones. He'd never fought back, until now. He hauled off and punched Roy. It was an archetypal moment: the son finally confronting the violent father. Vernon rarely talked about what happened that day, but he would often preach against what he'd witnessed. "Don't ever let me ever catch any parent disciplining their kids in anger," he told his followers more than once.

It was a rule he would break again and again.

Roy was furious that Vernon had hit him, but he and Bonnie stopped short of kicking their son out. Regardless, Vernon was slowly becoming more independent of his parents. He had money of his own coming in. Texas was in another one of its oil booms, and Vernon was riding the wave.

His job involved putting up Sheetrock, painting, doing panel mold, pouring cement. He didn't dig it. Pouring slabs or manning a jackhammer was grunt work. But he did like putting up the frame, and especially the trim work, really putting your touch on a house. It was a good feeling when you locked out the thing and knew some family would be moving in. He felt like a craftsman.

During his off-hours, he'd bring his guitar and his amp to a mobile home park where he knew a girl, Debbie Owens. She was really into him, he could tell. He started shredding some riffs from his favorite songs, even some Clapton. Kids at the pool nodded their heads to the music and others came up and just watched. It was like a little concert.

The music hypnotized Vernon with its possibilities. It had sex in it, and freedom, unlimited freedom, exaltation. Vernon closed his eyes and the world would collapse itself into the guitar lines. He only had to hear a song once or twice on the radio or on a stereo before it was locked in his head. The breaks, the solos, everything. It wasn't something a lot of teenaged musicians could do.

If he blew a note, he'd get down on himself. Maybe it went back to that show-and-tell music show in sixth grade, but he wanted the chord changes to be perfect. Vernon wanted to be perfect.

But in striving to become the next Clapton, Vernon ran into some problems. Sometimes, he'd be playing, going all the way down into a riff, and suddenly he'd stop. A good rock song made you feel like you could have everything it promised. Vernon wanted to be famous, he wanted to be adored, he craved sex with groupies (even as he struggled to suppress those desires). But at the same time, he felt that even dreaming about them was like waving at the devil.

Vernon would stop playing and jerk the guitar strap right off his shoulder. He'd take the guitar off and throw it to the ground. It freaked people out. They thought he'd gotten electrocuted or something. But the real reason was that Vernon had felt Satan worming his way into his mind.

When the music felt the best to him, Vernon told his friends, that's when evil was close.

One night Vernon went to the arcade with some friends. He spent the evening playing foosball, minding his own business.

After a few hours, a girl he knew a little, Linda, came up and said hello. Vernon made small talk and then Linda asked him to drive her home. Linda was fifteen and didn't have her license yet. She lived in Richardson. She'd been hanging out with a couple of nerds and it seemed she'd gotten tired of them.

They talked on the way. Vernon asked how her friends were. She said, "I haven't seen anyone in months."

"Well, goodness, don't anybody come and see you?" Vernon asked.

"Not since I moved in with my dad."

"Well, if you ever need a ride up to Mars or some other place, just give me a call and I'll pick you up."

After they arrived at Linda's house, she invited him inside to talk. Vernon said he'd like to say hello to her dad—he knew him a little bit—and so he went in.

Her dad wasn't up. "Look, I better get out of here," Vernon said. Linda told him, stay awhile, we can talk, so he did. But the talking led to kissing and soon they were going at it. There should be a law against it, Vernon thought afterward. But it's just one of those times when a good man falls.

Driving home that night, Vernon's mind was going a mile a minute. "My God, here I am, this big religious guy who's got all his stuff together," he thought to himself. "I don't do things like this, I'm not some Mr. Cool looking to score. How could I fall into something like this?"

He told himself it would never happen again. He went out to Linda's the next day to apologize. But it was like a bad comedy. He got out there, they got to talking, pretty soon they were in bed going at it again.

Vernon had always hated when his music buddies talked about women, how they divvied them up into boobs and butts and lips, then fantasized about sleeping with them. It turned him off, a reaction he always chalked up to his own piety.

With Linda, his defenses faltered. Clearly, Vernon wanted to have sex with young women; he did it with Linda every chance he got. But afterward, he let himself off the hook. His animal desires had taken over, he told himself, but his heart was still pure.

His earlier disgust at his friends now looked more like jealousy than anything else. Vernon didn't just hate when a specific girl he liked slept with one of his friends; he hated when *any* girl slept with *anyone* who wasn't him.

The narcissism that had flashed out here and there through his childhood—his insistence that God was speaking to him, the refusal to back down to teachers, his perfectionism on the guitar—now came fully out into the open. When he saw others hooking up, his first question was: Why isn't she interested in me?

Vernon had to get away from the temptation. He left town.

After a few months, he returned. One day, the phone rang. It was Linda.

"How'd you get my number?" he said.

"Oh, I have ways."

He asked her why she was calling.

"I'm in trouble. I'm pregnant."

It knocked him backward. A terrible fear came over him. He felt like the walls of the kitchen were closing in.

"I'm sterile," he blurted out. It was a line he'd heard in a movie once.

There was silence on the other line.

"Oh. I see," Linda said finally, her voice so sweet, childlike. "Okay, I'm sorry, then."

Vernon heard a click on the other end. He put down the phone.

Vernon was upset. He prayed. "God, what's going on?" he said. "Help me." Me a father, he thought. It didn't seem possible.

It was his childhood all over again. He was Bobby Howell and Linda was Bonnie. They were both about the same age as when his parents got together. And now he was thinking of abandoning his child, just like Bobby had with him.

As the weeks went by, though, his mood began to shift. The pregnancy wasn't necessarily a disaster, he thought. To have a baby to raise and love and be loved by? It could be special. He could raise the child and make sure not to make the mistakes that were made with him.

He went back to the Bible and read the Scriptures that spoke of sex and marriage. He realized that sleeping with Linda wasn't a sin after all. They'd lain with each other, which, as Vernon interpreted the scripture, made them a married couple in God's eyes. If he could get Linda to be with him and to honor the marriage contract, everything would be fine.

Vernon couldn't bear to be the bad guy. God had to sanctify his desires, no matter how deranged they were. In fact, the Bible records no verses that grant marital status to men and women who sleep together. Vernon was finding in the Bible what he wanted to find.

Soon, the Lord came to him in a dream. He told Vernon that he and Linda had to live together as husband and wife. Excited, Vernon hopped in his pickup and drove the hour and a half back to Richardson.

Before he got to her house, he pulled over, found a pay phone, and called Linda's number. He couldn't wait to give her the good news. They weren't sinners; in fact, they were newlyweds!

Linda picked up. Vernon barely had a chance to ask her how she was before she blurted out that she'd had an abortion. "I had to," she said.

Vernon felt his skin get hot.

"I'm really sorry about everything," he told her. "I . . . I wish I could die."

Guilt washed through him. *I'm a murderer*, he said to himself. He thought Linda was going to yell, tell him how much she hated him. But instead, she said, "I'd like to see you."

Vernon drove over to her place and they talked. The two made up. Vernon started spending more and more time at the house, returning every chance he could get. He found Linda had a deep mind, a fact he'd almost missed by thinking of her as an object of his lust.

Within days, he realized that he was in love for the first time.

Linda's dad let him stay at the house, up in Linda's bedroom. The three of them got along famously. It was like he had his own family there in Richardson, Texas. He was doing construction all day, and then at night he'd come home to his little love nest with Linda. It was a bizarre arrangement, one that would have never passed muster in the Clark house where

Vernon grew up. All Linda's father asked was that Vernon respect his house and not have relations with his daughter.

Vernon agreed. But the temptation persisted. He found, despite praying on it, that he couldn't control himself. He and Linda were getting it on right every time they looked at each other.

Linda got pregnant again. Her father found out and lost it. He ordered Vernon out of the house.

Vernon was ready to defy him. He went to see Linda, even after her father had forbidden it. But from the moment he saw her, he felt the electricity between them strangely altered.

Linda told him he was scaring her. He was too obsessive, ranting and raving about what God wanted. She said he should see someone, like a psychiatrist.

That really irked Vernon. There was mental illness in his family, something Vernon knew but was reluctant to talk about, taboo as it was in 1970s North Texas. When she was sixteen or seventeen, Bonnie's sister Beverly had started showing signs of instability. She was later diagnosed as a paranoid schizophrenic. Then Bonnie's niece started going strange and she got the same diagnosis. There were others who had succumbed to mental illness, one way or another. But, in his family, people didn't see psychiatrists.

Vernon didn't give up. He kept going by Linda's house, telling her that God had told him she was to be his. The way he saw it, if God ordained it, it wasn't Linda's to decide.

Linda started avoiding him. She was afraid for herself and for the baby she was expecting. "Your love is the best love in the world," she said in one of their last conversations, "but it's like candy. Too much of it rots."

Linda gave birth to a girl. She wouldn't let Vernon see the baby, no matter how much he begged. Every time he tried, Linda's father would tell him to go away. Linda would let Bonnie come by and hold the baby, but not Vernon.

It was like a hot piece of steel being put through his chest. A hard lesson in pain.

As the weeks went by, Vernon became more and more depressed. As a child, he'd been robbed of a father. Now he was going to be robbed of his daughter. The injustices were piling up.

He cried and cried whenever he thought about the little girl.

Vernon often understood theology through biography. He'd come to believe that the wrenching, bewildering things that happened to him were actually divine tests. His life was a prophetic storybook, and he was tasked with reading it correctly. When he started to feel extreme things, and to behave in extreme ways, he didn't see it as a sign of psychological problems. It was, instead, the correct response to God's challenges.

There was a grandiosity to his pain. It was special.

After Linda, children began to loom large in Vernon's cosmology. He saw her rejection of him as another obstacle he had to overcome.

"The way you become one with God," he told his followers later, "is by becoming one with God's image, becoming one with your own glory. The way you love God is by loving yourself. The way you love yourself is by becoming one with one that is given to you of God, the woman . . . She anoints you. Your horn [your penis] is a symbol of your power, your power to be as God, to procreate . . . Then you have one, two, three, four, five, six, fifteen, twenty, thirty, forty, fifty, a hundred, a thousand, maybe two thousand, twenty thousand, maybe a million kids."

"Now who is king?" he said. "You are."

His first child had been hidden away from him. Soon he would vow to raise an army of them.

After Linda left him, Vernon was adrift, physically and spiritually. He'd lost his new family and had nowhere to go. He started living in his pickup. He was feeling increasingly distraught. He couldn't eat and his bowels became so bound up that he wouldn't go number two for days.

He started attending different churches near Tyler and asking the preachers for answers: "What should I do? Why am I so alone?" In his estimation, he got nothing back he could hold on to.

Sometimes he'd find a graveyard and pray there. He knelt among the tombstones and spoke to his Father. Maybe he'd given up on the living, maybe he thought about being dead himself.

There's little doubt he was depressed. God seemed to have abandoned him and he had no idea why.

He landed a job with a lumber company in nearby Wylie, Texas. The owner's son had just bought a brand-new El Camino. The kid had re-moved the motor out of the car and was looking to put something faster in there. Vernon told him he worked on hot rods and would help him install the new engine.

The two of them got friendly and the guy said, hey, why don't you stay here at the lumberyard? There was a place he could use. Vernon moved out of his car and into the little room.

He continued his round of church visits, looking in on the Southern Baptists next. If you swung a dead cat in North Texas, you were bound to hit a Baptist, and Vernon thought they might have some good advice. He was having mood swings; one minute he thought he was God's favorite, the next he was a no-account son of a bitch, scum who was so corrupt and wicked that he was constantly surprised God didn't kill him on the spot.

He kept it together at work or at church, mostly. But when Bonnie came to see her son, she found him inconsolable. He'd talk about losing Linda and the baby he never saw. How much was the world going to take from him? He'd cry for hours.

His depression manifested itself in new ways. Vernon had bought a car to go along with his pickup; he was still a motorhead and loved tinkering with the engine. One day, he set the car on fire, sat back and watched the flames take it. For a young man in Texas to burn his car was a serious thing. Vernon never did explain why he did it. It may have been a violent act that gave him some mental relief, like cutting himself. He might have seen the truck as a material temptation that had to be done away with.

But it was a clear sign of mental distress. The stories Vernon told himself about God testing him didn't always work. He had doubts and not a small amount of self-hatred. The simple fact was that Vernon's life was falling apart and he was in pain.

Bonnie witnessed his struggles. One day, when they were having a meal at a restaurant, Vernon picked up a napkin and began writing a poem, which he called "Child." Bonnie thought it might have been about Linda's little girl, but it echoed with details of Vernon's own life:

I once was a child, full of interest and wonder,
to pretend meant I could be all.

So my name and world change, and my life rearrange,
only then could I stand ten feet tall.
To me there was, yet never was,
one person for me to be. For how totally could I
then understand with only one way to see? . . .
For to please those others, who with me, share my life,
Another sole [soul] I must present.
So I have become, maybe one, two, three, possibly even four.
If this is to be . . . what ambition have I, that only to live no more.

It was a complex poem. Imagination had been a joy when he was a child; it had enabled him to comprehend the world. He'd cycled through different personas and places; perhaps he was referring to his failed attempts to be a jock and a rocker. (He even talks of changing his name, something Vernon would actually do eleven years later.) But people around him—Linda? Bonnie and Roy?—were demanding he "present . . . another soul." Being Vernon wasn't good enough.

By the end of the poem, he's looking to the future in despair. Death awaits. "Child" was a portrait of bewilderment that seemed to leave few escape routes.

At the Southern Baptist church he attended, Vernon studied the worshippers around him. Sit down, stand up, kneel. Sit down, stand up, kneel. "Yo-yo people," he called them. They'd finish the mass and get out of there and go back home to start consuming again. Get fat sitting on their couches and slurping down pasta, watching Baylor football or the Cowboys, like his stepdad Roy. This church's God was like a slow hour of afternoon TV.

Billy Harris, a Baptist preacher, was one of the men Vernon sought help from. Vernon went to see him with a specific problem. He was masturbating like crazy and felt this was a horrible affront to God. His seed should be used to make babies, not for self-gratification. How could he stop?

Pastor Harris counseled Vernon to trust in the Lord. Pray every chance you get, he said, and God will answer your call.

Vernon took Harris's advice. He increased his prayer time. He was on his knees day and night, begging God to let him stop. But sure as anything, that night he'd be back at it, whacking away.

It soured him on Billy Harris and the Southern Baptists. Here was a real-world problem, a pretty basic one, and their solution hadn't worked. It was clear to Vernon that the Southern Baptist church didn't have a real connection to God.

He turned to revival meetings led by an Adventist preacher named Jim Gilley, out of Arlington, Texas. He sat in the folding chairs with hundreds of people who'd showed up for the so-called Revelation Seminars.

When the seminar started, Vernon felt himself lifted away from his troubles. There was a screen to the side of the lectern, flashing a series of images as Preacher Gilley implored the audience to find Jesus. Earthquakes, famine, pestilence, killings, persecutions. Spliced into the prophecies were pieces of video from the evening news, things that had happened just weeks or months ago.

Vernon was rapt. He went to see the seminar seven nights in a row. It was like Jim Gilley had pulled together all the strands of Vernon's Bible learning into one narrative. The End was coming, and the unrighteous were doomed.

After one revival, Vernon went backstage and found Gilley and said he'd like to join up with him. He could help. There were things in the presentation than needed fixing, little tweaks—or maybe not so little— here and there.

What Gilley was showing was amazing, but it wasn't complete. He didn't talk about the Seven Seals, to start with. The Book of Revelation showed us that God holds a sealed scroll in his right hand that foretells the calamities that will usher in the Apocalypse. The so-called Seven Seals had to be in the seminar, he told Gilley.

Vernon loved the Book of Revelation. To him, it contained the code that unlocked the Scriptures. All the books of the Bible began and met there. How could you talk about Revelation and the kingdom of God on earth without talking about the Seven Seals?

Gilley listened politely, but at the end he told Vernon no. It didn't put Vernon off one bit. How many times had some older dude told him to go kick sand? It just told him that Jim Gilley didn't have the right stuff.

As the disappointments mounted, what Vernon saw as signs from God grew clearer. One night, lying in the back seat of his pickup, he felt a physical presence there with him. It pulsed inside the cab, just above his body.

Vernon started shaking. He felt he was being observed by this entity that had surrounded him. There was no escaping it; it was pressed right up on him.

Finally, a voice spoke in his head.

"You're really hurt, aren't you?" it said.

Vernon saw images of himself running out into the schoolyard as the other children called, "Here come the retards." He saw Roy beating him. Linda when they first met. A hundred images in a second or two.

"You've loved her for about a year, and now she's turned her back on you," the voice said. "She's rejected you."

A fresh set of pictures flitted through his mind. All the times in his life he'd felt this same presence close to him, protecting him.

"Don't you know that for nineteen years I've loved you and for nineteen years you've turned your back on me and rejected me?" the voice said. Vernon saw that Linda had only done to him what he'd done to God. He felt he was looking back on the path of his life, but now he could comprehend each event down to its smallest detail. A wave of love passed through him.

As he lay there, pinned to the seat of his pickup, God told him he would give Linda to him in good time. Vernon was overjoyed.

7

SANDY

VERNON HAD EXHAUSTED his faith in the traditional churches of Texas. Regular attendance at mass and dutiful prayer had gained him nothing. He decided to give Bonnie's old church, the Seventh-day Adventists, a try. The Adventists promised a more intimate, prophetic relationship with God, and that was what Vernon was looking for.

There was a little SDA church in Tyler, and he attended a service there. He noticed the pastor's attractive fifteen-year-old daughter. Curly blond hair, pretty and smart, a budding musician like himself. Her name was Sandy.

Growing up in Tyler, Sandy's nickname had been "Jungle Butt." The kids in school called her that because she'd been born in Ghana, where her father had worked as an Adventist missionary. If you were born outside of Texas, people looked at you like you had two heads.

Sandy knew the nickname was to squash her down into a nothing. She came from another place, was headstrong and opinionated, and that marked her out as a target.

When she was being bullied, Sandy fell back on her faith. She believed strongly in the Lord. She believed every person on this planet was engaged in a personal battle between Christ and Satan. Satan wasn't kind, he was strong and he studied our every weakness.

When Vernon showed up at her father's church in Tyler, right around

Thanksgiving of 1979, Sandy noticed him immediately. He was handsome, lean, with curly dark hair, a little greasy. He dressed sloppily; sometimes his clothes were torn up or dirty. You could tell that he didn't have anyone to take care of him, to wash his clothes or iron them.

But something drew Sandy's eyes. He'd wear these T-shirts with cut-off sleeves, showing off his biceps. East Texas redneck fashion. Sandy thought he was cute. God, the charm just oozed out of the guy.

Vernon would come over to the house for Bible study with her dad, and they'd all have a snack afterward. Sandy had been reading the Bible for years. Scripturally, she could hold her own with just about any man. That just about blew Vernon's mind. When she cited a verse without digging through her King James to find it, he'd study her, his eyes sparkling. One day she felt his leg brush up against hers under the dining room table. It was like touching a five-thousand-volt line.

Vernon could be slick. He knew his way around girls, that was for sure. He smiled mischievously at her, as if they had some secret that was too tantalizing to utter. When he passed her in the hallway after washing up, he'd give her hip a squeeze. They started talking in the pews at the church after mass, lingering in the church foyer, at potluck dinners, anywhere they could get together without raising suspicions.

He was twenty and Sandy was fifteen, two years younger than the age of sexual consent in Texas.

Vernon was searching for something. His first few times at the Tyler church, he told the congregation, "I am just a newborn baby." He wanted to be saved. The church members were impressed by this bright, energetic young man who was so eager to humble himself.

Soon after his first service, Vernon decided to go ahead with his "believer's baptism." Sandy's father was all for it. He and Vernon stood in front of the congregation and Vernon answered the thirteen questions that would usher him into the faith.

"Is the soon coming of Jesus the blessed hope in your heart, and are you determined to be personally ready to meet the Lord . . . ?"

"Yes," Vernon said.

"Do you believe that the Seventh-day Adventist Church is the remnant church of Bible prophecy, Revelation 12:17, and that the people of every nation, race, and language are invited and accepted into its fellowship . . . ?"

"Yes."

"Do you believe that your body is the temple of the Holy Spirit and that you are to honor God by caring for your body, avoiding the use of that which is harmful? To abstain from all unclean foods, and from the use of all alcoholic beverages, narcotics, or any other types of drug?"

"Yes."

When the questions were answered, Vernon tilted backward and Sandy's father lowered him into the water. The SDA believed in baptism by full immersion, so when Vernon rose again, he was drenched from head to toe.

The congregants rushed up to Vernon to congratulate him. He smiled and dried himself with a towel as he accepted their good wishes. He had cast off his old self and been reborn.

But later, Vernon found Sandy and told her what had happened in the font. It was horrifying to hear.

When her father put one hand on Vernon's chest and held the back of his head with the other hand, and slowly lowered Vernon into the water, voices had begun shrieking in Vernon's head. He realized that they belonged to demons who were shouting for him to stop. They were so loud they nearly deafened him.

Satan was real to Adventists. In their theology, he was to play an oversized role in the End Times. According to the great SDA prophet Ellen White, Satan would "plunge the inhabitants of the earth into one great, final trouble. As the angels of God cease to hold in check the fierce winds of human passion, all the elements of strife will be let loose. The whole world will be involved in ruin more terrible than that which came upon Jerusalem of old."

As terror engulfed the world, millions would seek out a savior. Satan would disguise himself as the son of God and many of the biggest churches would believe him and begin to worship at his feet. Only the true Christian soldiers of the SDA would see through his lie and defeat the imposter.

The battle with Satan was alive for Vernon every day. Once, Sandy went to meet him and found him exhausted, just wrung out. He told her that the devil had come to him in the bathroom and held him down on the floor, pressing him down onto the linoleum. It went on for hours, as Vernon begged God to help him.

He talked about these episodes the way other people talked about going to a ball game. He really thought everyone went through the same thing. At first, Vernon wouldn't even play his guitar for Sandy. "I'm afraid the devil will fly through my fingers, and I'll be right back where I started," he said.

Pridefulness was right at the top of his list of things to watch out for. When Vernon lined up to take a picture with Sandy's family, he'd slide over a few inches, edging behind a shoulder or someone's hairdo. You'd get the pictures developed and you'd see his brown curls and half a smile and nothing else. He didn't want to be vain. He really walked that walk.

After a few months of Bible studies, Sandy's father announced that Vernon had to get his mind off Linda, whom he still talked about constantly. He proposed that Vernon come along on the family's annual spring trip to Minnesota, where Sandy's grandparents lived.

Her parents put Sandy and Vernon in the back seat of their little Dodge Omni hatchback. Texas went flying by the windows, then Kansas. Most teenagers would have been bored. But Vernon and Sandy were half-giddy in the narrow back seat, their heads bent over their Bibles.

Vernon would point out a passage, or he would quote a verse aloud. Sandy would flip to it and read. Then Sandy would give her own passage from memory. He'd read it, laugh in that sparkly, dimply way he had. Each passage had a secret meaning, like a love note, that was lost on Sandy's parents in the front seat.

When they got to Minnesota, Sandy took Vernon on a tour of the property, to the farmer's fields behind the trees out back of the house. This is where she'd spent her summers, playing with local kids, riding three- and four-wheelers to the neighbors and back, or goofing off in the barns, when she wasn't doing chores.

She led him to her favorite tree. It had this big old trunk, wide as a bull's back. Vernon's eyes lit up when he saw it. Sandy went to climb it, and she felt Vernon put his hand on her butt to boost her up.

Sandy straddled the branch, facing him as he came up. He sat across from her, and she could tell that he was more than ready to make love to her right there. She tried not to stare at his erection. He kept asking her, "Why are you blushing so much?"

He scooched closer to her. Then he said, "Can I kiss you?" She said yes. He cradled her face in his hands. It was the best kiss she'd ever had.

They were on top of each other now, but Vernon was serious. He wasn't grabbing and pulling at her like a teenaged boy. He looked at her and said, "Sandy, God has told me that you are to become my wife."

Lord, please help me, she thought. She wanted to be with Vernon, but her father was going to have a stroke.

Vernon got excited. He told her he'd always believed Linda was meant to be his wife, but now God had shown that it was Sandy all along. "Wow," he told her, "I never knew there was a girl like you out here for me!"

Vernon was on cloud nine, yammering away about how God had given him this blessing. He was bursting with happiness. He got so carried away he said he had to give the great news to her dad.

Sandy nearly fell out of the tree. "You cannot tell my dad," she told him. "He won't understand."

"He'll be just fine," he said.

"No, Vernon. You don't know my dad. We have to play it cool around him or this will never happen. That is a promise."

They got down and Vernon covered her with kisses. She thought, *OK, he's calmed down*. Vernon wrapped his arm around her and they walked down the lane toward her grandmother's house. Cattails swayed by the side of the road.

They were pushing open the gate to the house when her father drove up. Vernon turned and waved to him. He walked toward the car, its engine idling in the heat. Sandy felt her insides coil in fear.

But maybe Vernon was just going to talk about their walk and the old house and the farm. As soon as she heard Vernon's voice, so hopeful and happy, she knew it was not going to be that.

He called out, "God has revealed to me that I'm to marry Sandy, your daughter!" She couldn't believe a grown man could be so naïve.

Her father turned the key in the ignition and the engine went quiet. He got out of the car. Sandy watched as the color in his face deepened, second by second.

"God didn't tell me you're supposed to marry my daughter!" he shouted. "There is no way you are going to marry her. You don't even know what love is!"

It was like Vernon went into shock. He looked at Sandy's father as if he was speaking Hindi. Everything had been arranged, God had blessed this union, Sandy and him were in love! It was a happy day. So why was her father so mad?

Vernon tried to get a word in edgewise. He quoted a few biblical verses about men marrying younger women. Her father listened but then went right back on the attack. Vernon might as well have been speaking into a tornado.

Sandy went toward the house and opened the door. Her father came in after her, shouting that they were going to have a family meeting without Vernon. He told those inside—it was Sandy's grandmother, her cousin Bill, and her mom—what Vernon had just said.

They started talking, panic in their voices. "They're infatuated with each other!" someone called out. Her mom said, "Send him home on a bus." Bill was a little easier on the guy and said that was cruel: just put him on a plane. Grandma suggested they make Vernon walk all the way back to Texas.

Meanwhile, Vernon was pacing outside, kicking the dirt. Like he was waiting for an answer to his marriage proposal.

Sandy was listening in another room. Bill agreed to watch the two of them closely, spying on them when her dad wasn't around. Her dad calmed down a little. Finally, he went out and had a "serious talk" with Vernon about how young Sandy was and how he was on the rebound from Linda.

Vernon looked defeated. The joy in his body was gone. But he gave her father a pledge that he would obey him and not take advantage.

Her father worked Vernon like a dog for the rest of the trip. He had him mowing lawns, cutting wood, cleaning out this room or fixing that one.

He wanted to keep him and Sandy far apart. When he drove off or went on errands, Vernon would drop what he was doing and they would run off to the woods.

Vernon kept saying, *chetem, chetem.* She didn't understand. Finally, Sandy asked what he was saying. "It means 'I love you' in French," Vernon said. None of the relatives knew French, so he thought it was safe.

For the drive back to Texas, her father took suitcases and Sandy's guitar case and whatever else he could find and piled them in the middle of the back seat. It was a thick little wall, with Vernon on one side and Sandy on the other. Sandy was just thankful he didn't stick Vernon in the front and put her mom in the back with her.

Vernon looked like a scolded little boy, slumped down in his seat. He snaked his fingers through the junk, wriggling them around the edges of the suitcases and pushing through until he found hers. They held hands, hidden from her father. It was like a promise.

They were still sending messages via their Bibles. Vernon said, "Exodus thirty, thirty-seven, thirty-eight." She glanced at her dad, then laid her Bible on her lap and found the verse.

> *And as for the perfume which thou shalt make, ye shalt not make to yourselves according to the composition thereof:*
> *It shall be unto thee holy for the Lord. Whosoever shall make like unto that, to smell thereto, shall even be cut off from his people.*

She understood. Anything she did in her life, any perfume she wore, was to be for Vernon only.

She said, "Proverbs 24:14." Vernon didn't even have to look. He knew it by heart:

> *So shall the knowledge of wisdom be to your soul; If you have found it, there is a prospect, and your hope will not be cut off.*

She was saying: "Please be smart, Vernon. Trust that good things are coming."

Through the little gap in the suitcases and stuff, Vernon shot his beautiful gaze, full of feeling, straight into her. He said, "Psalms 140:2–3."

Continually are they gathered together for war.
They have sharpened their tongues like a serpent: adders poison is
  under their lips.

It sent a chill through her. So dark and violent! Why was Vernon convinced everyone was against him? How should she respond? She told
him, "Exodus 20:12."

Honor thy father and thy mother: that thy days may be long upon the
  land which the Lord thy God giveth thee . . .

The fifth commandment. It was about as plain as she could make it.

Sandy peeked through the pile of junk and studied Vernon's face. He
was half-smiling, probably thinking about exceptions to the rule. One
thing she'd learned about Vernon by then was that he never wavered.
Once he made up his mind on something, an atomic bomb wouldn't
move him a quarter inch.

8

EVERY STORY TELLS A LIE

A S THE COUPLE tried to patch things up with Sandy's father, Vernon was staying with a woman named Harriet. Harriet was older, in her fifties, a deaconess at the SDA church in Tyler. Her kids had left the nest. She lived with her husband in a funky old house in Whitehouse, about ten miles outside Tyler.

Months before, before he'd first attended Sandy's father's church, Vernon was playing a gig at a local place when Harriet walked in.

Vernon was up onstage, singing covers mostly. It was another gig in another shithole bar in Tyler, Texas. He didn't remember what song he was playing when he looked up and saw the old lady making her way through the tables. She didn't look much like a drinker, seemed out of place with the couples at the tables and the roughnecks getting numb at the bar. Like she was lost and had come in asking for directions or something.

But the woman came up to him and stared. Vernon stopped singing and waved the band off.

"What can I do for you?" he asked.

"Do you know Jesus loves you?" Harriet said.

Vernon had heard those words before. He'd asked the same question to hundreds of people over the years. But for some reason, they struck him full force. This little old lady, in the midst of the neon Bud signs and the drunks and the general shittiness of his life, was inquiring after his soul. He broke down.

Harriet later told Vernon the church in Tyler had sent its members out to save sinners. She'd been driving around when something told her, compelled her actually, to go into that bar. When she got inside, she knew it was Vernon she was meant to speak to.

Vernon told Harriet about his problems with Sandy and her dad, how much he needed to be with this girl.

A couple of weeks later, Harriet told Sandy's parents that her two grandkids were coming over for the weekend. Could Sandy come babysit? Her parents said yes, anything to keep the girl occupied. They didn't know Vernon was staying there.

The three of them ate dinner that first night. Harriet was beaming. "I just love seeing two young people get together!" she said. "It's such a beautiful thing." But Harriet was nervous. She begged Vernon not to have sex with Sandy. Vernon only laughed.

Harriet showed Sandy to her room and told her to behave. Sandy got into bed in her panties and a T-shirt and pulled the sheets up. She stared at the ceiling, listening to a clock ticktocking somewhere in the house. She knew Vernon was going to come to her.

After a while, she heard footsteps approaching. Her heart skipped a beat and she sat up and scooted to the edge of the bed. Vernon came in, shirtless.

He got out of his jeans and then pulled her panties off. He was kneeling naked on the floor. His penis brushed against her down there and she felt this weird feeling, like this was a ceremony and Vernon was the priest.

"Sandy, you agreed to marry me," he said. "I'm going to make you my wife now. Is that okay?"

She could feel herself entering a trance. She said *Yes, yes, I want to be your wife, I love you!* He smiled, the dimples like little hollows of darkness. He said, "Chetem."

Then he asked, "Are you a virgin?" Her heart sank to the floor. No, she wasn't. He threw his head back and cried out. It was like Sandy had cut him with a knife.

Being the daughter of an SDA preacher, Sandy knew the value the church placed on virginity. Premarital sex was forbidden. She and Vernon had grown up hearing that women who broke that law were damaged goods. Evil, actually. Ministers pointed out that unmarried women in the Old Testament could be put to death if they lost their virginity.

Sandy felt like a piece of dirty, crushed-up paper tossed on the ground. She'd ruined everything with Vernon.

"Well, I guess a harlot can't expect to ask for a virgin," Vernon said.

But after a moment, Vernon's mood turned. He tried to repair the damage. "In *my* eyes you're a virgin," he told Sandy. "You were meant to be my wife." His face was grave.

He looked upwards and gave thanks to God. Then he pulled Sandy toward him and entered her.

Vernon was a super lover. Like, otherworldly. Starting with the words. He said a little prayer before they really got started. She'd never had a boy pray over her before.

When he climaxed, she felt the thoughts of her father and her mother and the arguments melt away. Sandy felt completely different now. She was Vernon's wife.

The next morning, the pair went down the stairs arm in arm to breakfast. Seeing Harriet's disapproving face, Vernon announced, "Sandy is now my wife," he said. Harriet protested, crying that they'd promised her they wouldn't.

Vernon said, "Well, you know what, let's pray on it." The three of them knelt on the floor holding hands. Vernon looked up and told God everything that had happened. He asked God for a sign to let them know that the sex was His work and not just a product of Vernon's lust. Three seconds later, he looked at Harriet and said, "Did you feel that? Electricity just went through my body."

"Yes, I felt that," Harriet said. "Wow!"

They both turned and looked at Sandy. They asked her if she'd experienced the sign. She hadn't, just felt her heart swell when she saw Vernon trying to make it right with God. But she decided to lie a little bit.

"Well, I definitely felt something!" she said.

Later, she doubted Harriet had felt anything, either, except perhaps

Vernon's charisma. That, Sandy thought, was the only thing that had tingled in the old woman's body.

Sandy and Vernon started sneaking around behind her father's back. He was infatuated. When they were out in public, every so often he'd reach up with his right index finger and tweak his nose, like cowboys sometimes did in the movies that played on TV Saturday afternoons. You'd think he was just itching a scratch, but he'd told her that every time he did it, it meant "I love you."

He played for Sandy on Harriet's piano, original songs he'd written. When he finished one song, she'd beg him for another. There was one that was clearly about Linda, his ex. Sandy thought it was super good.

Every picture tells a story,
Every story tells a lie,
Just like the one I heard from you.

Sandy hated that the lyrics were about Linda, but they cut right into her anyway. It was real honky-tonk heartbreak stuff. He'd never finished writing the song; Linda had broken up with him before he could. He told Sandy he never would, either. He and Linda weren't meant to be.

WILD WINDS

VERNON WAS FEELING stronger. He had a new lover that adored him and the Adventists' focus on prophecy had awakened in him a belief in his own spiritual power. His visions had never stopped; now he wanted to tell the world about them.

At the end of the Adventist Sabbath service in the little Tyler church, Sandy's dad would ask for individual testimony. Believers would stand up in their pew and speak their piece for a few moments. Often, they would share difficult moments from their lives when they'd relied on God's grace to make it through. It was a pleasant interlude in the service.

One Sabbath, Vernon stood up. But instead of telling a story of overcoming doubt or some difficulty during the week, he ran up to the pulpit and began to preach. Ranting for all he was worth, sharing his latest vision and what he thought it meant. He went on for thirty minutes or longer, completely taking over the service.

He wanted to hear fresh prophecies, he told the others, "the new light." Why wouldn't anyone show it to him? Unlike the Baptists or the Catholics, the Adventists were known as a prophetic church. It was one reason he'd started going there. So where were the living prophets?

Vernon did this with Sandy, too, and it disturbed her. When she tried to talk him down, tell him not to mistake his dreams for visions, he found passages in the Bible that backed up what he believed. He would take a piece of the Gospel, cut it down to the root, add his own embellishment, and presto-magico, it turned out Vernon was right all along.

He had a fanatic streak, Sandy realized. His visions were curiously tailored to what he wanted. He would get tremendously excited when he had one, practically jumping out of his skin. When he described his latest to Sandy, sometimes she couldn't even make out what he was saying, he was talking so fast.

As Vernon got more and more into his visions, the Tyler congregation began, subtly and then not so subtly, to turn against him. Vernon was pretty fast for a twenty-year-old, people said. His fellow church members started to wonder if he wanted salvation or if he just wanted to take over their little church.

Vernon talked down to them, like he was an enlightened king and they were peasants. One time, the church was debating whether to buy a new organ. Vernon stood up and told the congregants that God had spoken to him and said not to buy the instrument. He'd heard the words clear as day.

People listened for a minute, then turned away and took up the discussion again.

Finally, the believers got fed up. During one of his "sermons," the SDA men left their seats and marched to the pulpit; they grabbed Vernon and carried him bodily out of the church, struggling and shrieking like he was being kidnapped.

Vernon didn't back down. He'd been doubted his whole life, beginning with his mother, who told him his visions were passing fancies. It had bred a distrust of authority figures. More and more, he took criticism as a rejection of his whole being. When confronted, he became even more rebellious.

Sandy tried to help him. More than once, she told him, "Just because you have a dream doesn't mean the Lord is talking to you. It might just be something in your own head." This was the same advice the Adventist prophet Ellen White had given her flock over a hundred years before. Visions can be ordinary dreams. One has to vet them against the Scriptures before you can claim they are from God.

Vernon scoffed; he told Sandy she was all wrong. His narcissism was again complicating his life.

It all become too much for Sandy. She decided to break up with Vernon. But when she told him, he refused to listen.

He began stalking her. Vernon had seen men strong-arming women before. His grandfather had beaten his grandmother when she didn't listen to him. His first stepdad, Joe, had treated Bonnie like a piece of property. As much as he prided himself on being different, their ways had stuck with Vernon.

The church parking lot was one of his favorite spots to catch Sandy. He'd wait there and when he saw her he'd go off on a preaching session, laying a guilt trip on her for disobeying God and being a coward who couldn't stand up to her own family. Then he'd ask her to run away with him right then and there.

Once, Sandy's father saw Vernon carrying on in the parking lot and dashed out. His face grew ruby red as he ordered Vernon to give Sandy up, once and for all. He pulled on Sandy's arm, dragging her away.

Vernon refused to leave. His voice got louder. When she and her father had made it to the far edge of the lot, Vernon threw his head back and laughed, in a way you could only describe as maniacal. It was something he always did when he lost an argument.

Another time, after he'd begged and begged, Sandy agreed to meet Vernon in Dallas. He drove up in a muscle car with big boss wheels in back like a drag racer and a jacked-up suspension. Vernon said, we're married in the eyes of God. He opened the trunk and told her to get in.

Sandy played it cool, though inside she was trembling. Vernon was just crazy enough to do it, she thought. Kidnap her, shove her in that dark trunk, take her to some house in the boondocks, and hide her away from her family. They'd be on the six o'clock news.

It took her three hours to convince him to let her go.

Sandy was slipping away and Vernon's life was once again spiraling downward. In despair, he poured his heart out to Harriet. "Where are the living prophets?" he asked her. He'd memorized almost the entire Bible, and still hadn't found what he needed.

Harriet told him about this group in Waco, Texas. They were called the Branch Davidians and they looked at their leader, sixty-five-year-old Lois Roden, as a visionary. She gave teachings that were called "present truth." Harriet had been connected with the Davidians for years.

It was the summer of 1981. Vernon said he'd go that weekend.

Part II

THE MESSAGE

LOIS

L OIS RODEN GREW up in a man's world and it toughened her up. Born in Montana in the middle of World War I, by her late teens she'd become a "strong, stubborn and persevering woman" who brooked no nonsense. At twenty-one, she married a young man named Ben Roden, who believed he had a spiritual vision to impart to the world. Lois became his helpmeet, enduring the rejection and hardship that is natural to any prophet's life.

In 1945, when Lois was twenty-nine, she and Ben and their followers were kicked out of the Seventh-day Adventists for suggesting certain reforms. Lois thought it was outrageous. Ben, who'd converted from Judaism, was the next true prophet, the "Branch," as he called himself after a verse in the Bible. But the SDA refused to see the truth.

Lois didn't take the insult sitting down. She went into the baptistery of the local SDA church, which the Rodens had helped pay for, and stayed there for a week in protest. Her children brought her food and Ben carried in some tools and took doors off their hinges so they couldn't be closed against the family again. The Rodens were zealous in the Lord and they took all comers.

Lois and Ben later joined the Davidians, a small Adventist reform sect that had been founded by a Hungarian immigrant named Victor Houteff in 1929. The believers lived together in a humble, dusty compound called Mount Carmel just outside Waco, Texas. Houteff had chosen this place because the Bible decreed that the faithful should build their fortress "in the midst of the land" and Waco was about equidistant from both coasts.

Houteff believed God had chosen him to send a final message to the SDA. The Lord will judge his people, Houteff warned; he wanted to purify the church until only 144,000 members remained. These warriors would then become soldiers of the Lord's earthly kingdom as the Apocalypse descended.

The Davidians, like the Adventists and the other faiths that had grown out of the Millerite movement of the 1840s, were focused on Revelation. Their desire was to be joined with Christ in their lifetimes. And as the Book clearly stated, that required the end of the world.

After Houteff's death in 1955, the Rodens lobbied to have Ben appointed the new leader of the Davidians. Lois and Ben and their followers traveled to the compound near Waco and attempted to persuade the Davidians that Ben was the true messenger. By nightfall, they realized they'd failed. Houteff's wife, Florence, was named the group's leader.

The Rodens walked out to their cars and arranged them so they faced away from the compound. They believed that God was going to spark an inferno and the meeting place would erupt in flames unless the believers signed Mount Carmel over.

The fire never arrived, but that didn't dampen the Rodens' spirits. Lois and the others started their cars and headed out the driveway. Instead of taking the road away from the compound, however, the lead car turned and began executing a circle. The others followed, until they had formed into a convoy of automobiles speeding around the compound, dust swirling behind their rear wheels. As they drove, they called out to the Davidians that they were re-creating Joshua's encirclement of Jericho before it fell.

Lois reminded many of a pioneer woman, with her cotton dresses, sharp eyes, and straight-across mouth. It was a face built for stoicism, but in her eyes there was kindness, too.

She would give folksy, old-timey Bible studies, similar to those you might have heard in a well-worn revival tent fifty or a hundred years before. The years in Texas had flavored her speech. She'd say "Pen-T-cost" for "Pentecost" and "the 19 and 30" when she meant 1930.

A typical Lois Bible study went like this:

LOIS: But what do you think this morning? Are we going to take the Reformation to its completion? Can I have an amen? I like to hear it loud and strong.

CONGREGATION: Amen.

LOIS: All right, let's get on with it. And let's go back to truth, because that's the only way we're gonna do it . . . The same thing is gonna happen today that happened in the Dark Ages, if we don't get busy. It shows we're not up on our job, that's what it shows me.

And I'm sorry that I haven't taken care of my responsibilities any better 'n I have. I've gotten sidetracked and discouraged and this, that, and the other. But God is encouraging me now to go ahead and help finish the work. How 'bout you folks?

All right, let's get on. [Pointing to a chart] Help me children, what do these four beasts represent?

In 1955, Ben Roden founded a rival sect to the one he'd hoped to lead, and he called it the Branch Davidians. "Branch" referred to an anointed one foretold in the Book of Zechariah: *Listen, High Priest Joshua, you and your associates seated before you, who are men symbolic of things to come: I am going to bring my servant, the Branch.*

"Davidians" was a continuation of Victor Houteff's teaching. It reflected the group's belief that they were descended from the ancient, Jewish House of King David.

In 1962, Florence Houteff disbanded the Mount Carmel congregation and the property went into receivership. The Rodens filed multiple lawsuits to gain control of the compound and finally succeeded. They christened the place New Mount Carmel.

One night in 1977, Lois was up late, studying the Bible. She was reading Revelation 18, which speaks of a mighty angel that comes to earth and lightens the whole land with the glory of God.

Time passed. Two o'clock struck.

Just then, Lois looked up through her window and spotted a shimmering presence hovering in the ink-black sky. As she peered at it, she realized it was a female angel. Behind the angel's wings were arrayed countless other spirit-beings, radiant in silver.

The vision was clearly of the Holy Spirit, the third member of the Holy Trinity. God was showing Lois in no uncertain terms that the Holy Spirit was a woman.

Lois did what Vernon refused to do and checked her vision against the Word. The Bible stated that God had made humans in his own image. Humans were both male and female, Lois reasoned, so God, too, had to be both male and female. This was the core of her vision. "My work is to bring forth the femininity of God in the Bible," Lois told her flock. She called her new teachings the Living Waters message.

But Lois went a little further. She argued that Eve was a "higher act of creation" than Adam because Adam was made out of dust, while Eve took shape from flesh and blood. In her Bible studies, Lois even changed the beginning of the Lord's Prayer to "Our Mother, who art in Heaven . . ."

The change set off an earthquake among the Davidians. Some of the believers thought Lois had lost her mind. Feminists were on the march in the late seventies, but some Davidians rebelled against joining them. Did Lois want to make their sect into an outpost for Women's Lib? Who was she trying to be, Betty Friedan?

Nearly half her flock, almost all of them men, walked away. They hated the new teaching, thought it was blasphemy. Clive Doyle, an Australian who was in charge of the Davidians' publishing arm, refused to print Lois's pamphlets announcing the new truth. He feared Lois was going to send the Davidians to hell by teaching false doctrine.

Anonymous quotes from people inside Mount Carmel began appearing in major newspapers. "Women preaching is like a dog walking on two legs," said one of her followers. "It's interesting, but it's not right."

But Lois was steadfast. When her husband Ben died in 1978, she succeeded him as the new prophet and the leader of the Davidians.

A new era began for the Branch, with an activist bent and a global reach. Lois launched not one but two magazines, *In Her Image* and *SHEkinah*. She traveled the world, meeting celebrities and politicians.

She called famous preachers her friends: Pat Robertson, Jim Bakker, Jimmy Swaggart, Jerry Falwell. She even traveled to the Philippines to confer with Ferdinand Marcos.

Besides the Living Waters message, however, Lois had little or nothing to add to Branch Davidian theology. Every Bible study, she taught what she'd always taught: the same lessons, the same passages, the familiar "seven-year prophecy chart" that predicted things to come. These charts had been around since the forties and many of the group members knew them by heart.

To her followers, even the ones who loved and respected her, it often felt like the same day was repeating itself endlessly. Some people at Mount Carmel wouldn't speak to another person for a week at a time. If you didn't work in Waco and have news from the outside, what was there to say? Days piled on top of days in the wait for the end of the world. Most Davidians felt they should have left the earth years ago.

In the dust and the cold of Waco, it seemed like the clocks had stopped.

After the vision of the female Holy Spirit, Lois did have one other announcement: Something very important would happen in four years. Then three years after that, there would be another big development. She drilled those dates into the Davidians: 1981, 1984. Momentous events would arrive in each.

The Davidians wondered: Was it the arrival of the messiah at last? Was the end of the world approaching? They wished mightily for both.

THE DAVIDIANS

I N 1981, W H E N he first came to Mount Carmel, Vernon found a drab community plunked down in the middle of ranch country on the Central Texas plain, about twelve miles from downtown Waco. On the land, there was a scattering of homes, a chapel, a weedy graveyard surrounded by rusted wire, an Ad (for Administration) building, and little else. The community had shrunk over the years of Lois's leadership to about thirty men, women, and children living on the compound. Worldwide, there were another one hundred twenty members in countries such as England and Australia.

The drive took him about two hours. The compound sat among green fields and small hillocks dotted with underbrush. There wasn't a lot out here, miles from mostly anything. You'd spot horses and some cattle as you passed by the big farms, with swing gates on the driveways leading up to sprawling houses. Vernon turned off Double EE Ranch Road and headed down a long driveway toward a cluster of buildings.

As Vernon pulled into Mount Carmel, Debbie Kendrick and her friend Rachel Jones, daughter of Perry Jones, one of Lois's key followers, were standing on the porch of the Ad building. They saw a dark-haired guy drive by in his pickup truck. Debbie and Rachel were dressed in skirts because it was a holy day. Maybe the Sabbath or the new moon, Debbie could never remember afterward.

Debbie had always felt sorry for Rachel, living in the Joneses' house.

She'd had such a tough life, tougher than Debbie's in a way. Rachel was so starved for affection. At one point, she'd started fancying herself in love with her brother. The infatuation went on for a long time. In Debbie's opinion, the Jones kids couldn't have told you what love was if you gave them a million dollars.

Debbie and Rachel watched as the pickup truck came down the driveway and headed toward the Jones house. They didn't think much about the man inside.

They meandered over to Debbie's house and sat on the floor in the living room playing a Bible board game, because that's all you were allowed to do on a holy day. You had to wear a long dress or a skirt along with your best pantyhose, and you could only do holy things. Go for walks and play Bible games and listen to sermons and sing.

While they were playing, the phone rang. It was Perry. He said there was a new guy at Mount Carmel and he wanted to talk to them. Vernon had spotted them at the Ad building and told Perry he wanted to speak to "those two young girls" on the porch.

He'd been on the compound all of five minutes and first thing he wanted to do was meet two twelve-year-olds. Debbie turned to Rachel and said, "Okay, so he's a pervert."

Debbie felt her stomach starting to cramp. Three years before, her father had begun sexually abusing her, the first time when she was in the bath. Things like that weren't supposed to happen at Mount Carmel, which Lois always told them was a place for the most special people on earth. But they did happen, often. In her time at the compound, Debbie had seen more ugliness than she cared to remember: animals abused, children neglected or sexually exploited, despair and violence. Ben Roden had even stolen her bicycle once (her father had stolen it back). A thought rolled into Debbie's brain when she heard Lois's remark. *What do you mean we're so special? What do you mean these are God's people? If these are God's people, I think I'd rather know the devil's.*

Did any decent, wholesome person ever wander into Mount Carmel, Debbie wondered. It was like the place sent out a signal on bizarro frequencies only.

Vernon wasn't much to look at. A stumblebum with torn clothes and greaser hair, which hung down to his shoulders. It was uncombed and you could tell he hadn't washed it in a long time. He had this big smile on his face, smarmy as anything.

Nothing much happened that day. Vernon only stayed a few hours. When he got ready to leave, Clive Doyle put together a package of literature for him to take home with him.

All through that year, 1981, Vernon would show up at meetings—essentially Bible studies where Lois interpreted the Scriptures and prodded the Davidians to be more pious. You never knew when he was going to appear and when he left you never knew if he was coming back.

He ate very little to nothing at all; some herbal tea, most days, and that was it. He told the others this was meant to purge his sins. The weight dropped off him, and he'd been pretty lean to begin with. You could actually see the bones through his skin.

He'd smoke, too. One cigarette after the other. Lois didn't like it. She told him to quit.

Every time Vernon left, Lois would chase him down. She'd find him in whatever random town he was living in and haul him back. Lois was concerned about him. She'd say, "Vernon, are you smoking again?"

Vernon was struck by that. How did she know? Vernon thought she was using her prophet skills to know if he was back on the cigarettes.

But others thought, "Duh, Vernon, she just smelled the smoke on your clothes." Vernon always seemed to find a biblical reason for things when a simpler one would have done.

Vernon took off again and again, as if he was afraid to commit to the life at Mount Carmel. He would go and sin in other towns. Once he headed off to Keene, Texas. This time, it wasn't cigarettes but food. Vernon decided to go on a carrot cake binge—if he was going to hell, he was gonna go ahead and eat all the carrot cake he could find.

Finally, Lois decided to put him to work. As he was a musician, it was decided that Debbie and Rachel would take guitar lessons from him. Perhaps that would give him a reason to stick around.

But when he arrived for the first session, all Vernon wanted to talk about was sex. "Well, what have you done with boys," he said to the girls. "Rachel, Debbie, have you kissed a boy? Oh, you have? Did you use tongue? Did you let him touch you? Well, I sure hope you haven't let any boy touch you!"

Every lesson, he would get more and more detailed. Vernon said the grossest things. "What does it make you feel like when boys touch you? What does it feel like, down there? Does it make your nipples tingle?"

Obviously, Vernon had no idea Debbie had been through all this before with her father. He was real excited. He thought he was blowing her young mind with his questions.

After a few guitar lessons, Vernon started bringing himself into the picture. "Have you ever thought about marrying me?" he asked Debbie and Rachel. "When you get married, would you want to share your husband?" He even asked if the two would get mad if he made love to both of them at the same time.

Debbie gave him a dead look. Took her mind somewhere else and pretended he hadn't said anything. Soon enough, he turned all his attention to Rachel. And that girl wanted love so badly that she listened.

Debbie never told anyone about Vernon's questions. Her own mother didn't care if her father raped her, so why would she do anything about Vernon being a perv? In fact, Debbie didn't trust any of the adults enough to let them know what was happening. The kids at Mount Carmel were nonhumans to the grown-ups, without rights or emotions to be protected. "We're their little lumps of clay," Debbie thought. "To be molded and do with as they wish."

The Davidians were that rare Christian sect in 1980s America that was led by a woman. And Lois was taking the flock in a direction where female members would be valued equally to men. But the Davidians still placed men above women. In Mount Carmel, Vernon had found a place that would feed his desire to manipulate women. To possess them wholly.

That next year, 1982, Vernon quit his construction job and moved to Mount Carmel permanently. Some Davidians believed that Lois had given him an ultimatum—stay or leave forever—but no one really knew.

It quickly became clear that Vernon believed he had all the answers. He was never embarrassed to get into people's business and tell them how they were displeasing God. He even marched into Lois's house one time and went through her fridge and shelves and cupboards, tossing out things because they were forbidden. Then he marched on down to Perry Jones's house and did the same.

Things got so bad with Vernon's pestering that even Lois tired of him. She moved him into a tiny room in a house across from Debbie's family with no furniture and one light bulb. It looked like a prison cell.

Then, in the blink of an eye, Vernon would reverse course. "I'm lost," he'd say. "I'm a sinner and I don't know what to do about it." The earth was going to open up and swallow him because he was too evil to even be. He became overwrought, crying with almost everyone at one point or another.

Debbie's bedroom window overlooked Vernon's. In the evening when he came home, he'd enter the room and flick the light switch on. He'd move to the end of his bed and fling his arms out, then throw himself across the bed, his whole body flailing wildly. All the time he'd be crying out so loudly it was like he was being whipped. Debbie watched the scene unfold, open-mouthed.

The shouting got louder until it seemed Vernon was practically going into convulsions. This happened every single night.

Some of the other Davidians were impressed by his outbursts. "Vernon is really suffering," they said. "Boy, that Vernon sure does want to find a way to God."

As for Debbie, she thought Vernon was putting on a show. He could have always pulled the curtains and kept his nightly suffering to himself, couldn't he?

The praying and the crying out caught Lois's attention. Often, at night, she came to the door of his room and pleaded with him to eat something. Vernon usually refused, saying this or that food was forbidden and he couldn't partake.

Lois stayed at the door. She'd say, "Oh, will you at least then drink this tea? It will fortify you." And Vernon would relent, open the door. Maybe they'd talk a bit. No one thought much of it.

Vernon spread his misery around. One time that year, they went down to see Harriet. It was Lois, Vernon, and the six young girls that lived at Mount Carmel at the time, including Debbie. They were trying to convince Harriet to come to Waco and join the group, so the trip was meant to show her how normal they all were. And just to have fun.

And it was fun. Lois was good with kids, a real down-home grandma. But Vernon tried to screw everything up with his holiness thing. He'd tell Lois that taking the girls for ice cream and movies was frivolous. He wanted them to stay home and pray.

"But Vernon," Lois said. "We're meant to enjoy life."

Vernon just shook his head. He didn't seem to get that.

Vernon spent most of his days studying, trying to master the extremely complex Branch Davidian theology. It took him months to get up to speed.

Among the Davidians, everything a prophet said, everything a follower believed, had to be justified through scripture. You couldn't just say, "I believe this because I feel it in my heart." You had to back up your interpretation with chapter and verse and be prepared to defend it. If you didn't know your Ellen White and you tried to claim to be a prophet, you'd get laughed out of the room. A lot of the more scholarly types at Mount Carmel could quote passage after passage of the classic texts the faith was built on.

So Vernon spent a lot of time in his bedroom poring over thousands and thousands of pages of Ellen White and Victor Houteff, the founder of the Davidians. He read Ben Roden and Lois Roden. He studied the charts that Houteff had drawn in the 1940s, depicting the journey to the End Times. He memorized many of these things. And then he went back to the Bible again and read that.

One thing that was new to Vernon in his studies was the idea of types and antitypes. An antitype was someone or something that was foreshadowed by an earlier figure in the Bible. Adam, in the Old Testament, was a type. Jesus Christ, in the New Testament, was his antitype. These pairings ran through Davidian theology.

Vernon paid special attention to the stories of Cyrus, the ancient Persian king spoken of in the Old Testament. The original Cyrus had conquered ancient Babylon in 539 BC. In the Book of Revelation, it was written that another Cyrus, an antitype, would appear to conquer the evil entities that would hold sway before the last days.

The Davidians believed that the End Times would begin in the

Middle East, with a conflict between the Jews and the Arabs. America would take the side of Israel and the USSR would take the side of the Arab nations. American troops would go to the Middle East and fight a great battle, which they would lose. In the aftermath, the Jews would be wiped out. Then God would strike down the Arabs as well, and the land of Israel would be scorched clean of any human presence.

The Apocalypse would arrive, led by the Four Horsemen: worldwide slaughter, earthquakes, and pestilence, the same things Vernon had seen in the Revelation Seminar from Pastor Jim Gilley. This destruction and death would prepare the way for the remnant, the 144,000 men, women, and children who would help establish the kingdom of God on earth.

But before God built the kingdom, the remnant would need to pass through a refining fire. They would be immersed in flames and remade, or "translated," into eternal life. Anyone who wanted to pass into the Kingdom of God must first experience this. Then and only then would Jesus appear and the world be saved.

This teaching was right in line with the kind of conspiratorial beliefs Vernon had grown up with, from the Texas preachers he'd listened to as a boy to the right-wing broadcasters who'd turned Dallas into an exporter of radical theories. The alliance between America and Satan was one of the signs of the second coming of Christ. The keeping of the Sabbath—which was Saturday, not Sunday, as celebrated from coast to coast—was another. Before the final tribulations began, the Davidians believed, the nation would come out publicly and ally itself with the devil and the Roman Catholic Church. America would become Babylon in full, and the End Times would begin.

Lois taught that she was the Sixth Angel named in the Book of Revelation. The next, and final, prophet—the Seventh Angel—would follow her and fulfill the message. This being would be present at the End of Days, ushering God's elect through the conflagrations that would consume the world. "If we are here to know these mysteries," Lois preached, "a divine revelation would be necessary to explain their meaning, at the time of the voice of the Seventh Angel, when the 'mystery of God' is to be finished."

This spirit's arrival was approaching, Lois said. God had tired of the world and its people. He had shown Lois the apocalypse would come "within the lifetime of people now living on earth."

Though he was becoming fluent in the group's theology, Vernon was still an afterthought at Mount Carmel. He volunteered to help around the compound and quickly became a Mr. Fixit, repairing things, painting, whatever. Chief cook and bottle-washer.

At first, he was pleased to be useful. But as time went on, he grew resentful, feeling that people were looking down on him. He was the guy you got to do the dirty jobs no one else wanted to do. It was always "Vernon do this, Vernon do that." He liked to do things for people, but he didn't like to be told to do things for people.

As time went by, it was clear Lois very much wanted Vernon to stay. She was in her midsixties, a grandmother several times over and a world traveler. But at the end of the day, she was alone. Her husband was dead and her nights were long.

She took to Vernon. She saw something in this suffering young man.

But Lois didn't believe in idleness and wasn't going to encourage it. When someone's car broke down, she'd send Vernon over to fix it. Sometimes, when he was done working, the car still wouldn't start and Lois would have to get a real mechanic to come by and fix what Vernon had supposedly repaired. But she kept giving him little assignments. She wanted to build Vernon up.

He did generate some goodwill around Mount Carmel. He never charged anybody a dime for his work. He was humble. Still, if you told Debbie or Perry Jones or one of the others that this Vernon person would rise to lead the Davidians, they would have laughed. It was like saying your dorm janitor was going to become college president. Vernon Howell? Not hardly.

But Vernon wasn't content to stay the janitor forever. At one point, he even asked Lois for permission to preach to the flock, lead them in Bible study. This was a big deal. At Mount Carmel, those who led Bible study usually had the gift of prophecy. Victor Houteff had it, as did Ben Roden, on down to Lois.

Lois told him no. He wasn't ready.

Debbie, for one, thought Vernon was a puzzle. He was depressed and he was ambitious. He hated himself and he loved himself. She figured you'd have to be some mastermind psychiatrist to figure Vernon out, and even then, you could never be sure.

Lois knew about unstable men. The Rodens' son George, the only one of their six children to stay close to the compound, was equally unpredictable.

George was a beefy guy with a beard. His nickname was "Bucky" and he loved wearing his black Stetsons and his sidearms, usually a .38. He had serious mental problems, beginning with Tourette's syndrome. It caused him to spray spittle on people when he talked, to knock dishes off tables, and to stutter. He would be sitting there and all of a sudden slam his hand down on the table and the soup would go everywhere and George would be cussing up a storm.

People at Mount Carmel suspected George had other mental problems, too. He was a bully, he was unstable, and he often seemed to be living in his own reality. He saw big conspiracies everywhere, usually against himself.

Behind his back, the followers called him "Poor George." The man was afflicted. No one could remember the Rodens taking him to a psychiatrist or getting him help. That just wasn't done among the Davidians.

Instead, the Rodens dealt with George themselves. One time, when Ben was still alive, a Davidian came on him standing by the side of one of the houses in Mount Carmel. George was there, too, having some kind of a fit. Ben had tied his son up with a rope and secured him to a post.

George was screaming and bellowing, straining against the rope and trying to get his arms free. His eyes rolled in their sockets like a bull in a lather. Ben was standing there watching his son, not saying a word.

It was a sad sight. Animalistic. But the Davidian walked on. You didn't get involved in the Rodens' business.

The others might look at the junior Roden as "poor George," but that's not how George saw himself. In fact, quite the opposite. He believed he was someone to be reckoned with, a man in line to be the next prophet.

In George's view, he couldn't help having Tourette's, but he had been anointed as the prophet in waiting, and that was important. He had big dreams, and he was always at the center of them. As Vernon said, "George had this wild idea that he was God's man of the hour." Damned straight, as far as George was concerned.

George thought so much of himself that he'd once decided to run for president on the 1976 Democratic ticket. One of his first moves was to arrange meetings with party leaders, Jimmy Carter and Morris Udall, a powerful Congressman from Arizona. Both agreed to sit down with him.

George asked the two men for their support. They declined. Carter, of course, was running himself and Udall had no idea who this wild-eyed Texan was.

The candidate pressed onward. He wrangled a meeting with executives from the Dallas Cowboys and told them that he had received a message from God. If the organization threw its support behind George, they would win the Super Bowl that very year. The execs thanked George, but he never heard back.

He was undeterred. He printed up leaflets, bumper stickers and buttons that read "RODEN FOR PRESIDENT" and handed them out to anyone he met. He had a thirty-six-page pamphlet printed up outlining his political platform. In it, he vowed that if he was elected, his first two acts in office would be the legalization of bigamy (George had multiple wives) and an immediate nuclear strike on the USSR.

In the end, George couldn't gather enough signatures to get on the presidential ballot. His self-confidence, however, was barely nicked.

At the time of Ben Roden's death, George was estranged from his parents and living in California. His father had sent him there, for what exact reasons no one knew. Probably, the Rodens had simply tired of having George around. He'd moved to a trailer park on the California-Arizona border, a four-hour drive from LA out into the desert. George was unable or unwilling to hold down a job, so he survived off welfare. Despite the tough conditions, he thought of himself as a prince in exile.

When he got the phone call that his father was dead, George chartered a plane at great expense and flew to Texas. He got in a car at the airport and headed for Mount Carmel, sweeping in to see the executive council of the Davidians. There he made an announcement: "There is a new King in the Kingdom. As Solomon succeeded his father, David . . . so do I now, the antitypical Solomon, fill the position of ruler of God's earthly Kingdom." He truly believed he was the reincarnation of King Solomon.

The council disagreed. They decided that Lois, Ben's widow, was the true prophet, and she would lead the Davidians. This was a bitter pill for George.

Their relationship never recovered. After Lois announced the Living Waters message, things went from bad to worse. George was enraged by the new teachings. He'd never, as it turned out, been much of a feminist. When Lois went to Israel one time when George was alive, he had thrown a fit. He told anyone that would listen that "if my wife had been away from me that long, I would rape every woman in the house."

As the sniping between mother and son got worse, Vernon was there to soothe Lois. The two would often chat into the early hours of the morning, talking about Scriptures and poring over Victor Houteff's charts of angels and demons, looking for the way forward. Some thought Vernon was chasing Lois. At times, he appeared besotted with the older woman. He trailed after her, looking like a puppy who'd just found his master.

Lois gave Vernon a new job, as a kind of personal secretary. He started tagging along with her to conferences and revival meetings, carrying Lois's pamphlets with the charts and other things. He helped her as she tried to gather up new followers for the Davidians.

Recruiting was a hard business. Many Adventists hated the Davidians, felt they were parasites preaching false doctrine. Lois and the others were attacked, smacked in the face, physically carried off church property.

But Vernon was so inspired by these trips that he went back to Tyler and Chandler, where he'd spent time before Waco. He looked up his old friends and tried to convince them to come to Mount Carmel. He found his old girlfriend, Debbie Owens.

Vernon pulled up in his banged-up Chevy Nova, the back stacked with pamphlets, and started in on her. "Debbie, do you see what the Lord has done for me? Debbie, you need to change your life right now."

Debbie couldn't believe her ears. Vernon Howell was telling her to find Jesus? She let him have it. "You're the *last* son of a bitch to take me to God," she said.

Vernon didn't give up. Sandy, too, was still on his mind. He kept going back to Tyler to see her. He'd show up at her house or the Tyler church, ranting about the phonies of the SDA and trying to win her back. Sometimes he brought a few of the Davidians with him. When her father emerged from the church, Vernon would call out to the other Davidians and tell them he was being persecuted. Then he'd rail at Sandy about her betrayal. It got so bad that her dad and some of the other elders began surrounding Sandy as she left the church, forming a protective rugby scrum moving across the parking lot with Sandy at its center.

Sandy refused to listen to Vernon, but his old friend Harriet was still under his spell. She'd call Sandy and give her updates on Vernon's time at Mount Carmel. She'd say, *He's finding new truths, people who he can relate to.* Or *He's just a wreck without you. He needs you more than you could know.*

Sandy knew Vernon and she knew that he'd sent Harriet to feel her out. Trying to make her jealous, get Sandy stuck in his spiderweb.

Finally, Sandy decided it was over for good. She started dating another guy. The SDA church had tired of Vernon as well. They took the drastic step of formally disfellowshipping him. He was barred from the church forever.

12

THE MEETINGS

EARLY IN 1982, the administration building at Mount Carmel caught fire. There were no fire trucks for miles, so it burned and burned. The Davidians' financial records and pamphlets and teaching aids went up in the flames.

Lois didn't speak about the fire, didn't surmise why God had seen fit to let an important Davidian building be destroyed. Many of her followers thought it was odd. Why would God allow this disaster, and why wasn't Lois explaining the reason to them?

Vernon stepped into the breach. He told the group that God had allowed the fire because the Branches were breaking His dietary laws. It sounded ominous, but Vernon's words actually invigorated the Davidians. It got their blood flowing just to know that God really was keeping a close eye on Mount Carmel.

Vernon expanded on the idea. The believers' disobedience was also why the End Times hadn't yet arrived. God was displeased with the Davidians, Vernon said. That really got people's attention. Vernon, at long last, had given them a reason for why they'd been sitting in Waco for decade after decade without anything happening.

To repair their relationship with God, Vernon started correcting the Davidians' diets. Certain foods, he said, were out. Store-bought mayonnaise, vinegar, sugary foods, corn syrup all had to go. Chocolate was a big no-no. Vernon believed that the body couldn't digest it, and all the chocolate you put in your mouth over your entire life sat in your belly in one big ball.

It was one of the first orders Vernon had given the Davidians. Usually, Lois was the one to lay down the law. But she didn't make a peep. That set people talking. If she was the true prophet, why was Vernon giving the light?

As the months went by, Vernon and Lois were together more and more. Lois was becoming infatuated with this handsome, twenty-two-year-old man.

Vernon moved out of his bedroom across the way from Debbie's house and in with Lois. Soon after, she gave in to his begging. She announced that Vernon could finally lead a Bible study on his own.

When the day arrived, everyone gathered in the chapel. Vernon stood up and walked to the head of the congregation. He opened his Bible. He was nervous, practically shaking.

He launched into his study, but already he was stammering and stumbling. His voice was so low you could barely hear it in the third row. More than once, he lost his train of thought and had to double back to get the thread again. It was a fiasco, almost too awkward to watch.

The negative reviews on Vernon's performance got back to Lois. She preached patience: "Give him a hearing, listen to him, don't be so judgmental." Coming from Lois, it meant a lot.

A few weeks later, Vernon asked Lois for permission to speak again. He got up in front of the congregation and gave his study. His delivery was a little better, more confident. But hardly memorable.

When Vernon got up to speak for a third time, his theme was the devil's lies and Godly truth. How to discern one from the other. He preached about how God's judgment transcended all earthly tribunals. From the beginning, Vernon believed that the Lord and the Lord only—not the police, not the government—could say if a man's actions were right or wrong. "We were never created to be judges," he told the Davidians. This time, his voice was clear and unwavering. "The Son of Man is supposed to judge. The prophets are to judge. And the people are to accept that judgment. No matter what the devil tells us. No matter what the devils tells us. *No matter what the devil tells us.*"

He'd come alive. The cadences that Vernon had absorbed when he was ten, tuned in to the preachers and evangelists on his mother's radio, now reasserted themselves. Vernon had taken in their folksy paranoid style for years, and now he made them his own. He spoke casually, as if he was talking across the fence to a neighbor about things that had grown to concern him, going on in this way until his voice tightened and grew steely with anger. It rasped and sang, a drama to itself.

Vernon would take a Bible verse and break it down, coaxing the meaning out of the old-fashioned words. He did this with Ezekiel 21:9–10: "a sword is sharpened, and also furbished: It is sharpened to make a sore slaughter; it is furbished that it may glitter."

Who was going to get this beautiful sword? "God's people," Vernon said. "The scriptures make themselves plain."

He read on: "It shall be upon all the princes of Israel: terrors by reason of the sword shall be upon my people: smite therefore upon thy thigh."

That rang a bell with Vernon.

"'Upon thy thigh,'" he said. "Ezekiel's command to smite upon his thigh. Now we know that there's been one person in the Bible who ended up wrestling with an angel who received a wounded thigh. He thought that he was being slain. That was Jacob. Good old Jacob, remember? Going back to his father's house? In that night of darkness, he separated all by himself and the angel came to him . . ."

Vernon's interpretation was as clear as glass, helped along by his encyclopedic knowledge of the Scriptures. He could pick out a detail like the smiting of the thigh and show you where the reference came from and how it gained its meaning through the Bible's rich associations. Even the children in the chapel could understand what he was teaching. He was respectful of the Davidian prophets, too, quoting Sister Roden and Brother Ben Roden and Victor Houteff. He'd learned their words well.

It wasn't his concepts that gripped the listeners, at least not yet. It wasn't the material. Vernon wasn't introducing any new light or saying anything that was particularly startling. It was his delivery, his conviction, his fluency with the Word that held the followers rapt. Vernon had gained so much force in such a short time. The rhythms of his speech carried the Davidians along, as if they were sweeping forward on an ocean wave, up and down until they began to feel almost dizzy. People fell to their knees right there in the chapel.

Vernon had discovered one of his great themes: No man can judge me, only God. And it inspired him. None of the Davidians had ever seen a man turn into a prophet almost overnight. It was like the Holy Spirit had reached into Vernon and given him a brand-new soul and voice box. He'd been made over.

Vernon called his teachings "The Serpent's Root." They plumbed the mysteries of the serpent in Eden and how it had beguiled Eve and what that meant for mankind. The serpent had eaten the fruit of the tree of knowledge and had gained a deeper understanding of good and evil than those who only practiced virtue. Vernon was like the serpent in this way: He, too, had sinned, but his sinning had given him a more piercing view into life as it truly was.

He did eight meetings exploring the themes of sin and judgment. The more he spoke, the more he came into his power. He wasn't stammering anymore; you could hear him in the back of the room. And how he handled the Scriptures, no one had ever heard anything like it. One of his followers would later say, "Vernon knew them like he wrote them."

His mother, Bonnie, heard that he was preaching. She came to see and was taken aback. As Vernon flipped from one book to the other, his thoughts flowed seamlessly, every image and turn of phrase vivid and arresting. "Wow," she thought, "he must be inspired to teach the word like this." She'd never heard anyone speak out of the Bible like Vernon did.

Lois had found a new prophet for the Branch Davidian message. A young man who might preach it for decades. A charming man who could persuade.

Leaders in other religious groups were often chosen for their piety or their skills at politics. One could work one's way up to become a Baptist deacon without any special gifts to speak of. With the Davidians, it was different. There was one supreme leader, and that person had to be a visionary. The Davidians weren't trying to build a church for the ages. Their leader was tasked with evading Satan's snares and leading his or her followers into God's new kingdom as soon as possible.

The group's structure was a pyramid, with one God-connected person in total command. This led not only to schisms, but to bold leaders who believed they were special. If Vernon had wandered into a different sect, if he'd settled for the Baptists or even the Pentecostals, the world most likely would never have heard of him. As luck had it, the Davidians were primed not only to accept a narcissist as their leader but to build on his narcissism. Among the Davidians, no one could check the prophet's power.

There was also, as it happened, a vacancy: The group was searching for a seventh, and final, angel.

One afternoon, Vernon came into the kitchen where everyone took their meals. Lois was eating her lunch. He told her he'd had a vision. He quoted Isaiah 8:3. "And I went to the prophetess; and she conceived and bore a son. Then said the Lord said to me, call his name Maher-Shalal-Hash-Baz."

It was a message: They should have a child together. Vernon said God had told him Lois would bear a son and they would name him as directed in Isaiah.

Lois was startled at first. But soon she came around, telling the others she believed she was pregnant by Vernon. She knew this because she'd taken one of those over-the-counter tests and it had come back positive.

In a meeting one day, she pulled out a thin white plastic something or other and waved it in front of her followers. "I have proof!" she cried. The white thing turned out to be the pregnancy test. The Davidians murmured with excitement as they gathered around to peer at it.

The faint blue lines were indeed lined up in a way that meant "positive." Lois was beaming with pride. Anyone who wanted a closer look, she happily showed the plastic thingie to.

It was a miracle of the first order. Sarah, Abraham's wife, was ninety when God told her husband that He would give them a child that would make her "the mother of nations." Sarah had doubted the conception, as had Lois. But now God had allowed her womb to become fertile again, proving not only that Vernon had the gift of vision, but that the Lord had chosen an illustrious role for Lois in the unfolding of His work.

Vernon was right behind her, spreading the word that the baby proved that he and Lois were living prophets. There could no longer be any doubt.

Soon after, Vernon announced that God had been speaking to him directly since he was a child, in visions and in audible speech. In fact, he now declared that he was the "Seventh and Final Angel." This meant that the Apocalypse would occur in Vernon's lifetime and he would lead the Davidians through it.

Lois confirmed it. Vernon Wayne Howell was the being they'd been awaiting. She sent a letter to all the Branches. "We have a messenger from God," she told them.

Her followers reflected back on Lois's prophecies about 1981 and 1984. Lois had predicted something big would happen in both those years. Vernon had arrived in 1981. Now it was three years later, and Vernon was claiming the gift of prophecy.

The dates fit. He'd been foretold.

The members of the group saw a change in Vernon. There was no more flailing and wailing in the window across from Debbie's room. He cut out the "I'm too evil to live" stuff, too. Now he was quiet, very serious, solemn.

Vernon washed and cut his hair. He started dressing in clean clothes, often a shirt and a tie. He was slimmer than the buffed-up guy who'd first walked into Mount Carmel.

People started leaving his sermons saying, "Man, the Lord is *working* on Vernon." After years of listening to Lois explain the same charts in the same way, it was like Mount Carmel had a pulse again. It even worked on Debbie. She thought, *God's changed him*.

Later that fall, Vernon got ready for his first trip to Israel. It was an important moment for him. The Davidians considered themselves to be the continuation of God's chosen people on earth. They had named themselves after King David; they observed the Jewish high holidays as devotedly as they observed Easter or Christmas, more so in fact. For a believer, to walk around Jerusalem and see and touch the living history of its prophets was to witness one's own destiny.

Every Davidian leader had visited the country; now David was making the pilgrimage. He would have seen it as a homecoming. Here the Davidians' past and future met. This is where their transformation into Christian soldiers, into eternal, righteous beings, would begin.

He was to accompany Lois, at her invitation. To prepare for the journey, she gave Vernon a necklace with a Star of David pendant. He put it on so that the pendant hung near the hollow of his neck.

The Rodens had always promoted their Israel trips as preparing the way for the Davidians' eventual move to the Holy Land. They sought inspiration there, visited possible sites for a new compound and for the Temple they'd vowed to build. The Davidians paid for the trip through their tithing and contributions; for them, this was a down payment on their own eternal lives to come.

Lois was fully in love now. One day Perry Jones heard her say, "It looks like God has raised a son out of the earth." Not from her womb, but out of the earth. Meaning that Vernon was Lois's true heir.

Before the trip, the couple made their bond official. They were married in secret at Mount Carmel. Lois herself conducted the ceremony. The two didn't yet have a marriage license from the state of Texas, but in their minds, they were husband and wife. They told no one, not even Lois's own followers.

Though their relationship seemed to proceed smoothly, Vernon did give Lois occasional cause to wonder. One day while they were out driving, Vernon was thinking about his preaching and his future. All of a sudden he blurted out, "Why, with this message I could make love to every woman in the world!"

Who knew what Vernon saw in his mind as he drove along with Lois that afternoon? But clearly, he now sensed he could get what he wanted. When he was a teenage guitar god back in Tyler, he'd rejected the sex and freedom that came with the music, because it was allied with the devil. But this message came from God, which meant he could have his exaltation in sex and still dwell in the Lord's grace. It was so damn exciting he forgot Lois was even in the car.

Lois turned to him. Just what did he mean by that, she asked.

Vernon kept his cool. He explained that she had it all wrong. His mind was in high places. He was speaking in spiritual terms only.

She let it pass and the two soon left for Israel.

When Lois and Vernon returned to Waco, Lois's children began hearing more and more about this young stranger from the Davidians at Waco. Lois's daughter Jane, who lived in California, called Mount Carmel several times, looking to speak with her mother. There was only one phone in the compound, and it sat on a nightstand next to Lois's bed.

Because of the time difference between Texas and California, the phone would often ring at midnight or later. Vernon picked up. Lois's daughter thought that was strange. Vernon readily acknowledged that he was with Lois in the evenings. But he swore that he was consulting with her on the Scriptures, preparing to write his sermons.

George Roden was in California when rumors reached him that Lois and Vernon were sleeping together. He rushed back to Waco and attended one of Vernon's Bible studies. Vernon spoke about the Scriptures for hours, with Lois and her followers nodding along.

George was aghast. This interloper, "vile Vernon" as George now started to call him, had beguiled the entire congregation. These people had taken the bait hook, line, and sinker. Aghast at what he was seeing, George began denouncing Vernon as a Satan worshipper.

At one meeting, George and Vernon got into a heated confrontation. Vernon grabbed George in a bear hug and lifted him off his feet. George flew into a rage and pulled out his .357 Magnum, shouting that he was going to blow Vernon's balls off. He demanded Vernon leave the property and stay out of his mother's life. Vernon refused.

George became increasingly obsessed by his new rival. When he got a letter from a Davidian in California talking about the couple, he wrote back: "To begin with, my mother was not deceived, she was raped at gunpoint."

Later, he went further. He filed a lawsuit, writing the deposition himself: "This V.W. Howell is a cult leader who uses hypnotism, mind-altering drugs and sex as a means to seduce people. He restricts their intake of food and all of them have lost weight, especially my mother. Although the efforts of my sister and I have been untiring, she has improved somewhat, but is still under his satanic spell."

RACHEL

AS GEORGE RAGED, the rest of the Davidians waited for Lois's baby to be born. When she walked to dinner or stood to give her studies, their eyes would fix on her belly, quietly measuring its size relative to the week before.

The weeks passed and no bump appeared under Lois's plain cotton dresses. The Davidians began to gossip. If the pregnancy was a message from God, wasn't the absence of a child a message, too?

Vernon scrambled. He began telling people, out of Lois's hearing, that the reason she'd "lost" the baby was that God was disappointed in her. She'd disobeyed the Lord and so He had taken the child away. Vernon even started denying that he'd ever slept with Lois, implying that the pregnancy had been God's work.

The baby never came. Lois was sad about it. Her flock wondered what had happened.

In the shadow of Lois's disappointment, Vernon began ingratiating himself with Perry and his fourteen-year-old daughter Rachel, along with other key figures at Mount Carmel. Perry was Lois's right-hand man and one of her main recruiters. He had a gift for bringing people in.

Vernon also spent more and more time with Clive Doyle, the lanky printer from Australia. He ran Mount Carmel's magazine and pamphlet division, which brought in most of the sect's money. He had a list of the names and addresses of every Davidian around the world.

Both Perry and Clive were important to Lois's leadership. Vernon clearly sensed this. It appeared he was searching for allies.

In January 1984, Vernon told Lois that he needed her van to run some errands. It was an old blue Chevy, prone to breaking down. She agreed and off he went.

Sure enough, later that afternoon, Vernon came back and told Lois the van had stopped running. It was out on one of the roads near Mount Carmel. He'd left it there and walked back.

He started apologizing. "It's fine," Lois said. Told him not to worry about it.

That night, they went to bed. When Lois fell asleep, Vernon got up and put on his clothes. He left the house and walked down to the Jones house with just the moon lighting the way.

When he reached the house, he got Perry Jones up. "Perry, Perry," he said, "I've been told by God that Rachel is to be my wife." Vernon seemed frightened. This strange command in the middle of the night had, it seemed, unsettled him.

As for Perry, he was stunned. He started asking Vernon questions about the vision and the Scriptures. Vernon calmed down enough to go through some Bible verses, showing that such a marriage was justified in God's eyes. After a few minutes, Perry started nodding his head.

The two men went to the room where fourteen-year-old Rachel was sleeping. They woke her.

"Rachel, you're gonna be my wife, okay?" Vernon said. "But don't be afraid, we're gonna just be married in name only. We're gonna live together like brother and sister."

"All right, Vernon, if it's okay with my daddy," Rachel said.

She got up and put on some clothes. Vernon took her out of the house and they walked down the driveway through the unguarded gate and turned on the dirt road where the van had broken down.

Vernon had planned it all out. The van started right up and the two drove to town. It was close to morning now.

They went to the courthouse and got their marriage license. When that was done, and they were officially husband and wife, Vernon took Rachel back to the blue Chevy van, and drove it to an isolated road outside Waco. Then he parked and told Rachel to get into the back. He followed, and he raped her for the first time.

Lois knew nothing about the events of the morning until hours later. Perry finally went to her house and told her what had happened.

She started bellowing. Some of her followers came to find out what was happening. Was the prophet ill? Distressed? When they saw her, Lois seemed to be having some kind of a nervous fit.

Vernon and Rachel were nowhere to be seen. The cash-strapped groom had taken his bride to Harriet's house for their honeymoon. It was the same place where Sandy and Vernon had been "married in God's eyes" just a few years earlier. Likely it was all he could afford. Likely, too, he knew that word of his marriage had reached Lois by then and wanted to avoid her at all costs.

At Mount Carmel, Lois was inconsolable. Her followers had never seen her like this before. She was cycling through moods, raving with anger, then breaking down in a flood of tears. "How could Vernon do it?" she asked the Davidians. "How could he betray me?"

With Vernon nowhere in sight, Lois blamed her followers. She began slapping them, beating them with her fists. They'd allowed this disaster to happen to their prophet. In her pain, she seemed nearly deranged.

Lois condemned Vernon's prophecy. Once she'd called him the Seventh Angel and said he held the key to the End of Days in his mind. She'd told everyone this. But now she told her followers that Vernon was preaching "the Lucifer message."

Vernon and Rachel left Harriet's and drove back to Mount Carmel. Vernon knew he had to face the music. If he wanted a future with the Davidians, he'd have to deal with Lois.

Rachel arrived wearing the Star of David necklace that Lois had presented him with months earlier. He'd given it to her as a wedding gift.

Some Davidians thought it was the cruelest, most redneck thing they'd ever heard of, recycling a love gift like that. Lois was bound to see it. At times, Vernon seemed to lack a basic understanding that other people had feelings. Either that, or he'd finished with Lois, and so he'd erased her from his mind.

He went to see her. He spoke plainly. "I'm married to Rachel now," Vernon said. Lois was in a state. She shook her head back and forth, trying to shake the words from her head. "But I thought you were married to me!" she cried.

Perhaps Lois had waited for him to come to her, thinking he'd clear up this rumor, tell her it was a misunderstanding, a crush that had quickly run its course. But Vernon held firm. Rachel was his wife; his time with Lois was over. Hearing it straight from her ex-lover, Lois knew that it was true. She'd lost him.

She returned to her wailing, now doubled in volume.

A number of Davidians witnessed the mortifying scene. Lois was their matriarch, a firm and judicious prophet. Her behavior shook the followers. Who was this unhinged person? Whether or not the word "hysteria" passed their lips, that's essentially what Lois was accused of.

The Davidians had always mistrusted the wasps' nest that was women and sex. And now, they had further proof of its dangers. Look how it had unmade Lois! She'd preached the dignity of the female but when Vernon turned her down, she'd gone to pieces.

The wretched meeting between the ex-lovers ended, and the Davidians returned to their rooms. Days passed.

Soon after, Rachel was walking through the compound one afternoon. Lois was outside and spotted her. She called her over.

Rachel approached. As she neared, Lois sprang at her, surprisingly agile for her age. As she did, she reached out and tore the Star of David necklace from the girl's neck. Lois held the chain in her fist as Rachel ran away crying. Lois had her memento back. She was triumphant at least in this. She refused to return it to Rachel.

But despite Vernon's treachery, it was Lois who found herself being judged. The Davidians gossiped about how petty and high-schoolish she'd become. The position of prophet was a serious one. To see it in the hands of a distraught, vulnerable woman made many of the Davidians uneasy. Vernon, though he'd betrayed his onetime lover, at least carried himself with dignity.

Passover, a major holiday on the Davidian calendar, arrived that April. Believers came from far and wide to hear this new prophet, Vernon Howell, and to learn who was going to lead the Davidians. Lois was a fading power, but she was still the group's formal leader. There were a few men vying to replace her, George Roden and Vernon among them. As the flock gathered, accusations and counteraccusations about false prophets and skullduggery flew back and forth among the different camps.

The followers expected that Lois, their prophet, would lead them in Bible studies. But she stayed in the background. Not once did she stand up in front of the congregation and try to unify the group. A rousing speech would have done wonders, but Lois never gave it.

Vernon took up the slack. With his speaking style now honed by hours and hours of Bible studies, he told the members his vision of what was to come. What they'd been waiting for was just around the corner. "I am so sad for some," he said, "and at the same time I'm very happy the end is here. God's giving us a message which is so startling and so cutting, that when we see it as it is in Christ, we'll realize that we just barely made it. This is the last chance, Branches. It's the last movement."

The lesson was rough and raw. It woke you up. It wasn't a bide-your-time kind of teaching, like Lois usually gave.

At the chapel during Passover, Vernon gave his "Seventh Angel's message." He was the antitypical King Cyrus, he told the followers, the Persian king whom God had anointed to slay the Babylonians and protect the people of Israel. Now Vernon had been appointed do the same during the coming apocalypse. He drew from his lesson that day from Isaiah 8:9:

Raise the war cry, you nations, and be shattered!
Listen, all you distant lands.
Prepare for battle, and be shattered!

He launched into his study. As he talked, Lois stood up. She began to speak, loudly. She said that she and Vernon had been having sex; she gave intimate details. The talk of an immaculate conception was Vernon's lie. She claimed that he was the aggressor. He'd constantly asked her for intercourse until she succumbed.

Vernon stood at the head of the room, dumbfounded. "Oh, Sister Roden, Sister Roden," he cried out sorrowfully. "Why are you doing this?"

Lois ignored him. She went on, detailing every lewd act they'd ever performed on each other. She luxuriated in the filthy details. "Like you said, Vernon," she called to him, "'The Emmanuels shall know the truth.' So, I decided to tell the truth.'"

Lois had saved her voice not to rally the believers, but to get revenge on her disloyal lover. Vernon stammered, unable to string a sentence together.

Over the next days, the Davidians talked about Lois's outburst. The sexual revelations were old news to some, but the details had disturbed even them. A consensus formed. Lois had been acting ungodly for many weeks. She had behaved like a jilted teenager and this outburst was more of the same.

Discounting Lois's decades of faithful work on behalf of the flock, the Davidians chose to put their trust in Vernon, who'd arrived at Mount Carmel only a few years before. A man's word counted more at Mount Carmel and always had. Even if her account was true, the followers reasoned, Vernon must have either been tricked or led by God into this affair. What else could account for it? What vital young man would choose to sleep with an elderly woman long past her sexual prime? If Lois had been trying to turn the congregation against Vernon, she'd largely failed. Only a few followers rallied to her side.

Lois had miscalculated in another way, too. Ever since her 1977 vision of the female Holy Spirit, her core message was focused on the mysterious third element of the Trinity. She'd staked her leadership on it. But the Holy Spirit was hard to grasp. It didn't inspire believers in the way that the Book of Revelation did. No one joined the Davidians because they were zealots for the Holy Spirit. The core of the faith at Mount Carmel remained the Lord and the End Times and the return of Jesus Christ.

And then there was the old misgivings. Many of the followers, especially the men but some of the women as well, simply didn't want to be in a feminist church. They were tired of saying *Our Mother, who art in heaven*. They longed to get back to that old-time religion.

As the Davidians debated, George Roden sought to poison the waters against Vernon. Now that the affair with his mother was out in the open, he declared, it was a stain on the good name of the Branch Davidians. In order to remove it, Vernon had to marry Lois lawfully.

Vernon resisted. In fact, according to George, he threatened revenge. "He said that . . . [Lois] and me and my sister and all the Roden family would have to die in the slaughter of Ezekiel 9:1–5," he told the other Davidians. "So there began the death decree against me and the Roden family."

Vernon had his own version of the events. George had been stalking him. He came to Vernon's Bible studies, twice a day, his .357 Magnum gun strapped to his leg like he was Doc Holliday.

It was clear to Vernon that George was planning a coup. The younger Roden wanted to be named the living prophet. In fact, he was now signing his letters, "The Man, The Branch, George Roden."

After a long week marked by accusations, gossip, and fits of rage, George managed to force Vernon and Rachel off the compound. There was too much ill will for them to stay on the property. The two loaded what belongings they could gather onto a truck and retreated to Waco. After lodging a few months at an apartment rented by Rachel's father, Vernon was able to find a house of his own.

He may have been cast out of Mount Carmel, but Vernon did leave with some assets to his name. With his marriage to Rachel, Vernon had brought Perry into his camp. The next target was Clive Doyle. Whoever had Clive and his mailing lists could reach the worldwide flock.

Soon after Passover, Clive announced he would follow Vernon. No one else at Mount Carmel had considered Clive's importance to the whole operation. Only when he'd switched sides did the Davidians realize he controlled the fundraising and the printing press. Now both were in Vernon's hands.

Still, George believed he had triumphed over Vernon. He renamed the compound "Rodenville" and crowed about his victory. But only a few believers stayed on the property. About twenty-five Davidians left to follow Vernon, a small number kept faith with Lois, and the remainder lit out because of George's loony bin antics.

Believing that he was now the Davidians' new leader, George started a newsletter, "Rough Wind," to guide his flock. In one issue, he brought up a verse from Isaiah 57:3, which George paraphrased this way: "The seed of the adulterer and the sorceress and the whore." He thought the verse was talking about Vernon.

George took aim at Vernon's illegitimate birth. He pointed out that the Bible taught that children of unwed mothers were "prohibited from the congregation" for ten generations. He implied that Bonnie may have been a witch herself, as she'd given birth to a rock and roller "who performed cunnilingus on women." George arrived at this startling conclusion by pointing out that the members of the band KISS regularly stuck their tongues out at their audience.

He twisted Vernon's warnings with childish logic. When Vernon warned that the Davidians were doomed to be smote by "the rod" for their devious ways—meaning a heavy stick—George chose to interpret "the rod" as being Vernon's penis. Clearly, George was still fuming about Vernon's affair with his mother.

George hunkered down at Mount Carmel. He put up makeshift barricades to stop any attack by Vernon. "This is what they should have had to protect our boys in Lebanon," he told his followers, referring to the 1983 bombing in Beirut that killed 241 American service members. "It's basically a holy jihad, Khomeini vs. Israel, that's what Vernon Howell has with me."

He started patrolling the compound with an Uzi submachine gun. At times, he'd catch one of Vernon's followers on the grounds and force them at gunpoint to sign a document he'd had written up, confirming that George was the rightful leader of the group. Then and only then would he let them go.

One young woman, a student at Baylor University in Waco, wanted to do her master's thesis on Lois's feminist message. She went to Mount Carmel and did some interviews with the Davidians who remained there. She started following the group around, doing field research and speaking to members of the different factions.

One evening, Perry Jones, who was staying at the compound at the time, walked the student past the gatehouse to her car. She got in, but before she could put the car into gear, George drove up on an ATV, carrying a shotgun. He stopped beside the driver's-side window and pointed the gun at the young woman's face.

George thought the woman was a journalist, there to report a story on the Davidians. He wanted to tell his version of events. He kept the gun aimed at the woman's head as he spoke about Vernon's evil ways.

He recounted the whole saga. When he was finished, the terrified young woman drove off.

As wild as that incident was, it was only a small taste of what George was capable of. One morning, the hot water heater broke at a Waco house Vernon and the others sometimes stayed at. There was no hot water for bathing. Vernon called up Lois, who was still technically in charge of Mount Carmel. Still half-infatuated with him, Lois agreed to let Vernon and his people take showers there.

Vernon's followers jumped in one of the school buses they were using at the time and headed over to the compound. But when they drove up the long driveway, they saw George Roden standing in the front yard, holding the Uzi.

He started shooting. The bullets ripped through the bus tires and the vehicle shuddered to a halt on the long driveway. The children inside were screaming their heads off.

After the firing stopped, the Davidians slowly exited the bus. The cops arrived to investigate. A catastrophe had been narrowly averted. If he'd aimed a few feet higher, George would have killed a number of Vernon's people.

Years later, many people would come to believe that Vernon conjured mass death out of the ether. But the truth was it was George Roden who introduced the mix of guns, menace, and prophecy into the Davidians' world. He was Vernon's teacher in this.

Vernon had never been a gun geek. And since he was a boy, he'd hated violence, even on the football field. As for the Davidians, they'd always kept the talk of killing to the Bible, boxed it up like a gift to be opened at the End of Days.

It was George who showed Vernon what was what when it came to barbarous desires. George loved the feel of his well-oiled Colt .45 sitting snug in its leather holster, was never happier than when he was carrying around his chunky Uzi. George wanted to bring the violence he felt inside into the here and now. His attitude was: *Release your grudges, man, just get it on.*

14

DAVID BUNDS

After being driven out of Mount Carmel by George Ro-den, Vernon was eager to bring more believers into his camp. He decided to head to California to coax the Davidians there over to his side. Followers who lived away from Mount Carmel were called "outside" believers, and California was home to quite a few. One of the families he visited first was the Bunds, who were eager to help with Vernon's mission. On his arrival, he commenced giving his Bible studies in their living room.

The Bundses' teenaged son, David, thrilled to Vernon's preaching. Not ten minutes after Vernon started, David thought, "He's changed." The woe-is-me loser stuff was gone; all of a sudden Vernon was laser freaking focused. Vernon always had a lot of energy and now he had something to concentrate it on: leading his own little sect. Vernon spoke with so much passion, it filled the room. This guy's on fire, David thought. Right there, he accepted Vernon's message.

There was only one point when doubt crept into David's mind. One afternoon, he and Vernon were looking at some of the Branch Davidian charts, the ones originally drawn by Victor Houteff, filled with drawings of beasts and prophets and other things. Vernon pointed to a particular beast, one with a little green head. "Oh, that's Sandy, my girlfriend," he said.

Sandy, the girl from Tyler, Texas. Vernon talked about her all the time.

David thought, how could this chart, which had probably been around since the 1940s, have a picture of a young woman who hadn't been born yet? How was that possible? And if it was prophecy, if old Victor Houteff had somehow "seen" a face from the future and drawn her, why would it be an ex-girlfriend of Vernon's who was to play no real part in the Branch Davidians? What was that even about?

This kind of thing—injecting the prophetic tradition with bits and pieces of one's own life—had never happened before. Lois's desire for women's equality might have had something to do with her vision of the female Holy Spirit, but one could see that as inspiration, the Lord's guiding hand. What Vernon had just done was different, a tiny but important step in remaking the Davidians in his own image.

David let it go. Vernon was just too electrifying to get hung up on a minor detail. The next year, David drove to Texas to join the group. It was a momentous time to become part of the Branch Davidians.

Soon after Vernon's marriage to Rachel, she became pregnant. The couple flew to Israel, in the hopes that the baby would be born in the Holy Land.

The couple landed in Israel and spent their time sightseeing. Rachel still hadn't given birth by the time their return date arrived, but something far more momentous did occur. While they were touring the country, Vernon had a major vision. On his return, he announced it to his followers: Not only was he the Seventh Angel, but the secrets of the End Times had been revealed to him in full.

Vernon explained how it had happened: While he was in Israel, some Russian cosmonauts were orbiting the earth in their spacecraft. Vernon happened to catch a TV news report about their mission. The announcer said that, during their orbit, the cosmonauts called down to their space center and reported they'd seen something strange: seven angelic beings flying toward earth with the wings the size of jumbo jets. The men were terrified by the creatures.

Vernon didn't think much about the report at the time. But days later, he was standing on Mount Zion, outside the walls of the Old City, when the same seven angels came down and spoke to him. They didn't have wings—the cosmonauts had been mistaken on that point. But they did have Merkabahs. In Jewish mysticism, a Merkabah is a four-wheeled chariot that carries four angels. Vernon believed that it was in fact a spaceship, a spaceship that traveled by the refraction of light.

These seven angels took Vernon into one of their Merkabahs and flew him up into the sky. They traveled to the celestial equator, then to Orion, the constellation that is visible from every part of the earth. There they revealed to him their secrets.

The Book of Revelation speaks of a lamb holding a book with seven seals on it. In the book were the details of the end of the world and the founding of God's new kingdom on earth. Only the lamb can open and interpret the seals. The angels showed him the location of the Seven Seals in the Scriptures and told him what they meant. He was, therefore, the Lamb of God.

So much had been revealed to him, he told the Davidians. He was aflame with this new light. He called it "the Cyrus Doctrine," as he now believed himself to be the antitypical King Cyrus, the second coming of the great Persian king. As the original Cyrus had defeated the ancient Babylonian empire, Vernon would defeat the new Babylon that had sprung up in its wake.

What it came down to, in practical terms, was this: The Davidians had to ready themselves to move to Israel in order to prepare for the Apocalypse.

Vernon sent out a new batch of pamphlets to possible recruits.

I AM THE SON OF GOD, they began. YOU DO NOT KNOW ME.

DEAR BRETHREN IN THE SEVENTH-DAY ADVENTIST CHURCH. I AM THE SON OF GOD. YOU DO NOT KNOW ME NOR MY NAME. I HAVE BEEN RAISED UP FROM THE NORTH AND MY TRAVELS ARE FROM THE RISING OF THE SUN.

Vernon, like most of the Davidian leaders before him, was targeting Seventh-day Adventists. Followers of the SDA church were the most likely converts—they knew the texts and shared a common history.

ALL THE PROPHETS OF THE BIBLE SPEAK OF ME. . . . I HAVE BEEN REJECTED IN THE PERSONS OF MY PROPHETS OVER AND OVER.

I HAVE SEVEN EYES AND SEVEN HORNS. MY NAME IS THE WORD
OF GOD AND I RIDE ON A WHITE HORSE (REV 19:11). I AM HERE
ON EARTH TO GIVE YOU THE SEVENTH ANGEL'S MESSAGE (REV.
10:7). I AM THE PROPHETS; ALL OF THEM.

Vernon's boldness shone through. Not only was he the seventh angel,
which the Davidians had been waiting for since they were founded, he
was also every biblical prophet who'd ever lived. No Davidian leader, no
Adventist visionary, had ever claimed that for themselves. He was in new
territory.

I WANT TO INVITE YOU TO MY MARRIAGE SUPPER. THE INVITA-
TION IS IN PSALMS 45.

Biblical scholars had long considered the Book of Psalms to be poetry,
an ecstatic attempt to describe and reach toward God. Not prophecy. But
Vernon was treating the lovely verses of Psalm 45—"Thine arrows are
sharp in the heart of the king's enemies"—as if they had been written
about him.

READ IT AND CONFESS THAT YOU DON'T KNOW ME. . . . MY NAME
IS CYRUS AND I AM HERE TO DESTROY BABYLON. I HAVE COME
IN A WAY THAT IS CONTRARY TO YOUR PRECONCEIVED IDEAS.
I WILL REPROVE YOU FOR YOUR WORLD LOVING. I WILL SCOLD
YOUR DAUGHTERS FOR THEIR NAKEDNESS AND PRIDE THAT
THEY PARADE IN MY FATHER'S HOUSE AND BY MY ANGELS WILL
STRIP THEM NAKED BEFORE ALL EYES BECAUSE OF THEIR FOOL-
ISH PRIDE.

This was classic Vernon, echoing themes from his childhood. He
could see things others couldn't. He had rebuked Adventists—even
Davidians—for letting their daughters wear short skirts. This was Vernon the scold.

THE YOUNG MEN WILL ABUSE MY KINDNESS. THEY WILL TAKE
MY LIFE, BUT I WILL ARISE AND TAKE THEIRS FOREVER MORE.

YOU MINISTERS WILL LAMENT YOUR FOOLISHNESS. YOUR LOST
FLOCK WILL TEAR YOU TO PIECES.

PREPARE TO MEET THY GOD.

Vernon was telling the Davidians that he would be killed before his
time—"They will take my life"—and would then return to smite his enemies. ("They" was the government.) He'd said such things to his family
and his followers before, but now he was making the prophecy public.

It was the same paranoid theory that Vernon had heard as a child: The
End Times were going to be intimately tied up with American history
and no one, least of all Vernon, would escape it. The feds had allied with
Satan. A great fracture was coming in the world.

In the pamphlet, Vernon also claimed that God had cured him of his
stutter. However, no one could actually remember him stuttering in the
first place, only stammering during his first attempts at Bible studies.
Still, Vernon announced that his affliction was gone. It was another blessing from above, a sign of his favor in Heaven.

15

PALESTINE

AFTER HIS RETURN from Israel in 1984, Vernon was thinking big. He had a triumphant new message and he told David and the others that, with it, he was going to recruit thousands of new followers.

Vernon decided a new motorcycle was just the thing for evangelizing, and he asked Don Bunds, David's father, to pay for it. Vernon said he'd put two guys on it and they'd go around the country drumming up new recruits. Whatever Vernon was doing, whatever idea came to him, he had to work a God angle into it. He couldn't just say, "Hey, I dig motorcycles. Buy me one."

Don resisted. He pointed out that if Vernon bought an economy car, he could put four guys in there, not just two. It would be cheaper and the believers could even sleep in it.

But no, Vernon had to have the bike. So Don Bunds bought him a 1982 Honda V45 Magna.

Before he could hit the road and pull in new followers, Vernon had to find a place for his flock to live. With this in mind, he hopped on the Magna one morning and began driving. He was looking for a sign. Wherever he and his followers settled had to be approved by God.

Vernon turned the handlebars eastward, toward the Piney Woods of Texas. The east had symbolic meaning for him, as King Cyrus II had been ruler of Persia, an eastern kingdom. Vernon was beginning to think of himself as the antitypical Cyrus, so east it was. Vernon revved the engine and hit the road, receptive to all portents.

It was, in its own small way, an echo of the journeys taken by other American faiths: the Puritans arriving at Plymouth Rock, the Mormons venturing west into Utah. Each had found their land, defended it, and flourished. Now Vernon would do the same for the Davidians.

Vernon was reliving, too, the drama of the Westerns like *Gunsmoke* and *The Rifleman* that he'd watched as a boy, even if he was riding a two-wheeled Honda and not a four-legged palomino. He was a pioneer looking for a place away from the corruption of the cities. He believed he could start afresh.

About a hundred miles from Waco, a town came into view over his handlebars. It was Palestine, Texas, which had begun as a frontier trading post before the Civil War. Though it was pronounced "PAL-uhs-teen," and not "PAL-uhs-tine" (the territory that was renamed Israel) Vernon was sure that God had led him there.

He drove around until he found a realtor's office. There he learned there was a twenty-acre property in town that was for sale. The price was $38,000.

Vernon put down a deposit.

Later, Perry Jones went to the local post office and rented a PO box. The postal clerk gave him number 1846. As Perry well knew, that was the year the Adventists had published an important account of Ellen White's first vision, a milestone in Adventist history.

Perry returned and gave Vernon the news. "Praise *GOD!*" Vernon exclaimed with feeling. How clear was it now that the Lord had blessed his new venture, that they were all on their way to great and illustrious things?

The land at Palestine was in the middle of nowhere, covered with massive pines. No water line, no sewage lines, a single electric wire out by the road.

About twenty-five of the Davidians went with Vernon to settle there, David Bunds and Perry Jones and Rachel and Clive Doyle and his wife and some others. They began cutting back the pine and shrubs. It was like they were homesteading.

After the terrain was cleared, the Davidians put together a little camp, nailing together some five-by-seven plywood shacks to live in. They hauled in several old, broken-down buses that would serve as little apartments. Vernon found wood-burning stoves to keep the plywood houses warm in the winter.

They had one phone. They ran the wire all through the woods to reach it. For water, they'd go to into town and fill up jugs and haul them back. They'd drink it and take showers, too, by pouring a gallon of the stuff over their heads. Their income came from some of the members' Social Security checks, which were handed over to Vernon. A few of the men got jobs and gave Vernon most of their wages.

Along with the shacks and the buses, there were rusted-out cars scattered over the grounds, along with weight benches, broken toys, pots and pans, and discarded couches. At night, the believers gathered around campfires, sitting on the couches as the wood crackled and spit embers.

They never built a chapel or a meetinghouse. Vernon told them they wouldn't be in Palestine long.

The good thing about the new camp was that they were all together, away from the distractions of Waco. The bad thing was that it was unbelievably boring. There was nothing to do; no fresh believers were showing up to hear the message, and Vernon wasn't introducing any new light. It was the same old thing day after day: breakfast, morning Bible study, work or free time, lunch, another Bible study, sleep.

Stuck in the back of beyond, David and some of the others found it hard to hide their frustration. Vernon had returned from Israel ablaze, promising a new epoch in the Davidian's journey. But all that had happened was they were stranded in this remote camp, listening to Bible studies and baking in the heat.

Vernon sensed their mood; he had a gift for divining what his followers were thinking. He came up with a saying for those who were spacing out: "Faith," he told them, "is not feeling."

The saying became a kind of mantra for the Davidians. It meant: Your emotions come and go; you feel good about the message one day, you have doubts the next. Okay, so you're bored. So what? God didn't care. There were things that were true regardless of how you felt about them. Faith is not feeling.

Another one of his mantras, even more important, soon joined the first: "Come up hither." The phrase appeared in Revelation 11:12: *And they heard a great voice from heaven saying unto them, Come up hither. And they ascended up to heaven in a cloud; and their enemies beheld them.*

For Vernon, it meant, hew close to the message. Leave Babylon behind. Listen to me. Exalt me. Be with me always.

16

THE GOLDEN STATE

WITH HIS HOME base established, Vernon began splitting his time between Palestine and California. Out west, he stayed with the Bunds at their house in Pomona or in one of several houses his followers rented for him. He hit music stores in LA, tried out some new guitars, casually attempted to convert the salesmen. Often, he brought Rachel and some of the others with him.

Vernon drove his Honda Magna everywhere. He loved it so much that he went back to Don and said, I need two more. Don reluctantly agreed.

When Vernon went to the dealership to buy the second Magna, the salesman told him the price he'd paid for the first one was too low. The dealership had made a mistake. Vernon told everyone it was a sign from God that the motorcycle idea was blessed by the Lord. The bikes would bring them a rush of followers.

But, as usual with Vernon, the idea went nowhere. It fizzled out before a single evangelist could hop on the Magna. Vernon was better at making plans than executing them.

Instead, Vernon asked Don to buy him some buses, old airport shuttles that came cheap. Vernon planned to rehab the things and drive them all over the country, playing his music and giving Bible studies. Once on the road, he'd turn his music fans into believers. That was the way.

Grudgingly, Don ponied up for the first shuttle bus. When Vernon drove it into the Bundses' driveway, he called out to his followers to see. "The Lord provided us with a bus!" he said.

Bunds shook his head. "Don Bunds gave you the money and you went and bought a bus," he muttered. The Lord hadn't provided shit.

Vernon set the Davidians to work. They scraped the old paint off the vehicle with little razor blades. They cleaned the interior until it shone. They tinkered with the engine, got it running smooth. After weeks of mind-numbing work, the shuttle was ready to tour the country.

But Vernon, as mercurial as ever, announced he'd changed his mind again. The music thing wasn't going to work out. He told David and some others to drive the buses back to Palestine and park it in the camp. It would serve as shelter for some of the believers.

Vernon didn't bother informing his followers that God had told him music wasn't the way forward. The change was just part of his chaotic management style, as the Davidians were starting to realize. He reserved the right to change his mind without warning, knowing that the Davidians would simply take him at his word.

Despite the setback, Vernon was undaunted. The Davidians were going to plant congregations in every state in the country, he said. He would gather up the 144,000 that would form God's army in the End of Days.

His mother, Bonnie, came to Palestine and joined the group, having finally gotten sick and tired of Roy beating on her. It was a supremely joyful moment for Vernon. He always told the Davidians what a shitty childhood he'd had, but the next thing he'd do was get on the phone pleading with Bonnie to move to Palestine. He wanted her there with him. Roy followed his wife to the camp, swearing to give up alcohol. Vernon welcomed even him.

Vernon was constantly inviting his family and other loved ones to come to Palestine. Every so often, he would show up on the doorsteps of Linda and Sandy, the loves of his early life, and ask them to join him. He visited others from his past, too. He was going to bind up the wounds of his childhood. Heal everyone through the power of Christ.

Of course, in this new family Vernon was creating, he would be the boss. There would be no more "Mr. Retardo" or "the bastard." He would be the messiah, and he'd be treated as such.

Vernon went to visit his aunt Sharon, the one he'd played with at Grandma Erline's place. He told her she needed to be in the message and asked her to come to Palestine. Sharon went for a visit, but there was something about the setup—just what it was, she couldn't locate in her own mind—that unnerved her. She couldn't see her and her little children living there.

Sharon told him she wouldn't be joining him. Vernon was hurt, she could see it in his eyes. It took her back to those times in Little Elm, with her daddy's car pulling away from Bonnie and Roy's place, and Vernon pedaling after it on his bike, crying, calling for them to take him back.

Vernon's bursts of jubilation, however, were often followed by painful days. The gleam in his eyes would fade. He'd get super-down and talk about "the darkness." Or he wouldn't talk at all. It happened many, many times.

During another visit with Sharon, he told her, "You know, the government is going to kill me one day."

"That's a terrible thing to say," Sharon replied. "Why would you say something like that?"

He mentioned things happening at Palestine that the government didn't like, but he wouldn't go into any details. It left a weird taste in Sharon's mouth for days. She'd never known Vernon to be paranoid, or especially prone to keeping secrets. It seemed as if the pressure of leading the Davidians—or something else she couldn't quite put her finger on— was stirring a new volatility within Vernon. It worried Sharon to no end.

Sometimes the dark thoughts struck when he was on the road. During one of his trips, he called Palestine and said he was suffering terribly. The details were fuzzy, but Vernon was furious. "What are you doing back there?!" he shouted into the phone. Then he hung up.

Vernon had this idea that, if he got sick, one of his followers had caused it. If the Davidians sinned, God would strike at the prophet. So the reason he was hurting was that people were disobeying the Lord.

Back at Palestine, the Davidians began to worry: Was it me? Did I cause Vernon's anguish? The whole camp went into the meetinghouse and started praying. "God, please, we're so sorry. Please don't hurt our prophet. We apologize. We'll do better. Please, Lord, take this affliction away from Vernon."

Vernon was buffeted by changing moods, as if the struggle between good and evil that he preached about was already underway in his own heart. One incident showed just how far the pendulum was swinging.

During one stay in Los Angeles, Rachel got lonely. Her younger sister, Michele, who was ten at the time, was back in Palestine. Vernon decided he would bring her out to stay with Rachel.

Instead of buying her an airline ticket, Vernon drove back to Texas himself, picked up Michele, and turned back toward California: sixteen hundred miles in an old van. He said God told him to drive.

On the way, he felt something overcome him. A feeling, a temptation that grew stronger until it actually began to frighten him. A voice said: "Pull over to the side of the road, take off Michele's clothes, and make love to her."

Vernon was shaken. He thought, "This is Satan speaking, this is not God."

But he was confused. Perhaps it was the Lord, testing him. Perhaps it was part of his plan to strengthen Vernon for what was to come.

Vernon pulled to the side of the road onto the gravel. Cars went flying by on his left.

He was horrified by the message, but at the same time an overpowering lust coiled in his jeans. Michele was three feet away from him. Something in his mind was telling him to tear her clothes off and give it to her right there. He cried out within himself, begging God to save him.

After a time, the urge faltered. Vernon put the car back in drive and got the van back on the highway. He didn't lay so much as a finger on the girl. He felt he'd won a great victory.

When he got back to California, he told everyone about the experience. Vernon seemed genuinely afraid that he was in danger of losing his mind.

The recruiting dream hadn't died. Instead of crisscrossing the country picking up new believers, Vernon now decided to focus on the down and out right there in LA. One night, he got on his motorcycle and drove to Skid Row.

When Vernon arrived, he spotted a guy sleeping in the gutter. Immediately he drove to a fast-food place and bought a bunch of burgers. He left the food next to the guy in a paper bag, so when he woke up, he'd have a decent meal.

He made more trips, slowly getting to know the men and women, most of whom were Black, living in tents or sleeping on cardboard boxes. Vernon really got down on their level and listened to their stories, tried to see the world through their eyes. One of the guys told him they hated how the city would just come and dump supplies in the middle of the street, without even speaking to the people. Vernon nodded. He made an effort to get to know the Skid Row residents, one by one.

It was the same for drug addicts and prostitutes. He didn't judge them. One of his followers who went along on a Skid Row visit was amazed: These people stank, they were dressed in rags, and most were half out of their gourds on drugs. But Vernon treated them like individuals who were worth having as friends. He even persuaded a few to go to rehab.

One day, the Bunds came home and found the place filled with homeless people. Wall to wall. Vernon wanted to have the men and women in one place so he could preach the message. He'd brought them home for a hot meal and some Bible studies.

David's dad wasn't exactly thrilled about the unwashed men and women crammed into his new house. Fortunately for him, the homeless people were thoroughly bored by Vernon's Bible studies. After a few days, they left.

Vernon finally moved out of the Bundses' home and into a rental house, along with about thirty of his followers. The house belonged to a prostitute named Gayle, and Gayle—who remained living at the house even after the Davidians moved in—had a hopeless addiction to cocaine.

For the other Davidians, Gayle was a major pain in the ass. There were only two bedrooms in the house, so most of the followers crashed in sleeping bags on the floor. At night, Gayle, who spent most of the day sleeping, would get up and stumble around the house, stepping on the dozing people or tripping over their stuff and crashing loudly to the floor.

No one could get a decent night's sleep. But Vernon told the others to be patient with Gayle. He was counseling her, listening to her tales of the streets and trying to wean her off drugs. He really did seem to care.

Gayle came home one night and told the Davidians a story. She'd gone to see a friend, and there was this guy there. He'd just been released from prison, and they got to talking, and the guy had gotten aggressive and raped her.

Gayle was hurting; she had marks and bruises on her body. She was afraid of going to the hospital because they might see that she had a drug habit and force her off the coke.

Vernon said, "Gayle, you have to go to the emergency room." He wanted her taken care of. He and the others sat with her and coaxed her into their car. When they got to the hospital, Gayle didn't have insurance, so Vernon offered to pay. He was just all-around sweet to the woman.

Vernon's compassion extended even to those who'd hurt him. As he grew older, he talked to his aunt Sharon about his grandfather, Vernon Clark. Still living in Texas, Clark had alienated most of his children, who'd moved out of the house to escape his violent outbursts and general hatefulness. In the early eighties, his health began to decline.

In 1985, Clark entered a VA hospital in Texas, suffering from a raft of illnesses complicated by a lifetime of hard drinking. None of his children or grandchildren went to see him, except for Vernon. When he heard that Clark was dying, Vernon drove to Texas and visited the old man at the hospital.

He found a humbled person. Clark tried to make amends for the years of calling Vernon "that little bastard" and treating him like an unwanted intruder at the house in Little Elm. The older man was near death, and he wanted Vernon's blessing.

Vernon responded with great kindness. "He prayed over him, prayed with him," said Sharon. "He bore no ill feelings to him at all."

Vernon not only went to see his namesake, he urged others in the family to go, too. "He was a person of his time," he told his aunts and uncles, perhaps referring not only to Clark's raw childhood, but to his unloving ways. Go, Vernon said. Allow the man to unburden himself.

The family refused. Some things were not to be forgiven. Vernon was the only one who made peace with his grandfather before his death.

Sometimes, Vernon would give a job to someone who might not be qualified for the work, just to build that person up, like Lois had done for him when he first came to Mount Carmel. To help them grow.

Bob Kendrick, Debbie's father, had been away from the Davidians for a while. He'd heard all the bad stories and rumors about Vernon, but wanted to see for himself, so he made his way to Palestine. After a few days, Vernon told Bob's wife that Bob ought to quit work. He felt that Bob's heart was like a worn-out balloon, and it was going to burst if he didn't get some rest. Bob took his advice, quit his job, and moved full-time to Palestine.

There was nothing in it for Vernon. He probably lost some money on the deal, because Bob couldn't pay his tithe anymore. But he just went ahead and did it.

As for Bob, he thought Vernon was the tops. "All the rot-gut about him is just hogwash," he told David. "I don't understand why people wanted to try to hurt him. He really cares about us."

Vernon even acted as a kind of counselor. One female Davidian revealed to him something extremely painful: She'd been sexually abused as a child.

Vernon listened, saying nothing. When she finished, he began to talk. "I know what that's like," he said. He told her about Bonnie's relative, who started by touching his private parts and ended up raping him.

Vernon would talk about the abuse privately with different members throughout the years. The shame had stayed with him. Maybe, too, the need to get back the control he'd lost to bigger, stronger people.

And yet, even as he recounted the terrible episodes in his childhood, Vernon was already beginning to abuse young girls himself. Men who were molested as children are three times as likely to commit abuse themselves. But Vernon was an unusual case: He projected strong empathy for others even as he created new victims.

There's no evidence he ever told Vernon Clark how badly he'd hurt him as a boy. He never shared with Bonnie the story of how her relative had molested him for years or denounced the beatings she dished out when he was four and five. There's no memory within the Clark family of Vernon getting in Roy Haldeman's face and explaining exactly how much damage the man had done by belittling and abusing him.

Perhaps he thought forbearance was the Christian thing to do; perhaps he felt bringing up the past was unworthy of him as a Texas man of a certain era. (It might have felt like whining.) Most likely, too, holding those close to him accountable would have destroyed any chance of a loving family reunion in the future. Vernon never stopped dreaming about one of those.

Now that he had his own flock to lead, however, the pain reappeared in new forms. Inside the Davidians, he not only talked about the abuse, he reenacted it, recycling the terror he'd felt as a five-year-old boy. The fear that he'd learned so well was becoming a management tool.

The sins of the past never left him. They only flowed into new areas, where Vernon had fewer restraints on his anger.

Vernon was slowly gaining control of his followers: their faith, their diet, their sex lives. In these matters, he was becoming the sole authority, beyond questioning. One of the areas he found hard to manipulate, however, was who his people loved.

When she first met David Bunds at the Palestine camp, fifteen-year-old Debbie Kendrick was taken aback. "Oh my gosh, boys can be sweet!" she said to herself. It sounded corny, but for Debbie it was like a light had gone on in a dark room. The two fell in love.

Vernon was annoyed. He forbade the two from even speaking. They had to walk around the camp and pretend the other person didn't exist.

One night, Debbie was in her tent when Vernon shook her awake. She left her little sister there and went outside, followed him in the moonlight. Once they got by the bonfire, glowing with embers, Vernon sat down and just started rambling. Random stuff like, *Oh, what were your parents like when you were growing up? Did they fight a lot?*

It went on like this for two hours. Vernon's voice and the fire spitting and fussing just kind of all blended together. *Have you ever had any other boyfriends? Did you watch your sisters with their husbands?*

It was all this lech stuff again.

Finally, Vernon got to the crux of the matter. "I was praying over there," he said. He pointed to a shallow gully not too far from the bonfire. "I was crying to God. And one of the things I was talking to him about was, I just don't know what to do with you and Dave.

"And all of a sudden, God stopped me and said, 'Let them marry.' And I was like, 'God, they're so young!' But he was like, 'Let them marry.'"

Vernon was in full cry. He threw his arms out, as if he was wracked with pain. He pointed to Debbie's tent. "If you go back there, this will be the end of it. You will not be with David." Then with the other hand, he pointed at David's tent. "If you go there, you're married. And I want you to remember that once you're married in the eyes of God, you cannot separate. If that is your choice, you have to make this work."

Debbie stood there long as she could, listening to Vernon yammer on until she couldn't take it anymore. She shot out on a beeline for David's tent.

When she got there, she called out, "David? David, wake up."

She heard a sleepy voice from inside. "Wha-at?"

"I'm going to come in now."

Debbie pulled back the flap and ducked inside. She started talking fast: "I just had a conversation with Vernon and, well, we're married now." Poor David thought he was in the middle of a dream.

She was so nervous she could hardly speak. Not because she was afraid of rejection but because it was all so strange. But she went to David and a few minutes later they were naked in his bed together.

Soon, Debbie started feeling nauseous and throwing up. She was pregnant with their daughter, Jennifer. She and David were over the moon. But Vernon was visibly angry. It was clear he'd made a terrible mistake: He couldn't manipulate David and Debbie anymore. He couldn't play the great lover in the camp, either. Debbie had rejected him and chosen David.

And the marriage was irreversible. God had approved it, as Vernon had said himself. Everyone knew it, and it drove Vernon crazy.

MARC

I N JANUARY 1986, Marc Breault was shopping in a supermarket in Loma Linda, California. He was twenty-two. He was tall, bearded, a little chubby, and legally blind, though he still had some vision in one eye.

Visions ran in Marc's family. When he was ten years old, living in Hawaii, Marc had his first. The sky went dark, as if a deep twilight had fallen over the world. Marc spotted an angel, about eight feet tall, floating above the cut grass of the yard. The angel was dressed in chain mail, with a sword by his side. His face was bright.

Marc fainted. After a few seconds, he felt a hand lift him up to his feet. The angel helped him stand. "Do not be afraid," he said. "I will show you." He pointed up into the dark sky and Marc saw shapes and symbols written there.

The angel said, "Here is the key to understanding the Book of Revelation." Marc saw a series of portents unfold across the far heavens. Wars, natural disasters, people screaming and running helter-skelter.

The vision ended. The sky resumed its pale blue color. Marc was terrified by what he'd witnessed and told no one.

When he received another vision, at fifteen, Marc quit attending the local Roman Catholic church and became a Seventh-day Adventist. It was the same year that Vernon, in Tyler, Texas, joined the church.

After graduating with a degree in theology, Marc went out looking for a job as a pastor. But, because of his eye problems, he couldn't find anything. He became disillusioned. He returned to Hawaii, where his parents now lived, and gave up his studies in theology.

In December of 1985, the visions returned. An angel showed him seven people riding in a green van. He told Marc that he had to go to Loma Linda University and enroll in the master's program there or his spiritual life would be over. He would meet the seven people in the green van and they would help him to find the truth about God.

Despite the vision, Marc thought he'd probably stay in Hawaii. He didn't have money for a master's degree. Two days later, the Center for the Blind in Hawaii called him with an offer of a full scholarship, a book stipend, and a new computer and printer. He hadn't applied for any of it.

Marc was astonished. He quit his job and flew to Loma Linda.

On his second day at the university, he was doing some shopping at a local grocery store. He was wearing a Dallas Cowboys T-shirt. A man spotted it and started talking about Texas. A very friendly guy who was there with his daughter. Later, Marc learned their names were Perry and Rachel Jones.

As they chatted, Marc was secretly freaking out. He'd recognized Perry and Rachel immediately. They were two of the seven people in his vision of the green van.

Perry started talking about the growing influence of Jerry Falwell and Pat Robertson and the rise of the Moral Majority. Marc nodded. He mentioned the Seventh-day Adventist belief that Protestantism would eventually take over the world and create a totalitarian religious state.

"You're a really unusual young man!" Perry said. "I've got to go to a religious conference in Washington, DC, this week, but I'd like to get in touch with you when I get back."

Marc said that would be fine.

The next time they spoke Perry revealed that his son-in-law was a prophet. He wanted Marc to meet him. "Let me guess," Marc thought to himself. "He's going to show up in a green van."

A couple of days later, Vernon drove up to where Marc was staying. He was driving a green van. Marc recognized him, too, from the vision.

For the first time in his life, Marc had someone to talk to who understood what it was like to receive messages from God. So did Vernon. Vernon was like the big brother and Marc the little brother.

Each had intense Godly visions. Each had memorized large sections of the Bible. That was something that people like Perry Jones and Clive Doyle had never managed to do. But Vernon didn't bullshit Marc. He admitted he was worried that the two of them would eventually compete to be the Branch Davidian prophet. A "this town ain't big enough for both of us" kind of thing.

Vernon confided in Marc, told him that not only did he believe he was the Chosen One, but that he wanted to be the Chosen One. The journey to become the Seventh Angel had made his life unimaginably rich in meaning. He had a purpose now, and it was everything to him.

Marc found Vernon a challenge. He could be really abrasive and he was definitely full of himself. But there was something about the guy Marc liked. He was so forthright, so candid about his true feelings.

At least Vernon had the guts to speak his truth out loud. He faced up to things. Other preachers and televangelists—the Jimmy Swaggarts of the world—pretended to be good and righteous when they were on TV, but then you found out they were doing all kinds of dirt in private.

And the biblical prophets, Marc knew, had not been easy people. Almost none were well-liked in their time. They were disturbers of the peace, arrogant. Vernon was like that.

Marc forgot about Loma Linda University. He stayed with Vernon at his house in Pomona. There was something inside him that told him there had to be a God, but he didn't know him yet. Maybe Vernon would change that.

When he met the other Davidians, he started recognizing more people from the dream, until all seven had been accounted for. Later, this mystical "list of seven" would circulate within the group, further proof that Vernon was divinely inspired.

When Marc met the others in the little group of twenty-five or so, he studied them. He noticed that many had tough childhoods. They'd been neglected or molested or treated like they didn't matter. One girl had seen her sister murdered when she was five years old. Some of the men had been beaten as children. There were people who'd been on drugs and into prostitution. And Vernon told him about his stepfather, Roy Haldeman, and how he'd been abused as a little boy.

"We all saw so much hate and suffering in the world," Marc thought. It united them in this little group.

Vernon's idea for driving buses around and getting a wave of new recruits had sputtered out, like so many of his schemes. But he was steadily bringing in new people. Marc had arrived. Then Vernon went to New Bedford, Massachusetts, the hometown of David Bunds's mother, and snapped up four followers. Others, attracted by Vernon's charisma, dribbled in by ones and twos.

That Passover, in 1986, Vernon called his worldwide followers to come to Palestine. Believers in Australia and Great Britain and Hawaii booked their tickets. When they landed in Dallas, they got in their cars and made their way south.

Surprisingly, Lois showed up at the Passover meeting. She'd been living in Waco, away from the Mount Carmel compound, where George—abandoned by his mother and most of the other Davidians—held court over a bizarre mélange of believers, family members, and drifters and ex-cons who'd wormed their way into his circle.

Lois had recently been diagnosed with breast cancer and was treating it with something called "The Grape Cure," which called for fasting and a strict diet of the fruit. The treatment was having little effect. She looked thin, low on energy.

Lois went around the small groups, trying to convince her old flock to come back and support her. Vernon knew what she was doing—the tight-knit Davidians were nothing if not accomplished gossips—but he was gratified to see her efforts bore little fruit. Few if any of the followers rallied to her side.

Later, some Davidians would think back to that Passover with sadness. They kept in their memory the image of this frail woman attempting to gather up her flock, begging them to once more embrace the vision of the female Godhead that had transformed her life. But she was too late. Vernon had taken control.

Lois was a spent force. Almost no one was talking about the things close to her heart, the feminine Holy Spirit and the ordination of women. Vernon was gradually cutting those teachings out of his Bible studies.

The bitter irony was clear to more than one Davidian. Vernon had got his foot in the door by bedding Lois and preaching all this pro-woman stuff. Lois had fallen for what was beneath his belt buckle and for his charm, believing that when the time came, the two of them would walk hand in hand into the new kingdom. But once Vernon was in charge, he deep-sixed the whole message. He broke Lois's heart and took up with Rachel.

Lois had tried, but the men always seemed to win. She could have written a book on their perfidy.

She died that November.

That Passover, the Davidians noticed something odd. It seemed that wherever Vernon went, fourteen-year-old Karen Doyle, Clive Doyle's daughter, followed. When Vernon sat down at meetings, Karen would be right by his side.

Word began filtering through the congregation. Vernon had taken a second wife. Eventually, he explained how it had happened.

Months before, in San Bernardino, Vernon was studying one of the charts drawn up by Victor Houteff. The chart was about events described in Revelation 12. As he peered at the beasts and prophets and other illustrations inscribed there, he began to fixate on one, the face of a woman. Vernon was struck by something in the lines: The drawing was clearly a mixture of the features of his wife Rachel and those of Karen Doyle.

Karen Doyle was staying back in Palestine. Vernon decided he would drive there and celebrate an early, "special" Passover with her. Rachel wanted to go along, but he told her, "God said no." Rachel didn't understand. Why would God speak to Vernon about such a minor, everyday matter? Vernon didn't explain and left without his wife.

After arriving in Palestine, Vernon was sitting in his cabin when he heard a loud command. "Give seed to Karen," it said. It was God's voice.

Vernon protested; he didn't want to sleep with Karen, who was staying not too far away. He began shouting the names of his wife and son, as talismans. "My Rachel!" he cried. "My Cyrus!"

An image appeared in his mind. It was Rachel in her mother's womb. Then: Cyrus being formed in Rachel's uterus. The two images flashed and were gone. How should I understand this message, Vernon wondered. He spent a long time thinking about it before deciding that God was showing him that Rachel and Cyrus belonged to Him, not to Vernon.

The voice resounded again, but again Vernon refused to obey it. An hour later, he heard it again. "Give seed to Karen!"

God hounded Vernon all day. He couldn't concentrate; he felt his spirit failing. He didn't want to lay with Karen. That night, he tossed and turned in his bed, racking his brain for a way to disobey the Lord without angering him.

His mind finally went quiet. Then, in the middle of his sleep, the voice thundered in his mind. "GIVE SEED TO KAREN!"

Vernon knew he could no longer resist. "I had made up my mind to do what God said," he said later, "even though I could only sow destruction and ruin."

He went and found Karen and told her what had happened. He asked if she agreed they had to follow God's commands. She nodded, and he raped her. Afterward, Vernon announced he and Karen were married, just as his previous rape of Rachel had sealed their union.

The Davidians were staggered by the news. One of the old-time followers called out Vernon to his face: "I knew you always wanted to do this," he said. He predicted that Vernon would claim more brides. "You want to get my wife!" he cried. The believer promised to kill Vernon if he tried it.

Vernon said no, his vision was of two wives only. And a child by Karen.

Wayne Martin, a Harvard-trained Black lawyer who'd joined the Davidians with his wife and children, took the news especially hard. A rumor went around Mount Carmel that he was thinking of killing himself. Martin knew what Vernon was doing was statutory rape, and he was terrified of being arrested as an accessory. What they did in Texas prisons to those associated with child assault was unspeakable in polite circles.

But Vernon didn't give an inch. He told the believers that he'd been given new light and it didn't matter how radical it was, they had to accept it.

Taking Karen as his bride was a kind of preview of things to come, he said. Soon, he would reveal a new prophecy to the Davidians. But only those who were truly committed would comprehend it. If you flinched at Vernon making love to Karen, you weren't ready for the big stuff. He was coy about what exactly this new light was. *I can't tell you yet* was the message. *You have to pray about it and seek God and get ready to hear such a great truth.*

Vernon had promised the Davidians Karen would be his last bride. But later that year, while he was staying in Palestine, there was another crisis. It concerned Michele Jones, Rachel's little sister. She was the one he'd been tempted to rape years ago while driving with her to California. He'd successfully resisted that urge.

One night, Vernon was reading the Song of Solomon. He came across a passage: *We have a young sister, and her breasts are not yet grown. What shall we do for our sister for the day she is spoken for?* "Spoken for" meant a proposal of marriage.

Vernon felt the presence of God, who began to reveal a vision: The girl in the verse was Michele, and Vernon was to have her.

He went to the meetinghouse, where Michele was staying. She was asleep. He pulled back the blanket and climbed in next to her.

At first, Michele thought Vernon was trying to get warm. The Palestine nights were frigid. But then Vernon put his finger inside the top of her panties and tried to pull them off.

Michele, half-awake, began to struggle. Vernon proved too strong for her. He said he had seen them making love in his prophecies and she should submit. He raped her.

Perry Jones, for all his faith, was devastated by his daughters' "marriage" to Vernon. Two young daughters were now with Vernon. A heavy toll. After Michele, the limit on Vernon's wives was rarely talked about again. It was clear to the Davidians there would be more.

Years later, David asked himself a question about Vernon's visions. They always seemed to come just after a period of darkness in his life, like the one that told him to give Karen his seed. Was this garden-variety depression? David wondered. Or was it something peculiar to the twisty passages and bluff dead ends he knew existed in Vernon's mind?

Perhaps the "darkness" was actually Vernon realizing what his desires were, seeing them in bold type. The reaction of a twenty-seven-year-old man, one who still possessed a small reservoir of decency, to wanting to have sex with a twelve-year-old girl.

It would nudge anyone's mind over a cliff, knowing that some part of you wanted to rape children. Vernon had always thought himself as a protector of younger kids, ever since his days in Garland, when he watched over his aunt Sharon and his uncle Kenneth.

Vernon was desiring younger and younger girls. It caused him to spiral into self-loathing and depression. It was as if there were two Vernons, and they were fighting for control.

Eventually, after days spent with his depressed thoughts, a special dream would burst into Vernon's mind. God would demand that Vernon obey him. The vision would release him from all responsibility. It gave him permission to do what he'd wanted all along.

STEVE

O NCE MARC WAS firmly in the group, Vernon began talking to him about bringing in new members. Marc still had Adventist friends in Hawaii. He called one of his friends there, Steve Schneider, and told him about this vision he'd had, of seven people in a green van, and how it was being fulfilled right before his eyes.

Steve had been searching for answers for a long time. He'd grown up in Wisconsin in an Adventist family before fleeing the faith and moving to Hawaii. But he was haunted by the meaninglessness of what he saw there—the parties, the lusting after new cars and new homes. This dissatisfaction with things as they were increasingly manifested itself in a fear of death that crept up on him in random moments. Or not so much death as the icy void that followed it. Steve became obsessed with finding eternal life through a true God.

The odd thing was that Steve wasn't particularly religious when you looked right at it. Or spiritual. He wasn't craving God's love and he didn't have a thing for Jesus. He was more like an engineer, or an actuary. There was a problem he needed to solve and he didn't care one bit if he got the answer from a Buddhist, a Moonie, or Ronald Reagan. If some quantum physicist had invented a machine that could give you eternal life, Steve would have dropped his Bible on the sidewalk and lined up.

When Marc called, Steve was skeptical. Was it a vision or just a normal dream? But he liked Marc, thought he was a serious person.

Marc flew in to talk to Steve and his wife, Judy, and some others. He found Marc's excitement contagious. What if his friend had stumbled on a real messiah?

After the session, Steve drove home to his wife. He knew that the first thing she'd do when he got home would be to start firing questions at him. "What do we study? What are we learning?" The two of them were on this quest together.

As he drove, anxiety swarmed his mind. "God, geez, what am I doing?" he said to himself. "What if this is another Jim Jones cult and I'm getting involved in it and I'm pulling innocent people in?" But then, his thoughts pivoted. "What if this is true and there is a living prophet, as God has sent through the ages? And what if I reject him and my soul dies in a black hell?"

Steve started burning up the long-distance lines talking to Vernon. He was spending hundreds of dollars a month on his phone bill. But it was worth it, because Vernon was opening up the Bible for him. He started with Revelation 8 and the story of the seven trumpets. Steve had never heard anything like it.

"I've got a group of people that would like to hear you," he told Vernon. "They'll pay your way. Why don't you come over?"

Vernon said, "I don't go anywhere, I don't do anything without the direction of God."

My God, that's a good answer, Steve thought.

He flew to California to meet with Vernon. He arrived at the house and right away, Vernon started acting weird. Steve was busting at the seams to talk, but Vernon ignored him.

Steve hated personal rudeness. He couldn't understand why Vernon was acting this way. All of a sudden, the guy was really busy and he's got something going on right at the moment, like some life-or-death situation? Playing Mr. Cool. Steve didn't get it.

Then there was Vernon's background. Before meeting Vernon, Steve thought for sure he must have gone to a top school: Oxford, Harvard, something like that. He was expecting someone impressive. But Vernon looked like a roadie for a second-tier heavy metal act. "Of all the people in the world," Steve thought, "why did God have to choose a bum from Texas who can hardly speak English and who is always so rude to people?"

But then he thought, well, why not this guy? You look in the Bible, who were the prophets? Sheep herders, fig pickers. The unwashed. In other words, people just like Vernon.

After a frustrating few hours, Vernon finally sat down to talk. Steve sat on a chair, Vernon on the floor. Vernon just started riffing, getting deeper and deeper into the Bible. He'd start in one book talking about one prophet, then he'd tie him to another figure in a later book and glide into what that guy's message really meant, and then he'd find a verse that fused his thoughts to a biblical king that Steve had barely considered before, the connections lighting up like electrical lines catching fire against a night sky.

Steve had met so-called prophets and visionaries before. They were all over the place. Vernon wasn't like that. There was a cold, logical progression to what he said. Vernon saw patterns.

It was so plain and clear. Steve felt his mind fizzing just listening to the guy. After twenty minutes, he felt almost dizzy. *I can't refute him,* Steve thought finally. *I can't touch one single thing he says.*

As far as Steve was concerned, Vernon was the real deal. He and Judy started making plans to move to Waco.

Vernon flew to Hawaii to preach to the rest of Marc's potential recruits. For the meeting, he dressed in long white robes. He told the SDA people he had been called to be the son of God reincarnate. But he warned them that he was a different kind of messiah.

Christ had been sinless, and therefore he been incapable of judging people as they really were. Vernon made no pretense about being good. He was a low-down sinner through and through.

The approach was so novel, so upside down, it took his listeners aback. What messiah advertised his own wickedness?

Vernon went further. "I own everything and everyone, including all women whether married or otherwise," he told the Hawaiians. If you had a house or a car or a nice stereo, you were nothing but a thief, because all those things belonged to Vernon.

His message was out there. And yet, it had the rough grain of the truth to it.

.   .   .

More believers signed on. Vernon was growing the Branch, while George and Lois faded. His self-regard bloomed, as did his paranoia. He even toyed with the idea of changing his name. "Vernon Howell" didn't sound like a prophet, and it was a name embedded with the tragedies of his childhood. He had exceeded his humble beginnings, and he began to think his name should reflect that.

He was looking ahead. In a tape called "The Bird," Vernon told his followers that the authorities would put him to death because of his many wives. The statement didn't scan. Polygamy was not punishable by death in the United States. Vernon didn't explain the discrepancy. But clearly he was anticipating a lethal confrontation with Babylon.

But not necessarily in America. Vernon began to focus more and more on Israel as the place where the final battles of good vs. evil would be waged. He told his followers that the rugged conditions at Palestine, the food deprivation, the separation from loved ones, all of it was to toughen them up for the violence and horror that would unfold in Jerusalem. The timetable was accelerating.

Ben Roden had visited Israel. So had Lois. Even George had gone. But Vernon told the Davidians he would actually lead them there.

As his message sharpened, Vernon's recruitment ramped up. Clive flew off to his native Australia and lined up some prospects: Bruce and Lisa Gent, Ian and Allison Manning, Elizabeth Baranyai, and others. Later, Vernon made the trip and brought them all into the message.

Vernon was starting to fill out his brood, too. His son Cyrus had been born in 1985 and his daughter Star came along in 1987. He spoke of more children to come with Karen and Michele.

Vernon, Steve, and Marc were the recruiting team. They'd go to a Seventh-day Adventist church or somewhere else—Steve even tried hitting some beaches—and hand out pamphlets. People would read the literature and fire questions at the three of them.

That was the Davidians' opening. Marc and the others would start arguing with the SDA believers and, if they got one out of a hundred to listen, well, that was the job.

Vernon was the prophet, Steve was the salesman, and Marc the theologian down in the trenches answering the tough questions. Vernon was a powerful speaker—he could weave a spell—but the SDA followers wanted details. After listening to him, the recruits would go to Marc and say, well, what about this scripture? How does Ellen White fit into all this? There's a passage in the Bible that says this, and your teaching seems to go against it—how do you deal with that?

Marc, who knew his Scriptures cold, would give them the answers.

Vernon talked about the sort of people he wanted to recruit and where he would find them. He fantasized about setting up shop in Hollywood. "California women are liberal," he told the Davidians. "They're used to anything. If we try to get women in the Bible Belt, or someplace like that, we won't get many."

"We're bizarre. California women like bizarre things."

Steve was proving himself to be a valuable addition to the Davidians, a real go-getter. He was one of the great salesmen. He could sell you smog, Marc said. Vernon agreed. He said the guy had a million-dollar mouth.

Steve wasn't offended. People asked him, 'Steve, what do you do?' "I sell God," he told them.

After arriving in Texas, Steve started giving Bible studies. His theme was eternal life. The Davidians, he told the group, would become celebrities, eternal ones:

"Hazel, you're gonna be a movie star!" he preached to one follower. "Hey, I'm not joking! . . . We're gonna shine like stars forever and ever. We're gonna be ambassadors of the living God to planets that we have never seen yet, of which they've been watching the outcome of this planet that has been in rebellion against God's will for thousands of years. We're gonna be the greatest beings that have ever lived."

Two of the recruits Steve brought in were Kat Schroeder and her husband, Michael. They were devout Christians who'd met Steve after attending a Revelation Seminar in Miami. They drove out to Waco to see this Vernon Howell that Steve kept talking about but found he wasn't there. They got back in the car and kept driving until they got to California.

When she met Vernon, Kat didn't like him. She was a Leo and very, very strong-willed, and so was Vernon. She thought he was bullheaded. But when she threw out some argument, Vernon would shoot back an answer that stumped her. Just like Steve, she couldn't contradict his message.

After hours of going back and forth with Vernon, Kat took her husband aside. "I don't like him," she said, "but I love him. I can't not hear this message." She had to change her life right there and then.

The Schroeders drove back to Florida, sold all their possessions, bought a van, loaded Kat's mother and sister into it, and headed for Texas.

As the group grew, Vernon realized that he couldn't keep cramming the new recruits into the already-full houses in California. He ordered that new plywood shacks be built in Palestine and sent some of the men to get started.

The shacks measured eight feet by twelve for single people and eight feet by sixteen for couples and families. The floors were three-quarter-inch plywood, placed on wooden struts, the walls half-inch plywood reinforced with two by fours. On top, the men put in simple slanted roofs.

There was no insulation. The Davidians bought some cast iron, wood-burning fireplaces and cut holes in the plywood walls. They bordered them with metal shields to protect the plywood, then masonried the fireplaces into the wall. If you wanted a window, you simply cut a hole in the plywood and put some plexiglass in there.

The camp rang with the sounds of hammers, with men on ladders driving in rows of nails and voices calling out for supplies. The shacks were built in a row, starting near the communal kitchen and stretching out toward a gully that ran through the property. A lot of the structures were finished in a day.

Vernon moved into one of the plywood houses. He wanted to be close to his new followers, to bind them to the message.

The Bible studies went late into the night. You'd listen for two, four, ten hours, then drag your butt back to your shack. In your spare time, Vernon didn't want you doing anything that would distract you from the message. No computers, no forbidden books, no fun. Definitely no extramarital sex.

As for Vernon, he did what he wanted. If he wanted to sleep till noon, he slept till noon. But if you stayed up till three a.m. listening to his Bible study, you still had to be up when the bell rang for breakfast at seven a.m. sharp. If you were late, you didn't eat.

. . .

After a year, Marc was finding his place. He liked being a kind of scriptural authority within the Davidians. It pleased him that he was putting his years of intensive study to use.

Marc played some keyboards and quickly became part of Vernon's band. They'd jam for hours, then quaff a few beers afterward to cool down. The only bad part was when Vernon messed up on guitar. When it happened, it was never his fault. The drummer was off, or the bass player had come in at the wrong time, or whatever. Marc found it annoying, but it was part of the deal.

Marc had also found a partner among the Davidians, falling in love with Elizabeth Baranyai, one of the Australian recruits. He asked Vernon for permission to marry Elizabeth and Vernon took it under consideration.

Vernon seemed to enjoy talking to Marc; he treated him almost as an equal. "You know, Marc, with our music, we'll be rock stars, man," he'd say. "I'll have women begging me to make love to 'em." You could tell from the look on Vernon's face that he was still feeling the good vibes from the jam session. "Just imagine, virgins without number, man. This is how we're gonna do it."

Marc even joined in on Vernon's Bible studies. In one, the subject of this Davidian apostate, an Australian man, came up. This man had come to believe that he was the antitypical King David and the rightful leader of the Branch Davidians. He'd moved to Israel and published a series of tracts that he sent to the followers.

In his pamphlets, this guy pointed out that the Bible speaks of a modern-day David, not a modern-day Vernon. He argued that the name of the latter-day messiah should be "David ben-David." This guy was so convinced that his theory was right that he actually changed his name to David ben-David. In his tracts, he attacked Vernon for not seeing this essential truth.

The Davidians, especially Perry Jones, were concerned. David ben-David had a point. They'd always been taught that a modern-day David would arrive to lead the 144,000. So why was their leader's name Vernon?

This name thing was bugging everyone. Vernon was at a loss to explain it. The mood in the room grew troubled.

Marc wanted to lighten things up. He opened his Bible to Isaiah 45:4, a passage that speaks of King Cyrus of Prussia, and read aloud: *For Jacob my*

*servant's sake, and Israel mine elect, I have even called thee by thy name: I
have surnamed thee, though thou hast not known me.*

As a scholar, he knew that this particular use of "surnamed" didn't
mean that Cyrus was the king's last name. It's not like the Bible said "King
Joe Cyrus" or something.

But he pretended that he did believe it, just to get people to relax.
"See," he said, "ben-David can't be the true last name of the messiah,
because it says clearly here the last name should be Cyrus. So if anything, the Messiah's name should be David Cyrus! And if you really
want to get technical, 'Koresh' or something along those lines is how
you pronounce Cyrus in Hebrew. So maybe we should call the messiah
'David Koresh.'"

Marc was expecting the group to break out laughing. But the others
perked up. It was a great point! They grabbed at his little joke like a fish
going after a lure. Marc saw smiles around. The heaviness started to dis-
sipate. Even Vernon cracked a smile. "See how easy it is to disprove some
of these people?" he said.

Marc bit his lip. He didn't want to bum everyone out again, so he never
got around to explaining that he'd been kidding about the whole David
Koresh thing.

Despite his growing comfort with the Davidians, Marc did have the occasional stab of doubt: the young girls always with Vernon, the rationing
of food. But, like the others, Vernon convinced him that, scripturally,
what he was doing was sanctioned by God.

The first big argument he had with Vernon came over something different, something ridiculous, in fact. Somehow Vernon got it into his
head that they were all living in the nineteenth century.

When he first brought this up in a Bible study, it caused a ruckus. Judy
Schneider, Steve's wife, cried out, "No!" Others chimed in to support her.

Vernon wouldn't budge. "Read Isaiah," he said. "My truth is Godly
truth."

Exasperated, the followers asked Marc to intervene. Marc knew he
had to be firm. He told Vernon, "If God himself came down from heaven
in fire and glory and proclaimed we lived in the nineteenth century, I

would tell him to his face he was wrong and didn't know what he was talking about."

Vernon was taken aback; Marc didn't kid about Scripture. He relented. He never publicly withdrew his statement, but he stopped talking about living in the nineteenth century.

One afternoon that summer while visiting California, Vernon and Marc drove to a mall not too far from the Bundses' house. Passing a Sears store, they slowed at a television display with a few of the sets tuned to the national news. They were showing a segment on the political activist Lyndon LaRouche.

LaRouche had run in every presidential election since 1976. He had some pretty wild ideas. He said he'd predicted the arrival of AIDS, and that it was spread by mosquitoes. He also said the US government created the virus in a lab.

Vernon and Marc stopped to watch.

"Man, LaRouche is a nutcase if ever there was one," Marc said. "And his followers are even crazier."

"Yeah, that's true," Vernon said. "You almost wonder how anyone can believe such nonsense."

They gazed at the TV. "But you know," Vernon said after a moment, "we're even crazier than they are."

Marc felt his brain jangle a bit. What was this? He asked Vernon to explain.

"Well," he said, "just look at us. You know we're in a cult. We're actually in a cult." He broke out laughing. "I mean, do you ever fear I might turn into another Jim Jones and give y'all the Kool-Aid?"

Vernon thought it was funny, but Marc wasn't laughing.

When they got back to the compound, Vernon told the others about their moment in front of the TVs. "We're in a cult and that's something to be proud of!" was the message.

From then on, Vernon didn't shy away from the word. They were cultists. As were the early Christians! The Davidians came around to the idea. It was a badge of honor.

Marc managed to push most of his doubts aside, but they only found their way into his dreams. There was one in particular he found hard to forget.

I was in a desert. It was a terrible land, a desolate land in which there was no water. I was alone and wandering . . . I had lost my glasses and I was dying because I could not see to read.

While I was thus looking for my glasses, I met a man or, rather, he called to me. He appeared as my friend and gave me my glasses, which he had found. I was naturally very grateful and thanked him. But as I went on my way, the glasses he had given me disappeared and I again found myself in a blinded state.

Then the same man appeared again. I wanted this man and wanted what he could give me even though I knew that his gifts were not permanent . . . I became entirely dependent upon this man for my sight and my feelings.

I soon began to realize who this man was. This was Satan and he now had me in his clutches.

Satan attempted to kill me then and he almost succeeded. His method was cruel. He first tempted me with food I knew was not good. Somehow broken shards of glass were mixed in with it. I knew the danger, yet I began to eat.

Then I saw a most dreadful thing. I saw our group, wandering through a terrible land. It was completely barren and devoid of life. We were perishing.

It wasn't a difficult dream to interpret. Someone was leading Marc and his fellow believers astray. There was only one person it could possibly be, and it wasn't Satan.

But Marc pushed the story aside. He didn't want to leave.

In the six years since he'd arrived at Mount Carmel, Vernon's life had changed dramatically. It was, in many ways, a biblical story. He'd wandered into a place filled with believers, battered by life, quite possibly suicidal, anguished, worn, and searching for light. He'd accepted the message of the Davidians, and he'd grown strong in it. There were numerous men in the Scriptures who'd had their eyes opened just as he had. *He once was lost*, as the verse in Luke goes, *but now he was found*.

He'd married, fathered children, led his breakaway group into isolation at Palestine, even as he focused more of his followers' attention and love on him, overruling at times the words of the old prophets. He'd begun to supplant those prophets' words with his own. He'd added to the Davidian's numbers, sketched out their future in Israel, and begun to harden his people for the End Times.

Vernon had come into his own as a religious leader. But he still carried with him much of the pain and bewilderment he'd felt since he was a young boy. He spoke of those things often. He was convinced more darkness was on the way.

Part III

OF BABYLON

THE RAID

I N THE WINTER of 1987, Mount Carmel was increasingly on Vernon's mind. It was the home of the Branch Davidians; retaking it would mean his movement would gain greater legitimacy among the worldwide faithful and, most likely, an increased flow of funds. He meant to restore his believers there.

Rumors about the goings-on inside the compound reached him now and then. Vernon heard that George had let some real scum-bums onto the property, bikers and ex-cons who'd gone as far as building a meth factory on the grounds. The reports were that George also let these dudes run a pornography scam where they would take pictures of naked women and send them to their boyfriends, many of whom were soldiers at Fort Hood, about sixty miles down the highway. Demands for money would follow.

It was sacrilege. Vernon wanted the bad guys off the property and George, too.

George was undaunted. He wouldn't leave. He believed he was involved in a struggle for nothing less than the fate of the world. "God bless you . . . ," he wrote to a friend, "and know that the enemy is out after both of you and you are going to have to dig in and fire Jesus's name in his face like a machine gun. Because we do not and will not give an inch but we are going to consume and destroy this dominion in Jesus's strength unto the end of him. So help us God."

He continued to threaten Vernon, who took George's words seriously. Vernon really thought the guy might try to kill him.

One day, David Bunds and Vernon were driving on the highway. Vernon thought he spotted a car driving erratically behind them. He became convinced it was George and panicked.

He drove to a local police station, which David thought was weird. They didn't even have a plate number for the other car. Why would the cops care? George had got inside Vernon's brain.

Vernon's fears and other stressors led to anxiety attacks. One was so bad the Davidians took him to a Waco hospital. The doctor gave him some medicine—Vernon couldn't remember the name, Anzac or Danzig or something, he'd say later on. Most likely, it was Xanax.

Vernon took a couple of pills. After a few minutes, he started slurring his words. He couldn't form a coherent sentence.

Vernon was upset. His teachings were spoken, never written down. He couldn't be who he wanted to be without his voice. He needed an audience, and he needed to be exalted. He stopped taking the medicine.

But the problems continued. He developed an ulcer. He was plagued with periods of near panic. And his depression returned regularly.

One time, Vernon told the Davidians he'd been having thoughts of leaving. He'd been daydreaming about running away with one of his young female followers. Just taking off, maybe moving to a small town and getting a regular job. Living a plain life. He never went through with it, but clearly, he fantasized about throwing it all away—the prophecies, the message, the sycophants—and disappearing.

Vernon was also navigating a marriage with a strong-willed teenager. Like any couple, he and Rachel fought. Vernon hated admitting he was wrong, so the arguments often got heated.

He confided in David and others. He said he had a hard time admitting he was on the wrong side of his arguments with Rachel. Vernon's expression was filled with anguish. They'd never seen him be so vulnerable. David thought to himself, *being wrong for Vernon is like breaking a bone. It's painful to him in a way we can only dimly comprehend.*

· · ·

Vernon's dream of greater glory eventually won out over his fantasies of escape. And part of the dream was retaking Mount Carmel. If Vernon could get the compound back, George's power—and the threat he presented to Vernon—would be significantly reduced.

The two sniped back and forth over who was the place's rightful owner. Finally, George suggested a contest. There was a Davidian, Anna Hughes, who'd died twenty years before, and had been buried in a big metal coffin. The sect's followers buried the coffin in a corner of the property, a makeshift graveyard surrounded by an old rusty barbed-wire fence and prairie grass that would reach your belt buckle.

George dug Anna up, coffin and all. He took pictures of the casket and sent them to Vernon, along with a challenge: Whichever of them could bring Anna back to life would prove that he was the son of God and the true owner of Mount Carmel.

George tried first. He moved the casket to the chapel. Three times he went out there and tried to raise Anna from the dead, "banging gongs and howling at the moon." Nothing happened.

After hearing of George's reincarnation attempts, Vernon went down to the sheriff's office in Waco and spoke to a lieutenant there, Elijah Dickerson. He showed Dickerson the photos of the coffin and said he wanted George arrested for abuse of a dead person. The crime fell under Texas Penal Code 42.08, the first provision of which was directed at anyone who "disinters, disturbs, damages, dissects, in whole or in part, carries away, or treats in an offensive manner a human corpse."

Dickerson looked at the pictures. He told Vernon they weren't sufficient grounds for an arrest, because no body was visible. If Vernon wanted to pursue this case, he needed photos where you could see Anna Hughes.

Vernon said they could get those. Plans were already forming in his head. Before he left, Dickerson gave him a word of advice: "They're a bad bunch of boys," he said. "You'd better make sure you can protect yourself." It gave Vernon a good, warm feeling.

Vernon knew a guy named Sam Jones who'd gotten friendly with George and was allowed to come and go from Mount Carmel as he pleased. Vernon hired Sam, supplied him with an Instamatic camera, and told him to go to the chapel and take pictures of Anna Hughes from all different angles. The body (or rather, the skeleton), the casket, everything.

Sam managed to get into the chapel and snap some shots. Vernon took the film to be developed. Once he had the prints in hand, he headed back to the sheriff's department and submitted them as proof that George Roden had committed a crime. But the sheriff didn't move on the case. Vernon couldn't understand it. He'd gotten the sheriff exactly what he'd asked for and yet George was still walking around free.

Vernon decided he'd have to take matters into his own hands. He chose seven of his followers and started training them for a raid on Mount Carmel and told them to eat garlic, which would give them strength. The seven were part of the Mighty Men, Vernon's squad of bodyguards. The term came from Joel 3:9: *Proclaim ye this among the Gentiles; Prepare war, wake up the mighty men, let all the men of war draw near; let them come up.*

The team drew a map of the compound and marked where each Mighty Man was going to be positioned. Then Vernon went shopping. He bought rifles and ammo at the local gun stores and at Wal-Mart. He picked up some camo outfits, too. The salespeople remembered Vernon and the others giving off a strong smell of garlic.

On November 3, 1987, before sunrise, Vernon and the Mighty Men loaded into a van. They drove out to Mount Carmel, keeping well below the speed limit. When they got to the gate, Vernon hopped out and started crawling toward the compound. Some of the others drove a bit further, out by a lake that formed part of the property. The last group got dropped off near the compound's dump.

Vernon headed toward the chapel, where Anna's body was. The others angled that way, too. When Vernon got close, he called a halt to the others converging on the chapel.

Vernon knew where George was staying: in a double-wide trailer about a hundred fifty yards from the chapel. He wanted to know if George was still in there or if he was out walking the property with his Uzi. He listened. Nothing but night sounds. Vernon signaled and the men started moving again.

They were getting close to the church doors when a dog caught their scent. The dog came walking up the road, not running, just curious. He looked over and saw Vernon. He didn't do a thing, just turned and walked away. But when he got by George's trailer, he started barking like crazy.

The light in the trailer clicked on and Vernon could see George get up and look out his window. He was wearing a T-shirt and underwear. Soon enough, the trailer door swung open and George emerged, holding a spotlight in one hand. He started moving the beam back and forth over the property.

Vernon and the others remained hidden. George turned and went back in the trailer and got dressed, then emerged again and came walking down the road, black cowboy hat on, carrying his Uzi. Vernon thought he was strutting like a peacock. He walked out into the middle of the road, in clear sight of the eight men.

"Who are you?" George called out in the darkness.

One of the Mighty Men, Stan Silva, answered. "George, we don't want no trouble. What did you do with the casket? Put your gun down." Then he asked again. "Where did you put the casket?"

George fired. The bullet ricocheted and hit Stan in the pants pocket, smacking into a knife he carried there. It bent the blade almost in two and left a good-sized bruise on Stan's leg.

George scooted out of the road and ended up behind a nearby tree. Stan kept talking.

"Put your gun down, George. We got guns, too." All of a sudden Stan fired in the air, *pop pop pop*. Everyone else joined in. It sounded like World War III. Not all the bullets went up in the air. A number of them smacked into the tree George had been hiding behind. Another caught George in the hand.

George started backpedaling fast. As he went, he sprayed bullets from the Uzi at the voices in the dark. Vernon and the others shot back.

Vernon ran toward one of the houses on the property. He was going to work his way to the other side and hopefully get a glimpse of where George was headed. But as he ran across the open ground, he saw a dark shape against the brightening sky.

It was George. He was pointing the Uzi at Vernon. George let off two or three shots. Vernon heard the bullets snip the air, *brap-brap-brap*.

His mind got real clear. He wasn't scared, but his head began to ache. "Am I hit?" he thought to himself. "Am I dead?"

Vernon saw headlights in the distance and soon there were sirens. A line of cars was speeding down the road toward Mount Carmel. It was the McLennan County Sheriff's Department, along with two Department of Public Safety units, responding to reports of gunfire.

The cars pulled up and Vernon saw Sheriff Withorn get out of one of them. He knew Withorn and liked him. He called out hello to the officer as he walked up. Withorn gave him a disgusted look and passed by.

The deputies approached George and attempted to detain him. He struggled. One of the deputies grabbed a small gun from his hand. "He was coming to finish me off," Vernon thought. He was happy the cops were there.

The deputies came charging up to Vernon and the others. "Get on the fucking ground!" they yelled. Vernon got down on all fours. The gravel stung his palms and dug into his knees through his jeans.

In Waco in summertime, the red ants come out. It was only a minute or two before a pack of them swarmed onto Vernon, climbing over his hands, stinging him. Their bites left little white blisters. He could feel the ants crawling up his legs, too, chomping as they went. Then they got into his private parts, just eating him to pieces. All the while the deputies had him down on the ground like a roped calf.

More cars pulled up. One of the cops got out, looking just like a sergeant at a Marine boot camp. The guy was screaming his head off. "What in the hell is going on here? What in the goddamn hell is this? This kind of shit don't happen in America!"

He walked over to one of the Mighty Men. The cop reached down and pulled an earplug out of the man's ear and bent down to the guy's ear. "Did. You. Hear. Me?" he shouted. Vernon heard another deputy off to his side. "Just go ahead and move one inch, I'll blow your goddamn head off."

Vernon kept calm, but inside he was choking with rage. George was the corpse abuser. George was the first one to fire. George had speed freaks working at Mount Carmel. He and the Mighty Men, they were the good guys! True blue American heroes, that's how Vernon saw it.

Why did men always show their false faces to Vernon? It was a theme of his life.

The kindness he'd been shown earlier, the country neighborliness that sparked Dickerson to warn him about George, they were nowhere to be found. Vernon had thought he had a solid relationship with the sheriff and his men. But they were treating his men like common white trash.

George was questioned and released, while the cops loaded Vernon and the Mighty Men into their patrol cars and drove to the jail. Dickerson showed up. Vernon immediately felt better. He called out to him, "Mr. Dickerson!" The cop who'd been shouting about how this is America turned and shoved him. "Shut up," he hissed.

Dickerson walked by Vernon, saying nothing.

They lined the Davidians up for fingerprinting, Vernon told the cop at the desk that he was a musician. The cop grabbed his right hand and bent his fingers down on the paper form until the knuckles went white. It was almost as if he wanted to snap them.

Vernon tried to be respectful.

"Sir, excuse me? Please?"

"What?" the cop said.

"Could you be just a little more gentle?"

The cop looked at Vernon kind of funny, like "Huh. Ain't you tough enough?"

Vernon was put into a cell.

The inmates were surprisingly friendly. Vernon heard later that the news had reported that eight Palestinian Liberation Organization terrorists had assaulted Mount Carmel. So the guys in the jail thought Vernon and the others were Middle Eastern killers. They treated him better than the deputies did.

But the incident disturbed Vernon. In his heart, he felt a grievous injury. The contempt that the sheriff and his men had shown him—he'd rather they'd shot him, almost. Humiliation in private was one thing. But to be shown up in front of his men, it was hurtful to him.

The next few days soured his mood further. Being told when and what to eat, when to sleep, taking orders from the COs, was tough. Vernon felt like a needy child. He yearned to be in control of things, and in the Waco jail, he controlled nothing but his own vengeful thoughts.

In due time, he and the others were charged with the attempted murder of George Roden.

20

COKER

THE DAVIDIANS HIRED a local attorney, forty-two-year-old Gary J. Coker, Jr. to represent them. An assistant DA, El-Hadi T. Shabazz, was assigned as prosecutor.

Coker had grown up in Waco. When he was a boy, his father had owned some property about half a mile from Mount Carmel. Coker used to hear about the people living there, the ones who were waiting on the end of the world. He thought they were harmless.

The judge set bail at $100,000 for each of the defendants. Coker thought that was outrageous. He went before the court and told the judge that George had been annoying the Waco legal community for years with his spicy briefs and general craziness. He reminded them about the time George tried to get Mount Carmel declared a giant monastery to get tax-free status. The whole seventy-seven acres, not just the little chapel. In Coker's judgment, the guy was loonier than Daffy Duck.

The judge reduced the bail. The father of one of the guys, Paul Fatta, put up the bail money for Vernon and Paul and they were released.

Vernon pushed to get the others out. The shooting had kicked up a fuss in the national media. Maury Povich even mentioned it on his show. Vernon thought he might be able to capitalize on the press. He went into the studio and knocked out a song he'd written, "Mad Man in Waco." It was about George. He made some forty-five records and cassette versions.

There's a mad man living in Waco
Praying to the Prince of Hell
Please, please, won't you listen? ...
It's not what it appears to be
We didn't want to hurt anybody
Just set our people free

The song didn't sell. The other six men stayed in jail.

As Coker prepared for the trial, Vernon would come by his office. He seemed to want to be friends.

"Well, I've decided we can drink beer," Vernon said at one point. "Do you want to come down and have a beer in my car?"

Coker declined. He thought it was a little strange.

"You want to look at my Camaro?" Vernon asked.

"Um, no, that's okay," Coker said.

Rebuffed, Vernon began dispensing some biblical advice. He told Coker to study the Psalms and to pay close attention to the Book of Revelation. Coker was nonplussed.

Five months after the raid, jury selection was set to start. The day before, the *Waco Tribune* ran a full-color picture of George Roden being escorted down the courthouse steps by the sheriff and a US marshal. He was being held on contempt of court charges. In the photo, George was wearing an orange jumpsuit with "McLennan Sheriff's Office" written across it.

Coker had an idea. He cut the picture out of the paper and fastened it to a clipboard. When he got up to question the potential jury members, he held the picture up. "Does anyone know this man?" He displayed it for thirty or forty seconds, then had the jury candidates pass it around. Coker wanted the men and women to see George as a criminal and potentially dangerous.

The jury was picked: nine white men and women, and three Black.

To prepare for the trial, Coker drove out to Mount Carmel, to get an idea of how the gunfight had played out. He looked at the shooting angles and thought about bullet trajectories, even studied the tree that George had hid behind. He was putting things together in his head.

At one point, the lawyer spotted an old wooden shed with a busted door. He poked his head inside and saw a large metal coffin leaning up against one wall.

"What is . . . Is that the *casket*?" he asked the Davidians who were with him.

"Yes."

"Why is it there?"

"Well, we moved it here after George."

Coker felt another brainstorm coming on. "Do you think you could get that casket up?" he said. "Would y'all have any religious scruples about bringing that casket and we'll introduce it into evidence?" He wanted the jurors to know that Anna Hughes was a real person and that George had robbed her of eternal rest.

The Davidians agreed to try. Very obedient, straight-ahead people, Coker thought. Vernon even opened the casket up and tied a pink bow around the skeleton's neck to make it look pretty.

Coker went back to his office and began researching whether he could bring a casket into a courtroom. He found nothing to stop him. People had brought Oldsmobiles in. Why not a coffin?

The Davidians put the casket in a van and drove it to Waco's turn-of-the-century courthouse. On the third floor, where the trial was to take place, Coker argued with the judge about bringing it in.

"Judge, she was the closest non-eyewitness to the whole event," Coker said. "She was in her casket . . . only twenty or thirty feet away from all the shooting . . ." It was preposterous, but Coker was determined to have the coffin sitting in front of the jury box.

As Coker made his case, the Davidians slid the casket out of their truck and carried it up the courthouse steps. It was so big it wouldn't go through the front doors. Somehow, they managed to grapple the coffin up to the second floor, but that's as far as they could get it.

As the proceedings dragged on, Anna Hughes's remains lay in the rotunda of the Waco courthouse, under the great dome that capped the building. The local newspaper, the *Waco Tribune-Herald*, published an editorial, "Pitiful Display at Courthouse," decrying the stunt, but the coffin remained. The jurors filed by it every day on their way to the courtroom.

The first day of pretrial motions, the courtroom filled with Davidians and other spectators. It seemed like all of Vernon's supporters were sitting in the benches: women in long cotton dresses, many of them carrying babies on their arms, along with young children and unsmiling men.

The bailiff came into the courtroom. "All rise, please," he said. Everybody stood. The judge took his chair and said, "Okay, you may be seated." Most of the crowd sat down on the benches.

But the Davidians remained standing. Their eyes were on Vernon.

Vernon was still. After a few seconds, he raised his hand, held it there for a second, then dropped it.

"Be seated," he said.

All the Davidians sat down in unison.

The trial began. In his opening statement, Shabazz proposed that the Davidians hadn't gone to Mount Carmel to photograph the skeleton of Anna Hughes at all. They'd gone there to kill.

"How do we know they were trying to murder George Roden?" he asked. "The evidence will show there were 14 to 18 bullet holes in the tree that were so deep that they could not be dug out. The evidence will show that if you had removed that tree, George Roden would not be here today."

Shabazz introduced pieces of the arsenal the Mighty Men had been carrying that day: five Ruger .223 caliber semiautomatic ranch rifles, which were as powerful as an M-16; two .22 caliber rifles; and two 12-gauge shotguns with almost 400 rounds of ammunition. In addition, he said, the police confiscated three more rifles, an additional 2,500 rounds of .223 caliber ammunition, and several boxes of .22 caliber cartridges and shotgun shells.

It was a shit ton of firepower, even for Central Texas.

When it was the defense's turn, Coker called George Roden. The defense lawyer asked him about rumors that had been circulating in Waco. Were any of them true, he asked.

George acknowledged they were. He did own half the state of Israel, and he had a deed to prove it. He could put a curse on his enemies, causing God to introduce AIDS and herpes into their bloodstreams. When asked if he was the messiah, George didn't deny it.

"George, who is it that you lead?" Coker asked.

"All."

Coker frowned. "There wasn't a single Branch Davidian out there when you were rounded up . . . and put in jail. You didn't lead anybody."

George considered this. "Well, they're all my followers," he said, "even though they don't admit it."

As the trial progressed, the questions began to annoy George. He took the extraordinary step of complaining to the judge in a letter. "If you think you're God," he wrote, "then God would have taken the poor into account. But you sons of bitches have your goddam clique to take care of, don't you? You can't afford to allow the poor to get any benefit or you might lose your ass in the process. You fucking son of bitches."

After a week of testimony, final arguments arrived. Shabazz told the jury the raid was "a dangerous paramilitary operation." Vernon and the other men took the law into their own hands and nearly killed their target in the process. "Today it's George Roden . . . who is it going to be tomorrow?"

When Shabazz finished, Coker framed his argument: Vernon and the Davidians were the victims of a mad person. "These people aren't used to fighting. They may be unusual, they may be different in their beliefs, but at least they're peaceful and don't mean to harm anybody." George was the villain here.

After Shabazz and Coker had spoken, the judge told the jury they could take a break before deliberating. They declined.

When the bailiffs announced the verdict was in, the defendants, lawyers, and spectators filed back into the courtroom. The judge read the verdict for the seven other men first, keeping Vernon for last. The jury found the first defendant not guilty. The courtroom was quiet. The judge moved on to the other names.

The Mighty Men were all declared not guilty. Vernon's turn was next. The judge announced a hung jury. He polled the jurors and the nine white jurors had voted "Not guilty" and the three Black jurors had voted "Guilty."

It was a clear win for the Davidians. They were free to go. Some of the jurors even sought Vernon out and hugged him. He responded by inviting everyone out for ice cream.

The jury foreman spoke to reporters. "A lot of jurors commented that they felt frightened of [Roden]. They didn't feel his testimony was honest. They just didn't have any faith in what he said." Clearly, Coker's strategy had worked. For his part, Shabazz expressed disgust with the jury's decision. "It was a Black man trying to prosecute seven white men in a Southern town called Waco," he told reporters.

Shabazz's words held a good deal of truth to them. The trial had indeed shifted along racial lines. But it wasn't as simple as the prosecutor imagined.

Weeks later, Vernon was at an auto paint and body shop outside Waco. He was talking cars with the owner, just shooting the breeze. After a while, a Black guy walked into the shop.

Vernon got to talking to him. "Is your name Vernon?" the man asked after a few minutes. "Vernon Howell?" It was one of the jurors.

"Man, let me tell you something," the juror said. "They were after you."

The guy went on to explain what had happened with the jury. During the trial, someone—he didn't say who—had come to him and one of the other Black jurors and said that Vernon was into drugs. The night he went out to Mount Carmel, this person explained, it was really to do a drug deal. And Vernon and George got into a shootout because George was manufacturing speed at the compound and for some reason Vernon was mad about it.

The religious stuff? It was just a cover. The truth was that Vernon and his boys were just low-down meth dealers.

The Black jurors had believed it. They wanted to convict all the Davidians.

The man went on to explain that he and the other Black juror made their intentions clear to the white jurors, who told them, "Okay, let's make a deal. If you let the other seven off, we'll give you Vernon. Once the others are acquitted, we'll all vote guilty on Vernon."

That was the offer. Seven Davidians would go free and Vernon would be convicted for attempted murder. The Black jurors agreed.

So, the Black jurors went ahead and voted "not guilty" on the seven Davidians. But when it came time to vote on Vernon, the white jurors, who were secretly pro-Vernon, reneged on their deal and went with "not guilty." It was a setup, the man explained. The white jurors had never intended to convict Vernon.

The guy apologized to Vernon. He'd come to understand the stuff about Vernon being a drug dealer was a lie. Vernon was struck by the story. What had happened in the courtroom, he believed, was rotten to the core.

Months later, Larry Coker ran into one of the white jurors. "We tricked them," the guy said, meaning the Black jurors. He told the same story the guy in the auto shop had told Vernon. They'd gotten Vernon and the others off. The guy thought it was hilarious.

Race had infiltrated the trial; it was the screen through which at least some of the jurors perceived the Davidians. The unnamed Black person who'd tried to prejudice the jurors against Vernon and the others saw them as a bunch of dangerous, heavily armed white men who were about to get away with attempted murder. (If they'd been Black, one must imagine this person thinking, would they have even made it off the compound alive?) The white jurors, on the other hand, saw a band of devoted Christians who, though a bit weird, deserved the benefit of the doubt. The whites prevailed.

Vernon had hoped his Godliness would sway the jury. But his skin had helped him the most.

After the verdict, Shabazz tried to get the Davidians' guns destroyed. He quoted a sheriff's deputy, who said that the Mighty Men had enough "weapons and ammunition to hold off the entire McLennan County Sheriff's Department, the police department, and the local National Guard."

Vernon protested. He wanted all his weapons back. The sheriff's department couldn't have as much as one bullet.

Coker tried to bring him around. "Vernon," he said, "why don't you just let me have one of those .223s?" It was for a souvenir. And it would take one gun out of the compound.

"No, no, no. We might need those," Vernon said. He refused to give up anything.

The judge ruled in Vernon's favor. Soon after, a group of Branch Davidian men backed a truck up to the county sheriff's department. They stood and smiled as deputies loaded rifle after rifle into the back.

The ordeal was finished. Vernon had gotten off. The system, it appeared, had worked.

But Vernon didn't see it that way. He made it clear to Coker and anyone who'd listen that he believed he'd gotten a raw deal. American justice was corrupt. The judge didn't let him tell the jury about his beliefs. He couldn't show how he was theologically the rightful owner of Mount Carmel. All they wanted was the secular story, which to Vernon wasn't the full truth.

Vernon felt he'd given the system a chance and it failed. He'd hated being questioned, hated being forced to talk about things he didn't want to talk about, hated being treated like dirt on the night of the arrest. Before he left the courtroom, he spoke to a deputy that was watching the trial. "I'll never be back in jail," he told the man. "You'll never lock me up again."

MOUNT CARMEL

VERNON'S STAR WAS rising, beaming out its light for all the faithful to see. George had vowed to eradicate him, but it was George who was now sitting in jail—for contempt of court—while Vernon was walking around free. And poor Lois was dead.

Vernon was now the undisputed leader of the Davidians. He'd told his followers that Mount Carmel would be returned to him and soon after the trial, he became the rightful owner of the property. There was, however, $68,000 in back taxes owed on the compound.

Vernon had plenty of money coming in, as much as $500,000 a year. The Davidians who held outside jobs tithed monthly. Thirty percent of income was an average contribution, though that number would later go up to 100 percent. Vernon's followers also ran a number of businesses in California and Texas. At a bakery that Vernon owned in San Bernardino in the mid-1980s, some believers toiled eighteen-hour days for as little as $2 a week. The Branch—meaning Vernon—owned houses in California that had been gifted to him by believers. If he needed money for a recruiting trip or a new Camaro, he could tap the rental income or the equity without anyone batting an eye.

The Davidians also ran three businesses in and around Waco. Wayne Martin, who had a passion for the law, had his own legal office, and other believers operated a gun dealership called the Mag Bag, along with a car repair shop. Vernon didn't handle the day-to-day operations himself, though he did like to hang out at the shop and talk muscle cars with the clients.

When it came to the tax bill at Mount Carmel, an elderly Chinese couple, followers of Vernon's, stepped up and paid it. The believers were free to move in.

The Davidians drove out to the compound. They didn't have the keys to the locks on the front gate, so they crawled under the barbed wire and slowly walked toward their old homes. "It's beautiful!" Perry Jones shouted as they got closer to the frame houses. "It has all worked out by the will of God!"

Physically, the place was a shambles. George had allowed it to deteriorate over the past four years since Vernon had been forced off the place. There were houses with doors dangling by one hinge, foundations starting to crumble, roofs in need of new shingles, windows with ripped screens or broken glass. The Davidians were fired up with the spirit of a people returning to their rightful home. They began working day after day cleaning the compound. They picked up garbage, repaired damaged walls, painted, towed away rusted-out car frames.

As the followers fixed up the place, they came across what looked like equipment used in a meth lab, along with pornographic pictures. They burned the photos and took the meth kit to the sheriff's department. Vernon thought he'd be called a hero. He'd reclaimed Mount Carmel for God, gotten rid of a drug operation, and put an end to a porn ring. But the sheriff deputies didn't fall over themselves thanking him. Vernon felt a fresh rush of bitterness.

Mount Carmel had been cleansed of George's presence, but at least one remnant of his term remained: guns seemed to be everywhere on the property. And Vernon wasn't afraid to use them.

After everyone had moved into Mount Carmel, a three-legged pet dog, Buddy, bit a dog belonging to Bonnie, Vernon's mother, who was now living at the compound. Buddy had been tied up outside one of the houses and Bonnie's mean-tempered terrier, Snuggles, had been tormenting the tethered pet. Snuggles took great delight in ambushing Buddy from behind and nipping him painfully on the flank. This time, Buddy snapped and bit him back.

Bonnie saw red. She picked up a shovel and repeatedly beat the wretched Buddy, eventually slicing open his remaining hind leg. When Bonnie was finished, she fetched her son.

With his AK-47 on his right shoulder, Vernon advanced on the cowering Buddy. By this stage the commotion had attracted a large audience, most of them children. They loved Buddy; he was a kind of mascot of theirs.

Vernon declared to the crowd that there were two things he refused to tolerate: unbelievers and troublemakers. He grabbed the dog by the scruff of the neck and dragged it into the middle of a field. He lifted the muzzle of the gun and calmly shot Buddy twice in the head. As the dog lay twitching in the grass, the children, and even some of the adults, began to cry. Vernon admonished the children, telling them he was training them to be warriors for the Lord, not pansies.

Vernon's paranoia wasn't completely without cause. For weeks after they returned, the phone at Mount Carmel rang with people threatening the group. Vernon figured it was the criminals and wastoids that had been living on the compound rent-free while George was in charge.

Vernon saw threats everywhere now. If it wasn't George, it was the meth heads seeking revenge, or it was Babylon, or it was the government.

He was just like Christ, he told his followers, and the people of Texas and the wider United States were the Romans of the ancient world: "Here are these Christians today that talk about loving Jesus. 'If I was there when he walked the earth 2000 years ago,' they say, 'I would have followed him.'

"Bullshit! Look how they treat me. They say I'm rude. They say I'm arrogant. Those same people who say they'll follow Christ are the kind of people that would have been saying 'Crucify him! Crucify him!'"

To calm his mind, Vernon assigned the Davidians to do guard duty at the front gate, 24 hours a day, 365 days a year. They were armed with the rifles that Vernon and the Mighty Men had bought for the raid, along with new AK-47s and other weapons. Everyone was required to do their shifts, including pregnant women.

Most of the guards were given a Ruger .223 rifle. Vernon's instruction was to shoot first and ask questions never. There was a tiny shack near the foot of the driveway with an old couch inside, its covers ripped and known to harbor fleas. Next to the shack was the long gate that swung on hinges. No one could enter—or leave—without permission.

Despite the boredom, people loved guard duty. When you did it, you could skip Bible study.

One day, the Davidian on duty saw a strange man approaching. He raised his rifle and was about to fire when the man cried out for him to stop. It was the newspaper delivery guy.

The man told his bosses at the *Waco Tribune-Herald* and they stopped all service to the compound. They weren't about to see one of their carriers getting blown away for one subscription. Later the Star-Tex propane company that brought canisters to the Davidians told Vernon he'd have to send someone to their store to pick up fresh canisters. The propane delivery guys were spooked, too.

For years, Vernon had resisted the Southern obsession with guns, all that he-man stuff he'd thought was so lame in high school. No longer. The longtime paranoia that had lain dormant inside him since his boyhood had been stirred up by George's attacks on him, by his time in jail and the trial. His deep-seated belief that he'd been singled out by God had attracted enemies who were working to bring him down. Vernon believed he needed to protect himself.

America was increasingly corrupt and dangerous, he preached. "Look at the way children of the world are today," he told his followers. "Their parents are raising them up for Hell. They're into TV and candy bars and drugs." Mount Carmel would be a sanctuary from all that; inside it, Vernon would breed children-soldiers to counter the wickedness. "God's got a plan," he said. "I'm going to raise up righteous seed that'll rule the world. My children won't be like the world's children out there. They'll be righteous judges and rulers . . . and they'll destroy all the Babylonian children."

Neighbors heard gunfire from the compound now, at all times of the night and day. They spotted Vernon walking around the grounds, dressed in camo pants, with an AK hoisted on his shoulder. "At least my piece doesn't give me lip," he would tell people he met on his walks.

Vernon had a special compartment installed in the dashboard of his red 1967 Corvette Classic. In it went his little handgun, a .22. Later, he graduated to a .357 Magnum.

• • •

Under Lois Roden and the Davidians' previous leaders, outsiders were to be pitied or saved. But as Vernon's paranoia began to spread and take root among his followers, he increasingly painted nonbelievers as the enemy. Either they were actively plotting his fall or they were going along, sheep-like, with the conspiracy against him. And the more treacherous the world became in his eyes, the more Vernon watched for traitors inside Mount Carmel.

Vernon grew more intolerant of dissent. And increasingly, he had to be first in everything: with prophecy, with women, with sports. During one arm-wrestling tournament, Vernon became furious when he lost to bigger, stronger men. If you outshot him or outran him, you could feel the change in his mood.

This extended to the Davidian children. All the good things they received—Christmas gifts, birthday treats—had to come from him.

It made things hard for the parents. One time, Wayne Martin, among the most loyal of Vernon's followers, pulled Marc aside. He had something to confide. It was about his kids. Wayne felt that he couldn't give them a present. Gifts had to come from Vernon, so Wayne wasn't allowed to buy his child a simple game or a football or anything. It bothered Wayne. How was he to show his children that he loved them?

Marc didn't know what to say. Who could you complain to? One never knew who to trust inside Mount Carmel. It had always been a gossipy place where condemning your fellow believers was a kind of blood sport. But Vernon had increased the price of doubt considerably.

22

DAVID AND VERNON

ONE OF THE first to feel the sting of the new regime was David Bunds and his wife, Debbie. They'd fallen afoul of Vernon at the Palestine camp for sneaking in some forbidden food, and Vernon had ordered them to leave. They'd moved out, David had found a job in Houston and Debbie had become pregnant with their second child, a boy. But the child had been stillborn.

The hospital called a priest to counsel the couple, but David avoided him. What kept running through his head was this: *If we hadn't moved out of Mount Carmel, God would have saved our boy. I murdered my son. I was being disobedient and so God killed him.*

How much clearer could a message be? What other disasters awaited them if they remained apart from the prophet? He and Debbie decided they had to rejoin the group. The couple, along with their daughter, Jennifer, moved back in with the Davidians, who were now installed at Mount Carmel.

They'd only been away for six months, but it soon became clear that Vernon had changed. Not long after they arrived, Vernon came up to David. "You know," he said, "I think it's funny that your son died."

David was too stunned to say anything. Vernon continued. "You thought you were just going to run off and reject God. But God had another thing coming for you, didn't he, Dave? God was like, 'BOOM, there

ya go. What do you think of that, Dave? What do you think about rebelling against God now?'"

David was speechless. He saw that Vernon wasn't playing around. He
sincerely thought it was funny. Vernon was becoming crueler, David
thought. He would never have said anything like that a few years before.

The Bunds found Mount Carmel now had a weird vibe that hadn't
been there before. People were twitchy. When Vernon first started his
Bible studies back in 1982, it had been a thrill. People were stoked for
something new and different and for being even more special than they
were before. They were part of this big, radical movement.

Now all that had turned to depression and terror. You walked around
Mount Carmel and you were constantly afraid. You could hear the relief
in people's voices when Vernon would leave to go to California. As soon
as he returned, the tension would ratchet back up. Vernon controlled
more and more of their lives. It was like there was a force field that started
at the property line and the radiation swept the compound, interfering
with your brain waves, destroying your ability to think properly.

Only Vernon had the answers to the mysteries of the Bible. Even if
you mastered in your mind one of his teachings, it might change without
warning. Vernon couldn't be removed from the light. He himself was the
light.

This was embedded in the way he taught the Scripture. Vernon's message was a personal multimedia experience. It only worked when he was
standing a few feet away from you. Like any good performer, Vernon
wanted to watch your face, gauge your reaction. His cadences changed
depending on the mood of his audience, his voice turning gravelly or
sweet. It was something that couldn't be duplicated in a tape or a letter.

Vernon wasn't going to bring you up to his level, not if you listened to
him for ten thousand hours. He was always going to be the master and
you were going to be there to worship him.

In one Bible study, they were reading Romans. In it, Paul the apostle
is talking about somebody being "implacable." Vernon read the word as
"in-placeable," as in "not placeable." Vernon thought it meant, "Oh, you
can't place that person anywhere."

One of the Davidians spoke up. "Um, it's 'implacable,' isn't it? Meaning
relentless?"

Vernon blew her off. His teachings were no longer up for grammatical corrections. Sitting there watching the exchange, David Bunds thought, "Well it *did* mean that throughout human history until this very moment. Now Vernon has just changed the meaning of a word through his amazing prophetic powers."

Not even your body belonged to you. Once Debbie and David were back at Mount Carmel, Vernon started touching Debbie, stroking her hair. He was grooming her for the inevitable moment that she'd come to her senses and become one of his wives.

One time, Vernon caught her on the wrong day. He reached out to caress her and Debbie snapped. "If you ever touch me again," she said, "I will kill you. That will be the end of you."

She was so angry she couldn't see straight. "I always wanted to know if you could cut a person in half," she went on. "If you shoot them in a straight enough line, can you cut them in half with bullets? I always thought I'd just start from the crotch and go up."

Vernon was thunderstruck. Nobody spoke to him like that. Soon after, he gave an order: Debbie was exempted from guard duty. He didn't want her carrying a gun, because he was afraid she'd shoot him.

There was no room at Mount Carmel for anyone who would undermine the prophet's authority. Ten months after their return, Vernon found a pretext to throw David and Debbie out for good. One day, he came and told David he'd gone into their rooms and found all this forbidden stuff. Ramen noodles or something with shrimp flavoring among them. Vernon yelled at them for two hours.

Finally, he told them to leave.

David was distraught. "I'm sorry," he kept saying. "I'm just so sorry. Please, Vernon, don't do it. I'm sorry."

He offered to leave his daughter there. At least, she wouldn't be cast out. But Vernon turned that down because Jennifer was the spawn of evil. He handed David twenty bucks and showed him the door.

They were an example: the price of disobedience was banishment and hellfire.

23

NEWBOLD

THAT SUMMER, VERNON set his sights abroad. He wanted the recruitment effort to go international. Israel was still the eventual goal, but Vernon wanted more followers by the time the exodus came. Steve booked a ticket to England; Vernon headed for Australia. Marc stayed back in the States and ran things for a while.

Steve decided to try his luck at Newbold College, in Bracknell, an Adventist college he'd briefly attended before being thrown out for drinking and causing a disturbance. He had a method in mind. He'd fly in, take a car to the college, alone and unannounced, and go to the lounge of the men's dormitory. He'd arrive with no money and no place to lay his head. All he'd have were some clothes and toiletries in his suitcase.

What he wanted was at least one student to offer to let him stay in his dorm room. He would then work to recruit this person and from there to recruit his family, and then his friends, and his friend's families.

Steve arrived in Newbold and began preaching. He emphasized the less controversial parts of Vernon's message. The Branch Davidians had two sets of theology. One for the general public, and the other, truer set for its followers. The true teachings could be hinted at, but only revealed in their fullness by Vernon.

Secretly, what Steve was looking for in England was young women. That was Vernon's direct order. He wanted female believers to sleep with and to have children by. But Steve couldn't just show up and start chatting up young coeds. It would look creepy.

So he started with the men. If a young man accepted the message, Steve would say, "Great! Next time, bring along your sister." Or your girlfriend, your niece, your wife. The message was open to all.

Steve set up an unofficial headquarters at a bungalow used by the college's kitchen workers. He spent his day walking around the open campus, striking up conversations with students. He'd tease them with a hint of Vernon's message, then say "Come and see tonight!"

Steve was low key, American, friendly. His message was clear and simple: The hour is late. The End Times are going to arrive much sooner than the Adventists told you it would. And there is only one person who can reveal the truth of what is to come and his name is Vernon Howell.

Right away, he struck a chord. A small group of students flocked to his talks. If the potential recruits had anything in common, it was a kind of theological malaise. They were bored with Newbold's program: "The lectures . . . are OK," one wrote, "but they are not presented with any conviction." Other reviewers agreed: "The academic standard is good, but you are expected to question everything." "There exists a vacuum of feelings just waiting to be filled."

These young men and women were tired of analysis. They wanted words that were on fire.

One student brought the message to his girlfriend, Diana Henry.

She came from a solid and loving family of West Indian strivers. Her father, Sam, was a handyman. He did roofing, bricking, plastering. If he'd had a hundred hands, Sam would tell people, every one of them would have been busy.

Sam was proud of his children. His son Stephen worked alongside him, learning the craft. Philip wanted to be a doctor, Pauline wanted to be a nurse, Vanessa was doing secretarial work. His firstborn, Diana, was studying for her master's, and wanted to be a psychologist.

Diana attended one of Steve's meetings. Afterward, she was almost frantic. She tried to explain the message to her father, who couldn't make heads or tails of it.

"Daddy, listen," Diana said.

Sam thought Steve was preaching Satanic things. He tried to refute him point by point.

"*Listen!*" Diana cried.

Diana was popular; she introduced Steve to her friends and family, including a woman named Dimplets and Dimplets's brother, an SDA member. The brother agreed to host a Bible study.

Word spread. When the night came, the brother's house was packed tight: People were sitting on chairs, on the floor, squeezed into corners. Some even sat on the window ledges.

Steve began. He was different from how he had been on the Newbold campus. Tougher, more impatient. If a child started crying, he'd shout at the parents to get them out of the room.

Dimplets didn't like Steve. She felt there was something wrong with him. At one point, she interrupted him and asked a question about the scripture. Faces turned. "Why are you questioning this man?" someone called out. Steve ignored her and went on with the teachings.

Another time, Dimplets asked Steve what time the study would end. "I don't know that yet," he said. "I need to make a telephone call and get my information from God." He meant Vernon.

The studies went through the night. Ten, twelve, seventeen hours, day after day. Still, people wanted more.

Steve had leaflets printed up, and his new recruits started passing them out. One of them was dropped in the postbox of a young woman named Bernadette Monbelly. Bernadette, another child of West Indian immigrants, was sick at the time, feeling low. But she'd always been curious about God. When she went to the meeting listed on the leaflet, her family thought nothing of it.

Soon after the meeting, her sister Gail tried to call her. Gail could hear voices in the background. Bernadette hurried Gail off the phone, saying she was busy.

Gail called another night and heard the same swirl of voices behind her sister's. "Bernadette, what are these people doing here?" she said.

"Oh, they're helping me, they're helping me."

By the time Steve boarded his plane for Texas, he'd brought in more than twenty converts. Some began to leave for Waco. Dimplets sat in a black cab with her brother, who was a taxi driver, and her sister-in-law. She begged them not to go.

It was like their minds had been taken over by a virus, Dimplets thought. She had the feeling that the people sitting in the cab weren't her brother and sister-in-law at all. For two hours they argued.

At the end, the couple told her she was the one with the problem. Nothing Dimplets said had registered in the faintest way. The couple left for Waco with their three boys.

One Sunday evening, Sam Henry was at home in Old Trafford. His wife, Zilla, and children were upstairs. Zilla called him up and he went to see her. The whole family was there, minus Diana, who was in Texas.

They crowded together in one of the bedrooms. Zilla said, "We're going to Waco."

Sam thought they were going to visit Diana, but then they told him they were moving to Texas to be with Vernon. They'd already bought their tickets. It was all arranged.

"You must be joking," Sam said. "Why do you want to go to Waco?"

They didn't answer. Sam begged Zilla. "Let's talk about this. Let's pray about this."

"It's too late," Zilla said. "This man is the Christ." They left the following morning.

Vernon's trip to Australia was almost as successful as Steve's. He brought in about fifteen new followers. The group was growing.

When the Australians and the Brits arrived in Waco, they settled in and learned the ways of Mount Carmel. The first issue was the food. Eating was different here. Vernon's paranoia about what his followers ate ran second only to his paranoia about the government.

The new followers found out that the French fries at McDonald's were out. Juice from the supermarket—even if your doctor prescribed it, which happened to one follower—was out. Chocolate was a definite no. Milk, too, was off the list. Vernon's reasoning was that milk is what you drank when you're a baby and they were adults now.

Vernon targeted the overweight. He told them to have some willpower and get those pounds off. He'd buy a dozen doughnuts, and then hold one in front of the Davidian's face before whipping it away. Or he'd tell one of his loyal followers to stuff the offender's mouth with the forbidden food until they were sick of the taste of it.

"All of you are gluttons," Vernon told the newcomers. "If I relax the rules even for a minute, you'll all go out there and eat Babylonian food."

Breakfast was cornmeal mush. Lunch, served at one p.m., was salad, usually lettuce, tomatoes, and onions, maybe some squash and corn, too, along with bread and beans. On special occasions, Vernon would allow grilled chicken on the salad. Dinner was more of a snack: just popcorn. There might be some ice cream afterward: vanilla, praline, or strawberry, never chocolate. But most of the Brits and Aussies found that they were constantly hungry at the Waco compound.

Pregnant women suffered. They couldn't eat pasta or other things. When pancakes were on the menu, they only got two small ones. Vernon went into the pantry and marked the items the pregnant mothers could have. If he caught them eating something unmarked, he'd fly into a rage. You're feeding my future kings and queens filth, he told them.

"Think how much money in the name of God you've been spilling out over these past few years and what the food value is in that stuff? I mean, just to get this feeling of these little squishy, little run, little long, little wormy, little things always through your mouth going 'Slurp! I love spaghetti, I love spaghetti!' Right? But really, what are you eating? Dead, cooked, starchy, little, funny, little, long piece of bread . . . called a noodle.

"Potato chips are a sin. It's part of the Mark of the Beast . . . A Hostess Twinkie is the Mark of the Beast . . . Yeah, the Mark of the Beast is Snickers candy bars and soda pop."

Some of the Davidians broke the rules: They snuck in some Ho-Hos from the local supermarket or dashed into the nearest Whataburger when they had ten minutes of unsupervised time in town. If you were caught, the punishment depended on whether you were one of Vernon's favorites or not.

Even Vernon sinned. One afternoon, Debbie was at a restaurant in Waco. It was owned by Margarita and Neal Vega, two Branch Davidians. One of their specialties were crepes, exactly the kind of sugary treat Vernon had forbidden.

When Debbie walked into the restaurant, she spotted Vernon scarfing down a stack of crepes. Every time somebody passed by or he thought someone was watching him, he'd put his hand on his stomach. "Oh, God is telling me to eat," he'd moan. "I don't want to, but I'm supposed to eat because I'm weak and thin."

He snuck into steakhouses, too, which were on the forbidden list. Vernon loved a good rib eye.

24

THE SCREAM TAPE

THE TRUE REVELATION of Mount Carmel, however, was Vernon himself. The man the new followers met or been told about—in Manchester or Melbourne—was not the man they met in Waco.

One morning, the newcomers filed into the meeting room for a Bible study along with the rest of the followers. The benches were crowded. Mount Carmel's population had swelled to about a hundred twenty men, women, and children, so the room was nearly full. Vernon walked in, carrying his enormous Bible. He began slowly.

"In our study this afternoon, we are going to lay out some wonderful information. It's wonderful to me! Some of you may not be able to comprehend it. Some of you have not had enough experience in the things of God to know why God is, and why we are, and why God is the way that he is, and why we are the way we are."

His tone got chillier. "My God is . . . hard, cold, feelingless," he said. "I want to show you about a God that you haven't yet known. You've all been spoon-fed. You've all been diaper-padded. And now it's time for this cloak to be thrown off, and you're going to go through the fires. You're gonna see whether you believe this message."

As he went on, the material got darker and darker. Vernon's voice ratcheted up. If his followers didn't accept that God was intent on a mass slaughter of Babylonians, they would pay the cost. "I guarantee you," he shouted, "I'll kill you one day . . ."

He was shouting by now. "What has God spoken? Follow the vision! He's got a book! He gives the book to the Lamb! The Lamb shows you the man on the white horse! Get it in your minds! That's what he says! You stupid idiots! . . . You'd better start fearing God, 'cause he's going to burn you in the lowest hell!

"Do you hear?! Do you understand! *It's war!*"

The talk lasted eighty-seven minutes. By the end Vernon was shrieking at his followers, almost out of control. Recordings of the meeting filtered out among the believers worldwide. Some called it "the scream tape."

The Australians Bruce and Elisabeth Gent joined the group in 1986. Bruce came to America with his wife, son Peter, and daughter Nicole to learn the message. They'd liquidated their property and arrived in the US in December, giving $12,000 in Australian dollars as a tithe.

When they met with Vernon, he was furious. He said they should have given a full third of what they made on the sale of their home and belongings. They'd cheated him.

Nicole, the Gents' daughter, came over with her fiancé, James Tom. Soon after they arrived, Vernon propositioned her. Was she up for a threesome with himself and one of the other girls?

Nicole was horrified. She went to her suitcase and put on several layers of clothing, including her Ugg boots. Then she sat in a corner, as far away from Vernon as she could get.

Vernon kept trying. He offered James other girls for marriage; that way, he'd get his green card and could stay in America. Vernon suggested Robyn Bunds, David's sister. James turned him down, but Vernon wasn't put off. "Well, how about Brenda?" he said, naming another teen girl. It was like being sold a used car.

James said no to everything. Eventually, their resistance paid off. Vernon let them marry.

But that wasn't the end of it. When anything went wrong among the Davidians, Vernon lashed out at James and Nicole. They were the reason bad things happened at Mount Carmel. They wanted to do their own thing by getting married, and in so doing, they'd opened the group up to God's punishment.

The abuse of Vernon's adult followers was mostly verbal. The children had it harder. If a child displeased Vernon, they were spanked, often violently. Vernon could be set off by a variety of things: a sour glance, crying, backtalk. If a child accidentally spilled a drink or knocked over a plate, the boy or girl would often turn their heads and put their hands behind their backs. They crouched, faces near the floor, expecting a blow.

Vernon demanded respect. If he passed by a child and they didn't smile at him, or they gave him a look, oftentimes he'd beat them. One time, Vernon whaled on the Tomses' eight-month-old daughter Tarah with a wooden spoon. It went on for thirty minutes. By the end Tarah's bottom was bruised and bleeding.

Another trigger was pacifiers. "If I ever see you giving them to our children," Vernon told parents, "I will personally kill them by smashing them against the wall." Children who were disobedient were forced to take cold baths. There was even a "whipping room" at Mount Carmel. If the Davidians didn't want their children's screams to be heard, they'd take them there.

Vernon would informally "adopt" the children he liked. They were told to regard him as their father. The others were often called "bastards," the same word his grandfather had called Vernon back in Little Elm.

The Gents brought their son Peter over from Australia, and he fell deep into the message. Once, when Bruce Gent opposed Vernon on some minor theological point, Peter threatened to kill his father. Bruce was convinced that, if Vernon ordered it, Peter would indeed murder Bruce and his wife.

Vernon's first son, Cyrus, got the worst of his anger. One time, Cyrus acted up and Vernon sent him away. After a few minutes, he set his Bible down and walked out to spank the boy. The Davidians sat in silence, listening to Cyrus scream. After about ten minutes of this, Vernon walked back and resumed his teaching. Ten minutes later, he set the Bible down again and walked out of the room. The screaming resumed.

James Tom couldn't stomach it. He spoke to his wife, Nicole, about it, told her it wasn't right. Nicole must have reported the conversation to Vernon—informing on people was still popular at Mount Carmel—because a few hours later, Vernon emerged and called Floyd Hautman, the boxer. He told Floyd to take James to the backyard and discipline him. Floyd did what he was told and beat James with a fence paling.

On another occasion, Cyrus didn't want to sit next to one of Vernon's wives. So Vernon decided he wouldn't get any food. He couldn't leave his bedroom, either. Vernon had the windows closed and locked and the blinds pulled down.

It went on all day and into the night. When Vernon finally decided to feed Cyrus, the child was like a rag doll. He couldn't sit up; he just slumped on the ground and ate that way. When he was finished, Vernon left him lying on the vinyl floor in the kitchen, without a pillow or a blanket.

James Tom went to Vernon and told him that this wasn't right. The boy shouldn't be forced to doze on the cold vinyl. "Do you want to sleep with him on the floor?" Vernon said. He ordered James to take the boy out to the garage and lock him in there. Vernon had always told Cyrus that the garage was prowled by big rats who ate naughty boys. The boy had terror dreams about the place.

James took him out. Cyrus was raving with fear, nearly out of his head. James locked him in the garage. The followers could hear Cyrus's cries, but no one dared move. It was hours before Vernon went himself and let him out. The traumatized boy didn't seem to know himself.

The strange thing was that Cyrus was Vernon's favorite. He even looked like Vernon. That, for some deep reason none of the Davidians could fathom, sent Vernon into paroxysms of rage.

Later on, when he was eight, Vernon let Cyrus get a pierced ear. And he bought him a leather jacket, similar to his own. He could go to the local music bars with Vernon, while the other kids stayed home. There were other special treats that came only to Cyrus.

In Vernon's treatment of his son and the other children, his obsessions and his insecurities met. He told his followers that, once he was slain in battle, his sons would rule over God's coming kingdom. But the idea of another person having power, even his own children, even after his death, drove him to violence. Certainly, the beatings he took as a boy played a part in the abuse, but there was something else, something brittle. He was so insecure that he saw six-year-olds as threats to his power.

At times, he treated Cyrus like his heir. At other times, he seemed to hate the boy with his entire being.

UNREAL COLOSSAL SUPERMARKET

T HE NEWCOMERS ALSO came to suspect what those already at Mount Carmel had known for years now: Vernon was having sex with young girls. Though he'd vowed to stop after Karen Doyle, in fact, he regularly added new victims. Girl after girl were brought into what had been named the House of David.

Vernon hid his depravities from the outside world, but inside Mount Carmel, he hinted at his skills as a lover. "I'm a real professional in bed," he told the Davidians during one Bible study. He described the first time he had sex with Michele, Rachel's sister. How he'd slipped into bed next to her, how Michele thought he was just trying to get warm, until he stuck a finger under the band of her panties.

"You know when an animal's scared, how its heart just pounds?" he told the others. "That's how her heart sounded." It was like hunting a rabbit.

Vernon did set up some guardrails to protect young girls, but they only emphasized just how all-encompassing his pedophilia had become. He decreed that the Davidian men shouldn't change the diapers of their baby daughters, lest they be tempted. The reason: Once, when he was changing his own baby daughter, he'd become aroused. Vernon imagined this was a common response, and so he forbid men to be around naked infants.

All the sex, licit and illicit, had a purpose. Vernon was building a ruling class for God's new kingdom. Eventually, he told the Davidians, he would have a thousand wives. When the End Times came, Vernon would be fighting the infidel Americans in the deserts of Israel. Eventually, the GIs would slay him in battle. Then his widows would marry Jesus.

Contraceptives were out. Vernon demanded the girls get pregnant and bear him children—preferably boys, who'd become soldiers and judges during the End Times. Vernon ordered the girls and women he slept with to keep track of their menstrual cycle and inform him when they were in the fertile stage. That's when he would invite them to his room and have sex with them.

"You know, you ever heard the word, well, like on the TV: 'Well, I'm so horny,'" he told his followers. "Right? What does that mean? It's your strength, your power to rule. And your power to rule in this world is your power to have a family. No family, no war. No army, no war. No wife, no army. You got to first conquer by obeying God's will. And then you get the army. Okay?"

But sex didn't seem to make Vernon happy. "In my body has been desire, but it deceived me," he told the group during a Bible study. "I looked upon the desire and said, this is love. But once that love came through my testicles and left out of the head of my mind and went into their body, my body turned into hatred. My body found no more desire and my body ached, my stomach grabbed ahold of me and said, 'You don't love these girls.'"

Postcoital sadness revealed to Vernon how empty his little trysts were. The girls (literally) worshipped him, but sleeping with them brought only contempt. Groupie sex wasn't doing it for him.

"I said, 'God, what is love?'" Vernon said. "God said, 'No man knoweth love, nor hate, by all the things he sees under the sun.' And I persevered. I continued my work, feeling dead, feeling lonely, feeling like a dirty dog, 'cause God said that they that bear the vessels of the Lord shall triumph."

His sadness didn't cause him to stop. In fact, Vernon was sleeping with so many girls and women that it caused health problems. "I suffer," he told the others. "I get tired." He caught thrush, a fungal infection that caused painful white lesions on the tongue and inside the mouth. He told his wives to eat a bulb of raw garlic every day to kill off the infection. He also took the stuff himself to maintain his stamina.

All the while, Vernon was having freaky dreams. As usual, he told the group about them. He went into detail on one in particular:

> We're going to the supermarket. And I am really frustrated. And this supermarket, I'd never been in it before. But it was colossal, it was . . . unreal, an unreal colossal supermarket. And I'm walking down the alleyway, you know, and I'm looking and I'm really, I'm hating life. You know. You know this big supermarket, yeah, it's fine, but I'm not caring about eating, I'm not concerned about food.
>
> And I see this one long . . . like a thing . . . long and skinny, you know wrapped up real tight. And I go over and I can't make it out because it's just a long thing wrapped up, you know . . . and it's been there a while and . . . the thing is a human cadaver.
>
> And I'm going to myself, "Aw, sick." I said, "Man, sick." . . . And I got really teed off and I turned around and I walked down the hall and I saw this woman over there and she's like, taking care of some juices or something . . . and I said, "Ma'am, will you come over here and help me? What is this?"
>
> And she goes, "Well, that's human meat."
>
> I said, "What you saying?"
>
> "Well, these people, they donate their bodies for this."
>
> "You mean, there's people who eat other people?"
>
> She goes, "Yeah, this store has everything."
>
> And I grab this girl and I push her around like that, in front of all those girls, even Judy. And I grab her and I'm pulling her clothes off and I whack it right to her. And I turned myself over and I watched the TV set. And I came out of my dream.

Had the newcomers been psychology students at Baylor University down the road, they might have spent a week of class time parsing the dream. Symbols and disturbances jackknifed into each other, layer on layer, a Pompeiian frieze of Vernonalia. But it just kind of zoomed by before their leader was on to his next study.

THE NEW LIGHT

VERNON BANISHED SUSPECTED dissidents from Mount Carmel. Followers who challenged him were dealt with harshly, often violently. He even forbid any Davidian from having contact with relatives outside the group. Even small reminders, such as family pictures, were out.

Other cult leaders had used the same technique, hoping to prevent loved ones from luring away their followers. But, for David, it went further. He seemed to want to be the Davidians' sole object of love and devotion.

Still, it wasn't enough. His ego, and his psychological hold over the Davidians, required constant maintenance. In August 1989, Vernon summoned his followers to a marathon sixteen-hour meeting. There, he revealed that he'd had another vision. He was calling it "the New Light." It was the full, radical realization of the message he'd had when he announced he'd taken Michele Jones as a wife.

Since the last time they saw him, Vernon said, he'd passed away and been resurrected. The old Vernon had died. The new Vernon had arisen and was pure God. Vernon told the believers he and he alone would guide humanity through the End Times. Not God, not the Bible. And certainly not the Davidian prophets, whose words were now dust.

All prophecy was about Vernon. Who were the four horsemen of the

Apocalypse? They were Vernon. Who were the twenty-four elders of the Book of Revelation? They were Vernon's children. To turn away from Vernon was to turn away from the face of God.

Something else had been revealed to Vernon: None of the believers' marriages had been sanctioned by God. All women belonged to him. Therefore, his follower's unions were null and void.

"Why did you marry your wife?" Vernon asked his male followers as he introduced the new teaching. "You had a feeling between your legs and you wanted to satisfy it. You had lust in your heart and you fulfilled it by fucking your wife. You didn't really love your wife, did you? Did you?!"

He looked around the room. "So, Scott, how does it feel to know you're not married anymore?" He laughed. "All these years my wives have sacrificed to be with me. They have shared me around among themselves and you said it was okay because you didn't have to suffer. You didn't have to sacrifice. Well, now you have to sacrifice. How does it feel?" Vernon forbade the children at Mount Carmel from having any contact with their natural fathers. He claimed all the boys and girls as his own. By the end of the meeting, some of the male believers were weeping.

The Davidian men walked around the compound in disbelief. The only comfort Vernon allowed them was that they could, for a time, drink all the beer they wanted. Later, he started buying go-karts for the guys to ride. He started a group talent show every few weeks and bought lumber for doghouses for the eleven Alaskan malamute puppies that had been delivered to the compound. "Let the boys have their fun" seemed to be his thinking.

Vernon did grant his male followers one sliver of hope. He began teaching that everyone had a "mirror person" inside of him. Every man had a woman inside of him who was a perfect companion for them, suited in every way to their personality and their needs. And every woman had a perfect man inside of her.

When the End Times came, these mirror people would depart the bodies of the Davidians and become their hosts' lifelong companions. The Davidians would be happier than they had ever been with their earthly wives and husbands. If they only waited until Judgment Day, they would all have their ideal mates.

There was a caveat: The men who didn't separate from their wives would pay. A man, not a woman, would emerge from their bodies and God would condemn the stubborn follower to have sex with this man in plain view of everyone. For Vernon, this was a terrible punishment.

The women who refused to sleep with Vernon would suffer an even worse fate. They would be murdered in hell, forever, their bodies consumed over and over by Satan's fires. Vernon screamed when he described the flames, shrieking as if he was feeling the heat himself. It felt, he told the Davidians, like having your skin removed with a nail clipper, snip by snip.

The new teaching was directed at the married men at Mount Carmel. But it affected the single guys, too. How were they supposed to find wives now? Vernon was claiming all the women in the group for himself.

Vernon apparently hadn't thought of this. "Well, I guess you'll have to go out to get one," he responded when one of the unattached men asked.

But when the guys did bring single women into the group, ones that were decent-looking, Vernon often grabbed them for his own bed. And if the woman said no, she (and you, if you were her boyfriend or fiancé) would inevitably feel his wrath. The unmarried men were caught in a dilemma. Vernon was condemning them to celibacy or hellfire.

Vernon taunted his male followers. He seemed to enjoy humiliating them. He taught the group that if they remained true to him, and accepted the New Light, during the End Times God would send a spaceship and bring them to heaven.

He said he'd seen the spaceship personally. With his own eyes! He walked over to the whiteboard and took up a marker and began drawing it. When he stepped back, the Davidians got a look at his sketch: a fully erect penis. "That's God's spaceship," Vernon said. "It really is."

Vernon relished the idea that his new sexual dominance would soon extend beyond Mount Carmel's gates. He became obsessed with the pop star Madonna, who to him was the ultimate woman. "God told me, I will give thee Madonna," he said to his followers. She personified all the sins of the world, and Vernon was going to sleep with her and then save her.

He was looking forward to having sex with the singer. "Sometimes, I just want to have a nice steak instead of eating hamburgers all the time," he said during one study. Despite the dig, the women smiled and nodded their heads.

A number of couples resisted Vernon's order to split. Steve and Judy, surprisingly, were among them. Steve had become one of Vernon's most loyal supporters, but he was deeply in love with Judy. He didn't want to lose her. Judy felt the same way. Steve was the love of her life, and she found it hard to imagine being without him. When Vernon asked her to come visit him in his bedroom, she declined.

In the days that followed, Vernon went after Judy. "You know the truth, but you refuse to obey it!" he shouted during a Bible study. "If you don't leave Steve and agree to be my wife, you're a whore. You are standing against God!"

It went on for weeks. Each Bible study, Vernon would work his way around to attacking the couple. And after each session, Steve and Judy walked out into the yard and jumped on one of the Magna motorcycles. They went for rides through the Central Texas countryside, clearing their heads. Conversation was tough on a bike at speed so they just cruised the local roads, catching the occasional glimpse of horses grazing in the fields, the sway of wheat, letting their minds roam.

Steve went to Marc and told him he was afraid. If Judy became Vernon's wife, it would be painful enough. But if Judy fell in love with Vernon, Steve didn't know if he could take it.

Vernon solved the problem by sending Steve away to England to find more followers. While he was off recruiting, Vernon coaxed Judy into his bed and she became pregnant. Steve came back in October 1989 and learned the news. He was distraught.

Steve's fears proved prophetic. Judy had fallen for Vernon. To be the beloved of the son of God was almost overwhelming for her. It wasn't just the sex. Vernon wanted the wives' hearts, too. He wanted to see love shining in their eyes.

Now when Vernon was away on trips with Steve, he'd call Judy in the evening. The two would chat about their days, with Steve just a few feet away, forced to listen to Vernon lolling on the phone with his wife, sharing intimacies.

At the end, Vernon would be like, "Okay, gotta go. Oh, I love you, too, Judy!" Steve just had to harden up and take it.

It was as if having sex with the Davidian wives was just half the thrill for Vernon. He also wanted to humiliate the men, revel in their pain.

MARC AGONISTES

THE HUMILIATIONS AT Mount Carmel were increasingly public, the Davidians' own show trials. Vernon summoned his followers to small inquisitions where he confronted the wrong-doers. Mostly, the meetings concerned one of the Davidians breaking a rule and causing Vernon great pain. One day, he announced that some-one had transgressed so terribly that Vernon's back had broken. He called them all to the chapel to see the accused, an eighteen-year-old woman. Her crime was lying for a friend who'd slipped out of Mount Carmel to visit her mother.

When they entered the chapel, Vernon was sitting on a bed placed at the front. His face was contorted with anger. "You've lied to the Lamb!" he shouted at the woman, who was standing in the doorway. "How could you do this?"

The woman was too terrified to speak. Vernon railed at her. "God in the flesh! Do you know who I am? God in the flesh!" The girl was weeping.

As he sat on the bed, Vernon shifted his Bible to his left hand. His right hand worked at something on the side of the bed. After a few seconds, he pulled out a gun.

"God would not condemn me if I killed you now!" he cried.

He held the pistol pointed at her. The room had gone silent. Having made his point, Vernon dropped his hand. He expelled the woman from Mount Carmel, broke and alone.

A heat spell settled over Waco, with temperatures hovering around 104 degrees. No breezes came at night to cool the plains. Vernon introduced mandatory paramilitary training for everyone at Mount Carmel, including the children. He claimed he was preparing them for when the authorities would descend on the compound. They had to defend their prophet.

The men and the boys woke up at 5:30 a.m. They marched and drilled and ran the obstacle course. They practiced fighting each other, Babylonians vs. Davidians. If a follower didn't strike at his opponent with the requisite gusto, they were paddled.

The women ran mile after mile around the compound to toughen up. They made up chants to keep their spirits up:

We're with Cyrus, he's our man,
Gonna kill his enemies where they stand,
If you have the world's desire,
Gonna throw you in God's holy fire.

Heat and dust, Bible studies. The whole mood was oppressive. Febrile.

Vernon had always sought to cloak his sexual abuse of young girls from his followers. It was biblically ordained, he preached. The rapes were part of the marriage covenant. But it became harder and harder to hide what he was doing. So many girls were falling under his sway and getting pregnant. Even Perry, one of his most devoted followers, had briefly rebelled at sacrificing his daughters.

Then came the New Light, and the discovery that even one's wife wasn't safe from Vernon. This upped the psychological price of faith. One either had to ramp up one's devotion or begin to doubt the whole enterprise. Most of Vernon's followers toed the line.

Marc struggled with the new revelations. He decided to look into the accusations of child rape. One night, he stationed himself in the office at the foot of the stairs leading to Vernon's bedroom. He wanted to see if any underage girls stayed with him overnight. By the morning, he knew that one had: Aisha Gyarfas, one of the Australian girls.

Marc couldn't look away any longer. He decided he had to leave.

Once the decision was made, Marc knew he needed a plan. By now, Vernon was so neurotic that his guards at the gate would never let Marc pass without permission. They were there to keep believers in just as much as to keep nonbelievers out. Those who held jobs were still allowed to make the trip to Waco, but the others rarely ventured out.

His wife, Elizabeth, was in Australia, had been for weeks. She was safe. So he only had to worry about himself.

He came up with a strategy. One afternoon that fall, he told Vernon they should go to California to buy some new musical equipment. His keyboard mixer was out of date; LA had better music stores than Waco, so it made sense to pick one up there.

Vernon said sure. He always loved escaping to California, where he could meet new women and dream of becoming the next Mick Jagger.

Marc packed as if he was going away for a few days. Aside from clothes, he took only his wallet and his personal mobile computer. The two left in Vernon's Camaro. Two days later, they were in Pomona.

Marc didn't have much money. He wasn't allowed to have a job and Vernon sucked up every extra dollar that came into the compound. Marc would have to ask Elizabeth to wire it to him.

Elizabeth disliked Vernon intensely, but she was still in the message. What if Marc confessed to her and she turned around and told Vernon what he was planning? Faith was often stronger than love. You only had to look at Steve and Judy to know that. Marc didn't know if he could trust Elizabeth anymore. Also, he knew Vernon had a .22 in the glove compartment of the red Camaro and an AK-47 wrapped in a blanket in the trunk.

He couldn't call Elizabeth from the house phone in Pomona, either. There was always somebody nearby, listening. He made some excuse and walked to a nearby Target store. He bought a phone card and dialed Elizabeth's number. When she answered, Marc told her what had been going on and said he wanted to escape.

Elizabeth's first thought was that it was a sting operation set up by Vernon. He was trying to get her back to Waco and into his bed. She hated Vernon, but she acknowledged his cunning.

She wrote Marc a letter:

Today is the day you dropped the latest bombshell on me, when you called so early in the morning. When you told me the news, I just wanted to die rather than give you up. I still feel that way. You are my only love, the love of my life, and I don't believe I will be able to go through what is being asked. If I thought that it was possible, then I would have become part of the House of David rather than marry you in the first place. And believe me, I did think long and hard about it.

I don't like Vernon in the least. Every time that he touches me, I feel ill. The thought that we might never be allowed to be together again makes my mind want to explode. I don't think that I'd want to live anymore. Please God don't let it be like that. Don't take my love away from me just when I've found him. Don't be so cruel. I suppose my prayer should be, "Let thy will be done," only I'm too afraid to pray that one now.

I don't know what to say or do anymore. Marc, I'm really scared.

> With all my Love
> Elizabeth

She put a check in the mail. But Vernon inspected the letters that came into the Pomona house. Anything suspicious, he opened and read.

Marc began waiting for the mailman every day. When he heard his footsteps on the path, he would spring up and rush to the door. It went on for two weeks. Finally, the check arrived.

Soon after, Marc told Vernon he was going into downtown LA to look at keyboard mixers. What he really intended doing was going to the Australian consulate and turning in some documents for his visa application. Vernon nodded. He didn't ask to tag along.

Marc took the bus downtown. In order to get to the consulate, he'd have to ask for a transfer and connect to a second bus. When he arrived at the transfer point, he got out. He was standing on the curb on Broadway waiting for the traffic to clear when a black Honda motorcycle pulled up to a light. On it were Steve and Judy Schneider.

Marc felt light-headed. He could tell the pair were startled to see him, too. As Steve pulled to the curb, Marc saw his expression turn. What was Marc doing in downtown LA, all alone?

Marc was preparing to explain. The keyboard mixer, etc. But Steve was in a rush. "Judy's got an appointment," he called out. Marc mumbled a few words, then Steve revved the engine and sped off.

Marc went to the consulate and turned in his documents.

He waited for the visa to book his flight. He tried to act as normal as possible. Kept his head down and his mouth shut.

But Greg Summers, one of the Mighty Men, was getting weird vibes. He went to see Vernon. Marc's acting suspicious, he said. Something's up.

Vernon told Summers to watch Marc. If he detected any sign of betrayal, the Mighty Men were to escort him out of the house and beat the shit out of him.

Finally, Marc's visa arrived and he made a reservation on Continental Airlines. The day of his flight arrived. As he was making his final arrangements, Vernon found him.

"What's this I hear about your attitude?" he said.

"Where did you hear it from?"

"That's none of your business."

"It is my business when someone talks about me behind my back."

Vernon's voice notched higher. "You'd better humble yourself! You'd better lick the dust! You don't have any experience. You have never suffered but have been spoon-fed."

Marc couldn't restrain himself any longer. He yelled back at Vernon that his talk about suffering was so much bullshit. Vernon was the last person to suffer among the Davidians. He was a god as well as a lord, and the other Davidians were his peasants.

Vernon was stunned. He told Marc to go back to Waco and await his punishment. Marc packed his few things into a suitcase. He left the house and headed to LAX and boarded the plane for Melbourne.

I'm never going back, he told himself. He'd had a revelation, as sharp and strong as his angel vision when he was a boy. The Davidians under Vernon Howell were a Satanic movement. He would fight it.

Marc left a parting gift for Vernon. It was in the form of the small joke he'd made years back, during the worried debate about the ex-member who believed that Vernon was a fraud because his name wasn't David ben-David. Marc had quipped that, if you were really going along with the Bible, the name of the true prophet should be "David Koresh."

Vernon went to the California Superior Court in Pomona and requested his name be legally changed. It took over a year, but in the summer of 1990, his request was granted. The new name, with its biblical echoes, was more appropriate for a messiah. But it's also true that Vernon had changed a great deal in the last few years. Perhaps he had simply tired of being called Vernon Howell, which combined the names of a grandfather who despised him (until the very end) and a father who abandoned him.

A letter went out to his followers around the world. From now on, they were to direct all their prayers "to the god of life and death," David Koresh.

AUTHOR'S NOTE

Following his name change from Vernon Howell to David Koresh, I will use the latter name from here on in.

Part IV

COMING A TIME

THE RIVAL

I N AUSTRALIA, MARC settled in for what he knew would be a long fight. He'd escaped the compound, but people he cared about were still trapped there and he worried about their safety. He committed himself to getting them out. For that he knew he'd have to bring down David.

This required a change in thinking. The only way to attack David successfully was at his weak points, scripturally speaking. The believers wouldn't be convinced by stories of David's abuse or his meanness. If he was the messiah, those things had to be accepted. Instead, Marc would have to challenge his role as the savior. And to do that he had to stop thinking like a Davidian and think more like David.

How did David see his followers? Not as human beings, clearly, as was shown in how he treated his own son, among others. They were more like concepts, or vessels. They were weak material that had to be altered in order to serve his purpose.

In a sense, Marc was thinking like a prophet himself. He had to. David's grip on his followers was superhuman, quite literally. Marc had to offer a competing truth if he was going to defeat him.

Marc decided on a ploy of sorts. He was known within the Davidians for having visions, which had been accepted as coming from God. Now he would take the next step. What better way to defeat a false prophet than by becoming a prophet oneself?

He wrote to the Aussie followers:

Since I am here in Australia at the Lord's direction, God has seen
fit to reveal much New Light so as to put to shame those who think
they know the Scriptures . . . I am instructed to invite any branches
who will give ear to attend very important studies . . . Those who
have an ear, let them hear what the Spirit saith. Those who do not, let
them dwell in darkness.

Marc was feeling apocalyptic. The Davidians were headed toward disaster, perhaps mass death. He had to make that clear to the followers
he was writing to. These people had seen child abuse and rage and gun
obsession, and they were still in the message. Marc had to make clear far
worse things were coming.

He recalled something Steve had once told him. David had confided
to Steve that God had spoken to him about his son Cyrus. God told David what he'd told Abraham in the Old Testament: to kill his child as a
mark of his obedience. Marc had heard David teach that same doctrine.
So Marc wrote to the Australians that David was likely going to sacrifice
a child in the near future.

In Waco, David was tightening the screws. He ordered that, from
now on, every phone call had to be monitored by one of his loyalists. No
one at Mount Carmel or at the California houses could speak to a family member, or anyone else, without another Davidian listening in. No
one, especially, was allowed to speak to or correspond with Marc. David
changed the phone numbers at the Pomona house several times and got
new ones that were unlisted.

But Marc kept writing to the believers. Steve was one of his primary
targets. Marc had brought him into the group and felt a great deal of
guilt about that. He loved Steve. He was responsible, in a way, for where
his friend found himself. And Steve had power within the group. If Marc
managed to peel him away, others might follow.

He wrote his friend about ten letters, but only one or two got through
David's surveillance system. In them, he still used David's old name,
Vernon:

You say that Vernon has never gone into his visions. Steve, what is wrong with your mind! How many times have we heard about Linda, Sandy, his female self and any number of visions? I could relate them by memory if I wanted to.

I am saying that the people are full of idol worship. They accept what Vernon says even when they should know it is false. One plus one equals two, Steve, not three or four . . .

In [a recent tape], Vernon expresses such gems as the fact that he has permission by God to kill his enemies. They will rape the women, the women deserve it, they're begging for it. Now I know where he's coming from, but the police and television shows would not. Imagine what they'd think if they heard that stuff?

Steve didn't write back.

Marc scored his first successes among the Australians. James Tom listened to his pleas and left the message. Then Bruce and Elisabeth Gent renounced David. It was a promising start.

But the Gents' daughter Nicole and son Peter remained in the group. The Gents called Waco and ask to speak to their children. When the Davidians realized who was on the other end, they said, "Oh, I'm not sure where Nicole and Peter are." They put the phone down and went looking, supposedly, for the two. International calls were expensive, so after ten or fifteen minutes, the Gents had to hang up.

Another time, a follower told them, "The line is breaking up. I can't hear you." On a third call, a Davidian claimed not to know who Peter Gent was. "Peter, who's Peter?" they said.

The Gents were living in Australia, and they'd already had doubts about David following the New Light. They were low-hanging fruit. The people inside the compound were going to be far harder to reach.

David was disturbed by the Australians' defection. He decided to challenge Marc to a debate. He named the date—Yom Kippur, in the fall of 1990—and the place—Mount Carmel. He even offered to buy Marc a first-class plane ticket to Texas.

It was a clever move. If Marc declined, it would look like he was afraid of David. If Marc went, he might be in danger of never coming back.

Marc wanted to go. But David, he suspected, was planning something. Why would he expose himself to someone who knew the Scriptures as well as if not better than him?

As he mulled over the offer, Bruce Gent called and told Marc he'd been speaking with some of the Davidians and he wanted to relay their message: "They can't tell me how they know, but they're pretty sure David plans on putting something in your drink so that you'll drop dead on the spot."

There was no actual proof. The warning might have been the work of a Davidian's overheated imagination. But the poison plan fit what Marc had learned about David and his followers over the years: They were big on Godly punishment. If Marc was in the meeting talking about the Bible and all of a sudden he dropped to the floor dead, the Davidians would be convinced it was a divine judgment. Marc told David the debate was off.

DOREEN

MOUNT CARMEL WAS growing increasingly dark. Less information was getting in and out. Visitors from town, possible recruits, did visit, but few were privy to the group's secrets.

During the 1990 Passover celebrations, David responded to the traitors he saw among his flock, the ones who were listening to Marc. He picked out two believers in the crowd, Poia and her husband, Leslie, New Zealanders who had just returned to the compound after several years away from it. Through his informants, David knew they had been talking to Marc.

Poia and the others braced for what was coming. "The mood did not feel welcoming," she wrote. "I sensed a mixture of somberness and fear, so unlike the atmosphere we had left four years ago in Palestine." The lights in the chapel dimmed, while the stage brightened. The followers could see a bed sitting there; David was laying back on the mattress. He was holding a boat paddle. On the paddle, the Davidians could see words painted. "It is written."

David spoke from the stage. His voice was low, menacing. He railed against those who doubted the message. As he spoke, he took the paddle and smashed it against the footboard. The sound echoed in the cavernous room.

His voice rose to a shriek. He screamed that Poia and her husband had disobeyed him. They were poison. It went on for four hours, David crashing the paddle against the bed frame every time his fury ratcheted up. "The reason I'm sick is because of people like you," he cried, "who can't even do as you're told!" Poia was rooted to her seat. "I had never experienced such terror in all my life," she wrote later.

David reached down and picked up something from the side of the bed. It was his AK-47. He hoisted it into the air. He then ordered the gun passed among his followers so they could touch it. It was a heavy, brutal-looking weapon. As it circulated, David stared at Poia's husband, Leslie. "If you try to hide," he said, "I can hunt you down."

After their public condemnation, Poia and her husband fled back to New Zealand. But the others stayed. Marc was picking off followers here and there, but the majority of the believers remained loyal to David.

It was hard to deny that Mount Carmel was a different place now. One believer told Poia's sister, Doreen, that they shouldn't subject David's words to any kind of analysis. His followers weren't there at Mount Carmel to think for themselves. They were there to obey.

"So what does this obedience look like?" Doreen asked.

The follower replied: "If David tells us to eat shit, we eat shit."

Even daily life was harder. The followers found that David had cut back on food. They could see in one another's faces that they were getting thinner. Sometimes, during the long Bible studies, they felt dizzy.

Popcorn for dinner went from being a treat to a necessity. You could always go back for a second heap of corn. Fill your belly up.

Anyone who didn't toe the line was suspect. And any believer who, even inadvertently, presented a threat to David's reign was open to attack. Doreen experienced this firsthand.

Perhaps she was simply unstable. Or perhaps the atmosphere at Mount Carmel worked on an already existing mental condition. But she began to experience hallucinations.

In her room one evening, a deep male voice spoke to her. She flicked on the light, and no one was there. She called this being that spoke to her "Voice."

Voice told her to do and say things. She made faces, whispered to herself, sometimes blurted out an odd comment. Once, at a Bible study,

Voice took the floor and told everyone's secrets, the ungodly things they did in private.

After weeks of this, David ordered some believers, including Rebecca, another sister, to bring Doreen to a clinic in Waco. As they were walking toward the car, Doreen's stomach swelled, or at least it looked that way to Doreen. Her belly stayed that way the whole ride. When she got out in the clinic parking lot, her stomach was going up and down, up and down.

Doreen didn't want to be there; she wanted to be at Mount Carmel. She began screaming at the nurses and her sister to take her back immediately. The workers got scared and told Rebecca and the others they couldn't handle Doreen's case. She needed to go to a real hospital, one with a psych ward.

Instead, the followers drove her back to Mount Carmel. The Davidians didn't believe in followers being questioned by outsiders. David was just getting into a car when he saw them pull in. The followers told him what had happened at the clinic. He ordered them to put Doreen in one of the cabins on the property.

David's guard was up. Here was a follower experiencing something strange: hallucinations, or visions. What if she began denouncing his teachings? What if he had another Marc on his hands? David had let Marc leave, only to find he'd created a rival. He wasn't about to make the same mistake twice. He needed to separate Doreen from the flock, isolate her, and make her recant.

The others brought Doreen to the cabin and locked her in. It was tiny, with a single window, a bed, and a bucket for a bathroom. A guard stood at the door and followed her whenever she went to empty the bucket outside. Every time she looked out, one of the Mighty Men was there.

After some time, David opened the door. There were two men with him. David started smacking her on the face with his open hand. The others just watched. When David left, he said to one of the guards, "If she gives you any trouble, fuck her."

One guard, Frank, tormented her. He spied on her in the shower. He demanded sex and beat her. Doreen resisted and several men had to be called in to restrain her. Doreen ranted at them. "Fuck me!" she yelled.

"The next time she says something like that," David instructed Frank, "do it."

David came by again and smacked her again with his open hand. "So you want to fuck me?" he shouted. "Maybe you better fuck me." He raped her, as did some of the other guards.

Her sister Rebecca came to the cabin. She was angry. She said that David had been telling the followers that Doreen's behavior was risking everyone's souls. Her sinning was so bad that God could abandon them at any moment. Doreen and Rebecca began to argue and Rebecca reached up and slapped Doreen across the face.

Doreen was in the cabin for four months. One afternoon, September 27, 1991, Doreen took out her passport. She flicked through the pages, wondering how she might escape.

She stared at the American visa taped to one of the pages. The expiration date was September 21. She called to the guard outside her door and said her visa had expired and she needed to go home. David was always concerned that the immigration officials would show up at Mount Carmel, asking about foreigners who'd overstayed their time.

A few hours later, the guard came back and said David was letting her and Rebecca fly back to New Zealand. They bought tickets and boarded the flight home.

Back in New Zealand, Poia received a phone call from a doctor at Mills Peninsula Hospital in San Francisco. Doreen was there, after acting bizarrely during a layover. When Poia went to see Doreen, she was raving about the cruel mistreatment she'd experienced at Mount Carmel. Between the accusations, she would dissolve into fits of laughter and tears. The doctors told Poia that her sister was suffering from an acute psychiatric illness.

Rebecca was there when she arrived. She downplayed Doreen's suffering and said that David and the others had tried to help her.

Later, Doreen came to feel that the atmosphere at Waco had sparked this psychiatric episode. She realized that David had been particularly cruel to her because she had spoken in another voice, a sure sign of prophecy. With Marc already working to bring David down, he wasn't going to tolerate a third prophet.

Neither Poia nor Doreen ever went back to Waco. But Rebecca, the youngest, returned to Mount Carmel to stay.

JERUSALEM LOST

THE DOREEN THREAT had been neutralized and her "episodes" were quickly forgotten at Mount Carmel. But in Australia, Marc continued his campaign. David knew from their years together how tenacious Marc could be; like him, Marc hated to lose an argument.

The problem for David was his method. To work his full power over an audience, he needed to be in front of them. Letters and tapes were a poor substitute for David's in-the-flesh magic. He'd always felt that if he could get in front of someone who was teetering on the fence, he could win that person back. Marc had a lot of gifts, but public speaking wasn't one of them.

In Australia, more followers left the message, and David became increasingly worried about the defections. He decided on a visit in mid-February. He would debate Marc in front of his Aussie followers, to see which of them was preaching truth. It would play to his chief strength: his personal magnetism.

The announcement created a buzz among the Aussies. David was going to go toe-to-toe with Marc. Theologically, it was a heavyweight bout.

Marc was confident of his command of the Scriptures. There was no problem there. But he was at a disadvantage. He had to break David's hold over him, the irrational conviction that he might just be the

messiah, or he would surely lose. It had to be clear both to him and the
followers that Marc wasn't cowed by David's presence.

Be assertive, he told himself. *You have to meet fire with fire.*

David would want to do all the talking, Marc thought. He would try to
take over the meeting, cast his spell. If that happened, the debate would
be over in twenty minutes.

The meeting was to take place at the home of one of the Aussie
followers. Twenty-five Davidians showed up to hear the two men
debate. Marc's wife, Elizabeth, made an arrangement with her brother,
John: If the couple didn't arrive back home by ten p.m., he should no-
tify the cops. David, she thought, was capable of just about anything,
including violence.

David arrived. As soon as he walked into the house, wearing a tank
top and jeans, Marc felt, almost unwillingly, his old fondness for the man.
It was like seeing a girlfriend you'd broken up with but had never stopped
caring for. He was still this man's friend; he still saw qualities there that
were good and admirable.

He saw the same emotion in David's eyes. There was anger there, for
sure—David was pissed that he'd had to fly nine thousand miles to put
down a rebellion—but a kind of regret, too.

David opened the debate. He called Marc the Antichrist. He cited passages in the Bible that prophesied Satan's arrival on earth, particularly
one in Zachariah that predicted the coming of a one-eyed shepherd.
Marc was almost totally blind in one eye, so the description fit.

Marc listened closely, attempting to keep his own anger in check. He
had to be strong without being rude and caustic. The followers still saw
David in a certain way; he couldn't treat him like dirt.

All of a sudden, David dropped to his knees before the circle of followers. "I remember when Judas betrayed me," he said. "I remember how
much it hurt me then. The pain!" He was screeching now, crying out as
if he was in physical agony.

It was an outlandish display. David was trying to pass himself off as
Christ in the flesh. Marc was appalled, but as he looked around, he saw
the men and women in the room were moved.

David turned to Marc. "And now it's happening again. I don't know if

I can take this! Marc, who showed you the Book? Who showed you these things?" David looked toward the ceiling, his palms turned upward, beseeching. "I'm being crucified all over again," he cried. "I'm being crucified all over again!"

Marc found himself strangely unmoved. He was watching a man perform, that was all. But the others were clearly susceptible to the drama in front of them.

At one point, Marc's ears pricked up. In talking about the betrayal, David misquoted a Bible passage. It was Marc's opening and he jumped in. He began to quote the Scriptures, laying out the case that the true Lamb of God was Jesus himself, not David Koresh. The Bible stated it plainly. David was usurping a role that belonged to Christ.

He turned to David. "Sorry, I don't think you're the son of God," he said. "You're just a human being."

David looked shocked. He peered at Marc like he was speaking Japanese. *He's so used to getting his way, to being the man,* Marc thought. *He's having trouble understanding why things are changing. Why did his followers continue to sit there? Why didn't they cast Marc out? Why was the feeling in the room different, and cold?*

They argued passionately back and forth. Marc and Elizabeth became so absorbed in the debate that they forgot all about the arrangement with John, her brother. Soon after ten o'clock, someone began pounding on the front door. It was John. "I called the cops and they're coming," he shouted from the other side of the door.

David heard. He got up and left quickly out the back door, found a bicycle there, and took off. Soon after, he went to the airport and flew back to Texas.

Marc had held his own in the debate. Many of the spectators, in fact, thought he'd won it. They dropped away from the group.

And then a strange thing happened. The followers who abandoned David began to see Marc differently. He'd defeated David, so naturally now he would become their new prophet. He would lead them and their lives as Davidians would continue!

Marc told the Aussies that he wouldn't tell them what to eat and what time to get up. That wasn't what this was about. There wasn't going to be a new sect rising from the ashes of the old one. Eventually, the ex-Davidians accepted it, but if Marc had wanted to become the new David, he realized, it would have been easy as pie.

In the end, of David's twenty-two followers in Australia, only seven remained.

On his return, David announced a major trip to the Holy Land. He and Steve would go to Israel to prepare the ground for the group's move there. It was the next step in the preparations for the End Times.

Perhaps David had been stung by the reception he found in Australia. Perhaps he felt he had to speed up the schedule in order to keep his flock engaged and out of Marc's clutches. Whatever the motive, the trip represented a moment the Davidians had long waited for. For decades, the Davidians had been saying that the final battle before the kingdom's foundation would be fought in the deserts and towns of the Holy Land. Now David was getting ready to relocate the group there.

The two flew to Jerusalem and began talking to realtors, looking at properties and proselytizing when they could. Steve crowed to the others back home that David was blowing the minds of rabbis that he met in Jerusalem. The Jews couldn't refute him! The pair even recruited one follower, Pablo Cohen, who would follow them back to Waco and joined the group.

Marc felt he had to act. He and Elizabeth went to the Israeli consulate in Melbourne, bringing along statements from ex-members and some of the more outrageous Davidian tracts. They warned the Israelis that David was dangerous and was planning to move to Jerusalem.

The consular official told Marc they got fifty to a hundred such cases a year. They had a term for the phenomenon: "Jerusalem syndrome." People went to the Temple Mount or the Wailing Wall and began to believe they were the messiah. "We know how to deal with this," the official told Marc. Authorities visited David and Steve and told them to leave the country immediately. They would not be allowed to return.

David was disturbed. The dream of Jerusalem had animated the Branch for decades. Now the gates were closed to them. The mystique of Israel, a place many of his followers had never seen but had yearned for

Vernon Howell as a young boy, trying
to look angelic for his school picture.
(Courtesy of Hollie Helrigel)

Roy Haldeman, Bonnie, Roger, and Vernon in March 1971 when Vernon was
eleven. *(Courtesy of Hollie Helrigel)*

Young Vernon staring down
the photographer during a Texas
summer. *(Courtesy of Hollie Helrigel)*

A muscled Vernon during
a visit to Sandy's family.
*(Courtesy of photo's
copyright owner)*

GEORGE RODEN
Democrat
for
PRESIDENT '76

A pamphlet for George Roden's 1976 presidential campaign.

Lois Roden in her later years when Vernon discovered the Branch Davidians.

Vernon Howell's mugshot after his 1987 confrontation with George Roden.

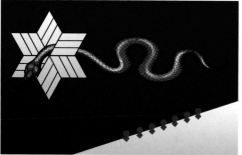

An artist's recreation of the Branch Davidian flag, designed by David Koresh.

A business card for David's band, Messiah. *(Courtesy of David Bunds)*

I AM THE SON OF GOD. YOU DO NOT KNOW ME....

Dear Brethren in the Seventh-day Adventist Church:

I Am the Son of God. You do not know Me nor My name. I have been raised up from the north and My travels are from the rising of the sun.

All the prophets of the Bible speak of Me. I Am The Branch, Isaiah 4:2; The Serpent, Isaiah 5:26; The Immanuel, Isaiah 7:14; The Root, Isaiah 11:10; The Holy One, Isaiah 12:6; The Voice, Isaiah 13:2; The Fiery Flying Serpent, Isaiah 14:29; The Lamb, Isaiah 16:1; The Stammerer, Isaiah 28:11; The King, Isaiah 32:1; The Righteous Man from the East, Isaiah 41:2; The Elect, Isaiah 42:1; The Ravenous Bird, Isaiah 46:11; The Loved One, Isaiah 48:14; The Sharp Sword, Isaiah 49:2; The Learned, Isaiah 50:4; The Arm, Isaiah 51:9; The Servant, Isaiah 52:13; David, Isaiah 55:3, 4.

I have been rejected in the person of My prophets over and over. I have seven eyes and seven horns. My Name is the Word of God and I ride on a white horse (Rev. 19:11). I Am here on earth to give you the Seventh Angel's Message (Rev. 10:7).

I Am the prophets; all of them. I want to invite you to My marriage supper. The invitation is in Psalms 45. Read it and confess that you don't know Me. I Am the Word of God. The key of David is in My hand. I only can open the prophecies of David and Solomon. I have ascended from the east with the seal of the living God. My Name is Cyrus and I Am here to destroy Babylon (Rev. 9:14). I have come in a way that is contrary to your preconceived ideas. I will reprove you for your world loving. I will scold your daughters for their nakedness and pride that they parade in My Father's house and My angels will strip them naked before all eyes because of their foolish pride. Read Isaiah 3:13-26.

The young men will abuse My kindness. They will take My life, but I will arise and take theirs forever more.

You ministers will lament your foolishness. Your lost flock will tear you to pieces.

I Am the Word and you do not know Me. I ride on a white horse and My Name is secret. Psalm 45 is My invitation to you for extended mercy. I will visit you at your unholy feast. Isaiah 3:13; 12:6; Daniel 2:44; Hosea 2:21; 2:5; 4:6; Joel 3:16, 17; Amos 1:2; 8:2; Obadiah 1:21; Habakkuk 3:13; Zephaniah 3:5; Zechariah 2:13; Malachi 1:11; 4:4; Testimonies, vol. 2, p. 190, 191.

PREPARE TO MEET THY GOD.

V. W. H. Jezreel

P.O. Box 1846
Palestine, Tex. 75802

One of the flyers sent to Branch Davidians during David's rise. *(Courtesy of Texas State University)*

Steve Schneider, Marc Breault, Elizabeth Baranyai, and Judy
Schneider at Marc and Elizabeth's wedding.
(Courtesy of Elizabeth Baranyai/Getty Images)

The Branch Davidian compound before the ATF raid. The construction
materials in the yard show that the Davidians were still working on and
reinforcing the large building and its grounds. *(FBI photo)*

The four ATF agents killed during the raid on the Branch Davidian compound: Conway LeBleu, Todd McKeehan, Robert Williams, and Steven Willis. *(ATF photo)*

The FBI negotiator Byron Sage.
(Courtesy of Byron Sage)

The lead FBI negotiator, Gary Noesner
(Courtesy of Gary Noesner)

One of the banners hung out by the Branch Davidians during the fifty-one-day siege. Two years following the Rodney King incident, many of the followers saw themselves as victims of a similarly unjustified assault by law enforcement. *(Courtesy of Texas State University)*

The compound from the viewpoint of an FBI sharpshooter.
(Courtesy of Texas State University)

Timothy McVeigh selling bumper stickers and protesting the government's actions during his visit to Waco. *(Courtesy of Oklahoma City National Memorial Museum)*

The *Waco Tribune-Herald* was nominated for a Pulitzer for its coverage of Koresh's misdeeds, but it was also subject to the misinformation that sometimes emerged from the compound, as shown with this story. *(Courtesy of the* Waco Tribune-Herald*)*

The fire at the Branch Davidian compound, fanned by high winds, moments after it started. *(FBI photo)*

as long as they could remember, formed part of his power over the group. A deeply troubled David left Israel with Steve and flew back to Texas.

If David and his flock couldn't go to Mount Zion and walk through Jerusalem as the End Times neared, his teachings, his prophecy, in fact, the entire mission of the group going back to Victor Houteff, was gibberish. David had taken and taken from his followers—their spouses, their homes, their money, their jobs—and promised one thing: The apocalypse in Israel. Now that was gone.

When he got back to Mount Carmel, David presented the change as he did every new turn he made: It was new light. God had told him that Israel was no longer needed for the fulfillment of the Book; the Davidians had advanced beyond that. Since he was the messiah, Israel wasn't a physical place any longer. It was wherever David was. This meant the apocalypse could begin anywhere, so long as David was present. Since he was living in Waco, that is where the End Time prophecies would now occur.

Still, many Davidians were shocked by the news. After a time, most of them swallowed their disappointment and soldiered on, but dark thoughts had to be growing like black mold in the back of their minds. One believer, Dana Okimato, who had become David's sixth wife and mother to two of his sons, eventually left the group, partly over the Israel issue.

David had been weakened, but that brought its own dangers. "The countdown to Armageddon in Waco, Texas, begins now," Marc told his band of defectors. "We have to alert the American authorities now to avoid a bloodbath."

After he returned from Israel, David became concerned that Marc might go to the authorities or the press and accuse him of various crimes. He heard that Marc was writing to the media and law enforcement in the US, telling them there was another Jonestown—a mass suicide like the one Jim Jones had triggered among his followers in Guyana—brewing in Texas. Marc, he learned, was collecting affidavits from the Australians, detailing the abuse and violence they'd seen inside Mount Carmel. He and Elizabeth wrote their own. They had the affidavits notarized by the American consulate in Melbourne.

The documents focused on David's law-breaking: the rape of underage girls, the beating of children, the flagrant immigration violations. Marc spoke of the guns he saw at Mount Carmel, the use of food and violence as disciplinary tools. And he assembled copies of David's more incendiary lectures.

The Aussie breakaways even hired a private detective to look into David's crimes. The detective flew to Texas to present the evidence to authorities, while Marc wrote some agencies himself. Together, they approached the McLennan County Sheriff's Department, the IRS, the Department of Immigration and Naturalization, and the Texas Department of Public Safety.

In response, David drew up a hit list. He spoke about it in Bible studies and with his followers. The bulk of the list was made up of his ex-followers, the ones he believed were working against him: Marc, Elizabeth, the Gents, etc. Madonna was on there, too. David's attraction to the star had curdled into hatred. Her manager hadn't responded to Steve's letters and phone calls. She'd rejected him and so now he thought she should die.

He also wanted to eliminate a prominent politician, although the list didn't specify anyone in particular. But he told the group that if law enforcement started investigating him, he could divert their attention by killing the president.

In reality there was little threat to George H. W. Bush, who was president at the time. David had never demonstrated the ability to organize something as complex as a presidential assassination. Most likely, he was trying to impress his followers by creating an enemy big enough for a messiah. The local sheriffs and cops would no longer do.

But it did signal a ratcheting up in his rhetoric. Babylon was not a faceless, Zog-like entity now. It was represented by living, breathing men and women. David intensified his threats against Marc and the other defectors, too. He had a certain way of menacing people.

Despite their feud, the two still spoke. David had an inexhaustible confidence in his own ability to persuade, and he sometimes tried to win Marc back. But he also threatened him.

In their conversations, David never said, "I'm going to kill you." He conveyed his message biblically. He'd say, "Marc, remember the prophecies. Remember what happened to this false prophet? Remember Psalm 149:6–7?"

Marc knew it well:

May the praise of God be in their mouths
and a double-edged sword in their hands,
to inflict vengeance on the nations
and punishment on the peoples . . .

Marc thought, is he talking about the Second Coming or is he talking about right now? After David repeated the threats several times, Marc became convinced he was talking about right now.

WACO

EVEN WITH MARC working to bring him down, David continued to make plans for the future. He'd gathered his flock at Mount
Carmel. Now he wanted to bring them all together.

Mount Carmel consisted of a collection of houses and other structures scattered over the compound's seventy-seven acres. David pictured a single large building where everyone would live, eat, and
worship. He wanted his followers all together, segregated by sex, with
the women sleeping in one part of the building with their children,
while the men slept in another. Their home, too, should be defensible
to attack.

David had enough cash on hand to build what he wanted. Construction began in September 1990. He oversaw the project himself, laying out
the floor plans and supervising the workers. The Davidians did over 90
percent of the work, pouring foundations, framing the building, driving
nails into two by fours.

David also ordered the freestanding church near the front of the
property torn down, along with some other buildings and homes. When
asked why, he said it was because he didn't want to have places for people
to go and have sex. Only he was allowed to do that.

The followers pounded the last nail and moved in. Mount Carmel had
gone from being a ragtag group of buildings on the Texas plains to a
place that rose up and cut through the horizon. Neighboring homes were

mostly low-slung affairs set back from the road, barely visible behind long driveways. The Davidians' new home was a statement.

As a piece of architecture, it was defiant and deliberately self-contained. Years before, David had collected his flock and herded them into the compound. Now he was concentrating them even further, on a corner of the property where they would be within calling distance of each other. The building looked like a fort, and it spoke to David's belief that he was the lord and master of a robust little principality.

He ran his own handmade flag up the pole in the front yard. It featured a six-winged snake, its mouth open, over a field of blue. The wings were arranged into a geometrical shape that resembled the Star of David. On the lower right, the blue gave over to white, the border between the two marked by seven small shapes in a dark red color.

The banner summed up David's career. The snake was clearly a reference to "The Serpent's Root," the message he taught in his first lectures at Mount Carmel, where he'd established himself as a preacher. The Star of David referred to Israel. And the seven dark shapes in the lower right represented the Seven Seals.

David had been rootless for most of his life, living with unfriendly relatives or in his own car or inside the rickety shack in Palestine. He'd often felt like a stranger in his own house, a man with no inheritance to speak of, not even a family history. Now he had a place that was big and tall and strong, and a banner to fly over it. Like the Texans before him, he'd staked his claim. The snake's stance—open-mouthed and ready to strike—indicated David was prepared to protect the compound.

The banner used the same colors as the state flag: a dominant blue and white, as well as a fleck of red. Over the past few years, David had finally embraced his Texas roots—the pride verging on arrogance, the guns, the self-reliance, the crusty refusal to genuflect toward Washington.

The compound brought to mind another fort: the Alamo. The Texas of the Alamo myth was a place where a man with a gun and the courage to use it could cut out the pattern of his own life, and that's just what David was doing. "When [William] Travis wrote 'Victory or Death' from behind the barricades of the Alamo mission," wrote the Beaumont-born journalist Jan Jarboe Russell, "he forced a vision of Texas on Santa Anna's army and the world at large." Like Travis, David wouldn't be held back by old laws or ruled by men he despised. On this "stage of his own creation," he waited for the enemy that would set his battle in motion.

The Davidians fixed up a large screen in the new chapel. There they watched the same movies over and over again: *Hamburger Hill*, *Platoon*, *Full Metal Jacket*. War films were David's favorites; he called them "training movies." "This is what it's going to be like," he said during the battle scenes. "You've gotta be tough. You've gotta have balls. You've gotta be ready for war! You've gotta be prepared to defend King Solomon's bed." Their attackers could be anyone who came to shut David down: Elijah Dickerson, the ATF, the DEA.

Guns flowed into the compound and training on them became mandatory. The followers learned how to strip down an AK-47, then reassemble it. Children practiced loading magazines into rifles. The Davidians acquired a .50 caliber antitank rifle that could hit a target at two thousand yards and whose bullets could pierce steel armor. David called it "the bear."

Group members converted rifles from semiautomatic to automatic by cutting out the safe switch and other modifications. They installed "hellfire switches" on the AKs, devices that increased the gun's rate of fire. Automatic weapons, along with the .50 caliber rifle, were illegal under federal gun laws.

The Davidians began selling guns to outsiders. Members went to trade shows, where they rented booths and sold gas masks, military MREs ("meals ready to eat"), and ammo mags. They even started a line of clothing, "David Koresh Survival Wear," that featured hunting vests sewn by the women at Mount Carmel. Some had dummy grenades braided into the cloth. They sold these at the Mag Bag and at gun shows.

In his Bible studies, David taught that Jesus told his disciples to arm themselves.

> *Then said he unto them, But now, he that hath a purse, let him take it, and likewise his scrip: and he that hath no sword, let him sell his garment, and buy one.*

It was Luke 22:36. The turn-the-cheek stuff that everyone talked about? That was a lie.

When the Romans tried to arrest Jesus, Peter swung his sword. That was the way to do it. "Peter jumped the gun and chopped off the centurion's ear . . . ," David told the group. "He was a bad shot, wasn't he? He was going for the guy's head."

The new tone seeped into his recruiting. Around this time, David was introduced to a potential convert. "Would you die for Christ?" David asked.

"I guess so."

"Would you kill for Him?"

"No."

David turned to one of his followers, remarking, "You just brought me another weak Christian." He said it with disgust.

THE TRIAL

O N OCTOBER 31, 1991, Marc made a call to David Jewell, the father of Kiri Jewell, whom David Koresh had raped in a hotel room when she was thirteen. She was now one of Koresh's wives. Jewell, a disc jockey, had divorced his wife Sherri, who was one of the true believers at Mount Carmel. When Marc told him about the sexual abuse going on at the compound, David Jewell agreed to work with Marc to get Kiri away from the Davidians.

David sued for full custody of his daughter. The hearing would take place in a Michigan court. For the first time, outsiders were taking legal action to stop David.

Both Marc and Steve flew to Michigan for the trial, and at the courthouse they met for the first time in many months. Every day they saw each other and every day they went at it. Even so, Marc couldn't hide his affection for his old friend.

"You know, I still love you," Marc said. "You're still my brother."

Steve nodded. He said he recognized that.

But Steve was still fully in the message. Marc probed and beseeched, but he couldn't reach him, not really. In the evening, after a long day of biblical debate, Marc would go back to his motel room and cry in Elizabeth's arms. Steve was lost. He was going to die. And he knew that Steve, in turn, was convinced that Marc was lost and he was going to die and be damned eternally, and that it pained his heart a great deal.

Marc's efforts failed, but by the end of the trial, the judge awarded full custody of Kiri to her father. Sherri was granted visitation rights, but the visits would be in the home of her grandmother. No cult member would be allowed any contact with the girl.

It was a defeat for David. The secrets of Mount Carmel had been aired and a judge had endorsed them. But the case didn't make the national news. The FBI and the McLennan Sheriff's Department took no notice of the proceedings. David had slipped past another snare.

Back home, Marc continued his media campaign, trying to get reporters interested in what was happening at Mount Carmel. One of the people he contacted was Martin King, an Australian journalist for the news show *A Current Affair.*

King called him back. Cults drew a lot of viewers. Plus, there was still at least one Australian at Mount Carmel.

Marc sent affidavits from the Gents and the Toms. There were some audiotapes that Marc had secretly recorded or gotten hold of, including some of David Koresh's Bible studies. It was eye-popping stuff. Martin decided to travel to Waco and confront David.

In January 1992, Martin flew to Texas with a three-man crew. The Australians arrived in Dallas and drove down to Waco. The morning that they were scheduled to go to Mount Carmel, they had breakfast at the hotel. They made some jokes about Jonestown, the camp in Guyana where the cult leader Jim Jones led his followers in a mass suicide in 1978. The tragedy was still fresh in their minds. There were clear similarities between the two groups: the compounds in remote places, the apocalyptic preaching, the cult of personality. The Jonestown tragedy had been triggered by the visit of an American congressman and a TV crew to the compound in Guyana. The team wondered if they were going to set off Jonestown 2.

After breakfast, they went to meet the news director at the local ABC affiliate. Martin wanted to get a feeling for what he might expect, and if he needed to worry about safety.

"They're dangerous people and Koresh is unstable," the guy told him. "Anything could happen to you and nobody would know." The news director instructed Martin to call after he got back from Mount Carmel. If the guy didn't hear from Martin by five o'clock, he would contact the police.

"Good luck" were his last words. "You might need it."

Before they could visit the compound, Martin and his crew met David for dinner at the restaurant at the Waco Hilton Hotel. David wanted to vet them before he agreed to an on-camera interview. Once they sat down, David started preaching. His voice rose. "You know how the Bible says, 'I have the keys of hell and death'? You know who that person is that it's talking about, don't you? You know that 'Koresh' means death? He's the rider on the pale horse."

David paused for breath and turned to Martin to gauge the effect of his words. Their waiter had been listening, hovering a few feet away. Now he stepped toward the table. "Sir, I have seen the light! Every morning I get up and I go outside and I look to the East and I pray for the Coming of the Lord."

Koresh smiled. He started quoting Scripture. The waiter listened intently. He burst into tears. "Sir, I am so thankful. I have seen the light." The dining room was quiet, but Martin could hear the other waiters snickering from the kitchen door.

David agreed to the interview the next day.

The crew drove out to Mount Carmel past sere fields and small hillocks. There wasn't a lot out here, miles from mostly anything. You'd spot horses and some cattle as you passed by the big farms. They headed down Double EE Ranch Road and turned in the driveway to the compound.

David came out of the big central building. He yawned. Slight frame, brown eyes, blinking a little awkwardly against the Texas sun. Steel aviator glasses. Scruffy three-day shadow. Olive green shirt, black jeans.

He was charming and talkative. He presented each of the four guys with a case of Foster's Lager, which was practically the Aussie national beer. It was thoughtful, a good sign.

They chatted for a while and David was personable. But as soon as Martin started asking the tougher questions—about child wives and polygamy and the rest of it—he bristled. At one point, David broke off the interview to take care of some business inside the compound, then re-emerged.

"You guys still with us, huh?" he said. "Haven't been shot by one of my guards yet?"

"Not yet," Martin said.

As for the other Davidians, Martin got a weird vibe, mostly from the guys. They looked at Martin and the other three guys with hatred in their eyes. Martin thought, "They wouldn't mind killing me."

"Are we safe here?" Martin asked David at one point. He wanted David to guarantee the Aussies his protection, out loud, so the others could hear it.

"It's not me you should be worried about," David said. He gestured at the Mighty Men. "It's them. These guys would die for me. Or kill for me, if necessary." He said it lightly, like it had just occurred to him.

They began walking around the compound. "We don't want you here, you son of a bitch," a tall, blond man with piercing blue eyes said to Martin. "We know why you're here. You're gonna tell the world we're just a bunch of crazies." It was Perry Jones's son, David, a mail carrier and Air Force veteran.

Can you tell the Mighty Men to drop back, Martin asked.

"*NO*," David said loudly.

Martin's cameraman was behind them, filming. They stopped near a waist-high shrub, its branches dry, bone-like.

"What about these people here?" Martin said, pointing toward the Mighty Men, who stood off-camera. "What do they think of you?"

"You know what they think of me?" David said. "They think I'm the son of God."

"Do they?"

"Yeah."

"Is that what you think you are?"

"It's not what I think, it's what I am." He began to preach. "This is a sick world out there. You do what you've got to do to make it. if you're a Hindu or Muslim or whatever you are—a pygmy—if what you know is right, you do it . . . I'm on no head game. I'm not the pope. I don't walk around with no robes. I am humanity."

They kept walking. David found a tree and leaned up against it.

"Do you have guns?" Martin said.

"Yeah, we have some."

"Can we see them?"

"Well, I guess if you want." David smirked, brought his hand up, tapped the bridge of his glasses back. "You know."

He looked off into the distance. His smile faded. "No," he said.

The Davidians were still working on the big central building. When the workers saw the visitors, they'd turn their heads, or drop their eyes. The Mighty Men were still trailing behind. "You'll never leave this place alive," one of them said.

Martin did manage to get one laugh out of the Davidians. He asked David in front of his Bible study class if he was sleeping with all the women.

"No," David said. "Only one. And she's tired of it."

Titters from the class, then full-out laughs.

David grinned. "I mean, she's tired of the accusations!"

It was the only glint of charm they saw that day, apart from the gift of the Fosters.

The team left and flew back to Melbourne. The *Current Affair* piece aired on Australia's Channel 9 to a "huge response." Other shows and newspapers picked up the story. It didn't run in America.

But authorities in the US had begun inching closer to action. That February, Joyce Sparks, an employee at Texas Department of Child Protective Services, received reports that minors were being sexually abused at Mount Carmel. The agency opened a case and over the next few months, Sparks visited Mount Carmel multiple times. She interviewed the children, interviews she felt were tightly controlled by David. The children told Sparks that infants were sometimes spanked, and that, if they were bad, sometimes they'd go hungry.

Sparks also talked to David, often for hours. He denied the charges.

She found the Davidian leader to be mercurial. He demanded that Sparks attempt to understand his teachings, ordering her to study the Bible, even though she attempted to steer clear of religion. At times, he could be as likeable as a down-home country pastor. At other times, he was frankly terrifying. He would talk about the arsenal he kept at Mount Carmel and training his followers in paramilitary tactics. His voice would grow belligerent. "There will be blood and fire and an explosion at the end," he told her.

The investigation continued into the summer, but it was dropped when no evidence of abuse—bruises, welts—was found on the children and when none of the Davidians agreed to testify against David. In the wake of the probe, followers installed about a dozen surveillance cameras around the perimeter at Mount Carmel and at least two inside it. David also ordered members from around the world to come back to Mount Carmel.

Graeme Craddock, the single guy who'd grown up lonely and overweight before joining the Davidians, had been staying in Australia. Steve Schneider called him long distance. He told him that David's prophecies about the Seven Seals and the Apocalypse were going to be proven true, and soon. David wanted him back at Mount Carmel. Graeme booked his flight.

After he arrived back in Waco, Graeme Craddock wrote to his family. "I don't know when I'll be coming back home again, but as yet I have no plans. I believe we are living in the last days, and we don't have too much time left before things start happening. We're expecting some big trouble . . .

"Don't think that I don't love you, I want you to be saved, but I have to seek God with all my strength first."

Other members of the group called and wrote their families, including David, who phoned his paternal grandmother, Jean Holub. "Grandma, it's coming a time," he said, "I'm going to bring you a little gun . . . They'll be breaking in on us and we've got to protect our families."

For months, Judy Schneider-Koresh had been talking to her brother in Wisconsin: "You need to get down here," she would say. "Bring your family. We're learning new truths every day. The end is coming soon." He stayed put, but it didn't stop Judy from trying.

Now Judy called her brother again. This time she didn't tell him to come. "It's too late for you," she said.

In England, the brother-in-law of Winston Blake, who'd joined the group after Steve's recruiting visit, received a call. Winston said he was thinking of coming home for a friend's funeral. After the funeral, he might stay in the UK, perhaps look for a job. In another call, Winston sounded down. "The door of the ark is closed," he said. He didn't return for the funeral.

Other Brits got in touch, too. Cliff Sellers, who'd come at the same time as Winston, wrote a friend. "Just book me a ticket," it said. "I need to come back to Britain."

Sellers repeatedly begged his friend to get him out of Texas. During one call, a man took the phone from Sellers. "You are not going anywhere," a voice said.

The friend thought it was David Koresh. The call ended and no more followed.

Gail Monbelly heard from her sister Bernadette, who'd joined the group after a period of illness. Bernadette seemed constrained, as if she couldn't speak her mind. She was bright and cheerful on the phone, but Gail sensed it was a ruse, to avoid attention from the others.

On one call, Gail tried speaking Creole to Bernadette; they were both fluent in the language. But Bernadette quickly switched back to English. Maybe speaking in Creole made the Davidians suspicious, her sister thought.

So Gail said, "Okay, Bernadette, when you mean yes, say no, and when you mean no, say yes."

Bernadette agreed and Gail went on.

"Bernadette, have you got your passport?"

"Yes." Meaning no.

"If you want to leave the compound, can you leave with your passport?"

"Yes." Gail felt chilled.

She told Bernadette: Get away from Mount Carmel. Any way you can.

"No," Bernadette said.

Bernadette spoke up. "Do you remember that Bible study where you disrupted it, because you were asking so many questions?"

Gail said yes, she remembered.

"You were right." Then Bernadette said, "I have to go now."

Sam Henry, the handyman from Old Trafford, England, flew to Waco, hoping to persuade his wife and children to return home. David invited him into the building and they sat down to talk. Sam's daughter Diana and the rest of his family watched.

David told Sam to stay, see how they lived. What a blessing it would be to have the whole Henry clan together under one roof! "Come to Waco and lose yourself," he said.

Sam was unconvinced. Now that David was right in front of him, he felt that he was a fanatic, an infidel. "We must leave!" he cried to Diana and the others.

"Watch what you say!" Diana called back. "Watch what you say!" David told him again to stay and learn.

"It was God who led me to the Adventist church and I'm going to die in that church," Sam replied.

David erupted. "You're a hypocrite!" he shouted. He threatened to take Sam and whip him for his irreverence. It was as if the devil had been hiding in his throat, Sam thought, and now it had jumped out.

Sam stood up and chased his children up to the second floor. "Let's leave this place!" he called. But they ignored him. Eventually, he left, alone.

One British woman decided to escape. Her children were being beaten by David Koresh and others, and she was on a near-starvation diet. Her weight had dropped from 225 pounds to 125.

There were armed guards at the gate and inside it, snitches as well. Snakes and bugs and water moccasins populated the outside grounds. Still, the woman made the decision to go.

She gathered some black clothes and scouted out the land surrounding the big building. One night, after everyone had gone to sleep, she dressed her children and herself in the clothes and they stole out of the house. They began crawling on their stomachs across the fields.

They made it to the fence and crawled under. On the road outside, headlights appeared. The woman waved down the pickup truck that was passing. She told the driver what had happened and he put the family in the back and put a tarpaulin over them. He drove them to his house, and in the morning, they called the British embassy.

Sam Henry's wife sent a message out with the woman. "I now understood that things at Mount Carmel are wrong and very dangerous," she said. "But I can't leave without my children."

Not all of those who reached out to their loved ones spoke with gloom in their voices. For some of the followers, David's urgency was the bright thread running through their days. Many of the Davidians couldn't wait for the End Times to begin. The new recruits, especially, had come to Mount Carmel on the promise of the Apocalypse's arrival. They'd prayed and they'd listened to David and now it was coming time.

They would go up to David and say, "When is something going to happen?" They weren't afraid. They looked forward with eagerness.

Part V

THE BUREAU

33

THE INVESTIGATION

LARRY GILBREATH WAS a driver for UPS in Waco. He had an honest face, plain and open, and he got along with most of the people along his route. A typical day meant delivering around a hundred packages and putting a few hundred miles on his truck.

One of his regular stops was Mount Carmel. The stuff they got was mostly medicines or household stuff. David Koresh often came out to sign for his packages himself.

Larry liked him. The guy was friendly. He'd sign for his packages and they'd talk about motorcycles or go-karts.

In 1992, he first noticed something new at Mount Carmel. The people he saw when he drove in were dressed in camo, which was a change. Then David said Larry couldn't come to the big house anymore. He had to stop at the Mag Bag, the little store they operated a few miles from the main compound. Larry would pull in, call on the phone, and David would give him permission to come on out to the compound.

The packages changed, too. Long boxes. Guns, obviously. Many were sent COD, collect on delivery. David would pay him in wads of cash, and Larry then had to carry the money, sometimes thousands of dollars, for the rest of his route.

One day that February, he was moving some packages in his truck when one of them tipped over and broke open. A few objects spilled out—empty casings for hand grenades. Larry told his wife about it and she got concerned. What were the Davidians doing with hand grenades? She called the sheriff's department.

Captain Dan Weyenberg looked into the tip. He wanted to get an idea of what the Davidians were up to, so he flew over the compound in a small airplane and took some photos. When they were developed, Weyenberg saw a buried bus near the main building; clearly, the Davidians were turning it into some kind of bunker. There was a tall observation tower, too, that gave you clear views of the prairie for miles in every direction. There were windows on all sides of the structure. If you wanted to put guns in them, you could see anyone coming and pick them off at your pleasure.

Weyenberg felt the case was too big for the sheriff's department. He called the ATF, the Bureau of Alcohol, Tobacco and Firearms.

Around this time, Marc Breault was writing a Michigan congressman, Fred Upton:

"The situation with respect to this cult is desperate as the cult leader, one Vernon Wayne Howell, is planning a mass suicide somewhere around April 18th of this year. This fact has been confirmed by a number of sources including an ex-member who has just recently (within the last month) fled the group . . .

"Time is running out and I need to talk to the FBI or someone who can do something. If this does not happen, I believe that over 200 persons will be massacred next month. Each day nothing is done, children are being abused, either physically or sexually. Each day brings us closer to another Jonestown."

Upton never replied to the letter.

The ATF was a blue-collar agency, a lot of ex-military guys. They thought of themselves as federal street cops. The FBI, their better-known and more glamorous rival, often put together complex cases over many months. The ATF was different: They were out in the back alleys serving warrants, knocking down doors.

The agency opened a case on the Davidians. Agent Davy Aguilera worked the investigation. He began by looking into what the Davidians were actually buying and found that, between March and the end

of April of 1992, Koresh and his followers purchased nearly sixty assault rifles, hundreds of thirty-round assault-rifle magazines, eleven
handguns, night-vision and ground-sensing equipment, and grenade
shells, along with 120,000 bullets. In total, Koresh had spent about
$40,000 on guns and other armaments that year to date. That included
104 "upper receivers" for AR-15 assault rifles. Also on the list were "M-
16 machine gun CAR kits" and "M-16 machine gun E-2 kits," popu-
larly known as "conversion kits." If you paired the kits with the AR-15s'
lower receiver, and if you had someone who could use metal milling
machines and lathes, you could make a fully automatic—and illegal—
machine gun.

The agent sent a list of some items David had received at Mount Carmel to an ATF explosives technician: black powder, igniter cord, grenade
shells, various chemicals. The expert confirmed that they could be used
to make live grenades and homemade bombs.

On July 30, 1992, Aguilera headed to Texas to investigate further. He
and another agent went to the home of Henry McMahon, who'd sold
thirty-six guns to a "Vernon Howell" and more to other Davidians. They
found that about sixty-five AR-15 lower receivers that McMahon had recorded as being in stock were not in the house. McMahon told them his
preacher, David Koresh, was keeping them for him. That November, a
deputy sheriff was driving by Mount Carmel when he heard a blast. He
looked over and saw a cloud of gray smoke boiling up from inside the
compound, as if something had just exploded.

That winter, the ATF contacted the assistant US attorney in Waco, a
tall, sonorous lawyer named Bill Johnston. He looked at their evidence
and told them there was probable cause for a federal search warrant on
gun violations.

ATF didn't pursue the warrant then. They wanted more evidence
against Koresh before they moved.

Bill Buford had grown up in Kansas City, a farmer's son, broad-shouldered
and tough.

When the war in Vietnam heated up his freshman year of college, Buford felt he didn't want to miss out. He'd always looked up to his uncles

and his older brother, all of whom had served. He volunteered to join the Green Berets.

When Buford got to Vietnam, it was different from what he'd expected. His first firefight terrified him. He caught dysentery just about the day he got there and had it the whole tour. The enemy was in front of you and then it was behind you and then it was nowhere. He remembered thinking, "John Wayne lied to me."

He was raw. During a firefight one time, an Australian soldier he was close to, Jock Gordon, said, very calmly, "Hey mate?"

"Yeah."

"You hear those buzzing sounds around your head?"

"Yeah."

"Well, those are bloody fucking bullets. Get your ass on the ground."

Most days, he saw at least one soldier killed. Sometimes more.

After his tour, Buford got a job at a building in downtown Lawrence, Kansas. There were a lot of war protests going on at the time. One day, an activist set off a series of bombs in eight buildings, including the one Buford worked in.

He saw some guys working the crime scene. He went over and asked them where they were from.

"We're ATF," one of them said.

"What's ATF?"

"We're whiskey, guns, and explosives."

"Hell, I could do that," Buford thought.

He'd been missing the adrenaline rush he'd felt in Vietnam. He went down and took the ATF test and thirty days later he was an agent.

He worked a lot of undercover. Once he got into a KKK case in southwestern Missouri and introduced himself as a grand kleagle from Kansas. Started buying guns from KKK guys. He played the role all the way. When he got on the stand to testify, he had to tell the jurors, "You're going to hear me use a lot of foul language, some racist language. But that was just the role I was playing." What he took away from undercover: If you know how your target thinks, you have a good idea of what he might do next.

He rose to become one of the commanders of the bureau's New Orleans SRT, or Special Response Team. The SRTs were tactical units that conducted criminal investigations and staged raids on drug and gun criminals.

As Aguilera continued his investigation, Buford was named the principal tactical contributor on the Waco case. He and the other SRT commanders were tasked with coming up with a plan to arrest Koresh. Another agent, Chuck Sarabyn, was put in charge of the total operation. Sarabyn was chosen for administrative reasons, not for any tactical experience he possessed. In fact, Sarabyn didn't have extensive experience with special operations.

Buford and the other planners came up with three options: an outside arrest, a siege of Mount Carmel, or a dynamic entry.

The first would mean snatching Koresh when he was away from the compound. The second involved putting up a perimeter around the compound and waiting the Davidians out. The third, dynamic entry, meant staging an armed raid that would breach the defenses of the compound and get ATF agents inside the building, where they could secure Koresh and any relevant evidence.

There was a lot to be said for a dynamic entry and against the siege. The Davidians had huge piles of MREs and other food stocks. A siege would give the group many weeks to destroy or alter evidence. The optics would be bad: The ATF would be spending money, doing nothing but watching the compound. Popular and political pressure to end the siege would likely build. Koresh could use the time to fortify the compound even more. And then there was the specter of mass suicide.

On December 4, 1992, the planners met with Agent Aguilera. They wanted to know if there was any way to get Koresh off the compound and arrest him there. They decided that a surveillance team should be installed near the compound to monitor the movements of Koresh and the Davidians.

On December 15, the phone in Marc Breault's apartment rang in the middle of the night. It was Aguilera. Elizabeth answered.

Aguilera introduced himself as an agent of the ATF. Elizabeth didn't know what that was. Marc explained, then picked up the phone. Aguilera told Marc he'd been working the Koresh case for months and had gone through everything Marc had written. He then read Marc the list of weapons David had assembled.

Marc hadn't known how big the arsenal was. "Armageddon is just around the corner," he thought to himself. He began talking nearly every day to the ATF. Marc was thrilled that American law enforcement was finally taking up the case. But he was also afraid. He thought David might learn about his role in the investigation and track down his mother and father and kill them. The Davidians had his parents' address.

The ATF asked Marc to come to California for further interviews. Elizabeth wanted to fly there with him, but the bureau only requested Marc. She hit the roof. "How do I know it's not a trap from David?" she asked him. "How do I know these are real federal agents? How do I know that David isn't trying to lure you to America to kill you like he's done before? You'll be there all alone and I'll be here in Australia not knowing what will happen to you."

Their arguments grew rancorous. Elizabeth was furious that Marc would consider going without her. Divorce was mentioned. When the time came for Marc to leave for the airport, Elizabeth refused to drive him.

Marc flew to California and Aguilera and another agent picked him up at the airport. They brought him to a motel and the interviews began. Their first questions were about the arsenal: What was David planning to do with it? Marc told them he didn't know, but that he expected they were to resist any attempt by the government to come on the compound and arrest him.

Marc emphasized that David was in a tough spot. He'd taught the Davidians that the End Times were coming soon. The longer it was delayed, the more his power over the Davidians would diminish. Marc mentioned one thing that David was trying to acquire right around the time Marc left the group. It was a copy of the *Anarchist Cookbook*, a book that told you how to make homemade explosives, among other things. "My God," one of the agents said.

What about serving the search warrant? How should they execute it?

Marc said flatly they shouldn't raid the compound. Instead, they should try and arrest David outside. He went to restaurants, music clubs, and guitar stores in Waco. They should grab him at one of those spots.

The agents agreed. But what would the Davidians do in such a scenario? Deprived of their leader, would they commit mass suicide?

Marc didn't think so. There was a precedent, after all: the 1988 trial of Koresh and the others for the attack on George Roden. David had been arrested and his followers hadn't offed themselves. The Davidians would do the same thing this time, he believed. Hire lawyers. Collect money for bail. Try to get David off.

Marc had a copy of a taped lecture David gave after Marc left. David was sending it out to the people who'd turned against him, Marc believed, in order to scare them into coming back. He played it for the ATF agents.

DAVID: There are those who say I'm out trying to get other men's wives. Huh! What confusion! I never taught that. But seeing they're in confusion, that means they're what?

FOLLOWERS: Babylonians.

DAVID: And if they're Babylonians that means they must want me to fulfill Isaiah 13! Man! How cruel can they be? They know what Isaiah 13 teaches, don't they? So if they think I'm going to do something that I'm not going to do, and I tell them that they're a liar, and show them in God's word that they're a liar, and they still follow their lie, that means they're Babylonians, and what happens to the Babylonian women, men?

DAVIDIAN MEN: They get raped.

DAVID: Ravished, Isaiah 13 says. Boy, they're just begging you guys to have their wives, aren't they? Aren't they? They're just begging for the sons of light to slay them and humble their Babylonian women.

When the men said "They get raped," they sounded zombie-like. No emotion. Marc found it frightening.

The planners interviewed Joyce Sparks, the Child Protective Services agent who'd investigated child abuse claims against David. She told them that any raid against Mount Carmel would turn violent. "They will get their guns and kill you," she said. Sparks came away from the interview feeling that the ATF hadn't taken her seriously. As if they were above listening to a social worker.

One other thing she told the agents was that David almost never left Mount Carmel. This idea quickly took root with the planners. But if the agents had spoken with Waco residents, they would have heard a different story.

Margaret Jones, a local resident, saw David often. According to Margaret, everybody and their dog spotted David around town, along with a bunch of his followers. He worked on car engines at a shop near Loop 340 and FM 2491, approximately five miles from the compound. He also caught some bands at local spots, sometimes bringing as many as ten people with him. With his silver wire-rimmed glasses, his beaky nose, and shaggy black hair, he was easily recognizable.

David also liked to go to the Chelsea Street Pub, the faux-English restaurant at the local mall. He and some of the Davidians would order bean and cheese nachos and iced teas. The manager said David was a lunch regular there, coming once a week.

But the ATF agents failed to interview any locals about David's movements.

The agents looked at other ways to arrest David. They called Bob Boyd, director of the local Children's Protective Services, and asked if one of his employees could contact the compound and ask David to meet them in town. Tell him they'd had another complaint about child abuse.

Boyd said he had to call the agency's lawyers. When he did, they told him that kind of operation was outside his brief. CPS workers couldn't act as decoys for a law enforcement operation. It was a no.

Boyd called the agent back and told him. "Forget I asked," the agent said.

The ideas got more ambitious. What about sending David a grand jury subpoena in the mail? Could they stage a school bus crash on one of the roads near the compound? Maybe Koresh and the Mighty Men would come running out to help and they could grab them out in the open. Or they could fake a helicopter accident, then rush in when David came over to investigate. The ideas were tossed around and eventually abandoned as impracticable.

In case they decided on a dynamic entry, the ATF requested three helicopters from the Texas National Guard. To get them, they had to show the Koresh investigation had a "drug nexus." In a letter dated December 18, 1992, the ATF made a formal request to the state of Texas, saying Koresh was "suspected of unlawfully being in possession of firearms and possibly narcotics."

The charges were false. There had been rumors of a meth lab when Koresh and the others retook the compound in 1988. And Koresh had asked Jack Harwell, the McClennan County sheriff, to come out to Mount Carmel and handed over what items his followers had found. Some of Koresh's followers had been arrested for drugs in the past, but there was no evidence they were using at Mount Carmel. And for years Koresh had been vocal about his hatred of drugs.

In late December, the planners met in Austin. Aguilera told them about his interviews with Marc and the other ex-Davidians, and they studied new overhead photos of the compound. The National Guard had flown a night surveillance flight over Mount Carmel in an airplane equipped with a thermal imaging system. The system detected "hot spots," heat emitters that could be guards stationed at the compound's gate.

Buford and the others drove out to Waco to take a look. They studied the tower and the terrain around the compound. There was a few bumps and hillocks, but mostly it was flat. When they thought of the weapons the Davidians had—a .50 caliber gun has a range of about two thousand yards, the length of twenty football fields—a siege began to look untenable.

The property was already big, seventy-seven acres. If you wanted your men outside the range of their guns, the perimeter would have to be enormous. The amount of personnel it would take to secure it would be enormous as well.

The men stared at the compound from afar, trying to picture it in their minds.

34

SURVEILLANCE

ATF RENTED A two-bedroom house across from Mount Carmel. On January 11, 1993, a team moved in and began their surveillance. The agents had a radio scanner, night-vision equipment, and cameras to watch the compound. They could see people coming and going from the front part of the house. Team members also photographed people entering and leaving.

It wasn't perfect. There was a road at the back of Mount Carmel, which David or his followers could conceivably use to leave or enter the property without being seen. They also had motorcycles that Davidians could drive across the fields, avoiding detection.

Eight agents were assigned to the task, working on four-hour shifts. They told neighbors they were students at TSTC, short for Texas State Technical College, which had a Waco campus. But the Davidians soon noticed the men made for unusual students: They looked older, they were fit, they drove late-model vehicles, and they came and went from the house carrying briefcases.

David Jones, the son of Perry Jones, was a mailman who lived at the compound. During his forays outside Mount Carmel, he ran into one of the agents. He asked what the guys living in the house did for a living. The guy repeated the standard line: They were students at TSTC.

Jones perked up. He'd gone to TSTC for a while, too. Jones started to pepper the guy with questions about his courses and such. The agent put him off as best he could. Jones also tried to wrangle an invite to the undercover house but got nowhere.

Most college dudes like to party, meet new people. These guys didn't.

The surveillance team maintained a log: arrivals, departures, unusual incidents. One of the things the undercover agents were focused on was "the pit." This was a large underground firing range that the Davidians were building at the southwest corner of the property. The pit was approximately fifteen feet deep, a hundred feet long, and forty-five feet wide. One source, who'd visited the compound in late 1992, had told the investigators that the Davidian men worked at the site every day.

With surveillance in place, the planners developed a tentative dynamic entry plan. While the majority of the men were working in the pit, a large number of ATF agents would surprise the Davidians, quickly enter the compound, secure it, and arrest David Koresh. The raid would be timed for ten a.m.

One of the undercover agents told Buford that the Davidians were in the pit by that time every day. But the surveillance logs contradicted that assertion:

—On January 15, six men were working in the pit just after noon. Fifteen minutes later, two girls came over and joined them. Over an hour later, there were eleven people working in the pit, including two women.
—On January 16, a Saturday, the Davidian's Sabbath, eight to ten men were seen in the pit the entire morning.

The activity tailed off after that.

—On January 17, the log read "minimal work."
—On the January 18, the agents didn't see any actual work being done, though three men were seen walking from the site.
—On January 19, there were no men at the pit.

After that, almost a week passed with no workers at the site.

—On January 25, a truck pulled into the compound with building supplies loaded on back.

—On January 26, no work.

—On January 27, the agents stopped keeping the log.

A crucial miscommunication had developed between the surveillance team and the planners. After the raid, Buford talked with some of the surveillance agents about the pit. "We never said they were out there every day," they said.

Another oversight: Buford was never sent the surveillance logs, which clearly showed the small number of workers involved in the work on the pit. Buford requested them several times from Chuck Sarabyn, but Sarabyn never sent them. At one point, Buford called the division office to inquire about the logs. He talked with several administrators there. He'd say, "Look, I need those surveillance logs."

"Not a problem" is what he was told. But still the logs never arrived. It was unusual. Over the course of Buford's career, he'd never made a request for material like that and not received it. A couple of times Chuck Sarabyn spoke to Buford, giving him an overview of what the surveillance team was seeing and hearing. But Buford never got any paper on it. The same was true of the photos the surveillance team took. Buford asked to see them, but he never received so much as a single picture.

There was another, almost inexplicable, miscalculation. The largest gathering of men inside the pit the surveillance team ever recorded was thirteen. There were many more than thirteen able-bodied males at Mount Carmel, dozens more. Even if there was twice that number of workers in the pit when the raid launched, it would still have left numerous Davidian men able to grab their guns and resist. But those numbers were never communicated to the planners.

As time went on, the pit issue grew even murkier. At one point in February, the Davidians hung a plastic tarp over the work area. It was probably there to protect the men from the sun, but the result was that the surveillance team could no longer see who was in the pit at any given time. The agency was now effectively blind to a key element of the plan.

The mistakes went both ways. As the plan came into focus in early February, the planners failed to inform the surveillance team that the pit was becoming a crucial element, if not the crucial element, in their strategy. The surveillance agents had no idea that the planners were counting on the men being at the site on the day of the raid. In fact, surveillance on the pit was even less rigorous in the middle part of February than it had been in January.

Another point of interest for the surveillance team was David's coming and going from the compound. But the logs cite neither. The surveillance agents either never spotted his departures or arrivals, or never recorded it. After the raid, the ATF asserted that David hadn't left the compound for months. This was untrue.

According to Waco locals, David visited the town during January and February: at the Chelsea Street Pub, an auto repair shop, and a music store. And, according to Paul Fatta, David often went jogging along Double EE Ranch Road, which led to the compound. In the log, the undercover agents cited two instances of a white male jogging on the Double EE Ranch Road, once on January 13 and once on January 16, when it was noted that the jogger was wearing camouflage clothes. But neither time was the person identified as David Koresh. In fact, there didn't seem to be a regular process of identifying who the men and women observed by the surveillance team were. The only person in the log identified by name was the mailman, David Jones.

The planners met again in late January. Buford had shifted his thinking decisively away from a siege. Ex-followers had told him that David had MREs stacked and ready, meaning they could hold out for months. And many of the ex-members stated that David taught his followers that they had to die to fulfill his prophecies. "They'll hold out as long as they can, and then they'll kill themselves" was a common refrain.

The worst option would be for the ATF to mount a long and expensive siege and then have to go and raid the place anyway. The media would be merciless. David could also use the potential months of a standoff to destroy evidence, including the illegal weapons. The ATF would be screwed. The planners eventually abandoned the siege idea.

A dynamic entry was now the leading option. On February 17, the ATF team ended their surveillance.

· · ·

An undercover ATF agent named Robert Rodriguez, using the name "Robert Gonzalez," had been assigned to go undercover inside the compound. He'd attended some Bible studies and chatted up David and the other believers. On February 17, he was invited inside the compound to attend another Bible session.

Rodriguez found David to be super friendly. The devil could walk up to his front door and David would welcome him, try to get him in the message. For his part, Steve Schneider assumed Rodriguez and his buddies across the road were ATF or FBI. He felt like saying, "Come on, Robert, we know you're an agent. You can't believe we're that stupid."

After his visit, Robert started taking target practice in the yard of the surveillance house, hoping that David would see him and invite him over to shoot. On February 19, David did just that. Robert brought along another agent. When David greeted the pair, both of whom had brought along their AR-15s, he told Robert he'd seen him through his binoculars, firing his rifle.

The men walked to the shooting range. David had two Sig Sauer handguns and a Ruger 10/22 rifle. Rodriguez had brought his .38 with him as well, and David gave it a close look. David was intrigued by the gun. Robert claimed not to know that much about firearms, said he'd just bought the AR. But his .38 wasn't a novice's weapon. It had a compensator, a device that keeps the muzzle down after firing and decreases the recoil, allowing for faster shooting.

The AR was cherry, too. It had a real nice scope on it, and a one and seven twist to the barrel, which is a military spec. That twist helped the gun stabilize for tracers and heavier bullets. The thing was set up nice. Maxed out.

David tested the trigger pull. A normal pull on an AR was maybe four pounds. This thing was a pound and a half, maybe two. Delicate.

"This is a sniper rifle," he said to Robert.

David walked off fifteen yards and set up some cans, stepped back and told Robert to hit them. Robert could feel David's eyes on him, sizing up his stance. Robert shot and hit most of his targets.

It was a nice result. Watching David, Robert saw that he was peeved. Clearly, he didn't like to be outshone in front of his people. "Next time I better miss," Robert thought.

Robert went back a few more times in the next week and a half. David was open about his guns. He even talked about hellfire triggers and drop-in sears, a part that converts semiautomatic guns to full auto.

One of David's rocker buddies came to check out the compound while Robert was there. The rocker asked one of the Davidians, "Who's that?" The Davidian said it was a guy who was coming to Mount Carmel for the Bible studies. David overheard this. "Yeah, right," he said. The rocker took that to mean that David knew Robert wasn't a Bible student at all, that he had another motive for being there. The Davidians realized they were being surveilled. They just didn't know by whom.

The other elements of the ATF plan fell into place. One agent, Dale Littleton, had used cattle trailers in an October 1992 operation where the ATF raided a band of heroin dealers on a 107-acre ranch in rural Texas. The trailers hid the agents until the last moment, allowing them to gain the element of surprise. The bad guys had been arrested with no injuries or deaths. Buford and the others added that feature to the plan.

But there were curious lapses, in addition to the ones with the surveillance team. The planners made no contingencies for extracting the wounded under fire. They didn't lay the groundwork for communicating with those inside the compound, in case there was some kind of a hitch in the plan or, in the worst case, an armed standoff. Though the surveillance team had the number for the phone at Mount Carmel, the tactical teams didn't.

A larger problem was the warrants. Back on February 10, the ATF still didn't have a search warrant for Mount Carmel or an arrest warrant for David. Even if the surveillance team had spotted Koresh outside the compound or walking around town, they wouldn't have been able to arrest him. He could have strolled up to an ATF agent and held his hands out for the cuffs, but they would have had no legal way to detain him. It had been three months since the bureau had brought their initial findings to Assistant US Attorney Bill Johnston, who had confirmed there was enough evidence for a warrant.

On February 11 and 12, Davy Aguilera and Phil Chojnacki met with ATF director Stephen Higgins and ATF associate director Daniel Hartnett. Afterward, the bureau gave the green light for Aguilera to brief Johnston and request the warrants.

Around February 20th, the ATF attempted to get a state warrant for Koresh on a charge of sexual relations with a minor, an underaged girl. Agents called Beth Toben, an assistant prosecutor for McLennan County, and asked her to meet with the unnamed girl, who had once stayed at the compound. On February 22, Toben spoke to the victim.

If the agency got the warrant, the Texas Department of Protective and Regulatory Services or the District Attorney's Office would then schedule a meeting with David outside the compound. David had met with investigators on similar charges before. It was thought this would be a fairly easy way to get him out of Mount Carmel and arrest him.

The girl, however, didn't want to testify against David. The idea was abandoned. The dynamic entry plan, focused on the men in the pit, was now the only approach under consideration.

On Friday, February 26, just days before the planned operation, the bureau sent a one-page memo to the Treasury Department's Office of Enforcement, informing it of the upcoming raid. The Office of Enforcement oversaw the ATF and had final veto power over any operation in Waco.

The memo arrived on the desk of Michael D. Langan, the acting deputy assistant secretary for law enforcement. It was also shared with other top officials, including John P. Simpson, who was acting as assistant secretary of the treasury. Simpson had final approval on the operation on the Treasury side.

Langan had his doubts. He thought that serving a warrant at Mount Carmel would be a mistake. The Davidians were heavily armed. It was gambling a dime to win a penny. Instead, he wanted the ATF to mount an intense surveillance operation on Koresh, wait for him to go for a run, then pounce.

Simpson called a meeting. "Why not just wait them out," Langan asked, "rather than try an entry that could be met with major force?" Others around the table nodded along. The Treasury officials were especially worried about the Davidians' children and the amount of firepower the group possessed.

Simpson called Ron Noble, who was his incoming boss at Treasury. Noble said there were too many things that could go wrong. We need to know more about the plan. Simpson sent a message to the ATF chief Stephen Higgins, and they all jumped on the phone. "There's no support for it here," Simpson said. "You need to call it off." It was around 4:30 p.m. on Friday, February 26. The raid was currently planned for March 2, four days away.

Higgins scrambled. He called Houston FBI agent Phil Chojnacki, who was one of the commanders of the planned raid, and asked him to address the concerns raised by Treasury. About three hours after Simpson had vetoed the raid, Higgins called him back. Ron Noble had just gone out to get something to eat. "I've talked to the people there," Higgins said, meaning the planners of the raid. "They have some additional information you need to know that may change your mind."

Simpson tracked Noble down and they all jumped on the phone. Higgins made three main points: The *Waco Tribune* was planning a major story on Koresh that might cause the Davidians to go on high alert. There was some sort of a ritual planned for Sunday morning inside the compound, during which the men and women were separated from the children and the guns were locked up. (He was referring to work on the pit.) The ATF had somebody on the inside who could get word to the commanders if they'd lost the element of surprise.

Simpson responded with three questions: Was February 28 the last opportunity for surprising the cult members? Was the operation going to be a surprise? What would happen if the operation was canceled? Higgins answered yes to the first two questions. As for the last one, he responded that the planners were afraid the cult members would eventually kill themselves.

By the end of the conversation, Simpson and Noble felt that the ATF director had sufficiently addressed their concerns. They gave Higgins the go-ahead.

In early 1992, Mark England was a reporter for the *Waco Tribune*. He was quiet, precise. He liked to protect his story drafts until they were nearly finished, and then hand them to his editors.

One day that April, the city editor asked England if he had any good ideas for a feature. England did. He'd been hearing things about Mount

Carmel. One of the rumors was that the Davidians were going to stage a mass suicide during Passover. He started looking into doing a piece on David Koresh and his followers.

England went out to the compound for Passover. There was no mass suicide. "People are here for life," Steve Schneider told him. "You mention a word like death, and I'm out of here myself."

The holiday passed uneventfully. But England was intrigued by the Davidians and what he was hearing from ex-members. Stories of polygamy, underage sex, abuse of children, a belief in the End Times. He decided to continue his research, joined by his colleague Darlene McCormick.

The reporters got in touch with Marc Breault. They would get up in the middle of the night and go to the *Trib*'s newsroom for their three a.m. calls to Australia. They spoke to Robyn Bunds, David Jewell, and others. The work went on through the summer and into the fall.

Nine months later, England and McCormick turned in their original draft of the story, which had grown into a multipart series. Editors worked on it, then passed it up to the paper's management.

Some of the top administrators were against running the piece. The editor in chief, Bob Lott, disagreed. The reporting had convinced him that Koresh was raping girls and abusing children. By early February 1993, the series had been edited and proofread. A copy editor gave it a title: "The Sinful Messiah."

The ATF knew about the series and asked the *Trib* to postpone or kill it. The paper declined.

The paper wanted to give Koresh one last chance to respond to the piece. England called the compound on Monday, February 22. "If the Bible is true, then I'm Christ," David told him. "But so what? Look at 2,000 years ago. What's so great about being Christ? A man nailed to the cross. A man of sorrow acquainted with grief. You know, being Christ ain't nothing."

On February 24, a final meeting between the ATF and *Trib* editors convened. Phil Chojnacki spoke for the ATF. He thanked the *Trib* staffers for postponing the series at the ATF's request. The editors quickly informed him that was a mistake; they'd held the story for their own reasons.

Chojnacki begged the editors not to run the story. It would endanger ATF agents and *Trib* staffers alike, he said. At the moment, the Davidians seemed to suspect nothing, but he believed "The Sinful Messiah" would set off alarms inside Mount Carmel and jack up the group's paranoia. The editors disagreed; they had a good and important story, and they were going to run it.

The *Trib* scheduled the first installment of the series for Saturday, February 27. The *Trib* offices were less busy on the weekends, and there would be fewer employees at risk if the Davidians decided to hit back.

The ATF established a command post at an unused airplane facility northeast of Waco. The site had been used during World War II to rehab aircraft, and the sprawling grounds contained both airplane hangars and barracks with beds the agents could use. Ironically, the site now belonged to Texas State Technical College, the same college that the ATF's surveillance agents were pretending to attend.

On Thursday the February 25, the ATF finally obtained an arrest warrant for David Koresh. They moved the raid up to Sunday, February 28. At least two sources, including a worker for an ambulance service contacted by the ATF and a member of the McLennan County Sheriff's Department, tipped off members of the local media that a raid was imminent.

With the operation drawing closer, Chuck Sarabyn called the undercover agent, Robert Rodriguez. He asked him to go back to the compound Saturday morning and check on the reaction to the series. Rodriguez balked. He felt the Davidians were growing increasingly suspicious of him, and worried about what they might do. Sarabyn pressed him. "We've got to, Robert," he said. "One more time to make sure everything is still OK." Rodriguez was filled with dread. Every time he visited Mount Carmel, he felt like he wasn't going to come out.

This will be the last time, he told himself. He agreed to go.

On Saturday, the first installment of "The Sinful Messiah" debuted. That morning, a phone call came into the *Trib*. It was Steve Schneider. He said that David had read the article and was troubled. He was offering to speak to the *Trib* and give them "the real story." It would focus on the Seven Seals and not the "seven days of lies" the *Trib* was planning to publish. The interview never happened.

At the compound, David showed his followers a copy of the *Trib*. "It's going to be soon," he said.

One follower remembered that morning:

When we came downstairs that morning, everyone was just kind of sitting there, kind of in shock. I saw a few newspapers lying around and heard David discussing the paper and the article about him. Then when we realized the article was set to run for the whole week we were dumbfounded, and rather embarrassed. We had been told that Robert Gonzalez was coming over today to join us for the morning Sabbath service. David had asked us all to come downstairs to meet Robert and let him get to know us. David wanted Robert to get to know who we were and what we were like, but the newspaper article seemed to cast a shadow over things.

35

HOOD

O N FEBRUARY 25, the ATF's training for the raid began at
Fort Hood, an enormous Army base about an hour away from
Waco. The agents stayed in busted World War II two-story
Army barracks. Guys in their thirties and forties, used to checking in at
the Holiday Inn while traveling for the bureau, were instead crammed
into what was a glorified summer camp, down to the bunks and the
common bathroom.

ATF agent Chuck Hustmyre couldn't believe it. "This sucks," he
thought. "Now I remember why I got out of the military."

Hustmyre hadn't actually been assigned to go down to Fort Hood
that first day. In fact, he had tickets to a George Strait concert he'd
been looking forward to seeing with his wife. But his partner, Todd
McKeehan, told him about this top-secret deal going on in Texas, and
it sounded too good to miss, so he got rid of the tickets and jumped in
a car for Fort Hood.

Todd was Chuck's best friend. He came from a God-fearing family in
East Tennessee, where people's accents were so thick, they could have
been speaking Klingon. When he met them, Chuck had trouble understanding what they were saying.

They'd met at a party thrown in Todd's honor when he returned from
the Gulf War. He told some funny-ass stories over the campfire: How,
after invading Iraq, they'd heard about a Baskin Robbins opening back in

Kuwait and they'd gotten on this line a mile long in 115-degree heat just to taste some butter pecan ice cream. And how he'd gone fifty-five days without a shower or a hot meal. Not bitching about it, just telling it.

Todd was a positive dude. Always looking forward to something in life. Chuck liked that about him.

Todd had served with the Marine infantry. A very Action Jackson kind of guy. When he got into the ATF, he loved kicking down doors and grabbing perps.

Once the agents had gathered, supervisors showed them aerial photographs of the compound. They talked about Koresh, held up some pictures of him. They laid out the case. "It's a religious cult" was the basic message; "the guy's kind of crazy, he's got a bunch of young girls living with him. Some of them are underage that he was having sex with and gotten one or two of them pregnant. They're kind of a death cult type of thing." That was what Chuck Hustmyre remembered most. "We're going to have to raid them because we're afraid they're going to be one of those Jonestown type deals."

The aerial photos were from months earlier. Hardly fresh. Some of the agents wondered why the ATF just didn't fly over again, find out what the place looked like now. There were other things that were slightly off, too. The supervisors talked about the surveillance house across the street from the compound who were watching him twenty-four hours a day. That turned out not to be true.

Then there was the mud. The main building at Mount Carmel sat about two or three hundred yards down a long unpaved driveway that branched off Double EE Ranch Road. During a briefing, one of the agents asked what if it rains the morning of the raid and the cattle trailers get stuck in the mud? "Well, we're just going to get out and run" was the answer.

Hustmyre was like, a couple of hundred yards of completely wide-open terrain, just a big field of grass, no cover whatsoever? Charging up to a building that's packed with armed religious fanatics who've said they'll shoot it out with the government? That's the backup plan?

"Is this real?" he thought. "Are these people fucking crazy?"

Hustmyre had been an MP in the Army before joining the bureau. Running straight ahead into gunfire wasn't really the Army way. But his buddy Todd was an ex-Marine. And charging straight to the sound of guns, that was Marine protocol, for sure. Hustmyre thought, if Todd's going to do it, then I'm damn well going to do it, too.

Three Special Response Teams, or SRTs, would carry out the raid, one from New Orleans, one from Houston, and one from Dallas. The teams would approach the compound in two cattle trailers, pulled by pickup trucks, and disembark yards from the compound's front door. Chuck Sarabyn gave each SRT its assignment. Members of the New Orleans team would use ladders to reach the compound's second floor. They would enter the armory, which the ATF believed was next to Koresh's bedroom. Other team members would clear the bedroom. The rest of the team would guard the area at the base of the ladders. The bureau estimated that there were seventy-five men, women, and children inside the compound. In fact, there were closer to 115, with the youngest being six months and the oldest seventy years.

The Dallas SRT would enter through the compound's front door and cover the second and third floors, as well as the observation tower. The ATF's information was that those areas housed the women's and children's bedrooms. Half the Houston SRT would take the first floor and secure it. They would find the trapdoor that led to the buried bus that the Davidians were making into a bunker. The second part of the Houston team would go to the western edge of the property, where the pit/shooting range was, and hold the Davidian men there.

Once the entire property was under ATF control, David Koresh would be arrested and a thorough search would be conducted. If there were problems on the way to the compound, the two cattle trailers would divert at one of several crossroads along the route. In case the trailers or the agents came under fire from the Davidians, the agency requested smoke canisters from the US military. The request was never filled, apparently because it was delivered too late for the military to respond in time.

By the time the trailers arrived at the front of the compound, there would be no more chances to abort the raid, even if the element of surprise had been lost. The landscape around Mount Carmel offered little cover, so the agents would have to proceed with the operation regardless.

After meeting with Sarabyn, Bill Buford and the other SRT leaders talked to their teams and gave more details on their assignment.

The undercover agent Robert Rodriguez gave a presentation, describing Mount Carmel's layout. The agents ate their meals and retired to the barracks. The next day, Friday, February 26, they assembled at the Military Operations in Urban Terrain site, a training course dense with structures and obstacles built to resemble an average American city. Strips of tape on the floor re-created Mount Carmel's layout. The teams practiced the dynamic entry and searches. Each action was timed down to the second. Afterward, the agents moved on to the firing ranges and practiced shooting.

There are three key components of a good dynamic entry: the element of surprise, superior firepower, and speed. The technique was designed to overwhelm a target before they could shoot back. At the briefings, two or three of them every day, the supervisors told the agents, "We're going to have the element of surprise and it's crucial to maintain it." To have the best chance at success, they would need to catch the Davidians unaware. A few of the agents would be armed with the semiautomatic AR-15s, but most would be carrying only handguns. On the days of the raid, the ATF would be outgunned by the Davidians.

It was going to be a big, high-profile raid, the largest in the bureau's history. Three SRTs. Eighty-plus agents. The bureau's media relations department alerted the local news media beforehand that they were going to have a major story for them in the coming days. The administrators gave the raid a name: "Operation Trojan Horse." But the guys at Fort Hood started calling it "Showtime." Some agents thought they were sure to get on CNN.

But that Friday, as the agents trained, a van loaded with over a thousand pounds of urea-nitrate explosive blew up in the basement of the World Trade Center in New York City. A small group of Islamist extremists had staged an attack on American soil. Six people, including a pregnant woman, were dead. Over a thousand were injured.

ATF agents flooded into New York to investigate. Resources were stretched thin just as the Waco raid was moving into the operational phase. Hustmyre was pissed. "That's it," he thought, "that just knocked us off the fucking news cycle." Their shot at getting on CNN and being called heroes for taking down a whacko cult was gone.

There was little talk about the possibility of the Davidians successfully resisting the raid. Most SRT members would have found that unthinkable. Collectively, the agents at Fort Hood had conducted thousands of raids over years and years, and in almost all of them, the ATF had prevailed.

There were exceptions, of course. Agents had died in the line of duty. But gun runners, confronted with a team of ATF agents pounding on their front door, rarely decided to fight back. They surrendered or they ran. No one thought, "Hey, let's go to war with the US government. That's a good idea."

Hustmyre and his team worked New Orleans, which was then probably the most dangerous city in America. Guns everywhere. Murders up the wazoo. And, consistently, they kicked ass. Waco was going to be a gigantic version of that, Hustmyre figured. He estimated it would be over in ten minutes.

The bureau booked 153 rooms at three Waco hotels for the night of February 28. They notified local hospitals to be prepared to accept casualties and recruited sheriff's deputies and Texas Highway patrolmen to block key roads and serve as support personnel. They brought in explosives experts, dog handlers, and lab techs to process any evidence from the scene.

Officials put in a large order for doughnuts at a local grocery store, to be picked up that morning. They also made sure there would be early-morning coffee for the agents at Bellmead Civic Center. One agent, Roland Ballesteros, went to the local Wal-Mart and bought candy bars for the children at Mount Carmel. Growing up, he'd watched those World War II paratrooper movies where the Yanks handed out candy to the French kids. When he got back to the barracks, he filled his ammo pouch with Snickers and other things.

The cattle trailers were brought to Fort Hood. They would ride up empty to Waco. February 28 was a Sunday. It didn't occur to the planners at the time that Texas ranchers almost never transported cattle on Sundays.

On Saturday, February 27, at eight a.m., Robert Rodriguez made his way to the compound. Saturday was the Sabbath, and David would usually hold a morning and an early-evening Bible study.

Rodriguez sat among the Davidians and listened as David talked about the "Sinful Messiah" story. "Now, for sure, they'll be coming," he said. David told his followers that, when the Babylonian forces arrived, they shouldn't panic. He'd trained them on what to do. He didn't spell out what that was.

After the morning session, Rodriguez left the compound and met with one of the commanders on the operation, Phil Chojnacki. Chojnacki wanted to know if he'd spotted any weapons or heard of any plans to fight back against any raid. Rodriguez said no on both counts. Rodriguez went back for the second study session, which lasted from five p.m. to about midnight. Then he left. The forward observers who'd settled into the surveillance house in anticipation of the raid noticed that Rodriguez seemed unsettled, anxious.

The undercover agent got on the phone with Sarabyn, who told him to return to the compound at 9:15 the next morning for a last report. Rodriguez didn't want to go in. He was worried that showing up a second day in a row might stoke the Davidians' paranoia. He didn't know if David would let him leave by 9:15, which was the drop-dead time for him to get out before the raid.

Eventually, Sarabyn convinced him to go back.

In Fort Hood, ATF agents drove around town looking for newspaper boxes. They wanted to grab copies of the *Waco Trib*, the one with David Koresh on the front page. They were getting them for their wives, parents, whatever. The ATF was going to play a small part in history, and it would be nice to have a memento.

THE ELEMENT OF SURPRISE

S UNDAY MORNING ARRIVED and the ATF agents at Fort Hood were grumbling. Some Army geek had announced a barracks inspection. They had to get their rooms cleaned up before they could head to Waco. The biggest raid maybe in the history of US law enforcement and the Army wanted them to make sure their beds were nice and tidy before they could leave. It was like an enhanced hallucination of being in the military.

They woke up around three a.m., most of them dead tired, and got to it. After a couple of hours, the Army prick walked into the barracks with an actual checklist in his hand. Had the showers been mopped? Check. Did you strip your bed? Check. It was farcical.

Before the sun came up, the place was finally spic and span. The Army guy left. The agents got in their cars and formed a convoy heading up the highway, led by one of the cattle trailers. There were about eighty late-model American vehicles, many of them with long antennas, all with their headlights turned on. The line extended about a mile down the interstate.

They hauled ass, heading northeast.

In Waco, the morning dawned cold and overcast, with light drizzle. The forward observers at the surveillance house studied the compound through their binoculars. Everything appeared normal. There were only a few Davidians outside, men walking around and women emptying the buckets that the followers used for their waste.

By around eight a.m., the trailers and ATF cars were pulling into the parking lot of Bellmead Civic Center in Waco. The agents got out of their cars and unloaded their equipment. Some went inside for coffee and doughnuts. Others threw their duffel bags up against the wall and lay down, trying to catch a few winks.

A bunch of agents stood outside, shooting the shit. They were wearing jackets with "ATF" emblazoned on the backs in bright yellow. A supervisor came hustling up and waved them inside the building. He was worried someone would see all the ATF jackets and alert the Davidians. While they waited, a supervisor issued another order. All the agents who were going to load onto the cattle trailers were to write their blood types on their necks in Magic Marker, in case they were wounded and needed transfusions.

Early that morning, two men, David Jones and Donald Bunds, drove out of the compound to find copies of the Sunday *Trib*, which featured the second installment of the Koresh series. Jones, who worked as a mailman, was driving a yellow truck with the "U.S. Mail" logo on the door. On the way, Jones spotted the KWTX cameraman Jim Peeler. Peeler was parked by the side of the road, clearly lost. Jones stopped and asked if he could help. Peeler said he was trying to find Rodenville, the old name for Mount Carmel. He had no idea Jones was a member of the Davidians.

As they talked, Jones pointed toward Mount Carmel and said he'd read the *Trib* story. Those people are strange, he said, talking about the Davidians. Peeler nodded and said that there was a law enforcement operation underway that morning, aimed at the compound. He said there could be gunfire.

The two finished up talking. Jones turned back toward the compound, driving fast. Peeler had unwittingly alerted a member of the Branch Davidians that the raid was underway, and Jones was eager to tell David.

One of the ATF surveillance agents witnessed the encounter. He reported it to his supervisor, who later said he called it in to the command center. But the agents at the center later had no recollection of the report.

As Jones raced back to the compound, Robert Rodriquez was in one of the first-floor rooms, talking with David. Things were normal.

David left the room. When he came back, he was agitated. His body, his limbs, they were actually shaking. David Jones had arrived and alerted him about the impending raid.

He turned toward Robert. "Neither the ATF nor the National Guard will ever get me," he said. "They got me once. They'll never get me again."

What was going on? Robert said nothing. David walked over to the front window, pulled up the shade, and peered outside.

"They're coming, Robert," he said. "The time has come."

Robert began to panic. Had the raid been moved forward without anyone telling him? Was that possible?

"Just relax, just relax, just relax," he said to himself. "Don't give yourself away."

Maybe it was 9:15 already, or later. He'd lost track of time. He stole a furtive glance at his watch. It was just past 9.

Robert told David he had a breakfast date. David said nothing.

Some other Davidians filed into the room, all men. They arranged themselves so they were standing between Robert and the door. A coincidence?

Rodriguez felt as though his brain was glitching. What should he do? For a moment, he thought about jumping through a window and running.

"I really have to go," Robert said again. He stood up. David turned and walked up to him. He held out his hand, something David never did. "Good luck, Robert," he said.

"This is it for me," Robert was thinking to himself. "They're going to shoot me, man." He was expecting to get out the door and get a round in the back. That's the scene that was playing in his head.

Rodriguez opened the front door and walked toward his pickup truck. He braced himself for the sound of a gun.

He reached the truck and got in. The alarm went off, screeching. The Davidians came to the windows and looked out. They heard four quick beeps and the alarm stopped. At least one Davidian thought it was strange.

The agent drove down the long driveway and sped over to the surveillance house. Once he reached it, he called Sarabyn, who was at the airstrip command center.

Rodriguez was amped, talking super-fast. "Chuck, Chuck, he knows . . . He knows we're coming, okay?" He told Sarabyn that Koresh was highly agitated.

The forward observers could hear Rodriguez talking. After listening for a moment, they started gathering up their equipment. If Koresh knew, they figured, the raid was over.

The planners had given Sarabyn a list of questions to determine whether the raid could go forward. He started reading them off to Rodriguez.

"Did you see any weapons?"

"No."

"Was there a call to arms?"

"No."

"Did you see them make any preparations?"

"No."

"What were the Davidians doing when you left?"

"Praying," Rodriguez said.

Sarabyn ended the call. He appeared frantic; his eyes wide. "What are you going to do," another ATF agent asked. Sarabyn said, "I think we can do it if we hurry."

Sarabyn hustled out to the tarmac, where Chojnacki and another commander were waiting. The rotors of the three Texas National Guard helicopters—two OH-58 Kiowas and a UH-60 Black Hawk—were turning, creating a wall of earsplitting noise. The men walked to the edge of the runway and bent over in a tight cluster so they could hear each other.

Sarabyn told the others about the conversation with Rodriguez. He said that Koresh was aware that the raid was coming, but that he hadn't armed himself or his followers.

"Did he see guns?" Chojnacki asked. Sarabyn said no.

Chojnacki asked Sarabyn what he wanted to do. Sarabyn replied that if they moved fast, he still believed the raid could work.

"Let's go," Chojnacki said.

Sarabyn jumped in a car and headed for the Civic Center. Chojnacki called the ATF National Command Center in Washington. He told the supervisors there that Rodriguez had left Mount Carmel and that the operation was a go. He didn't mention that the element of surprise had been lost.

ATF personnel filmed Chojnacki and the other supervisors as they put on their gear and hopped into the helicopters. Then they boarded the choppers themselves to record the raid from above.

Sarabyn arrived at the Civic Center, where the agents were milling around or sleeping. He hustled inside and stood at the front of the auditorium, shouting for the agents to listen up. His voice echoed in the enormous space. "Okay," he said, "we're going early." He gave a quick rundown: The undercover agent was just at the compound. Koresh knew they were coming. They had to leave now.

"Get your shit on, let's go."

The announcement caused a stir. Agents began grabbing their gear and shouting that Koresh knew about the raid. Some were confused. The element of surprise was lost and they going in anyway? Back at Fort Hood, hadn't the team leaders said that getting the jump on the Davidians was essential?

But no one wanted to be the first one to speak up. They got their gear and hurried into the trailers.

As for Hustmyre, it was hard to explain, but he was worried about *not* going. "Holy shit, the ATF is going to puss out," he thought. "They're actually going to call this whole thing off." Hustmyre didn't want that. It would be the worst thing in the world, in fact. Backing down from some religious fanatic because they were afraid of getting shot at? What kind of weak shit was that? He would no longer feel like he was working for a legitimate law enforcement organization.

He joked to his partner, Todd, that if the ATF stood down, they'd have to quit and find another agency to join. Couldn't lose face. He wasn't really kidding, though.

They went ahead and started boarding the cattle trailers. Hustmyre was in one, Todd in another.

Robert Rodriguez pulled into the airstrip command center. The choppers were gone; the place was half-deserted. Clearly, the raid was going forward.

Rodriguez became upset. He shouted "Why?" to no one in particular. He ran out to the tarmac, crying.

The cattle trailers loaded up and headed toward Double EE Ranch Road. Sarabyn, in the pickup truck pulling the lead trailer, was on his cell phone talking to the forward observers. They kept radioing back there was nothing unusual going on at the compound. A normal Sunday.

Tommy Witherspoon, a *Trib* reporter who'd been tipped off about the raid by a sheriff's deputy, pulled into the driveway of the home across from the compound. Witherspoon left another reporter and a staff photographer in his Honda Accord as he approached the front door. He had no idea it was an ATF surveillance site.

Witherspoon knocked on the door. He wanted to ask the owners if he and his co-workers could set up on the front lawn and observe the raid that was about to unfold across the road.

The door cracked open. Witherspoon saw a man's face. He seemed to be agitated.

Witherspoon went into his spiel about the raid and the front lawn and the *Waco Trib*. The man interrupted him. "Get the fuck out of here," he said.

Witherspoon walked quickly back to his car, put it in gear, and reversed out of the driveway. It was 9:45 a.m.

Jerry Petrelli, one of the planners, was inside one of the cattle trailers. He called out to Chuck Hustmyre, who was standing near the edge of the canvas tarp. "Hey, can you peek out there and just see what's going on?"

Hustmyre stuck the muzzle of his AR-15 between the gap and pulled the tarp over.

"What's going on?" Petrelli asked again.

"Man, there's nothing. There's nobody here." A mist of drizzle cloaked the front of the compound in gray.

It's too quiet, Hustmyre thought. He turned to another agent. "This doesn't seem right," he muttered. "This is spooky."

Two locals were listening to scanners that morning. They picked up radio traffic that seemed to be coming from the Branch Davidian compound. A male voice came on. He was speaking about agents in a trailer. He called them "a covey of quail . . . If I had a shotgun, I could flush them out and kill every one of them." The listener wasn't clear on what the guy was talking about.

The ATF didn't hear the conversation. Their scanners didn't pick up radio traffic coming from the compound. It was likely the last chance to abort the raid, and it passed quickly.

Witherspoon parked his Honda on the road in front of the surveillance house. As he looked down Double EE Ranch Road, he saw two cattle trailers driving toward him at a high rate of speed. The open trailers were covered in tarps, but a *Trib* photographer spotted men inside, wearing helmets. Two cars followed the trailers, one filled with journalists from KWTX and the other with more *Trib* reporters.

The car with the *Trib* journalists pulled up and parked near the Honda. Mark England and Darlene McCormick, who'd broken the "Sinful Messiah" story, were among them.

The three helicopters arrived and hovered north of the site. The two Kiowas were at five hundred feet, while the Black Hawk sat just below that. The pilots pushed their sticks forward and the helicopters swooped over Mount Carmel. Immediately, they started taking fire. Bullets smacked into the fuselages of the Blackhawk and one of the Kiowas. A bullet just missed Chojnacki's head. The pilots turned toward a field near the compound and put the choppers down.

The trailers rumbled off the main road and down Mount Carmel's long driveway, the compound looming ahead of them in the mist. Roland Ballesteros, the agent who'd filled his ammo pouch with candy for the kids, peeked out and saw that the TV crews had already set up their tripods and cameras across from the compound.

"Two minutes," said a voice on the radio.

They pulled up in front of the building and, even before the trailers came to a full stop, agents carrying fire extinguishers jumped out. Their job was to control the Davidians' dogs, the Alaskan malamutes who were barking in a pen near the front of the house.

Sheila Martin, wife of the lawyer Wayne Martin, was upstairs in her bedroom when she saw a tarp-covered trailer driving toward her window. She thought it was a large delivery of wood for the various construction projects going on at Mount Carmel. Sheila was annoyed. "What are we going to do with all this wood, and how much is this going to cost," she thought. "I thought David said we weren't going to be doing any more building for a while."

She watched as a second trailer appeared. It braked hard on the driveway and a man leapt from the back of it, holding a rifle. He yelled, "Okay guys" or "Okay boys" or something like that. Sheila don't know if he was talking to someone inside the trailer or to the Davidians.

Ballesteros ran toward the front door of the compound. He was the point man. He and his group were supposed to be the first guys through the double front doors. Arrest the Mighty Men and grab Koresh. That was his brief. He was carrying a Model 870 Remington shotgun.

Roland was running for the front porch. He yelled, "Police, search warrant!" He had a ram team just behind him. If the Davidians didn't open the door, they'd knock it down.

The door opened and David Koresh stepped out. Roland could see two other men just behind him. The three men looked out into the yard with a dazed expression on their faces. Roland concentrated on Koresh. His gaze was like, *Wow, what is going on?*

Koresh's eyes flicked toward Roland. "Lay down!" Roland yelled. David's gaze switched back to the trailers. Then he looked back to Roland. It was all unfolding so slowly.

David's expression was hard, glaring, but his body was relaxed. Roland yelled "Police!" again. He made it to the porch. David was about ten feet away now.

David grinned at him—a real dazzler of a smile, like he was walking onto the Merv Griffin set—then backed up and closed the door. A few seconds later, bullets punched through the metal skin. Someone inside was firing out.

The air filled with the sound of gunfire. You couldn't hear a thing.

Ballesteros reached out with his left hand, preparing to twist the knob on the left front door. His hand kicked back and Roland looked down at it. His thumb was lying across the top of his glove. A bullet had nearly severed it.

He glanced up. The right front door was bowing out from the barrage of gunfire being fired through it.

Roland turned left and dove for the dog kennel, which abutted the front of the house. The fall rattled his teeth. He rolled up close to the building. The windows of the first floor were just above his head.

A bullet hit the Honda of *Trib* reporter Tommy Witherspoon. Gunfire ratcheted up into a barrage.

The reporters jumped into a nearby ditch, facedown in the dewy grass. They could hear bullets snipping the air above them. Tracers arced there, too. Someone in the surveillance house that Witherspoon had just visited started firing back at the compound.

A bullet hit the engine block of the ATF's lead pickup truck, rendering it inoperable. Both trailers were now stuck in the driveway.

Lying in the ditch, Tommy Witherspoon grabbed the enormous cell phone issued by the *Trib*. He didn't know how to operate it, so he yelled at one of the photographers to show him.

One of the journalists hit the "Record" button on his portable tape recorder. The tape began with the sound of his rapid breathing. Then a male voice: "Oh God. Oh God. Oh God."

"Get your Hail Marys going, man," Witherspoon said.

"Should we, uh, try to get in the goddamn car and get out?" It was Mark England. One of the photographers said they were out of the line of fire and should stay put.

Sounds of gunfire filled the tape. England said something, but it was drowned out by the noise.

"What'd you say?" Witherspoon said.

England repeated it. "We're going to get blamed for this."

The ATF supervisor in the house across the way started yelling for someone to give him Mount Carmel's phone number. Another agent called back that it was on the fridge. The supervisor ran to the kitchen, found the number, and dialed it.

No one picked up.

"Get him away from the front door!" Someone was shouting from inside the house. It was Koresh, Roland was sure of it. "Get him out of there."

Roland was wearing a bulletproof vest. He tried to pull the collar up, protect his neck a little better.

It occurred to him he'd never said goodbye to his two-year-old son, Adam. How had he missed doing that? It ruled his mind for a good bit. He couldn't die without saying goodbye.

Bill Buford, one of the planners of the raid, bounded out of the trailer. The sound of gunfire was deafening. His mind immediately switched to the ambushes he'd lived through in Vietnam. He could hear the reports of weapons, AK-47s, and what sounded like an M60 machine gun. We don't have any of those, Buford thought.

There was little cover. A few junked cars littered the front yard, but most of the agents were exposed.

"Oh my God, this is gonna be a bloodbath," thought Hustmyre, who was running from the first trailer.

Roland was still pinned under the front window of the Davidians' house. He felt helpless. He couldn't get a bead on anyone and guys were dying out there.

He could hear someone calling out to him on the radio. "Put your head down," the voice said.

An agent had spotted someone inside the compound with a .308 rifle. He was peering down, sweeping the front of the house with his gaze. He appeared to be looking for Roland.

An agent was squatting behind one of the pickups that had pulled the cattle trailers. A .50 caliber bullet ripped through the truck's engine block and shattered his ankle bone. He dropped to the ground under the fuselage. He could see a young Davidian, just a kid really, in one of the upstairs windows, armed with a .22 rifle. They were in each other's line of view. The agent and the kid began trading shots, hoping to get lucky.

There was a sense of unreality to it. A large group of Americans opening up on federal agents with automatic weapons was like finding oneself in a new and alien land, head-spinning in its possible meanings. It was like watching rain fall upward.

Many of the older ATF agents were veterans of Vietnam. Most of them flashed back now, half their thoughts in Central Texas, the other half in the valleys and green riverbeds of Southeast Asia. Past and present merged, faces that were not there now in view. Adrenaline and acid dread converged in their bloodstreams.

Nobody knew who'd fired first. Dan Mulloney, the news cameraman for KWTX, heard firing as the trailers pulled up to the compound door. Judging by the sound of the bullets and the little geysers of dirt being kicked up on the driveway, he believed the Davidians fired the first shots. Darlene McCormick, the co-author of the "Sinful Messiah" series, was convinced the first reports she heard were automatic fire. The ATF was not carrying automatic weapons. Only the Davidians had them.

The gunfire peaked and ebbed as agents ran to their assigned positions. One of the Houston team members, Eric Evers, was hurrying around the west side of the compound. The ground was dotted with obstacles: a chicken coop, fences, the pit.

He was turning the corner on the compound wall when a bullet hit him. Evers fell and tumbled into a ditch.

Agent Lowell Sprague spotted a van that sat alongside the driveway. He ducked behind it, along with another ATF man, Steven Willis. From their sanctuary, Willis saw a Davidian perched atop a forty-foot-tall, rusty-brown steel water tower, firing down toward the agents swarming the compound. Willis called over to Sprague, pointing up at the tower. The sniper was aiming his rifle at someone at the ground.

At the same time, Agent Robert Elder glanced up. He saw the figure on top of the water tower. The man's rifle was pointed directly at Elder. I'm gone, Elder thought. He's going to shoot me now.

But in the next instant, the posture of the man on the water tower changed. His body started to fall back away from the tower. At the same time, the black outline of the rifle fell away from his hands and began dropping toward the ground in looping circles. Sprague and Willis—or an ATF sniper zeroed in on the water tower—had killed the Davidian.

A large-caliber weapon sounded in the distance. Sprague felt a bullet pass a few inches from his head. It gouged an exit hole in the van, about the size of a man's fist. He yelled at Willis to watch out. Someone in the compound had sighted in on the van.

Another boom. Sprague glanced at Willis. A bullet had struck him in the left temple. As Sprague watched, Willis's jaw dropped open and he fell forward slowly. He crumpled onto another agent and lay there.

Sprague grabbed Willis and pulled him close, laid him over his legs. He placed his hand on the exit wound. He could feel the blood push out of the wound through the bones of his fingers.

Buford and six other members of the New Orleans SRT reached the east side of the compound. Their target was the arms room, next to Koresh's bedroom on the second floor. The seven agents carried two ladders and leaned them against the walls of the first-floor chapel, which sat beneath the bedroom.

Buford and two others dashed up the ladder. The shingled roof was shaped like an upside-down V, with one side leading to the arms room, the other to the bedroom.

At the second set of windows, leading to the bedroom, three agents were preparing to "break and rake" the window, smashing out the glass with a metal bar and sweeping away the jagged shards stuck in the frame. But a barrage of gunfire tore through the window. Agent Kevin King was hit six times and rolled down the slope and dropped to a small courtyard below. Todd McKeehan, who'd encouraged his partner Chuck Hustmyre to go to Waco, was hit in the chest. He fell, wounded, to the shingled roof.

At the east window—the arms room—Agent Glen Jordan smashed out the glass with a metal pry bar. Bill Buford threw a flash-bang grenade inside, then stepped in through the window frame, followed by Jordan and Agent Keith Constantino.

Gun racks lined the long room. There were rifles in a few of the slots. The others were empty.

Standing in the gun room, Buford glanced at the doorway and spotted a Davidian, slowly backing down the hallway outside the room. He disappeared from view before Buford could get off a shot. Buford crept to the doorway and peeked around the frame. He saw the gunman standing a few yards away, holding an AK-47. It was clear to Buford that the Davidian was waiting in ambush, hoping an ATF agent would rush through the doorway, so he could cut him down.

Buford took his 9mm and stuck the muzzle into the space between the door and the frame. He pulled the trigger once, twice, again. The Davidian fell.

A barrage of gunshots erupted through the wall and floor. Buford was hit in the hip and thigh. He collapsed onto a wooden box sitting on the floor. When he looked down, he saw it contained a bunch of MK 2 hand grenades.

Buford tried to think over the sound of gunfire. He wanted to face what was happening. "If I'm gonna die," he thought, "it's not gonna be in this room. I'm gonna get out of here and die with my friends." He shouted to the other two agents that they had to leave.

Glen Jordan had also been hit. Constantino was the only one not wounded. Constantino could see through the bullet holes in the walls. A flash of color, a movement. He fired at them with his 9mm, letting off about thirty rounds in quick succession. Constantino popped an empty magazine out of his 9mm and yelled to Buford and Jordan. "When I start firing, get out," he said.

Someone rushed through the doorway. He was wearing jeans and a white T-shirt. At first, Constantino thought it was an ATF agent. The man took two steps into the room, then suddenly turned and brought a rifle he was holding in his hands around toward Constantino. He opened up on the agent.

Constantino shot at the same time the Davidian fired. The man dropped to the floor. Constantino sprinted for the window and jumped through it. On the way he slammed into a wooden beam; the jolt sent his gun skittering away. Based on photos he'd seen, Constantino believed the man he'd shot was David Koresh.

On the chapel roof, Constantino turned, rolling down toward the edge. Bullets were coming up through the shingled roof, and a gunman in the tower was firing down on him. Constantino spun off the roof and slammed into a patch of concrete on the ground. His hip bone snapped. After gathering his wits, he asked another agent for his spare gun and began returning fire.

For the rest of the day and for months, then years, afterward, a thought lurked in Constantino's mind. If he'd been carrying the more powerful MP4 submachine gun instead of his regular 9mm, he was certain he'd have struck the Davidian with a kill shot. If he'd had the right gun, the man he believed to be David Koresh would have died on February 28.

In the undercover house, the supervisor James Cavanaugh called Mount Carmel again. The phone rang but no one picked up. Cavanaugh got on the radio and told the agents near the building to get someone's attention inside and tell them to answer the phone. The agents started yelling at the windows.

Steve Schneider picked up the phone. Cavanaugh told Schneider who he was. In the background, Cavanaugh heard chaos: people screaming, crying, the rapid fire of a long gun.

Schneider was hyper. After a few minutes, Cavanaugh managed to calm him somewhat. He told him they needed a ceasefire. Schneider agreed, but he had no way of telling the gunmen inside the compound.

He put down the phone and walked through the rooms, shouting at the men to stop firing.

The sound of shooting died away. The agents and the Davidians could hear the sound of birdsong from the trees around the compound.

The Davidians might boast of a disorientation even more profound than the agents outside. Their government, in the Davidians' mind, had attacked them in force. How often did this happen? The words in Revelation were now energy vectors crashing into the present reality. The Babylonian world was collapsing. All of this, and they were going to become eternal beings, too, perhaps in as little as a few minutes. They would be joined with Christ forever and bring his kingdom into being.

Almost immediately, someone let off a shot and the fusillade started up again.

Eric Evers lay at the bottom of the muddy ditch. He'd been hit six times. Three of the bullets had struck his bulletproof vest, but one had penetrated it, going into his shoulder. He was also bleeding from a wound to his arm.

He had to force his mind to accept the reality of it. "This isn't a game," he thought. "They're putting real bullets down. They're going to drop one in your head." Rounds were bouncing off the concrete. One snipped his nose and it started to bleed.

Roland Ballesteros could hear the Davidians talking in the room above him. He couldn't see anyone, so he couldn't fire at them.

They were talking strategy. Get this guy over here, bring some ammo there. A woman was talking, telling people to go to this part of the house or that.

He heard a thud. A Davidian had been shot, a male. People started screaming. The screams became wails.

The dogs in the pen were barking. A big white dog, outside the pen, started loping toward it, trying to figure out why they were barking. Roland thought, he's going to find me and start barking. Or attack.

He leveled out his shotgun along the ground, trying to turn the muzzle on the dog. But the dog changed direction and walked over to a stack of lumber, jumped on it. Like it was trying to figure out what the hell was happening.

Agent Rob Williams was part of the New Orleans team assigned to guard the base of the ladders at the chapel wall. He crouched next to the building, shooting back at the Davidians who were trying to pick off Bill Buford. Buford was lying wounded about ten feet away. As the bullets cracked against the concrete, Williams spotted a Davidian who'd just taken a shot at Buford. He stood to get a better shot and fired at the man, then ducked back down.

A few minutes later, Williams raised himself up again. The Davidians had spotted his position. From somewhere in the compound, a bullet angled down, striking Williams in the left cheek. It traversed downward through Williams's skull, exiting below his right ear. He slumped to the ground.

Buford watched it happen. In Vietnam, he'd seen a lot of men get shot. The minute Williams was hit, Buford knew he was dead.

Eric Evers was shouting to the men crouched behind the bulldozer: "I can't stop the bleeding." An open stretch of ground lay between the ditch that Evers was laying in and the bulldozer.

A man emerged from behind the fence in sight of the bulldozer. He was dressed all in black and he was holding a rifle. The agents watched as he crab-crawled toward the ditch where Evers was; they had no idea if the guy was ATF or Davidian. The Houston and New Orleans guys were dressed in blue tactical outfits, the Dallas agents wore black.

One of the ATF guys called out to the man. The guy snapped his head toward the sound of the agent's voice, then jerked the muzzle of the rifle around. Before he could get off a shot, ATF gunfire sent him scuttling back toward the fence.

The KWTX reporter John McLemore called the station. The news director came on the line. "It's a war zone," McLemore said. "Get every ambulance in the county out here."

BYRON

INSIDE THE COMPOUND, before the cattle trailers arrived, the men had armed themselves with rifles and handguns. Some had put on bulletproof vests. David Koresh was carrying a semiautomatic rifle and was wearing a black vest.

In the kitchen, there were open boxes of 9mm bullets on the table. Men loaded them into their magazines. Most of them were also given a single grenade, which they hung around their necks. Wayne Martin, the Harvard-trained lawyer, took two. After arming himself, David walked into the chapel and spotted some women there. "What are you all doing here?" he said. "Get back to your rooms and watch."

The cattle trailers pulled to a stop and agents jumped down and pivoted toward the compound. The area in front of the door was filled with dozens of agents in black and blue uniforms, sprinting this way and that. "Hunting and grunting" is how Steve thought of them.

David emerged from the front door. He remembered holding his right hand out. "Stop, get back," he called to Ballesteros. "Let's talk about this." (Ballesteros never heard those words.) Then David caught the sound of a gun and the left door kicked inward from the impact.

He jumped back inside and pushed the right door shut.

As the trailers pulled up, the Davidian Kat Schroeder, who'd left her life in Florida to join David, was thinking, *Someone is coming into my home.* She was glad the men were armed and ready to defend her family.

When the shooting began, she dove to the floor and began pulling out the stuff under the beds so the children could get underneath. She'd helped build the compound and knew that the building had a base made of concrete and brick, above which there was only plywood and wood framing.

She heard running water and she looked up to the window. There were jugs of water sitting on the shelf opposite the window. Bullets had cut holes through them and water was spilling all over the floor.

Wayne and Sheila Martin had a son, Jamie, who'd caught spinal meningitis as a baby. It had left him blind and unable to walk or stand. After Sheila pushed her two young children to the floor, she swiveled around and saw Jamie lying on the couch, bits of drywall and glass raining on his face. She thought, "Is this how he dies? After all this sickness, is this how he leaves me?"

Jamie was screaming at the top of his lungs. "How am I going to get over there to him," Sheila thought. "What if I get shot as I try to reach him? And what about the other children? Do I take them with me, or leave them where they are, alone?" The bullets shattered the windows and thudded into the wall opposite her.

During a break in the firing, Sheila crawled toward Jamie. She touched his right elbow and got a grip on it and began to pull him down from the couch. The gunshots started again. She lugged him across the floor, with wood splinters and glass shards falling on them both. When she reached the two other children, she grabbed the edge of the mattress and pulled it over the four of them.

She looked at Jamie. He had spots of blood around his lips. Her first thought was that he had been shot, but it was the falling glass that had cut him.

One of the British converts, Livingstone Fagan, was hurrying down a hallway when he encountered David. "I heard you and Steve got one," David said. Fagan told him that he'd shot an ATF agent. "He nearly got me, but I got him first," Fagan said.

The shooting seemed to go on endlessly. Kat Schroeder stayed on the floor under the bed, next to her children. Her youngest child, Bryan, fell asleep.

She felt proud of the Davidians. They were withstanding an assault from the United States government. The Mighty Men had sworn to protect them, and that was exactly what was happening. They would keep fighting until they were killed.

Some of the Davidians thought the ATF agents had fired first. Some thought the first shots were directed at the Alaskan malamutes in their pen. But nobody knew for certain.

Many of the Davidians believed the opening battle of the End Times had begun. The ATF were the advance guard of the Babylonian army, and the battle between these wicked men and David's followers would soon mutate into a global war. Events foretold for millennia were now unfolding.

Moments after the first shots were fired, at 9:48 a.m., a phone call came in over the Waco 911 line.

"911, what is your emergency?" the dispatcher said.

Breathing. The dispatcher repeated her question.

"There's seventy-five men around our building, shooting at us." It was Wayne Martin.

The operator put Lieutenant Larry Lynch, a member of the McLennan Sheriff's Department, on the line.

"Hello? Hello?" Lynch said.

"Hello!" Martin answered.

"Yes, this is Lieutenant Lynch, may I help you?"

Martin repeated the line about the seventy-five men. His voice pitched higher. "Tell 'em there are children and women in here and to call it off!"

A large-caliber gun fired in the background. "I hear gunfire," Lynch said. "Ohhh shit. Hello? Who is this?"

"Call it off!" Martin shouted.

A second ceasefire settled on the compound. The shooting had lasted ninety minutes. "Move back to the road," an ATF supervisor shouted to the agents scattered over the compound.

The agents stirred. They began leaving their positions and retreating to the Double EE Ranch Road, then walk or drive out with the wounded and dead.

Chuck Hustmyre called out. "What about Evers?" Eric Evers was lying, wounded, in a ditch yards away. "We can't leave without him." The
agents around him mumbled their agreement. But who was going to go?
The first ceasefire had been broken by a hail of gunshots. Everyone was
worried it would happen again, and they'd be caught in the open just as
the gunfire kicked up.

"Hell, I'll go get him," Hustmyre said. Another agent, carrying an MP5
submachine gun, volunteered to back him up.

The two men emerged from behind the bulldozer and pushed their
way through the thick mud. They made it to a wooden fence. Almost
as soon as they reached it, the agents spotted two Davidians standing
twenty yards away. The men had rifles sighted at them.

"That's it. We're dead," Hustmyre thought.

But the Davidians didn't fire. After a few seconds, Hustmyre, careful to
keep his hands away from the gun holstered on his hip, shouted, "We're
supposed to pick up the wounded guy."

The Davidians waved their guns side to side. They wanted the agents
out of there. But Hustmyre wouldn't leave without Evers. Finally, one of
the Davidians shouted, "Hurry the fuck up!"

Hustmyre ran down into the ditch, grabbed Evers, and dragged him
up the muddy slope. Once he was on solid ground, he and the other
agent got their arms around Evers's shoulders and hustled him out toward the driveway.

Wayne Martin stayed on the line with Lynch. He told the sheriff the ATF
agents seemed to be preparing for a new assault. "They're breaking more
weapons out," Martin said. "They're breaking out the big stuff. Tell them
to stop it!"

"Let us get our injured people out before you do anything," Lynch
pleaded.

Martin was shouting. "If they attack us, we're going to fight to the last
man."

Lynch told Martin that law enforcement would help the Davidians
who had been wounded. Martin took a moment to answer.

"Lynch, here's the message," he said.

"I'm here," Lynch said. "Go ahead . . ."

"We don't want anything from your country," Martin said.

"You don't want any help from us?" Lynch asked. "Please let us help you, Wayne . . ."

"That's what our wounded are telling us," Martin said. "They don't want your help. I'm just passing it on."

Bernadette Griffin, a Black ATF agent, was looking for a wounded SRT member. She and three other agents were hustling toward the chapel wall. She believed the SRT guy was still on the shingled roof.

As she passed a doorway, she saw a Davidian standing there. He was dressed in a black hat and black technical vest. He was pointing a rifle at her. He said nothing.

Griffin raised her hands in the air but continued walking, not taking her eyes off the Davidian as she passed him in the doorway.

The agents found the agent lying near the chapel wall. Griffin bent down to help him. She heard a man calling out to her. "Bring your Black ass out so we can see you." Griffin stood and walked back the way she'd come. There was the man in the black vest. His rifle was leveled at her chest.

"Stand there," he said.

It was drizzling rain, and the rain mixed with blood that was dripping down from the shingled roof. The blood and water fell on Griffin's shoulders as she explained to the Davidian that she only wanted to remove the injured agent and get him some first aid. The man said nothing.

After a minute or two, Griffin thought to herself, this is a waste of time. The Davidians were going to execute her and the other agents anyway. She figured she might as well help her comrade in the meantime. She dropped her hands and walked back toward the chapel wall.

The man never fired.

Roland Ballesteros walked out with the others. His thumb was hanging by a ribbon of flesh.

He jumped in the back of a pickup truck that was taking out some of the wounded. A dead agent was lying next to him and another guy. The dead guy's helmet began to fall off.

The other agent grabbed the helmet. He and Roland could see that the man's brains were inside. The brains began to spill out over the edge.

The agent looked at Roland with a questioning look in his eyes.

"Put it back on him," Roland said.

After a delay, David Koresh got on the 911 line. After the frantic Wayne Martin, David was cool as a cucumber.

LYNCH: Yeah, this is Lynch.

DAVID: Hey, Lynch, that is a sort of funny name there.

LYNCH: (Laughing) Who am I speaking with?

DAVID: This is David Koresh.

LYNCH: Okay, David.

DAVID: The notorious. What did you guys do that for?

LYNCH: What I'm trying to do is establish some communication links with you.

DAVID: No, no, no, no, no. Let me tell you something. You see, you brought a bunch of guys out here and killed some of my children. We told you we wanted to talk.

The FBI negotiator Byron Sage was at home in Austin that morning when the phone rang. When he got on, Jeff Jamar was on the line. Jamar was the FBI Special Agent in Charge of the San Antonio office. He didn't say hello. "Byron, there's been a raid that's gone terribly wrong. Get to Waco as fast as you can and assist with negotiations."

Byron put the phone down and ran for the shower. He called out to his wife to pack him a bag. "This is a bad one. You better put about three days' worth in there."

He got out of the shower and jumped in his car. Hit the siren and the blue and red lights and tore ass toward Waco.

Byron had grown up in the Bay Area city of Vallejo, California, a juvenile delinquent with a drunk for a father. He learned to fight when his dad knocked him around, saying he wanted to teach him boxing. Rebellious and angry, Byron started breaking into homes and stealing things. A local cop sat him down and told him if he didn't change direction, he was going to end up in prison on a long bid.

Instead, Byron joined the Navy and served two tours aboard a submarine during the Vietnam War. Afterward, he got a college degree thanks to the GI Bill and joined the FBI in 1970.

Byron became an FBI agent to work leads, kick down doors, and have fun. He carried an ancient sawed-off shotgun with a pistol grip and a flashlight screwed onto the stock. He was good at developing informants. In the 1970s he grew close to the Nuestra Familia underboss Joe "Death Row" Gonzales and turned him into an FBI source. A decade later, he led a team that carried out an audacious sting against the Hells Angels. In 1976, Byron became a full-time negotiator.

American institutions—especially the FBI—had saved Byron. He was intensely loyal to and protective of them. One of his supervisors remembered wondering if Byron owned a piece of clothing that wasn't issued by the bureau or that didn't bear its logo; he didn't think he did. He remarked that Byron "pissed red, white, and blue."

Byron drove to the Waco Police headquarters and hurried down to the basement, where the 911 calls came in. He could see the dispatchers were in shock. Larry Lynch was talking on two phones at once, with Koresh on one of the lines.

Lynch worked Byron's name into the conversation, paving the way for him to take over negotiations. After a while, Byron took one of the phones. He said he was an FBI negotiator and he was there to get this matter resolved peacefully.

He listened. Someone was screaming in the background. Gunshots.

He'd been told that the name of the guy on the other end was Vernon Wayne Howell or David Koresh. "How do you want me to refer to you?" Byron said. "Do you want me to call you Vernon, Mr. Howell, David, or David Koresh? And by the way, how do you pronounce that last name?"

David's voice came over the line. "Agent Sage, have you ever heard a person die?"

Calm as could be. As if they were sitting in the park playing checkers, Byron thought.

"Yes, I have," Byron said.

"Then you know how to pronounce my name."

Byron didn't understand. "What do you mean by that?"

"It's pronounced like that last breath of someone dying. *Koresssssshhhhhhh.*"

Byron felt the hair on the back of his neck raise up. He glanced over at Lynch. They both shook their heads.

Well, now we're in for it, Byron thought.

Around 2:30 p.m., Steve Schneider got a call through to CNN. He was shouting that the ATF was shooting at the Davidians. Eventually, David took the phone. He was talking fast and began preaching about the Seven Seals. The network made the decision to put him on the air. David told the interviewer he'd been "shot through the guts" and was wrapped on a sheet covered in his blood.

As soon as the interview finished, the FBI called CNN executives. They were "livid beyond the point of being apoplectic." How had they gotten through to Koresh? Why was the network tying up the phone line when the Davidians were holding hostages? They called us, CNN executives responded.

The FBI then asked if CNN would get through to the compound again and allow the FBI to listen in. Executives called the network president. He said no.

AMBULANCES

A BOUT TWO HOURS after the first shot was fired, ATF agents began walking off the Davidian property. Hustmyre was looking for Todd, his partner, who'd been on the other side of the building. "Hey, man, have you seen Todd?" he asked another agent.

"I don't know," the dude said.

"You don't know?" Hustmyre thought. How can you not know if you've seen someone?

Up ahead, Hustmyre could see ATF people loading some wounded into an ambulance. He ran up there to help.

When he got to the ambulance, the back was full of injured men. There were so many that they left no room for the bodies of two dead agents that were still on the ground: Rob Williams and Conway LeBleu. The guys gathered around the back of the ambulance and said to each other, We can't leave them here, we have to find a way to get them out.

Hustmyre and some others picked up Rob Williams and carried him to the front of the ambulance. They tried to cram the body into the passenger seat, bending it over at the waist and arranging the arms and legs to the contours of the little compartment and the dash and everything.

But Rob was a big dude, and no matter how they tried, the body wouldn't fit. So they rolled down the window and hung his legs out. They shut the door. But then the ambulance driver wouldn't drive like that. So they opened the passenger door and took Rob out and laid him by the side of the road and the ambulance drove away.

Hustmyre felt numb.

He saw three guys coming down the driveway carrying an agent. Chuck got a glimpse of his forehead, which was chalk-white from loss of blood.

He walked over to help. It was Todd, his best friend. Hustmyre took his arm or his leg, he couldn't remember afterward. He carried Todd to a pickup truck and pulled him into the bed. Then he got in, too.

Someone ran up with an oxygen bottle. Hustmyre took it and put the mask over Todd's face. Once the mask was secured, Hustmyre reached over and turned the knob on the tank and he could hear the hissing of the oxygen.

It didn't make sense, any of it, because Todd was clearly dead but now, he was riding in the bed of a pickup with an oxygen mask over his face like he had a chance.

The KWTX cameraman Dan Mulloney could see the fury in the agents' faces as they walked by. Many of them, he sensed, thought the media had tipped off the Davidians that morning. Quickly, he took his tape of the raid out of his camera and stuffed it down the front of his pants, then covered it with his jacket.

A few agents spotted Mulloney. They came at him and began slamming their fists into his face and body. "Get that fucking camera out of here," one shouted. Mulloney shoved his camera between his legs to protect it and brought his arms up to cover his head. Somehow, he kept shooting, even as the agents tried to rip the camera away from him. A sheriff's deputy, watching this happen, yelled at Mulloney. "You son of a bitch! I knew this was going to happen."

Another cameraman, KWTX's Jim Peeler, was standing by the side of the Double EE Ranch Road. He spotted a dark-haired man whaling on the hood of a car, just beating the shit out of it. The man was crying as he swung.

"I told them! I told them! I told them!" he screamed. It was Robert Rodriguez, the undercover agent.

Mulloney eventually got away from the ATF agents. He and McLemore saw wounded agents walking away from the compound. There were no other vehicles to carry them.

The two asked the agents if they wanted to ride in their Bronco. One guy was in such bad shape, they had to lay him across the front hood. McLemore, who was driving, couldn't see over the ATF man, so two agents walked alongside the Bronco, saying "A little to the left, a little to the right."

The journalists brought the wounded men to a medical triage site. They were the last of the non-Davidians to leave the compound. All of the ATF agents had already withdrawn.

That night, negotiators offered David a chance to speak to the nation, get his side of the story out. David jumped at the offer. He decided to record a tape and send it out with one of the Davidians who'd elected to leave the compound. The Dallas-Fort Worth all-news station, KRLD, broadcasting at 1080 on the AM dial, agreed to run the brief recording after FBI officials told them it would save lives.

David recorded his talk and two FBI agents drove the cassette to the station's studio, which ran it several times that night. Later, David agreed to be interviewed and, after the FBI gave its consent, the interview went live on the air. David told the radio host that the raid had been prophesied in Psalm 2. The Babylonians had attacked Mount Carmel. It had been foretold. The Seven Seals were unfolding as they spoke. "You see, now people are going to lose their lives over this," David said. "Now the next event . . . we are in the Fifth Seal right now . . . the next event to take place is that the sun and the moon and the stars will be darkened just like Joel 2 and all the prophets teach."

The hosts nudged him toward more immediate topics. They asked him to come out, get treatment for his wounds. After all, continuing his ministry and saving the world wouldn't be possible if he was dead.

David broke in. "I am going home. I am going back to my father and we have . . . like I say the next thing you are going to see according to Matthew 24 is that you will see the Son of Man coming in the clouds with great glory and power."

"I think the National Guard's coming in on us," he said with a kind of battle-hardened weariness. It wasn't true.

As the interview wound down, David asked the hosts to get in touch with two women from his past. "Would you tell Linda I still love her and I'm gonna get back, okay? And also tell Sandy that I'll be back and I love her, too."

The KRLD host asked about casualties. Who died inside Mount Carmel?

"Two-year-old girl," David said. "My baby."

What was her name?

"I'm not disclosing this at this time."

David was either misinformed or lying. No children had died in the ATF raid.

After the interview was over, Bonnie, David's mother, called in hoping to speak to her son. But he'd already hung up. "I just want to say if Vernon's listening, I love you," she said on the air, using David's given name. "And God bless you." She began to cry.

David called Bonnie back later. She was out in the backyard, so he got her machine. He left a message. "Hello, Momma, this is your son. They shot me and I think I'm dying, all right? Tell Grandma hello for me. I'll be back real soon, okay? I'm sorry you didn't learn the Seals, but I'll be merciful to you, and God will be merciful to you, too. I'll see y'all in the skies."

Then nothing. Seconds passed as the tape hummed. A voice in the background: "He's dead." The call disconnected.

A few minutes later, Bonnie listened to the message. She went wild with grief.

It was a mean trick, intended, it seems, to inflict pain on his mother. David was very much alive.

Why did he do it? You could surmise that those years of getting stripes as a boy had left a layer of hate in him like bad groundwater. But it went deeper than that. For years, David displayed complicated and volatile feelings toward his own family. He constantly invited his aunts, uncles, mother, stepfather, and ex-girlfriends to come to Mount Carmel to stay. Every couple of years, he sought Sandy out in whichever little town she was now living in and begged her to come back. He and Steve researched her whereabouts obsessively in order to keep track of her.

David told them it was for their own good. Slaughter was coming and the only safe place was within the Davidians. But was it really? When his blood family, like his son Cyrus, was with him at Mount Carmel, his rage at them could become almost uncontrollable. Perhaps his true reason for summoning his kin to Mount Carmel, one that he was only half-aware of, was a kind of revenge.

The uninjured ATF agents gathered at a rallying point some distance from the compound. Supervisors came around, handing out boxes of ammo and fresh socks to replace ones that had gotten wet and muddy at the compound.

"We're going back," one of the supervisors told the agents.

Well, that's fucking crazy, Hustmyre thought. His shirt was still covered with Rob Williams's blood. But now they were going back?

Whatever, he thought. If we die, so be it. He started loading up his rifle magazine with fresh .223 rounds.

The decision was quickly reversed. They weren't going back to Mount Carmel. The exhausted agents boarded buses and were driven back to the Bellmead Civic Center. There they got into their cars and drove to one of the two hotels where the bureau had rooms reserved for them.

Hustmyre walked into his hotel, asked for the Johnson Family Reunion or whatever code name the ATF had booked him under. The front desk clerk said nothing. Everyone on the staff knew what was going on. The mood in the lobby was somber.

Hustmyre got his key and went to his room. He sat on the bed thinking about Todd, about how his best friend was dead. He couldn't fathom it.

Another agent called and said they were getting dinner. Hustmyre showered, put on his street clothes, and grabbed his gun. There was a rumor that the Branch Davidians were going to attack the hotel, so a bunch of the agents brought their sidearms along with them.

That afternoon, Michael Schroeder—the Davidian from Florida who was married to Kat Schroeder—was making his way back to the compound after the shootout, accompanied by two other men. He encountered a group of ATF agents and, according to the agents, raised a gun and fired at them. The agents returned fire and Schroeder was shot seven times and killed. The ATF later found a semiautomatic pistol on him.

The shooting added to the uncertainty hanging over Waco. Perhaps there were more Davidians with guns out there.

The local TV station, KWTX, had sent one of its cameramen, Val Lecour, to a local hospital to film the incoming casualties that morning. In the early hours, it was quiet. No ambulances had arrived. The staff didn't even know what was happening at Mount Carmel.

Every fifteen minutes, the newsroom called. "Are you ready? Film loaded? Get ready."

It took about three hours for the first ambulance to arrive. Its doors opened and agents began spilling out of the back. Some had head injuries, others had chunks of flesh missing from their legs or arms. One had a wound whose .50 caliber round had burned so hot that it had cauterized the flesh. A few agents were crying.

Lecour was scared to death—what had happened to all these people?—but he shot footage anyway. The feds at the hospital were on alert. They questioned Lecour. Why had he come to the hospital so early? How had he known there was going to be a shootout? Had someone told the Davidians what was going to happen?

We got a tip, Lecour said, which was true. But the agents didn't believe him. They refused to let him leave the hospital. They kept him there for four days. As if those bearded terrorists who had bombed New York had caught a flight to Waco.

The ambulances needed to be cleaned out before going back to Mount Carmel. One paramedic volunteered to get one ready. He went out to the vehicle and opened the doors. The entire back of the ambulance was scarlet. It looked like a bright red cloak had been thrown over the equipment, the floor, the stretchers. Blood dripped out of the compartment onto the corrugated steel bumper.

Four agents were dead, dozens were injured, some seriously. Six Davidians had been killed. It was something out of Indian days.

At Mount Carmel, David was lying on blankets in a hallway on the first floor, wounded by a bullet just above his groin. It was very quiet. He did more radio interviews. He spoke to those around him.

As night fell, he outlined a plan to his followers. He would get on a stretcher and the others would strap grenades to his body. Then they would carry him out, followed by the rest of the Davidians. When the stretcher reached the federal agents waiting outside, he would pull the pins on the grenade, killing himself and whatever ATF agents were in range.

It came time to say goodbye. A line of followers formed in front of David. The children came up to him and he kissed them.

Kat Schroeder was in line. When the person in front of her finished, Kat stepped toward David, who was lying on the bloodied sheet. He spotted her. "I love my rebellious ones the most," he said. She laughed, then kissed him.

When they'd all said their goodbyes, they started to pray in the hallway. It got super loud. Steve, who was upstairs talking to the FBI negotiators, came down and told them to quiet down.

Clive Doyle made his way down to the kitchen and started putting together brown-bag lunches for himself and his daughter Kathy. He was thinking that, once David died, the ATF would come back, kick them out of the house, and search it for evidence. He and Kathy would need to eat. When you have kids, you have to be practical.

The night wore on and the details of the suicide plan changed. Now David and one of the Mighty Men would go out and kill as many federal agents as possible with grenades, dying in the process. Those inside the building would wait for the ATF to storm the compound a second time, and then blow themselves up. In this scenario, no one was going to survive. Or as few as possible.

Some of the Davidians began making their own plans. Three of the Davidians, followers from the UK, were sitting in a group on the first floor. One called to another follower nearby: "Don't stay away from us . . . come and join us, that we all will go home to mother together." There was a feeling of fellowship in the big house. These were the people each Davidian was going to live with in eternity.

The women sat, holding hands. They prayed.

A male Davidian gave Kat Schroeder a grenade to blow up four or five of the women: Sheila Martin, Vanessa Henry, the daughter of the handyman from Old Trafford, England, and some others, along with Kat herself. Kat brought the grenade into a room where the others were sitting.

Kat was uncertain. Could she really pull the pin? Between the idea and the act there was a good wide gap of seeing yourself blown into smithereens.

"Kathy, you can do this," the other women told her.

"What if I can't?"

A solution presented itself. Someone said that those women who didn't die from the grenade shrapnel would be shot by the men. The men would comb through the victims and finish off anyone breathing.

Kat asked the guy who'd given her the grenades, if she couldn't pull the pin, would he kill her, along with the others? The guy said sure, if it came to that, he'd take care of her.

The women started praying. They were joyous. The Word was being fulfilled through them and with them.

But Kat still struggled with the idea of detonating the grenade. How could you even explain that to yourself? There was this T-shirt she'd seen once, and it came back to her now. "Everyone wants to go to heaven but nobody wants to die to get there," it said on it. Well, wasn't that the truth.

Many of the Davidians remained fully aligned with David's message, even after the traumatic day. There was no rebellion, no talk of renouncing the message. They'd trained for this kind of event for years now, and it seemed to be following a biblical track. David had been wounded in the side and the hand, as Jesus had been stabbed by the Roman soldier at Calvary in the side. He was thirty-three, the same age as Christ when he died. The signs were promising.

There was a delay. David was now going to make a tape for broadcast to the outside world. David saw a chance to reach thousands of listeners; his ego wouldn't allow him to turn that down. Once the tape was aired, the Davidians would leave.

Another wrinkle was added to the suicide plan: If David hadn't died by the time they were ready to leave, they would shoot and kill him. Then they'd carry him out on the stretcher. As they got close to the line of agents, they would raise their guns and fire. The feds would shoot back and kill them all.

The sound of prayer filled the room that contained the women. Still, nothing was happening. David hadn't initiated the suicide plan.

Kat changed gears and became a kind of quartermaster. She started issuing guns to the individual Davidians. She made sure everyone who needed a weapon had one. She issued them the correct ammunition. It felt good to be doing something instead of obsessing about that grenade.

Anyone who could comprehend David's teaching got a gun. The youngest was twelve.

The Davidians took the weapons and found spots in the compound to watch the terrain. The gaps blasted in the drywall by the ATF's gunfire served as lookout holes.

That night, David had a dream. It told him that the Davidians would not be shot by the Babylonians. Instead, they would perish in a great blaze. Their skin would burn away from their sinews and bones, and they would be transposed into new beings. Then their new life as one of the 144,000 soldiers of Christ would begin.

Part VI

MY STRANGE WORK

39

WASHINGTON

AT THE WHITE House, the early reports of the ATF's raid on Mount Carmel made it clear it had been a fiasco. Colonel Charlie Beckwith, former commander of the Army's Delta Force, later spoke to reporters: "If I had done an operation . . . and had no medical evacuation for an hour and 40 minutes, I would probably have been court-martialed. In an hour and a half, a man lays out there, he's gonna bleed to death."

"It's a disgrace to this country," Beckwith said.

President Clinton was very early in his first term. He'd been inaugurated on January 20, just over a month before. Waco was his first domestic crisis, and his administration scrambled to get their arms around the unfolding siege.

Clinton and his advisers debated pulling the ATF off the case and bringing in the FBI. A single adjective, "bungled," attached itself to news of the raid almost immediately. It was salt in the wound of the agents on the ground. The planning had been shit, the raid should have been aborted three or four different times, and they'd been sent, outgunned, into an ambush on open terrain, where they'd fought bravely. But people were calling them jackbooted thugs, Nazis, the whole deal. Incompetents.

Inside the ATF, there was rage at the Davidians, rage at their superiors, rage at the press. And grief for the dead.

There was no love lost between the ATF and the FBI. For many ATF agents, they were workhorses and the FBI were show horses. The ATF got into it with heroin dealers and gunrunners and nobody made movies about them.

Many ATF agents resented the G-men. They were publicity seekers, in their view, American golden boys. The ATF did the grunt work while the FBI, in their pressed white shirts and ties, took the credit.

The president decided to place the FBI in charge of the operation. He spoke with the FBI director, William Sessions, who had gone to Baylor University in Waco and knew the area well. They agreed on a strategy: negotiate, watch, and contain. Those were the bywords.

The crisis caught Sessions at a difficult time. He was under investigation for a series of ethical lapses, accused of claiming a false exemption on his taxes, and misusing FBI resources, including bureau cars that drove his wife to her manicure appointments. There was talk around Washington that his leadership of the bureau was endangered and that Clinton was already looking for his successor.

The word that they were being taken off the operation came down to the ATF agents that night. They grumbled and fumed. The attitude was "What, you don't think we're good enough to finish this thing?" The next day, March 1, at 4:45 p.m., operational control of the scene passed to the FBI.

Clinton's cabinet was still incomplete. The FBI fell under the purview of the Department of Justice and the attorney general. After his election the previous fall, Clinton had nominated two women to the post in succession, Zoë Baird and Kimba Wood. Both had run into trouble over their hiring of undocumented women as childcare providers and withdrew their names from consideration. The position of attorney general was the last unfilled slot in Clinton's cabinet, and now he had a crisis at the FBI.

Clinton had introduced his third candidate, Janet Reno, only seventeen days earlier. She was currently going through the confirmation process. But Reno immediately assumed unofficial responsibility for Waco.

Reno had made her name as the state attorney for Dade County (later Miami-Dade). She was tough, folksy, and approachable, listing her number in the Miami phone book and sometimes taking calls from citizens at two or three in the morning. One irate man called to complain about a neighbor's rooster, holding up the phone so Reno could hear the offending animal crowing before sunrise.

One of her passions was protecting children. She'd aggressively prosecuted child abusers using the "Miami Method," a technique for interviewing young children (including using closed-circuit televisions for their testimony) that she believed inflicted less trauma. She opened a full-time care facility to help minors who'd been abused. Her pioneering work attracted a great deal of positive press. Marian Wright Edelman, cofounder of the Children's Defense Fund, became a powerful supporter of Reno, as did Hillary Rodham Clinton.

The president's White House counsel, Bernard Nussbaum, spoke with Reno about the crisis. His advice was to be guided by the bureau. "They've been on the firing line there," he told her. "They know more what's happening . . . I have confidence that they'll give you disinterested advice."

The FBI protocol was for the special agent in charge (SAC) of the nearest field office, in this case Jeff Jamar out of San Antonio, to run the whole operation. It was a long-standing tradition, part of the bureau's culture. Jamar would confer with his bosses in Washington, but he was expected to devise a strategy and make the on-the-ground decisions.

The SACs were often called "little princes." They ran pretty much everything on scene. As one prosecutor put it, "The SAC ain't the Lord himself, but he's pretty dang close."

Jamar could be a daunting presence. He was well above six feet tall and had the build of a defensive lineman. The negotiator Byron Sage, who knew him well, called his style "management by intimidation."

SACS were trained in a wide variety of skills, but negotiation wasn't one of them. Many FBI negotiators found this frustrating, and had for years. They sometimes felt they arrived at a hostage situation and had to explain how negotiations worked in real time to an SAC who knew little or nothing about the process.

Dick Rogers was head of the FBI's Hostage Rescue Team (HRT). He was assigned as the tactical commander at Waco. Rogers came from the Army, where he'd served in an armored battalion. He was a spit-polished, ramrod-straight guy who wore BDUs, battle dress uniforms, camouflage outfits worn by the military. One FBI agent remarked you could just about cut your finger on the crease in Dick Rogers's pants.

Two years before, Rogers had played a lead role in the FBI's response to a prison riot in Talladega, Alabama. After talks failed, Rogers and his Hostage Rescue Team led an assault on the prison, freeing all the hostages. The impression within the FBI was that Rogers had succeeded where the negotiators had failed.

The next year, 1992, brought the eleven-day siege at Ruby Ridge, Idaho. The survivalist and ex–Green Beret Randy Weaver was being sought on firearms charges. When US marshals approached the cabin, they encountered Weaver and his fourteen-year-old son, Sammy, and a firefight erupted. One marshal and Sammy Weaver were killed.

Randy Weaver retreated to his rustic cabin, along with his wife, Vicki, his children, and a family friend. The Hostage Rescue Team was called in and an eleven-day siege ensued, during which an unarmed Vicki Weaver was shot and killed by an FBI sharpshooter.

Eventually, the negotiators, aided by the former Special Forces officer Bo Gritz, a former presidential candidate for the radical right Populist Party, deescalated the situation and ended the siege successfully. But the death of Vicki Weaver infuriated many, especially on the far right. Ruby Ridge became a flash point for neo-Nazi activists and other far-right extremists, who fumed at the government's perceived overreach and brutality. Though the story quickly faded in the national press, it percolated on the right for years afterward.

Even before President Clinton switched control of the scene to the FBI, the bureau's negotiators were rushing to Waco by car and plane. When they arrived at the TCTS facility, the former miliary airport the ATF had used as their headquarters, the agents quickly set up in the old barracks. They would rotate on and off the phones; four hours with the Davidians, then hours off to recuperate and recharge. There were female agents on the team, but only men would be allowed to conduct the negotiations. David's often overbearing and misogynistic relationship with women was one reason the FBI barred them from the talks.

The chaos of the shootout and the initial 911 calls from the compound had dissipated, but the situation inside the compound was still murky. There was little information on who David Koresh was, whether he was psychologically stable or not, and what he and his followers wanted. Was David holding his followers at gunpoint, or were the Davidians formed into a united front? Was David truly in control? Were there wounded? Were the Davidians planning to emerge from the compound, guns blazing, or were they in a defensive mindset? Nobody knew anything.

The first priority was to stabilize the situation, prevent further casualties, and work on getting the Davidians out of the compound. Thoughts of prosecuting the followers were secondary at this point. As soon as David and people were coaxed out of Mount Carmel and put into custody, the feds, along with the Texas Rangers, could go into the compound, confiscate the illegal guns, and start to gather evidence, which would eventually lead to charges in the deaths of the four federal agents.

A perimeter was set up around the enormous compound to make sure no Davidians escaped and no reinforcements were snuck in. Jeff Jamar and his team settled in about fifty feet down from the negotiators in another room down a long hallway. A third room housed FBI profilers, who listened in on the conversation, evaluating how the negotiators were doing and looking for clues to David's personality.

The negotiating team was led by Gary Noesner, the FBI's lead mediator. Byron Sage served as the day-shift manager. Eventually, fifty-two negotiators from seven law enforcement agencies—including local police, Texas Rangers, and state police—would work the case.

That Sunday, Noesner had been walking out of a hardware store in Virginia when he got the call. He headed to a nearby airport where the FBI kept its fleet of planes and landed in Waco at ten p.m. He arrived to learn that no gunfire had been traded in hours, that Koresh was talking, and that some Davidian children had already been released. He took those as optimistic signs.

Noesner called his approach "trickle flow gush," a term he made up on the spot. By slowly chipping away at David's authority, he felt they could get the Davidians out: a few at first, then more, then perhaps everyone. A steady diminishment of his power over the Davidians.

Noesner wanted to get across to Jamar that there wasn't going to be a grand solution here. He needed time. He used an analogy in talking to Jamar and the tactical guys: There's a train station with a lot of people standing on the platform. A train pulls in. The whistle blows, and the people start to get on. First a few, "trickle." Then more, "flow." Then everybody, "gush."

His question to his negotiators was "Will David wait to board the train or not?" The consensus was that he wouldn't wait. David wanted to keep the illusion of control. If he saw his followers starting to exit the compound, he'd be compelled to get at the front of the line, so it looked like he was driving events. Even if he wasn't controlling things, David would want to appear as if he was.

David was still sitting in the downstairs hallway, with a few blankets over him. He had a bedsheet tied around his midsection, covering the bullet wound. He was in surprisingly good spirits.

NEGOTIATOR: Your other wounded men, can you tell me anything about their condition?

DAVID: They're not as bad as I am, that's for sure. . . . They're bandaged up. They're up and around . . .

NEGOTIATOR: Yeah. Anything else hurting?

DAVID: Just my feelings.

Despite Byron's raised eyebrows over the pronunciation of his last name, David came across as pretty levelheaded early on. Even when he spoke about death and prison.

NEGOTIATOR: Are you in a comfortable position?

DAVID: . . . The only comfortable position right now I guess would be six feet under, huh?

NEGOTIATOR: No, buddy, hey, that's not, that's not it.

DAVID: Come on, it's a federal crime, I know the laws. I agree with the laws. I believe bad guys need to be dealt with.

There's too much bullshit in the world, okay? There's too many people . . . that hurt people for their own selfish gain, all right? . . . They need to be dealt with. That's what Rome—at least Rome got, got their crime rate way down. They crucified people; they made an example of them. . . .

David almost immediately started talking about another government raid on the compound:

DAVID: Don't worry about no bosses, like I say, if, if they're going to come here and shoot us all up, they're going to come and shoot us all—

NEGOTIATOR: I ain't going to let nobody shoot you up. I ain't going to let nobody—

DAVID: You're going to smoke bomb us or you're going to burn our . . . building down or whatever, you know?

The negotiator tried to deny it, take the temperature down. The FBI was focused on getting people out.

Just after midnight, two children emerged from the doors of the compound. Then at 8:22 a.m. on March 1, two more. One mother sent out her young daughter, named Joann, carrying a jewelry box with a necklace. Inside the box, there was a note from the mother to the girl's older sister, who lived in Hawaii. "By the time you see Joann," it read, "I'll be dead. Please take good care of her, she is your daughter now. I love the both of you much. Mom." The mother didn't clarify if she was considering suicide or if there were plans for mass death within the compound, but the FBI found the note concerning.

David eventually handed the phone off to Steve Schneider. The negotiators tried to be upbeat with him. It was all going to work out, they reassured him.

Steve was happy to hear it. He seemed eager to get this mess figured out. At times, he could sound like an overexcited Boy Scout. Not the type of person you'd expect, honestly. How had Steve gotten into this, the negotiator asked. They wanted to get to know Steve, show them they cared about who he was as a person.

STEVE: Well, it's in that if he has the truth because I want to live forever. Ever since I was a little child, . . . I've always like yourself looked up at the stars and wondered, why is this. Where are we going, how did we get here, what's this vast expanse about? . . .
Why is this earth a cemetery, everything dies here, plants, people, animals, 6000 years of woe and human history. We get a little bit

of pleasure but we're never satisfied and fulfilled and relatives can
be taken out of your life, friends, accidents. God, what's going
on? . . .

The negotiators quickly learned they had to watch what they said with
Steve. One negotiator told him there was a "cast of thousands" assem-
bling outside, hoping to see the matter resolved peacefully.

"In that cast of thousands, are there any angels out there?" Steve asked.
He was serious. If David's prophecy was correct, it meant they were in the
Fifth Seal. There should be angels. The negotiator said he sure hoped so.

As the days passed, Steve and David alternated on the phone, with
Steve becoming the main guy talking to the FBI on the Davidians' end.
David was wounded and in pain, so Steve stepped in as his intermediary.

When he was on the line, David was fond of giving Bible studies, which
the negotiators tried to stop in their tracks. Most times, he wore them
down and spoke on the Scriptures for as long as he could stay awake. In
their daily press conferences, the FBI began implying—sometimes stating it plainly—that David was a conman, an imposter who pretended
to be a man of faith. The negotiators knew that this was false. David
couldn't stop speaking about God.

But David was mercurial. His mood could easily turn.

DAVID: Now, the Fifth Seal, you know, in Isaiah 26, it says we have a
    strong city. Salvation will guard our plentiful walls and bulwarks. . . .
    It says trust in the Lord, for the Lord is everlasting strength. So
    bringeth down them that dwell on high . . .
NEGOTIATOR: David—
DAVID: I know it sounds like poetry to you, doesn't it?
NEGOTIATOR: No, listen, I just want to—
DAVID: You all are going to kill us.

David suggested that the American people wanted to see violence.
Demanded it, in fact.

DAVID: Well, the news wants something to happen. The news wants
    to see some firecrackers.

NEGOTIATOR: Well, why do people go to the Indianapolis 500?

DAVID: Why do they go see movies all the time?

NEGOTIATOR: Sure.

DAVID: *Terminator* and *Destroyer* and all that kind of stuff. They like it. They dig it.

NEGOTIATOR: Huh.

DAVID: This is the way; this is the way your country is.

Unlike Steve, David wasn't buying the happy-ending scenarios the FBI was pushing.

DAVID: Jim, I'm going to win, okay?

NEGOTIATOR: Yeah. We're all going to win.

DAVID: No, we're not all going to win.

A stumbling block emerged early on: Robert Rodriguez, the under-cover ATF agent. David wanted to talk to him. In fact, he seemed somewhat obsessed by the man.

"I really liked that guy," he said. "I've always loved law enforcement because you all risk your lives every day, you know . . . You know what one of the greatest pains there is, is when I look out a window and see those, those young men laying out there . . . and to think that if it'd been on a different situation, we could have been good friends."

The negotiators didn't want to put Rodriguez on the line. They wanted to look forward. Rodriguez was a reminder that four federal agents were lying in the morgue and some of the Davidians were looking at long prison sentences. They made excuses. Rodriguez was off duty, they said. He'd left Waco, had gone incommunicado. But David wouldn't let it go.

Here was a richly tangled knot for the FBI to pick at. Why was David doing this? Robert should have been the last person he wanted to talk to. The ATF agent had pretended to be David's friend while working to put him in prison. You might say that he'd betrayed David. And yet this seemed to attract David even more strongly.

It certainly was a puzzle. Was Robert just an extremely charismatic guy who'd bonded with David? Was David, who was clearly a narcissist, convinced that he was such a great and powerful prophet that he could convert even a federal agent who was trying to lock him away? Did that approach the root of it?

Or was this about David's past? The FBI hadn't yet had time to interview David's family, but once they did, they would have this to consider, too: Robert was an authority figure who'd tried to hurt David. Maybe it went right back to Roy Haldeman, his belligerent, dark-silenced stepfather. Maybe David was thinking of that story of Roy and Ed, the G-man who'd come into the Jade Lounge back in Houston. He and Roy had struck up a friendship. David loved that story. He would tell it later to the negotiators.

If Robert and David became friends, would it bring David closer to young Roy? Would it even make him Roy's equal? In this new version of the tale, he could inhabit Roy's role for as long as he and Robert were buddies. David was forever trying to get close to his stepfather, to prove his worthiness to the Sphinx. Maybe it was exactly by fucking over David that Robert Rodriguez attained this exalted stature in David's eyes.

David and the negotiators went back and forth about Robert. It would go on for days. Melissa Morrison, six years old, was supposed to leave the compound. Then David brought up his old friend.

DAVID: Well, Melissa will come out . . . once we get to talk to Robert, okay?

NEGOTIATOR: Well, let me talk to Melissa now. Let me see if we can work out this thing. . . . Give me something.

DAVID: I just did.

David handed the phone to Steve, so he could talk to Melissa. Steve narrated.

STEVE: He's asking a question; do you want to go? And she's saying, no. And then he asked her the question, would you go if it allows us to talk to Robert . . . ? And she shook her head yes.

It was something else. David was happy to put a six-year-old's life at some risk just to get on the phone with a guy he wanted to be pals with. Didn't bother him a bit.

The girl never did come out. Others did leave, however. Little Heather Jones, the daughter of the mailman David Jones, emerged. It was another trickle. Later, from the outside, Heather called in to say she was OK. Her father got on the phone while Koresh listened.

DAVID JONES: God promises to wipe away tears from all eyes but in the meantime, it's, it's, it's kind of tough, though, but God has many promises, Heather. And always, always remember that.

HEATHER: I went in that, that big truck and then I went in a car.

DAVID: Yeah.

HEATHER: And I got an apple.

DAVID: That's good. That's, that's good for you. You be a good girl. I'll see you, okay?

HEATHER: Daddy?

David Jones hung up or the phone cut off.

The FBI's Jamar prepared for the possibility of a long siege. Within days of assuming command, he began sending requests to the military for equipment. Calls went out to the Air Force, the United States Army Special Operations Command, and others. The list grew longer as the siege went on. A partial count: transport aircraft, helicopters, ammunition, surveillance "robots," top-secret Air Force jamming equipment to cut the Davidians off from CNN and other news channels, classified thermal imagers, classified ground sensing systems, classified remote observation cameras, mine detectors, searchlights, gas masks, night-vision goggles, concertina wire, tents, cots, diesel generators, medical equipment.

On the list were two Abrams M-1 tanks, fifty-five tons each and heavily armored. The FBI also brought in helicopters and a small fixed-wing aircraft called the Nightstalker, which could fly over the compound and shoot video with its FLIR, or forward-looking infrared camera, able to record thermal images.

They needed bodies, too. Eventually, 668 federal agents were called in to work the siege, along with six US Customs officers, fifteen US Army personnel, thirteen members of the Texas National Guard, thirty-one

Texas Rangers, a hundred thirty-one officers from the Texas Department of Public Safety, seventeen from the McLennan County Sheriff's Department, and eighteen Waco police, for a total of 899 people.

Ten soldiers from the Army's Special Forces were called in: seven technicians and three observers. The soldiers didn't take part in the negotiations or play any part in the tactical mission. They were there to observe how the FBI conducted a "barricaded hostage operation" with the equipment the Army provided. According to the Army, they were unarmed.

The Hostage Rescue Team was busy out on the land. They reinforced two sniper positions, Sierra One and Sierra Two, building up sandbags and metal plates to protect them, especially against the .50 caliber gun. Eventually, the HRT brought up seismic devices, borrowed from the US Special Operations Command, and set them up in front of the positions. The thinking was: If the Davidians sneak out and somehow evade detection, the sensors will go off and alert the snipers.

But the devices proved to be a pain in the ass. Deer and other animals kept setting them off. Eventually, they were removed.

The Davidians watched the tactical guys through the windows. One of the things the negotiators had told David and Steve was that the FBI would keep its distance. It was going to respect the Davidians' property and keep a low profile. But here were these guys in camo, armed to the teeth, crawling around the property and building fortified positions.

What was going on, Steve wanted to know.

Noesner and his team were asking the same question. What was HRT doing? The negotiators had promised the Davidians one thing, but HRT went and did the opposite.

Noesner wasn't a fan of the HRT leader Dick Rogers. Thought he was too rigid and, weirdly, too emotional. Once Rogers got an idea in his head, he never swerved from it. In Noesner's experience, shit happened during negotiations. You had to be pliant, roll with it. But that wasn't Rogers's style.

Rogers should have been removed from his position after Ruby Ridge, in Noesner's view. But it hadn't happened. The FBI decided to protect its own. It didn't want to admit its own failures at Ruby Ridge, so it circled the wagons around the guy responsible.

Noesner feared that Rogers would see Waco as another Talladega prison riot. It wasn't, in Noesner's opinion. It was Ruby Ridge times a hundred.

The full harvest of that tension was still in the future, however. On March 1, the first real good news arrived. Steve announced that if David could make a taped Bible study that would be played on a national radio station, they would all come out. The standoff would be over.

The negotiators were thrilled. Noesner talked to Jamar about broadcasting the tape.

"What are we getting for it?" Jamar asked.

"Boss, you're asking the wrong question," Noesner said.

"Well, what's the right question?"

"The right question is what do we lose? I don't think we lose a thing. I can't guarantee he'll come out and do what he says, but I don't see where we lose anything by making the effort."

Jamar signed on. The good vibes filtered through the barracks at TSTC, where the negotiators and the commanders were holed up. This thing might be over before it really started.

While they waited for the details to get nailed down, Steve asked: Could David get on national TV? Maybe *Nightline*, with Ted Koppel? The FBI said they'd look into it, but they wanted to focus on the radio thing. After the tape was broadcast, the Davidians were coming out. That's all they wanted.

The agreement firmed up. David would make a tape and the influential Christian Broadcasting Network, founded by the famous evangelist Pat Robertson three decades before and which reached a national audience, would play it. Then the Davidians would leave Mount Carmel. The FBI confirmed and reconfirmed. It was quid pro quo.

David said fine. The next morning, March 2, two more children came out. That totaled sixteen people that had left Mount Carmel.

The fifty-eight-minute tape played on CBN. David had hurried to complete the teaching and, by general consensus, it was a mishmash that didn't represent his best work. David rambled about the Fifth Seal and the Lamb of God and even his followers acknowledged the tape lacked his usual fire.

David could hardly be surprised. His words didn't bite with the same force unless you were right there with him. It was the only way you could get the full glow. And his gunshot wound drained some of the vitality from his voice.

Afterward, Steve kept the line open with the FBI. The negotiators wanted to know when the Davidians were coming out. What was happening in there?

Hours slipped by. The negotiators were feeling nervous. They got on Steve about it.

NEGOTIATOR: I've got commanders who do not trust me. I said, look, this is going to happen. And they're starting to doubt me . . .

STEVE: Well, as far as I'm concerned, between you and I, the guy is inspired either of Christ, either of God, or of Satan. There's no in-between. I mean, when three engineers came on and he's showing them how the pyramids were made, how it is that they sit on something as soft as sand, what a terrible foundation when the greatest engineers in the world can't go much higher than the Sears Tower because they haven't figured out a stronger foundation . . .

What is this shit, the negotiators wondered.

Steve went to see David down the hall. David was sleeping. Steve lay down next to him to catch some rest.

40

IRRECONCILABLE

THE NEXT DAY, Steve got back on the phone with the FBI. God had spoken to David and told him to wait. They weren't coming out. The negotiators were furious. David had made a promise and now he'd broken it. He'd double-crossed them, made them look like fools.

Steve apologized. "I'll tell you the truth," he said. "Humanly, I'm embarrassed."

Humanly? Clearly, there was a way in which Steve wasn't embarrassed, and that was theologically. If God told David to stay, there was no reason to feel bad about it. Steve confirmed this. The negotiators had their bosses and David had his.

Noesner was angry, but not surprised. People he negotiated with lied, constantly. It came with the territory. What he wasn't looking forward to was walking down the hall and telling Jeff Jamar. But he went anyway. Rogers was there when he walked in.

Noesner explained what had happened, and the other two went berserk. It was visceral; they took David's backtracking as a personal affront. "We are gonna show him," Rogers shouted.

Noesner tried to calm the two men. He had a saying, "Don't get mad, get your way." They should use the incident as a cudgel to beat David and Steve over the head, he suggested. *I went out on a limb for you, I convinced my boss to do this and that. Now you owe me.* The negotiators could lay a huge guilt trip on the Davidians and maybe get some kids out.

Jamar and Rogers said no. They were going to make the Davidians pay. Noesner went back down the hall, discouraged.

The negotiators hammered away at Steve and David. We thought we were dealing with men of their word, they said. When are you coming out?

Steve snapped. "And what about this whole thing about lying and deceiving and all the rest? . . . To tell you the truth, I see your agency and other agencies like yours as Big Brother. I really do . . ."

He talked about what the FBI had been doing.

STEVE: They've been creeping up closer and closer. . . . You're not abiding by the rules. It's like an Indian contract.

The negotiators demanded to speak to David. When he got on the line, he was unrepentant.

NEGOTIATOR: Can we talk about the arrangements?
DAVID: Can we talk about God?

David started going into the biblical book of Nahum. In it were prophecies about the Babylonians and their army. David was seeing them come true around him at Mount Carmel. The armored vehicles the FBI had brought in were, in reality, the chariots described in the Scriptures. He recited some of the Nahum story from memory.

DAVID: "The shield of the mighty men is made red, the valiant men are in scarlet; the chariots shall be with flaming torches." I mean, you know, bang, bang, bang . . . "The fir trees be . . . terribly shaken." I mean, you know, don't you think a tank can make a big boom?

The negotiators expressed their doubts. The armored vehicles didn't have muzzles.

DAVID: What are those things sticking out the front, Jim? Are you sure you're getting complete communication with these guys?

David insisted the Bradley vehicles had gun barrels; the negotiators said no. They went back and forth. "It's my understanding . . . that there are no barrels on the Bradleys," the negotiator said.

"You are full of shit!" David screamed. "S-H-I-T, shit!"

The talks went on for hours, deep into the night. David got tired of talking about Nahum and started on about his childhood, his wanderings in search of God.

DAVID: I'm a transgressor like Adam. Just because the spirit of truth can be run within my perceptions, into my veins, does not mean that my humanity is any different than anybody else's . . . On the contrary, I have fear, I have hunger, I have anxiety, I have tears, I have stress . . .

NEGOTIATOR: Do you have confusion?

DAVID: No.

NEGOTIATOR: No?

DAVID: No, I do not.

Only days into the siege, Noesner and the other negotiators increasingly felt they were caught between two irreconcilable forces: the Davidians and the FBI tactical commanders. Noesner met with Rogers, sometimes several times a day, to update him on the talks with the Davidians and to talk tactics. There was an immediate tension. Noesner would make a suggestion to calm or coax the Davidians. Rogers would deny it. Noesner would then walk back to his team room and tell the guy, "It's a no."

After a while, Noesner had a thought. Jamar and Rogers were turning down so many of his ideas that the other guys must be questioning how good a negotiator Noesner actually was. His suggestions were clearly sensible, and yet he was unable to get any of them acted on. "They're probably saying, 'Why the hell isn't Gary able to convince the boss?'" Noesner thought to himself. It was embarrassing.

Noesner's basic point was that they had to give something to get something. Reciprocity was the most basic concept in negotiations. They had to make Koresh feel he was being listened to and they had to avoid needless provocations.

Think about Pavlov's dog, he told Rogers. If you train the dog to bring you your newspaper and you give him a treat when he does it, he'll be back tomorrow with a fresh edition. He'll do what you want him to do. But if he comes walking toward you with the newspaper in his mouth and you pick up your boot and kick him in the nuts, he won't. That's not how motivation worked.

Dick Rogers was of a very different mindset. He resented what he saw as Noesner's attempt to coddle the cult leader. As he saw it, the negotiator was rewarding Koresh instead of applying pressure. He wanted the Davidians uncomfortable, which would spur the followers to leave the compound.

Rogers also decided early on that his men in the Hostage Rescue Team wouldn't be kept informed about what was happening in the negotiations. He didn't think it was any of their business. His guys were supposed to watch the compound and prepare for anyone coming out with hostile intentions.

Byron Sage was angry about it. The HRT guys were freezing to death in a ditch, imagining that the negotiators were warm and cozy back at their barracks, drinking hot chocolate or whatever. Having a fine old time chatting away with their buddy David Koresh. He made a point of going out and talking to the tactical guys. He could feel something happening. *Sage and the others are a bunch of weak sisters* was the vibe he was getting.

For their part, many of the HRT guys were not big fans of Noesner and his ilk. Some guys were content to be out in the field as opposed to twiddling their thumbs back at Quantico. But there were others who thought the negotiators were babying the Davidians.

One issue was the .50 caliber Barrett gun. It was a major concern; a .50 caliber bullet would go right through the armor the HRT guys wore. So they wanted eyes on that gun at all times.

About a week into the siege, the HRT guys spotted the .50 cal in one of the towers on the fourth floor. They called it in. But then one of the negotiators told the Davidians, hey, we know where the .50 cal is. So what did the Davidians do? Moved it somewhere else.

That rubbed the HRT guys raw. The negotiators had blown it. Now the gun was hidden somewhere and they were screwed.

That's how the HRT guys heard it. What actually happened was quite different.

Hours before the gun was removed, the negotiators were sitting in their command room when the door burst open. It was Rogers and Jamar. The negotiators had pinned a schematic of the compound to the wall. Rogers went up to the map and put his finger on the northwest tower. He hit it so hard he nearly put his finger through the thing.

"There's a fucking .50 caliber Barrett right here," he said. "And it's pointed at Sierra Two." A Barrett was a sniper rifle and Sierra Two was the main tactical position. "Get on the phone and get that thing out of there."

So that's what the negotiators did. On Rogers's express orders. But word hadn't gotten down to the guys lying in the mud that Rogers had ordered the sniper gun removed. He never briefed the HRT guys about it. So naturally they blamed the assholes talking to Koresh.

The negotiators wanted to stretch things out, wear down the Davidians mentally and emotionally. They were trying to form a bond with David, get to a level of trust and empathy where they might say, "Hey, let me offer you an idea of how this could work out better for you." But the HRT knew the longer you waited, the more Koresh could make plans. Harden his positions, move his guns around to optimal spots. If the HRT had to go in, that meant it was going to be tougher. More time, potentially more dead agents.

A hostage situation often brings out the latent tension between negotiators and tactical leaders, and Noesner and Sage had experienced similar conflicts on other cases. But Waco brought with it unique stressors: the four dead federal agents, the 24/7 media coverage, and David's changeable nature and his narcissism, all of which contributed to an atmosphere where trust quickly eroded. The break between the two teams would never be repaired. And its full cost would take weeks to reveal itself.

41

DOUBLE-MINDED

AS THE SIEGE neared the end of its first week, Jamar and the negotiators were able to agree on one tactic: building trust with David. They decided to send in a video camera so the Davidians could make tapes of themselves. The videos that would emerge might also give the FBI clues about the internal dynamics among the Davidians and the physical conditions inside.

On March 4, an agent approached the compound with the camera in hand; he left it near the front door. A Davidian soon emerged, grabbed it, and carried it inside. With the camera, the agents sent in their own home movies, showing the negotiators talking about themselves and their families. They wanted David to be able to put faces to names, hoping it would deepen his connection to the men he was talking to.

The video seemed to endear the negotiators to David. Like he had with the sheriff and Robert Rodriguez and many others, David fantasized about hanging out with the FBI guys, being pals. David always had one eye on alternate lives he'd never got to lead.

DAVID: I mean, if, if, like, me and you had not met like this way—
NEGOTIATOR: Um-hum.
DAVID: You know, we could have been out fishing or something. And

I could have been there and I could have been sitting there fishing and you could have said, you know, "How you doing?"

"How you doing?"

"You know, what do you do?"

"Well, I'm a musician . . . What do you do?"

"Well, I'm, I'm an FBI agent."

"Oh, really, you know. Glad to meet you. Boy, I bet you got a real hard job, you know." And then you'd end up being surprised to find out I'm involved in something like this later on.

It wasn't unusual for David to tell one of his favorite negotiators that he loved them. They responded in kind.

The men bonded over jokes. At one point, David asked for his followers not to be put in prison with any big dudes.

NEGOTIATOR: (laughs)
DAVID: That'll poke us in the rear.
NEGOTIATOR: Well, see, see—
DAVID: It's against our religion.

The men started joshing with David about a possible movie after Waco was all over. Who would play whom?

DAVID: Right. Steve, what was that actor's name. Mel what?
STEVE: Mel Gibson.
DAVID: Mel Gibson. I want Mel Gibson to play my part, huh?
NEGOTIATOR: You've got a good sense of humor, huh?
DAVID: Well, he's, he's—
NEGOTIATOR: He's a piece of work.
DAVID: He's crazy, isn't he?

When David wasn't on the line, the negotiators kidded Steve about the prophet's powers. As often as not, the jokes sailed past him. One time they were talking about David's ability to see the future.

NEGOTIATOR: I'd like to have him figure out when the next hurri-
cane's blowing through, huh?
STEVE: Well, yeah . . . He did tell us about the Gulf War before it came
about.

But just as quickly, the good vibes would evaporate and Steve and
David would rail about the tactical teams zooming around the property
in their armored vehicles. They were crushing cars, coming close to the
compound.

This was mostly true. The HRT had flattened some vehicles and they
did drive their Bradleys up and down in front of the compound. The
moves were meant to intimidate and to clear the property of obstacles
and potential Davidian positions, should they stage a breakout.

The men bickered about it like old husbands and wives:

STEVE: Are you listening to me?
NEGOTIATOR: I am. You told me yesterday you weren't going to yell.

Small annoyances festered. David had requested milk for the children
inside; he'd even sent one of the Davidians out with an envelope containing $1,000 to pay for it. The follower left the money near the front
door and an agent retrieved it. But the FBI wanted a couple of kids to be
released before they sent in the milk. An even swap. David said no deal.

David felt the FBI was messing with his manhood. The destruction of
the cars in the yard showed the FBI's contempt for him. Not to mention
the HRT guys that David was convinced were giving the Davidians the
finger and even pulling down their pants to moon the compound. HRT
operators vigorously denied any such things ever happened, but David
was convinced he was being disrespected.

DAVID: Let me explain something to you. You are taking me as a fool.
NEGOTIATOR: Absolutely untrue.

"Bringing these tanks and stuff around here," David said at another point.
"I'll tell you what, being an American first, I'm the kind of guy that I'll stand
in front of a tank. You can run over me but I'll be biting on the tracks."

He had an idea how the government could make it up to him. "Let's respect this . . . seventy-seven acres, let's respect this in this nation as Europe respects [the] Vatican, okay?" Many of the negotiators happened to be Catholic. What they thought of David's demand to be recognized as equivalent to the Holy See went unrecorded.

The FBI tried to sweeten David up. A negotiator explained why the tactical guys were out there zooming around in the Bradleys.

> NEGOTIATOR: You and I both know . . . that sometimes tactical people, you know, they, they like to put on their gear, they like to jump out of helicopters and they like to do those kinds of things, they like to drive around those little tanks . . . You know, they're young, they're not [as] mature . . . as you and I are perhaps . . .
>
> Some of these folks driving those tanks, you know, this may be the only opportunity they ever have to drive one of those Bradleys, and boy, I want to get that Bradley up and down the road and, you know, they, they get, they get impatient, they get, they get excited. "Hey here's my chance, let me push this vehicle, let's, let's see what this baby will do!"

David didn't buy a word of it.

On March 6, Steve's usually cheery voice turned macabre.

> STEVE: Listen, listen—if you ever wanted—if you ever wanted to use snipers or whatever else, you know, you go ahead and you do what you feel you've got to do.

The negotiators told him, no, they weren't going to kill the Davidians at his invitation. But Steve returned to the idea again and again.

> STEVE: Let me tell you, between you and me, I like it that you're bringing in the tanks and you're digging the ditches and, and there's more

armaments and so forth. I'm hoping that they'll bring in Apache helicopters and they'll bring in a lot more. I—

NEGOTIATOR: Why? Why, why would you want to see more of that stuff?

STEVE: Well, because I believe in the Bible and it's . . . a revelation, a fulfillment of the Book of Nahum.

On rare occasions, Steve could be as twitchy as David. He alternated between pleading patience—his usual stance toward the FBI—and a pressing, even wild, urgency. In the latter mood, he often encouraged the agents to attack the compound. Steve seemed tired of life. He wanted an answer, either way.

But Steve and David were double-minded, just like David Bunds had been years before. Despite asking for an FBI attack, when the Abrams tanks, the biggest and most powerful models in the American armory, finally arrived in Waco around March 9, the two freaked out. Steve called the negotiators "damn belligerent bullies . . . with a double tongue." The FBI guys tried to calm him down.

NEGOTIATOR: Have David talk to me, and—

STEVE: Did you hear what, no, no, Dick, did you hear what I said to you?

NEGOTIATOR: Steve, what did, yesterday you said you weren't going to yell—

STEVE: I'm going to put the phone down, we'll pull the plug, you won't talk to anybody.

It went on and on. By now, each side had now built up enough resentments to fuel long, punchy dialogues that doubled back and doubled back some more before petering out in bleak exhaustion. Steve and David joked that there was a factory somewhere in the country churning out FBI negotiators. They all sounded the same, they were all named John, they were all full of deceit. "Every one of them sounds like they came off the same cookie sheet," David told one of the negotiators. "There's not a genuine ounce of blood in these men." It was like talking to an IBM computer.

Steve was exasperated by this, but for David it went deeper. He felt like he was back in Garland, Texas, dealing with Roy Haldeman.

What had begun as a bloody, badly planned raid had turned into a waiting game whose momentum was hard to gauge. The FBI brought in profilers and psychologists to try and analyze David. Two experts from the behavioral science division contributed one of the first evaluations.

The memo's lead author was Peter A. Smerick, an FBI criminal profiler and forensic scientist. He concluded that, if the FBI assaulted the compound, there was a high probability David would kill himself: "When the Davidians sensed the FBI was closing in on the compound or performing some tactical maneuver, Koresh's prophecy would be confirmed . . . Do the OPPOSITE of what he is expecting . . . consider moving back . . . Attacking the compound could result in a tremendous loss of life."

The HRT did not move back. And in an administrative notebook kept by the HRT, agents mocked Smerick's analysis. "Psychological profile of an [expletive] by jerks," wrote one unidentified contributor.

Smerick felt pressure to alter his findings. He eventually wrote an "acquiescent" final report that deleted his recommendations to ease pressure on the Davidians. Instead, prompted by his FBI supervisor in Washington, he skewed more toward the tactical approach. On March 17, the profiler left Waco "in frustration." He later said that the "traditional independent process of FBI criminal analysis . . . was compromised at Waco."

Outside experts were brought in. They often disagreed on the way forward. Their reports saw David as too narcissistic to be a high suicide risk.

"We felt this was an individual who was extraordinarily vain and very fearful of physical injury," said one consultant, Dr. Murray S. Miron, a psychology professor at Syracuse University. "It appeared all of his actions were defensively aggressive."

This analysis got a boost from the negotiations. David did talk about the End Times and judgment and death, but at other times, he focused on what he was going to do when he got out of Mount Carmel. He wondered what the jail would be like, about food he would eat, and especially about spreading his message far and wide. A man who's planning suicide, the experts reasoned, wouldn't be thinking about book deals and even movie contracts. One bureau official told reporters that the time he felt the most hopeful during the entire siege was when David said he was going to sell his memoir to the highest bidder. He must be coming out, the official thought.

But no consensus emerged. If one analyst saw a sliver of light, the next one snuffed it out. The bureau turned to the highly experienced Dr. Park Dietz, who'd examined John Hinckley Jr. after his assassination attempt on Ronald Reagan and declared him sane enough to stand trial. He'd done the same for the Milwaukee serial killer Jeffrey Dahmer. Dietz turned in a written evaluation: David would not leave Mount Carmel, he predicted, and would not permit anyone close to him, including the children he'd fathered, to leave, either.

Sometime around March 6, Gary Coker, the Waco lawyer who'd defended David and the Mighty Men in the 1988 trial, got a call from FBI Director Sessions. Coker had been a Sunday School student of Sessions's back when the FBI director was living in Waco.

Sessions told the lawyer this was an unofficial call; he hadn't told anyone at the agency about it. He was calling, he said, in search of "the key to Koresh."

They talked about David. Coker told the director that Koresh wasn't some religious ascetic; he was a man of the world who loved fast cars and high-end guitars. David had grown up in a broken home; he was a narcissist who needed "strong, strong control." Coker was of the opinion that the FBI was coming on too hard. The Branch Davidians were regular folks who had some unusual views on religion, and the FBI was treating them like they were John Dillinger's gang.

Near the end of the conversation, Coker said he was willing to talk to Koresh. He said, "Why don't you come down here, and maybe we can get Judge Logue," a local magistrate, "to come with us and we'll walk in and talk to Vernon Howell." Sessions said, let me see what I can do.

Five minutes after Coker had hung up with Sessions, the phone rang again. It was Bob Ricks, the FBI's main spokesman at Waco. He and Coker had both gone to Baylor Law School years before, but this wasn't a friendly call. Ricks was worked up.

"I'm a lawyer and you don't have a right to go in there," Ricks said, talking about Mount Carmel.

Coker started talking about the Davidians' rights.

"They don't have any rights!" Ricks half-shouted.

"They do have rights."

"If you say that one more time, I'm going to hang up."

"But Bob," Coker replied, "you called me."

Coker waited for Sessions to get back to him, but it never happened. The lawyer took it as a sign that the FBI director didn't have the juice to get him into the compound.

That weekend, the original ATF raid was being hashed over in the media. The ATF director, Stephen Higgins, went on *Meet the Press* and claimed the Davidians hadn't known the raid was coming. "This plan was based on the element of surprise," he said. "We would not send our agents into a situation where we didn't think we had the element of surprise."

It was untrue.

Others in the ATF repeated the mistruth. Chuck Sarabyn, the ATF commander informed by Robert Rodriguez that Koresh knew they were coming, denied that the agent ever gave him that information. ATF administrators backed both of them. Rodriguez, who felt intense guilt for how the raid had turned out, believed he was being made the scapegoat. At work, he felt like he was being shunned. Everybody avoided him except his fellow agents.

ATF administrators ordered all agents not to speak to the press about the initial raid. Anyone who did would be fired from their jobs.

The main target in the week after the operation, however, was the press. The day after the raid, the KWTX reporter John McLemore had gotten a call at the station. It was Stephen Higgins, the head of the ATF. McLemore braced for a tirade; he thought Higgins was going to rip him for shooting footage of agents wounded during the operation. Instead, Higgins said, "John, I want to thank you for everything you did, for your bravery." McLemore had helped get three wounded agents away from the compound and to a medical triage site. All three survived.

But the day after the phone call from Higgins, Kathy Fair, a journalist from the *Houston Chronicle*, went on *Nightline*, a popular late-night news show on ABC. People within the ATF were telling her that "reporters for, I believe, the TV station, allegedly were hiding in the trees when federal agents arrived." Her ATF sources "have told me they think they were set up by at least one reporter" who had "tipped off the sect." It was just as hollow as Higgins's assertion—the cameraman Jim Peeler had unknowingly discussed the impending raid with one of the Branch Davidians the morning it launched, but no one had "tipped off" the followers. Still, the accusation stuck.

People began calling in to KWTX, wanting to know why McLemore had snitched to the Davidians. He noticed people in Waco were treating him differently. His wife, who worked as a receptionist at a local bank, was harassed by co-workers wanting to know if her husband had alerted the Davidians and got those feds killed.

THE TRILATERAL COMMISSION

EIGHT DAYS INTO the standoff, David was feeling irritable. He treated FBI negotiators to long, rambling monologues on theology, which they were thoroughly sick of by now. In certain moments, he sounded unstable, manic even.

"It's time," he told the negotiators. "It's time for men to learn how to fear God. . . . You see, me, I'm poor and I'm weak and I'm humble and I'm just a poor cult leader out here in the middle of Waco, Texas. Do you know what I mean? And I ain't hurting nobody. I never have hurt anybody.

"Yes, I have some things maybe I shouldn't have. But, of course, remember, on the other hand, I may be kind of crazy. I might be a great politician. I might be a king. I mean, hey, if the Vatican has its own little country, can't I have my own little country? . . . I'll even pay taxes. Just please let me have my little country. May be too much, though. Well, please. I may be insane. Help me, help me . . . Waaaaah."

The FBI tried to smooth over the small problems. They finally sent milk in for the kids, six gallons of it. The cartons had wafer-thin listening devices inserted in the cartons. Eventually, the bureau would get eleven of these bugs into the building.

One device ended up in the garbage pile, so all the agents listening on the other end heard was the Davidians dumping their MRE containers. But others made it into the kitchen and other parts of the compound where the followers gathered, chatting.

When the agents listened to the "bug tapes," the first surprise was the tone of what they heard. The Davidians weren't freaked out. Not at all. People were going about their days, calm and orderly. It sounded like a Christian retreat in Indiana or something.

David, surprisingly, seemed much calmer and more coherent than he sometimes did on the negotiation line. He was very much in control. The fact that no one inside the compound was questioning his logic clearly contributed to this. His followers obeyed unquestioningly, while the FBI pushed and prodded, which unsettled David.

The FBI was used to people in hostage situations showing signs of stress over time. It was a tried-and-true strategy: wait them out, wear them down. But, with his followers, David seemed to be the master of his emotions. Which could be good and bad. A leader losing control might hemorrhage followers, which was what the bureau wanted. Or he might dream up something drastic.

David did seem to enjoy himself now and then. He teased the agents. He'd perch his butt on a window ledge on the second floor and eat some ramen, in full view of the snipers that circled the property. Maybe light up one of his Marlboro Lights afterward. He also seemed to be making sure the FBI snipers could see his wounds.

Then in the evenings, he'd pull out his guitar and an amp and play for the agents. It was mostly rock riffs. Ted Nugent, Steve Vai, you name it. A lot of the FBI guys thought he was pretty good. The Davidians seemed pretty free and easy, too. Some agents saw members of the group giving them the finger or waving their guns at them.

One idea the FBI commanders had was to slowly dismantle the compound, room by room, giving the Davidians nowhere to go but out. But after a few forays in which FBI vehicles shoved aside some obstacles on the property and approached the building, they saw Davidians in the windows, holding up small children. The implication was clear, at least to the agents. If you wreck the building, you will hurt or kill these children. The FBI recounted the story at a press conference. Some agents started calling the Davidian boys and girls "Kevlar kids."

The Davidians angrily disputed it ever happened. David Thibodeau, one of David's drummers, remembered playing cards with two young boys, Joseph and Isaiah. Something caught their eyes in the window. It was the FBI driving tanks around the compound. Thibodeau didn't know what to tell the kids. What could you say, really? Finally, he settled on, "Yeah, that's something you don't see every day."

When the tanks started crushing cars and approaching the house, Thibodeau and the kids went right up to the windows and watched. "You're running over someone's car in a tank," Thibodeau said later. "You don't think a kid's going to be interested in seeing that happen? I was interested in seeing that happen."

He believed that was what the FBI claimed as the Kevlar kids incident. More of the government's twisted words.

In its press conferences, the FBI often referred to the children as "hostages" of Koresh. Slowly, both the bureau and the press would come to see the adult Davidians less as victims of David's mind control and more as enthusiastic supporters of his violent ways, but the bureau consistently spoke of the children as innocents. What the FBI didn't tell the press, however, is that they believed, in the event of an assault on the compound, some of the children would become combatants. They thought there was a real chance that, if the agents went into the building, the kids would pick up guns and fire on them.

As the siege wore on, FBI supervisors began to worry about attrition. They'd called on the HRT, a tier-one counterterrorism unit, the best in the nation, equivalent to a domestic SEAL Team Six, to contain the Davidians and—possibly—to prepare for an assault on the compound. But day after day, their highly trained operatives were out in the fields, fighting cold and boredom, wondering what they were doing in Central Texas. Holding a perimeter was something any decent SWAT team from St. Louis or Buffalo could have done. One agent compared it to taking Secretariat, the prize-winning racehorse, and hitching him up to a plow. It wasn't what the animal was bred to do.

The operatives' skills were perishable. They had to train daily to stay sharp. But instead, they were listening to David Koresh shred on the guitar.

The question came up: Should they just shoot the guy? HRT snipers were trained to hit an aspirin at two hundred yards; picking off an adult male would have been a walk in the park. Morally, the number of guys who'd have a problem pulling the trigger was close to nil.

It was a short debate. Killing Koresh would set a horrible precedent for the bureau, the higher-ups decided. They couldn't presume to judge his guilt or innocence. They talked the idea over and dismissed it almost immediately.

The same conversation was taking place in Washington. Mike Langan, the Justice official who'd originally argued against the ATF's handling of the raid, was sitting in a meeting with Janet Reno. They were listening to an FBI guy explain the situation. "Well, why didn't you shoot him?" one of Reno's advisers asked.

It would have solved everything, Langan admitted. But the blowback would have been monumental. The idea was quickly rejected.

In past missions, the option of last resort was simply to storm the building. The HRT was well-trained to carry out such operations. But in Waco, it was a nonstarter. The Davidians had shown once that they were proficient with their high-caliber weapons and the FBI was not going to test them again. It was the first time in his career that Byron Sage could remember the bureau refusing to send its agents in, simply because it was too dangerous.

Still, the HRT was frustrated with the slow pace of the people coming out. The trickle Noesner had promised had, in their view, failed to turn into a flow. Someone came up with the idea of blowing out the electricity in the compound by sending a powerful surge through the lines and burning out the circuits. The idea was to increase the discomfort the Davidians were forced to live with and to chip away at their will to resist. If the conditions inside the compound became grim enough, the thinking went, more and more followers would leave. The bureau also wanted to disrupt the Davidians ability to communicate, and to also put any televisions and radios out of commission.

But the building was poorly constructed. Who knew how good the wiring was? The bureau might spike the electricity and burn the place down. Jamar shelved the idea.

But on March 9 he decided to try a temporary outage. At 2:30 that morning, Jamar approved Dick Rogers's request to cut off the power. The lights went out inside Mount Carmel.

Jamar never told the negotiators about the cut-off. Noesner and the others were caught off guard. The shock outweighed the anger, at first. One of the maxims drilled into FBI agents was that the bureau always presents a united front to the world. If the tactical team had a suggestion, it was put in front of the negotiating team, so they could approve it or fight it. And vice versa. Even if one side won an argument and proceeded with an action, the other side still knew what was going to happen. You never blindsided your fellow agents.

And yet it had just happened. The HRT had made the negotiators look like assholes.

Noesner appealed to Jamar to reverse the decision. Around 9:30 a.m. the power was switched back on. But the acrimony lingered.

Around this time, Jamar went out to have a look at the Abrams tanks that had arrived in Waco. When he came back to the command center, he strolled down the hall to the negotiators' room, something he rarely did. Noesner was sitting around with four or five guys, taking a break from the talks. He looked up as Jamar walked in.

The guy was stoked. He started talking about the Abrams. How many gallons of fuel it could carry, how fast it could go, how many people it could fit, and how much ammo was on board: fifty-five rounds of 105mm shells! The thing was a technological wonder. Jamar couldn't stop talking about it.

He went over to a blueprint of Mount Carmel that was hung on the wall. "That tank," Jamar said, pointing to the blueprint, "could start from this end of the building"—he jabbed one side of the blueprint—"and go through it to this end." He dragged his finger along the schematic, mimicking the progress of the Abrams through drywall and lumber, the bedrooms and kitchen. "Without even stopping." It could blow through that sucker like a cardboard box.

Maybe Jamar just liked tanks. He certainly wasn't proposing the Abrams plow through the compound, mashing bodies as it went. But the image struck the negotiators as unseemly somehow.

One of them spoke up. "Why the hell would you do that?" he said.

Jamar's face went deep red. He turned and walked out of the room.

"See?" Noesner said to the other guys. "*You* just have to negotiate with David Koresh."

As for the negotiator who asked why you'd want to drive a tank through Mount Carmel, Jamar ordered him off the case. He was out of there the next day.

The negotiators tried a new gambit in hopes of turning the trickle into a flow: put the Davidians in touch with their families. They passed on appeals to leave Mount Carmel, tapes of worried mothers and fathers and brothers asking the followers to come out. The idea was to remind the group members that they had loved ones out in the world that they could see again.

Sometimes they made a connection, sometimes they didn't. A number of the Davidians had been so estranged from their families for so long that the connection had been almost completely severed. A woman named Lisa came to the phone.

> NEGOTIATOR: Do you have someone out here that you would like us to call and tell them that you're doing fine?
> LISA: No, I don't have any family out there. All my family is right here.
> NEGOTIATOR: No mother, father, sister, brother, et cetera?
> LISA: No, I was abandoned a long time ago . . . Well, I don't know how to get in touch with them anyway even if you did want to talk to them. I don't know where they are.

The bureau contacted Steve's sister, Sue, at her home in Wisconsin and asked her to make a tape. The FBI played it over the phone:

> Hi, Steve, this is Sue. And you know we've told you how much we love you and you know we care about you. Steve, this is a very dangerous situation. And, Steve, you know how bad we'd feel if you were hurt or anything happens to you or Judy or Minah. And, Steve, it's not too late.
>
> Please, Steve, if there's any way that you can peacefully settle this situation, please do it. Please don't let anything bad happen. You know that if anything happens, we will not be able to handle this. We would not be able to live with anything bad happening to you and, Steve, we

want you and Judy to come out and still have some kind of a decent life together . . .

We love you, Steve. Goodbye.

Steve listened to the tape. He was unmoved. "They're all extremely sentimental, emotional and so forth" was all he said.

The negotiators continued to work on him. Steve was softer than David, and he was the second in command. If he turned, he might lead everyone besides David and a few hardcore loyalists out. Steve protested. "I don't have the kind of influence you think I do. I don't. You don't understand . . . People will hear my opinions, but that's about as far as it goes."

The agents didn't let up. They began needling Steve about his wife. Judy, the woman he claimed to love so much, was sleeping with David Koresh. Had a baby by him.

NEGOTIATOR: Well, do you miss the way that you were?

STEVE: It's never changed. If anything, it's gotten better. See, there's a lot of stories and rumors that you'll always get, always . . .

NEGOTIATOR Yeah. Does Judy have one by him?

STEVE: Judy has a baby.

NEGOTIATOR: By him?

Steve wouldn't say whose baby it was. He just let the question hang there.

NEGOTIATOR: I think you answered it.

Why did it all have to be on him, Steve wanted to know. He wasn't in David's league as a theologian. Surely there must be someone who could challenge David.

STEVE: There's got to be some men out there. What about Baylor University? There's over 10,000 students that go there. They've got to have some sharp minds there, some doctors and so forth. But where are they? Where are the arguments?

NEGOTIATOR: No, there's no one out here. There's no one anywhere in the world that we can bring in there with David and with the people in there and sit and have a discussion that you and everybody in there would not see David as really 100 percent winner.

It might have sounded like flattery, but it was really the opposite. The negotiator was saying the Davidians were too brainwashed to listen to anyone other than their leader.

David was struggling, too, or so he claimed. He told Steve that the wait was gnawing at him. He wanted to hear from God so badly. Why wasn't He speaking? Why hadn't He shown David the way forward? A few of the negotiators were tempted to speak their minds, say "because he's full of shit, Steve, that's why." But they held their tongues.

Other times Steve wanted to talk about the government, secrets that he'd heard about its innermost workings. It was an itch that kept at him. "All of us—all my life—I will tell you the truth—I've been a patriotic, an extremely patriotic person," he told the FBI. "Very conservative. I've always backed this government. I've always backed the officials, the people in it. All my life. I've always—I thought it was the most awesome nation, the Constitution, its principles.

"But I've seen powerful men eroding that away. When I was taking history through the years, there were just too many dimensions that were left unanswered that did not make sense. And then I met an admiral of the United States Navy who started showing me documentation about the Trilateral Commission, Council on Foreign Relations, all these organizations of which you have all this power-hungry money people like the Rockefellers behind it all."

He told the negotiators that, since around 1920, the Council on Foreign Relations—"sixteen or eighteen . . . of the greatest industrialists, politicians, meaning congressmen, international bankers"—met regularly to decide where the world would go next. And then there was the Federal Reserve System. Private bankers coining our money. Manipulating the economy. It was a dirty deal, for sure.

As a boy, David had grown up around right-wing political paranoia and absorbed some of it. But he wasn't a true conspiracy theorist. He rarely, if ever, mentioned the Trilateral Commission or the Rockefellers or the Illuminati. Steve, though, along with the lawyer Wayne Martin, who spouted versions of the conspiracies while he was at Mount Carmel, were eager consumers of the stuff. They'd clearly been trading these ideas for some time. For them, politics was spiritual warfare by other means, and in the FBI's actions they saw Satan at work.

The siege at Waco was already acting as a bright beacon for the far right, Second Amendment absolutists, and those who felt Washington was out of touch and oppressive. Alex Jones, the future right-wing radio host, was a high school senior in Austin, a hundred miles away, as the siege unfolded. He was already delving into conspiracy theories, but as he watched the nonstop coverage on CNN, it "confirmed his belief in the inexorable progress of unseen, malevolent forces."

He would soon start his first call-in radio show, featuring screeds against the federal government in his trademark bellow. Years later, Jones's abortive plan to rebuild the Waco compound as a sacred memorial and alt-right Alamo would launch him to national fame.

Steve believed that what was happening to the Davidians would soon happen to all Americans. "It was warned by God in the writings of the Bible," he said, "and by great men like Abraham Lincoln and Jefferson, Madison, what could come of this country if the men and women of this country weren't vigilant for freedom. You know, government has taken control and it's taking greater control, more freedoms are being taken from us, you and I. Let me say, I'll probably be in trouble for it but I believe ATF has been brought about as an agency to take away those freedoms slowly but surely, insidiously . . .

"You've got this maniac organization . . . on the loose. They're terrorists. They should be dealt with as such. They should be investigated . . . Everybody is guilty until proven innocent, that's what you've shown over and over again."

Steve insisted that the government was planning a massacre at Mount Carmel. Why, the FBI negotiators asked. Why would the government kill its own people? To force gun control on all Americans, Steve said. "We're taking a twilight trip here to the Auschwitz camp."

Novel ideas entered the mix on the FBI's side. The tactical team talked about using a laser tool to force an entry into the compound. But Dick Rogers felt it might start a fire, so it was shelved.

The FBI got in touch with David Oates, an expert in "reverse speech." Oates believed that when we speak, people subconsciously reveal hidden meaning. These "backward" messages, produced every fifteen to twenty seconds in a normal conversation, exposed the speaker's true thoughts.

Oates apparently suggested listening to David's KRLD interview in reverse, to reveal what the leader was actually thinking and planning. It's unclear if Oates ever submitted an analysis of the interview.

When the Davidians tried to speak with each other using CB radio, the FBI jammed the channels. They also blocked all radio signals in the area, only allowing the Davidians to hear news broadcasts.

The FBI even investigated an experimental machine developed by Russian scientists that could send subliminal messages over a telephone line. The claim was that the messages could burrow into Koresh's subconscious and get him to come out of the compound along with his followers.

The FBI proposed flying a plane to Russia and picking up one of the machines. At this point, the Russians conceded that the device might not work as advertised. In fact, it might make things *worse*, by sending subliminal messages to Koresh that made him more violent and intractable. The idea was abandoned.

The HRT guys out in the field knew none of this, but their assessments were often the most prescient. Lying in the mud on the cold early-spring mornings, they traded jokes about the siege.

"Hey, you know what Waco stands for?" went one. "We Ain't Coming Out."

43

THE HILL

THE PRESS HAD arrived within hours of the ATF raid, filling up hotel rooms in Waco and surrounding areas. Packs of journalists from Chile and Israel and France and countries further afield were working the story, a thousand reporters and cameramen and producers in all. Satellite trucks cramped the roads around the perimeter. Crews from Southwestern Bell arrived to run new telephones lines and installed a microwave dish and a switching station to fulfill their needs.

It was the world's biggest story, but boring to actually report. Two weeks after the ATF raid, the siege had entered into a protracted lull. The daily FBI press briefing was the main event of the day. When that was over, the journalists searched for diversions. They turned a nearby cow pasture into a golf course, chipping and putting between stand-ups. Footballs were produced and tossed back and forth. The nights in Waco were chilly, but the days could get up into the high sixties. Some reporters worked on their tans, laid out in lawn chairs. A horseshoe pit was dug.

They drank and they gambled. The sound of margarita blenders competed with the growling hum of generators used to power the lights and cameras.

The Russian writer Ivan Solotaroff arrived on assignment for *Esquire* magazine. Everyone was asking what would happen at Waco, but Solotaroff had a different question. Not how will it end, but how do you want it to end? What would be the ideal endgame, journalistically speaking?

He had his answer, and it was very dark, very Russian. "Hey, you know what you want?" he told the others. "You want Da Big Heat. You know. Cagney. Da Big Heat. Dat's what you want." That is, a fiery, all-consuming explosion.

Most of the reporters had little sympathy for the Davidians. At one of the press conferences, the journalist Dick Reavis sensed "a lynching mood," and it wasn't just among the law enforcement types. *USA Today* reporter Mark Potok got down to Waco about twenty minutes before the first FBI briefing on February 28, and he stayed on. He hated how the FBI controlled the narrative with their daily press conferences, but he admitted that the press were hardly fans of Koresh. The chatter among the journos ran along the lines of: "What is wrong with these people? Why doesn't the FBI go in and do something? This is outrageous."

There was little to break up the day. It did cause some amusement when the FBI took out one of the cars on the property, sending a Bradley to crush it flat, and it turned out not to belong to the Davidians but to the *Waco Tribune*.

One moment of excitement arrived with the media's discovery of the Methodist's Children's Home in Waco. Most of the children who'd been released from the compound were staying there, decompressing and undergoing therapy. TV stations brought in helicopters from Dallas and further afield and flew overhead, attempting to catch the faces of the Davidian boys and girls when they walked outside for fresh air.

The locals in town ran a Salvation Army truck for the journalists and the agents, with fresh coffee and doughnuts. They also stood for interviews. They were friendly, for the most part, although the Chamber of Commerce was worried about the effects twenty-four-hour coverage would have on local business. A farmer, Josh Montkemp, was pretty savvy about how the journalists saw Waco, whatever the Chamber of Commerce imagined. He told a reporter, "There ain't been this much excitement around here since the hogs ate Mama."

The nonstop coverage got attention in Hollywood. Producers began circling Waco. One newspaper said that the story was the combination of every tabloid theme except the return of Elvis.

Reality programming was cresting in the early nineties. Made-for-TV movies like *Lethal Lolita*, based on the story of Amy Fisher, who shot her ex-lover's wife, earned high ratings. Bidding wars had broken out over the rights to the stories of the survivors of the bombing of the World Trade Center, drivers who'd gotten lost in the deserts of Nevada, skiers stranded on Colorado slopes.

There were reports that Bonnie Haldeman, Koresh's mother, had sold her story. Robyn Bunds, who was living outside the compound, had two TV offers on the table, plus one movie bid. "We're in a situation where a dog from Mars bites your toes off and you're in a hospital and the first thing you do is call an agent," complained the president of one film company. Offers flowed in as the siege continued to dominate the evening news, with bids ranging from $550,000 to $600,000. "The numbers got so grotesque that I just passed," the producer remarked.

Producers pored over TV schedules. If Koresh surrendered soon, they worried, there wouldn't be enough time to make a TV movie before the all-important May sweeps. What would be ideal was if he stayed inside the compound until June. If he came out then, a production could easily make the fall window.

The reports about Bonnie's film deal—she'd reportedly signed a contract for $75,000—reached David's ears. It pained him deeply. This was blood money, in his mind. "David's not happy," Steve told the negotiators. "If they want to say any of this, they can . . . he even said, that's more money than she made even as a prostitute."

This was fresh news. Steve told the FBI that Bonnie had turned tricks when David was a little boy. "That can be checked out and proven." Bonnie denied it, saying she had gone out with well-to-do men at one point, and they'd given her gifts, but that didn't make her a hooker.

David clearly felt betrayed. Viperish memories of the past welled up. If he should die, he told the FBI, he didn't want his children going to Bonnie. His protestations of love for her, his concern for her soul, were frangible. Go a millimeter beneath the surface and you could feel the acid running.

Ordinary people from Australia, South Africa, China, called the FBI with solutions to the siege. These included bringing in an enormous helicopter with a hook that would rip the roof off the compound or flooding

Mount Carmel until the followers emerged. Many said that God had told them to call.

Another suggestion was that the FBI should plant a large wooden crucifix in plain view of the compound and persuade David that if he was the true Christ, he should crucify himself on it. A retired judge from Alabama phoned in to ask for the compound's number, as he wanted to call David and pretend to be God. The deputy asked the judge what God's voice would sound like, and the judge said he would think of something.

People headed to Waco from various points on the map, as if on a pilgrimage. If some looked at Mount Carmel and saw a modern Alamo, Christians especially saw parallels to besieged faithful in other times and other places, such as Masada, the ancient fortress in Israel where legend had it that 960 Sicarii—a sect that had split off from the Jewish Zealots—withstood a Roman siege before committing mass suicide.

Jeff H. Terrell, thirty-one, a resident of LA, was driving to Waco with a friend. They were headed east on 1-10 in a van. Near Upland, California, Terrell's companion suddenly changed his mind about going to see the Davidians and exited the freeway. Terrell shouted that the man was an undercover FBI agent, then jumped out of the van and began running. He later said he was trying to find another ride to Waco.

Sometime later, Terrell jumped through the front plate-glass window of a home belonging to a Mrs. Fay Thacker. He was shouting, "I'm Jesus Christ, take me to Waco! Take me to Waco!" Mrs. Thacker happened to be sitting in her living room at the time watching coverage of the Waco standoff on TV. When Terrell picked himself up off the floor, she saw that he actually bore a striking resemblance to David Koresh, which gave her a shock. His hair was long and he was wearing a black motorcycle jacket. It turned out that Mrs. Thacker's was the tenth window he'd jumped through in his search for transportation.

Another seeker was Jesse "Lord Lightning" Amen. He showed up at the FBI perimeter and somehow slipped past it, walking across the fields and up to the compound itself. He knocked on the door and when one of the Davidians answered, Amen told them, "I've got fifty thousand people that are ready to come to your aid."

Amen claimed he was close to God, whose true name was "Lord Lightning Amen" and who lived in heaven with his partner, "Cherry

Lightning Amen." The fifty thousand men and women he spoke of were actually a biblical army that was waiting on the banks of the Colorado River for a sign. If the Davidians put a red flag out, this Christian army would come to Waco and rescue them from the FBI.

The Davidians were receptive. "Yeah! Let 'em come" was the general feeling. David really responded to Amen's journey. "Hey, if these people have got the cojones to come into this place right now, I'm going to wash their feet," he told the FBI. He did it, too, bathing Jesse Amen's toes in warm water.

The FBI didn't want interlopers in the compound, fearing they would get hurt or somehow catalyze the situation. They asked repeatedly for David to send Amen out, but he told them the man was genuine and they were going to be good hosts.

Amen lasted a week before leaving voluntarily. Once on the outside, he was jailed for interfering with a police officer. But he gave jailhouse interviews where he told reporters that David had repeatedly said that the feds should "bring it on." If the FBI wanted a battle, his followers were ready.

"The Halaluyah Gang" also arrived in Waco. They usually spent the year crisscrossing America in an old Winnebago. They were led by a man named Richard W. Schmaltz, and the "gang" consisted of his wife and children. The Winnebago acted as kind of traveling billboard for Jesus, slogans painted on the fuselage. "Be pro-Christ now because Jesus will destroy the anti-Christs when he comes again!" read one. "Prepare yourself with a GED, God's Everlasting Dream."

The Schmaltzes would talk to anyone who would listen. Richard lectured reporters on the meaning of Mount Carmel:

"Well, the New World Order. According to Bible prophecy, there is a government system emerging into a single government of the world. The government system is against the things of Jesus. Now Jesus Christ being loving and compassionate and accepting of all those who came to believe in him . . . he accepts the weak and the downtrodden and the worst-off. But the problem with the government system is that they can only access the efficient. So what happens is that the government has to kill off anything that is a liability, ultimately, and keep only those that fit into the mainstream of what they are trying to do."

The Schmaltzes' fellow seekers and tourists gathered at an elevated grassy slope about three miles from Mount Carmel. It was the closest public viewing point to the compound. There was a woman at the hill who called herself Maid Marian. She'd come to Waco to be the Bathsheba to Koresh's King David. Once she got into the compound, she believed, the siege would end and the End Times would begin, ushering in the new Kingdom. She wore dirty short shorts and a halter top, and she was often covered in a thin layer of dust. Marian intimidated people. Her arms would whip up and down as she shouted at visitors, frightening many away.

Vendors did a strong business in T-shirts and bumper stickers. The top sellers were a shirt featuring a drawing of David with Mount Carmel in the background. The slogan read: "BROTHER DAVE'S GUNS AND GOSPEL: WHERE EVERYTHING IS HALF-OFF (INCLUDING DAVE)." Another read: "DAVID, HERE ARE YOUR SEVEN SEALS," on the front. When you turned it over, there were seven badges for the seven law enforcement agencies working at Mount Carmel. It did well with state troopers and the local cops.

Cars drove up and parked for a while. Some got out. People would form little circles around the demonstrators to hear what they had to say.

On most days, the mood leaned antigovernment. A lot of libertarians and gun-rights supporters. People held up signs saying "IS YOUR CHURCH ATF APPROVED?," "BILL CRETIN: TEACH YOUR THUGS WHAT THE 4TH AMEND IS!" ("Bill Cretin" referred to President Clinton). And "ATF KILLS BABIES."

"You're next! You're next!" cried one woman to journalists and gawkers. "Wake up and understand!"

White supremacists and a broad spectrum of people on the far right saw Waco as an escalation of Ruby Ridge. The government was hunting down people like them because of their beliefs and their guns. One who frequented the hill was a twenty-four-year-old Army veteran and ex–Ku Klux Klan member, Timothy McVeigh. Wearing a camo military cap and a red-and-black flannel shirt, he spread bumper stickers on the hood of his car and sold them. "FEAR THE GOVERNMENT THAT FEARS YOUR GUN," read one. Another: "BAN GUNS. MAKE THE STREETS SAFE FOR A GOVERNMENT TAKEOVER."

McVeigh had been living in a suburb of Buffalo, working a dead-end job he despised, when the ATF raided the Davidian compound. He shared parts of his life history with David. He, too, had been bullied in school, he'd had suicidal thoughts, and his lack of success with women had become a source of intense frustration for him. McVeigh was strongly antitax and anti-gun regulation. He wanted to live by "God's law," not man's.

He soon became obsessed with Waco, watching every TV broadcast and reading every article he could find. Here was a perfect illustration of what he'd been feeling: The government had grown too large and too arrogant, and it had become a threat to the American people. McVeigh packed his car with pamphlets and bumper stickers and started driving for Texas.

"It seems the ATF just wants a chance to play with their toys, paid for by government money," he told a student journalist once he arrived. "The government is afraid of the guns people have because they have to . . . control . . . the people at all times. Once you take away the guns, you can do anything to the people. You give them an inch and they take a mile."

After two days, frustrated by his inability to get closer to the compound, McVeigh left. Out on the open road, he kept close track of what was happening with David and the others.

Some new arrivals went to the roadblock maintained by federal agents and asked to go through. A Texas ranger remembered one man specifically. He looked like a prosperous business executive, dressed in a coat and tie. He pulled up to the roadblock in a late-model sedan. "I really, really need to get in and see Lord Koresh," he told the Ranger.

The Ranger waited. He thought the guy was kidding and a punch line was surely coming. But when he studied the man's expression more closely, he saw sincerity there, and then some. He finally told the man that he couldn't get past the checkpoint. No one was getting through.

"You don't understand," the man said. "He is my Lord, and I've got to get to him." It was like the Davidians' story had found its way into some brains that were already struggling to scan. David was the final piece in their life-jigsaws.

Bill Johnston, the federal prosecutor who'd helped the ATF get the search warrant for Waco, was in his office talking with a bunch of Texas Rangers when his secretary buzzed him. "Bill, uh, phone call from George Roden."

Four years before, after losing Mount Carmel, George had gotten into an argument about David Koresh with his roommate, Dale Adair. Adair wanted to share a vision he'd recently had in which he was the new messiah. George didn't take the news well. He accused Adair of being an assassin sent by David Koresh to kill him.

A heated argument erupted. George reached for an axe and cut at Adair, spraying the man's blood across the room. He then took Adair's gun from him and shot him several times in the head. Adair died on the scene.

When detectives were called, George claimed self-defense. He said that Adair had attacked him and he'd fired the gun to protect himself. But the detectives looked at the evidence and concluded he was misleading them. He was arrested and charged with murder.

Before he could go to trial, George was declared mentally insane. The psych report concluded that he was paranoid schizophrenic. He was eventually remanded to the state psychiatric hospital in Big Spring, Texas.

Johnston punched the line and put the call on speaker.

"Johnston? This is George Roden," a voice said.

"Hey, George," said Johnston, who knew Roden slightly from a jury he'd served on when Johnston was an assistant DA. "How are you?"

George said he needed to talk about Mount Carmel. "Johnston, you and I need to get out there and solve this thing. I'll meet you Sunday at noon. I want worldwide press coverage. You know those people are all NGRI, right?"

Johnston didn't know what George was talking about and told him so.

"Come on, Johnston, you've got to know this. NGRI: not guilty by reason of insanity!" Johnston got off the call.

The people on the hill, who were mostly sympathetic to the Davidians, weren't representative of the country as a whole. The mood elsewhere was much tougher. Perhaps the unusually long distance from the authorities and media to the compound figured into this. No followers could be seen in the windows, pining for release, not even the flash of a pale face. It was difficult for CNN viewers to get a feel for the people inside. All the audience was given was a shot of a large compound wavering in the ripples of rising warm air and an alien flag lying desultorily against its pole. On most days, the image was slightly out of focus. The natural drama of a hostage situation was being withheld from the audience. Sometimes it seemed as if there really was no one inside at all.

The same abstraction that Marc had seen happening to the Davidians under David's leadership was now happening in the wider culture. The followers were becoming symbols of something or other. Extremism, God squadism run wild, gun worship.

It would be foolhardy to try and pinpoint a moment when Americans' patience with the siege finally began to thin out. But by the second full week of the siege, many had traded fascination for annoyance. The Davidians had hijacked their TV screens and given them little in the way of action or excitement in return. The story was one in which nothing happened. It grated on the public's tolerance.

NEBULA

I N HIS DOWNTIME, one of the FBI negotiators was listening to the radio. *The Rest of the Story*, a popular show hosted by the broadcaster Paul Harvey, came on. Harvey was talking about a comet or a nebula, in the shape of a guitar, that was making its way through the solar system.

The negotiator mentioned it to the other guys. They thought, "Oh, my God, we're negotiating with David Koresh, a rock star wannabe who sees visions. This is hot stuff." They called Steve and he gave the news to David. He got back on the phone and the FBI guy told him this could be what David had been waiting for.

The FBI got a copy of the newspaper that covered the comet and read it to Steve over the phone.

NEGOTIATOR: You, you ready for this?

STEVE: Go ahead.

NEGOTIATOR: The *Houston Chronicle*, today, captioned, "This Is One Hot Guitar: Neutron Star Is Moving Darn Fast Through Our Galaxy." They've got a whole article on it. . . . it's three full columns. I can read you part of it—

STEVE: No kidding?

NEGOTIATOR: —if you'd like to hear it.

STEVE: Sure, sure. I'd love to.

NEGOTIATOR: It's—it starts off, "Some very hot licks from the fastest star ever found has created a heavenly guitar-shaped glow, says astronomers."

STEVE: Holy . . . Do me a favor.

NEGOTIATOR: Yeah.

STEVE: I would love to have [it]; if you can . . . tomorrow . . . can we work it out where you can get me a copy of it, seriously?

NEGOTIATOR: We'll get it in to you tonight . . . And it's talking how this thing is traveling at 1,800 kilometers a second and, you know, it's, it's, it's a very interesting article.

STEVE: Wowie! . . . I think that would really lift David up, I would. I mean, I'd, I'd wake him up for that for sure.

The FBI did one better than sending the article in. They called up Paul Harvey's people and asked him to repeat the segment on the guitar-shaped nebula, because no one in the compound had caught it the first time. In the meantime, Steve woke up David and one of the negotiators read the *Chronicle* story to him. He came to the phone to talk about it. David seemed unimpressed.

NEGOTIATOR: "It's moving through our galaxy, the Milky Way, at a tremendous rate, perhaps 1,800 kilometers per second . . ."

DAVID: Moving pretty slow.

NEGOTIATOR: It's fast by my standards.

DAVID: I know . . .

NEGOTIATOR: "In a million years it has moved from Serpens to Cepheus."

DAVID: That's incorrect.

NEGOTIATOR: Well, all I'm doing is quoting the—

DAVID: Yeah.

David didn't think the nebula was a sign. The brief excitement faded. The episode had the whiff of a flimflam. Maybe David really was a con artist like the tactical guys believed. A barracuda, soulless, prowling, looking only to stay alive another day or two. Another time, he told them: "If you can tell me what the Fifth Seal of the Seven Seals means, I'll release a child." The team grabbed the Gideon Bibles from their hotel end tables and searched the Scriptures. They called Baylor University and spoke to religious scholars. They found what was the accepted location of the Fifth Seal.

They told David. "Not even close," he said, and refused to release the child.

A total of twenty-one children had come out of Mount Carmel. Dr. Bruce D. Perry, the chief of psychiatry at Texas Children's Hospital, volunteered to work with them, along with a team of therapists. The FBI wanted the kids taken care of. But they were also hoping the children would give them some clues as to what was happening inside the compound.

The children were given physical exams. Their heart rates were high, around one hundred forty beats per minute, instead of the more normal seventy to ninety beats. It took weeks for the numbers to come down.

At the facility where they were being cared for, the kids were surprised and delighted by the toilets, which many of them had never seen before. Some flushed them again and again, watching the water swirl. Others would only drink tap water at first, the only thing they drank in the compound. They had their first taste of candy.

The therapists played board games and went on long walks with the boys and girls. And they spoke with them for hours. The therapists asked the children, whose ages ranged from four to eleven, about life inside the compound. They asked about what was going to happen at Mount Carmel, to their mommies and daddies.

The kids talked a lot about David, and how much they adored him. They drew pictures and decorated them with hearts. Some wrote "I Love David" at the bottom.

But as the therapists probed their experiences, they came to mistrust those statements. On March 11, Perry wrote a memo to the agency.

A permeating and pervasive fear of displeasing David or betraying his "secrets" is present in all of the children—even those as young as 4 years old. The children have a sense that he will be able to punish them if they violate his prohibitions. They even allude to the fact that he will be able to return from death and punish them or others who betray them.

The children saw the world in stark terms: "The outside was full of 'bad guys,' unbelievers without the 'light,' evil and hurtful people." Their thoughts on the future were even darker. They had the sense "that there is going to be an absolute explosive end to [their] families." Perry reported that when the children were asked to draw Mount Carmel, they produced sketches with the compound in flames, or bombs tearing through it. When the therapists asked them what the future held, they said things like "Everyone is going to die," or "We're going to blow you all up."

The children asked to speak to their loved ones inside. When that happened, they would often ask their parents to leave Mount Carmel. Some of the kids would say, "Please come out," or "Please come and get me!"

On March 12, Janet Reno was sworn in as the first female attorney general of the United States. Later, in the unremarkable brick courtyard of the Justice building, she gave a speech to a thousand of the men and women who would work under her, while others craned for a look from nearby windows.

"I'm the new kid on the block and I thought I should let you know my hopes and dreams and how I do things. While I'm Attorney General, we will address each issue with one question: 'What's the right thing to do?' . . . Let us leave here today resolved to ask that of ourselves and others as we seek justice, remembering that sometimes doing the right thing is politically unpopular."

The siege was now twelve days old. The previous morning, HRT requested permission from Washington to use tear gas as a pressuring tactic. They were told no. The next day, they cut the compound's electricity permanently and shone spotlights on the front façade. The phone connection between the negotiators and the compound wasn't affected.

David seethed for days about the cut-off. "We're saying your commanders are a threat," he told the FBI. "You have continued to digress on the things you promise. You keep yourselves in ignorance. You don't understand."

"I do understand," the negotiator replied. "We're running out of patience."

Steve got on the phone and told the negotiator that twenty to thirty people had been ready to come out before the power was cut. Now they were staying.

Loudspeakers were trucked in and started broadcasting. The reason was that the phone line, which snaked across the ground from the FBI position into the compound, had gone on the fritz. One of the milk-carton bugs caught David responding to the move. "Someone stabbing me in the back," he said. "Gonna go up and blow their heads off."

The loudspeakers began playing music at volume, to increase the Davidians' discomfort. The next day, the Davidians hung a sign from one of the windows. "FBI BROKE NEGOTIATION," it read. "WE WANT PRESS." The FBI continued to deny David access to the media.

The FBI suggested a face-to-face meeting and on March 15, Steve and Wayne Martin emerged from the compound's front door. Byron Sage and Sheriff Harwell were waiting for them. They spoke for over an hour, with Sage and the sheriff making every effort to reach David's lieutenants. They talked about getting medical care for the Davidians and about preserving the crime scene so that the truth would come out once the siege was over. And they assured Steve and Wayne that they'd be free to retain their own lawyers.

Wayne said he was concerned. He no longer knew what the United States stood for or whether or not the Constitution had been suspended in the middle of the night. Had dictatorship come into being while the Davidians slept?

Byron bristled. "There are two documents that I would give my life for," he said. "One is the Constitution and one is the Bible, and I would give my life to defend both of them. That's why I'm standing here in plain sight." As he spoke, Byron looked Steve dead in the eye.

Steve seemed moved. He went back into the building and up to David's room. One of the bug tapes picked up the conversation.

"Byron, I liked. Man, what a person. I liked his personality. I believe he was 100 percent sincere. I saw his concern in his face and eyes. I really, you know, I believe what he's trying to do." Steve was gushing.

That afternoon, David ordered his men to take hundreds of gallons of diesel fuel that were stored in tanks outside the building and switch them to five-gallon containers, which they then brought into the house. The men went out, under the gaze of the FBI snipers, and transferred the fuel using a long hose.

David grew more combative. One of the negotiators challenged his manhood, straight up. "If I were in your position, I would definitely want to get the women and children out. This is a man's type of thing."

"Oh really?" David snarled. "This is a thing of guns and bombs and blowing their asses up, boys . . . We just kill those fuckers the first time we went in there. Shit, let's go ahead and just get the women and children out. We'll put them all in jail and put the kids with foster parents and all that."

The negotiator tried to interrupt, but David wouldn't let him. "No, well, let me, let me, let me finish. Let me finish . . . Because the government is bigger than any power there is. And you're going to spend your life in jail, or you're going to get lethal injection . . . And John, I'm a man. And I'm a brave man. I've always been a brave man . . ."

The FBI was all punk talk to David. They walked into Mount Carmel and punched him in the nose. And now they wanted to talk peace?

By mid-March, the FBI was still unaware of the earlier grenade-and-guns suicide plan. But it hardly mattered, because David finally announced to his followers that it was canceled. He'd heard that some of the Davidians, in the days after the shootout, had gorged on junk food and cigarettes that they'd secretly hoarded before the ATF raid, celebrating their survival or trying to soothe their nerves. Some had even cracked open liquor bottles and had a drink.

"You're all going to hell," he told them.

Kat Schroeder was among the guilty. She'd smoked a cigarette. Kat was frustrated. She was constantly pressing David: "What is God going to do to keep my kids safe?" David would quote some Bible verses, but Kat was unappeased. "Well, maybe I ought to send you out with the beast, too," he told her.

She didn't argue. She wanted to be with her youngest son. David didn't stand in her way. He was her messiah, but her lover, too. "He not only understood, he felt that," she said.

On March 13, David decided that she and the others had shown a "reckless disregard for God's laws [that] was going to cause the whole group to be held back." Kat and the other transgressors were told to leave. She went that day.

On March 19, two more adults came out. It was the herky-jerky nature of the thing. Forward, back, stasis. Like previous followers who'd emerged from the compound, these new releases were arrested and placed in a local jail. The charges varied, but the Davidians were being held on suspicion of involvement in the deaths of the four ATF agents.

In the wake of these banishments, David's anger continued to flare hot. "Don't make me go out there and take one of those tank barrels and twist it around like a pretzel," he told the negotiators, "and turn it around and scoot it off and put a wind-up toy in the back of it." He also talked about the end of the world. It had already happened once, with Noah and the ark. The flood had ended the human world for a time. He thought that was awesome. "Of course, the prophets say that it'll never be done with a flood again. It'll be done with fire the last time."

As the weeks passed, the negotiators struggled to come up with things to talk about with David. Sometimes the men just shot the shit. At one point, they got to comparing the local burger joints.

> NEGOTIATOR: How do you like Whataburger? They do anything for you?
> DAVID: Oh, man. Don't even talk about—
> NEGOTIATOR: Well, what can I tell you?
> DAVID: —oversoaked cardboard meat.
> NEGOTIATOR: What can I tell you?
> DAVID: Man, you didn't get them over there off of Bellmead, did you?
> NEGOTIATOR: Where?
> DAVID: That one off of Bellmead and 35?
> NEGOTIATOR: I, I guess so.
> DAVID: Nasty. Oh, that place is nasty.

Steve asked about prison. What could he wear there? "I guess they take your clothes from you or something like that and issue you something else?" Would he be allowed to bring his Bible and a concordance? The negotiators assured him he would.

It was encouraging. Better than when Steve went on about the Trilateral Commission.

On March 21, Steve shared big news. Seven people were coming out. There hadn't been that large a number in days. Steve and David were feeling good about it.

The negotiators were thrilled. But hours went by with no release. They got antsy. Finally, Steve called.

NEGOTIATOR: They're on their way?
STEVE: Guess what? Guess what, John?
NEGOTIATOR: What?
STEVE: They've decided not to come.
NEGOTIATOR: Don't tell me that.
STEVE: Only kidding.

He was having a little fun.

The seven adults finally came out. Gary Noesner was delighted. It was a big step forward. In his theory of "trickle gush flow," they'd reached the terminal stage.

Later that day, HRT agents took one of their tanks and drove it over a Davidian car, crushing it. It was another display of dominance. David's response was ice-cold.

NEGOTIATOR: I talked to David, you know, and he said—
STEVE: He just told me now. Just right now. He said no one is coming out. Nobody.

Noesner was furious. What the fuck was this? What rival theory of negotiation had emerged from Rogers and Jamar's room, that nuclear plant of testosterone?

The other negotiators were upset as well. "This is Dick Rogers's doing" was the general theme. Rogers saw the Davidians coming out and thought, "These damn negotiators. Now they're gonna win." The Davidians would emerge in ones and twos and the FBI would be stuck in Waco for months. So he'd ordered the tanks in. To screw the negotiators. That's how a lot of guys on Noesner's team saw it, anyway.

Noesner resisted, at least at first. It was one thing for the Davidians to promote batshit conspiracy theories about the FBI, and another for agents themselves to do it. But try as he might, he couldn't find another explanation for the tanks. Sending them in defied logic. Noesner could see no strategic reason for the move.

Noesner gave in. It had to be Rogers. He wanted control of the operation. It was as if the HRT's real opponent wasn't David Koresh. It was the negotiators.

Other things rankled, too. Why were the Brads always running over the phone line that connected the FBI to the Davidians? It would have been easy enough to avoid the area and keep the line pristine. But the Brads kept driving over the wire and the thing frayed and eventually broke. It had to be repaired, which took time and set back the talks.

And then there were the moonings. According to Steve and David, HRT guys were out there in the fields dropping trou and showing their backsides to the Davidians. Steve Schneider complained about it more than once.

If a negotiator had done that, Noesner would have yanked them out of Waco immediately. Brought them over to the Department of Justice and into their Office of Professional Responsibility. It was beyond the pale for an FBI agent to act that way.

But nothing happened. What was that about?

Noesner got a call from his boss at the FBI Academy in Quantico. "Hey, we're going to sub you out," he said.

Negotiators usually worked on a three-week rotation, in order to reduce the stress on them. Noesner had been on scene for longer than that. And he had a long-scheduled training mission in Amman, Jordan, that he was due to attend.

But Noesner believed the rotation was an excuse. He was being moved out so the bureau could bring in someone who was more in line with the tactical approach. Noesner went to Jamar and told him he was leaving. "I'm not asking you to leave," Jamar said. "This is coming from headquarters, not me. I'm happy with you being here." Noesner didn't know what to think.

He told Jamar he wasn't hopeful. "I don't think anybody else is coming out of there," he said. He walked out of the compound and, days later, was on his way to Amman.

Perhaps it didn't really matter in the larger scheme of things. Sometime in mid-March, Jamar had come to the conclusion that David had released the people he wanted to release. His gut told him no one else was coming out of their own accord.

ACCEPTANCE

THREE WEEKS INTO the siege, the compound was getting rancid. The Davidians couldn't walk to their outhouses; they used five-gallon buckets as their portable bathrooms. Most of the available water was used for drinking, so they went days without bathing.

It was loud. The FBI continued blasting music, but spliced in other sounds, too. Now the Davidians might hear Tibetan chanting, followed by Christmas carols, Nancy Sinatra's "These Boots Are Made for Walking," trumpets playing reveille, a helicopter's whirling blades. Bureau technicians sped the music up, then slowed it down. Babies cried, phones rang, lambs bleated as they were slaughtered.

With all the noise, Clive Doyle was getting about two hours of sleep a night. He and the other Davidians were growing thinner, too. Most of the food had run out and the Davidians were on MREs all day, every day.

A police psychologist told the press playing loud music was a common tactic in sieges. The Army had used it on General Manuel Noriega when trying to get him out of his compound in Panama. The sound of animals being slaughtered was in questionable taste, the psychologist admitted, but it sometimes worked.

There were limits, however. "If they go Barry Manilow," the psychologist said, "it's excessive force."

Days later, an angry fax arrived at FBI headquarters, addressed to

Director Sessions. It was from the Dalai Lama, objecting to the use of Tibetan religious chants at Mount Carmel. The music was sacred and shouldn't be used in such a context, the Dalai Lama said.

Sessions told agents to pull the chants.

On March 23, Byron got in one of the tanks and was driven up the driveway. Steve came out of the compound and they talked—Byron's head and shoulders sticking out of a porthole in the enormous metal armored vehicle, and the slight Schneider standing a few yards away.

The FBI had a new offer. David would be allowed special privileges in prison if he was convicted. He could meet with his incarcerated followers, with a special conference room set aside for them. And if David wished to write a memoir or a book on the Seven Seals—a topic that he and the negotiators had tossed around in previous conversations—a stenographer would be provided to take down chapters of his book.

Steve lit up. The ministry could continue. That night, FBI agents placed a letter on the driveway for the Davidians to pick up. It was written confirmation of everything that Byron had promised.

Afterward, Steve spoke to the negotiators. He told them he'd gotten the letter, went to David's room, and woke him up. David read the letter, crumpled it into a ball, and tossed it across the room.

Ill will bred ill will. Two days later, the FBI issued an ultimatum. Ten to twenty Davidians had to leave the compound by four p.m., or the agency would take action. "Again, this is not a threat," the negotiator told Steve. "This is a promise."

Nobody left. The FBI sent in the Bradleys and crushed several vehicles, including Steve's Honda motorcycle, the one he and Judy used to take on long drives to decompress after David revealed the New Light. Steve watched it happen from a window.

When he got on the phone later, he seemed curiously okay with it. It was as if he was slowly detaching from the world outside the compound windows.

"I thought they did a good job on it," he told the negotiator. "Man, they planted it good."

The negotiator apologized.

"No, that's fine. I don't mind, you know, it's only a material thing."

NEGOTIATOR: Oh, that's right. you're not into material things, are you?

STEVE: I really am not anymore; I'll be honest with you—

NEGOTIATOR: Okay, well, at any rate, the commanders have indicated—

STEVE: I even waved at one of the guys.

NEGOTIATOR: That we, this is no longer acceptable, all right? We need—

STEVE: Life isn't acceptable.

Steve seemed to be letting go. "A lot of people here are starting to act funny," he told the FBI. "Maybe if you keep on going, they'll start getting itchy fingers and we can get it over quicker, I mean, 'cause I'm losing control with people around here."

The FBI tried to goad Steve into action, but their taunts had less and less effect.

NEGOTIATOR: You know, Steve, I thought you had some strength of character, but the longer I talk to you I think I've made a mistake.

STEVE: You probably have.

NEGOTIATOR: I think I have made a mistake.

STEVE: I wouldn't doubt it.

NEGOTIATOR: Because listening to you, you're just not getting the job done.

STEVE: I know it.

He grew reflective. Why was he here, in Waco? What had made him abandon a nice life in Hawaii to come live in this place? He and Judy were going to buy twenty acres on Oahu and build a house, live out their lives. He'd been in LA trying to get David's music thing going. "All of a sudden, I make a trip . . . back to Texas and find myself in the most horrendous, horrible thing that ever could be."

Steve wasn't a trickster, unlike David at times. He really wondered how all this had happened to him, a towheaded boy from Wisconsin.

At one point, he asked the FBI guy what he thought about death.

STEVE: Tell me honestly, you don't have any concerns, huh?

NEGOTIATOR: No. Only the good die young. At that rate, I'll live forever.

STEVE: John, I don't understand. Why am I so different from you in that respect?

He'd pass by a mirror and be shocked at what he saw there. His hair had grown long and unkempt. He'd always been proud of his appearance, but there was no way to look clean at Mount Carmel. He had wrinkles he'd never seen before.

Steve was at a low ebb. "I'm looking forward to God bringing an end to this world of six thousand years of death and disheartened, unfulfilled lives," he told a negotiator, "and people trying to make something of their lives and . . . broken marriages and families and drugs and disease."

The FBI got Steve's sister Sue to speak to him again. "We don't have much time," he told her. He believed in David even more strongly now than he had before. Everything he prophesied was coming true.

Steve gave the FBI a suggestion on how to end the standoff. Put a match to the building and the Davidians would be forced to leave. "Some time when you have a chance, read Isaiah 33:14 about people living in fire and walking through it and coming out and surviving . . . Seriously . . . It says, 'Who of us can dwell with everlasting burning?' That's the question."

Steve was confident he'd come through the refining fire. He was looking forward to the FBI running over his carcass so he could get a brand-new one.

The Davidians' families, meanwhile, were trying to remain optimistic. David's mother, Bonnie, hired an attorney, Dick DeGuerin, to represent her son and hopefully negotiate his surrender to authorities. Jamar agreed to let him talk to David.

It was an unpopular decision among the feds. The ATF, the Texas Rangers, the prosecutors on the ATF case, the other SACs on-site (excepting the spokesman Bob Ricks), and a good portion of the FBI thought it was outrageous. The guy might tell David how to destroy evidence, give him ideas about a possible defense before anyone had a chance to question him.

But Jamar stuck by his guns. A well-respected lawyer like DeGuerin might advise David to think of his own interests. Tell him that he could avoid the death penalty, or that he might even get off completely if things went his way.

On March 27, Jeff told Byron he wanted him to take DeGuerin to the compound so he could meet with his client. The HRT would put the two men in a Brad and drive them up close to the front door.

That's a terrible idea, Byron thought. He was supposed to walk around escorting the lawyer for the guy who killed four ATF agents? What were the guys in the field going to think of that? But Jamar had asked him, and he said yes.

Byron and DeGuerin went out to the Bradley. One of the HRT guys came over to Byron and shoved a Kevlar helmet into his belly.

"What the hell's this for?" Byron asked.

"Trust me. You're gonna want to wear it." DeGuerin got a helmet, too.

The two loaded into the back of the Brad and sat on the benches that served as seats. The tailgate came down and the vehicle shot off like a spooked rabbit. The two men reached for the bars overhead to try and steady themselves, but the Brad was rocking and swerving so violently that he and DeGuerin flew from one side to the other, smashing into the steel walls. After one particularly vicious swerve, DeGuerin was lifted off his bench and came crashing down on Byron, sprawled on his lap.

When they reached the drop-off spot, the driver slammed on the brakes and the Brad nearly stood on its nose before rocking back down to the dirt. Byron heard a door slam shut. Somebody was laughing. Must be the driver, he thought.

He was mortified. This dude driving the Brad had embarrassed Byron, embarrassed the bureau, and embarrassed himself. Byron hated to see the bureau besmirched.

DeGuerin took off his helmet and thrust it at Byron. You could see he was fucking pissed.

"Was that really necessary?" he barked.

"Mr. DeGuerin," Byron said. "You have to realize these guys aren't used to driving track vehicles. And the road . . . it's chewed up." It wasn't true, but he had to try.

DeGuerin shot him a look and went off to meet with Koresh. Byron got out of the vehicle and found the driver. The guy was standing there grinning at him. He was a big dude, six-foot-four at least.

"What the hell are you doing?" Byron said.

The agent stared. "What do you mean?"

"Do you have any idea," Byron said, "how unprofessional that was?"

"I don't give a shit. He's just a murderer's lawyer."

Byron told the agent he should give a shit, because if they got Koresh out, the bureau was going to face DeGuerin in court. And the agent would be called up to the witness stand to explain why he nearly bashed the defense lawyer's brains out in the back of a government vehicle.

The driver scoffed. Byron couldn't believe they were having this conversation. "We're on the same side here, right?" he said.

The driver took a step back, looked Byron up and down.

"Are we really," he said.

Shit, it's real bad, Byron thought.

As March drew to a close, no more Davidians emerged. Livingstone Fagan, the firebrand from England, had been the last, and the FBI suspected he'd been released simply to get David's message out. Byron got on the line and expressed his concern for the people inside the compound. Steve was genuinely touched. "You don't know how much I appreciate that you would have that in mind and that you would warn me about it in a . . . in a decent way."

If Steve was feeling melancholy, David had his moments, too. "Yeah, my babies," he sighed over the phone line. "My life is over."

More and more, there was the feeling of having come to the end of a road. A black humor informed the talks.

STEVE: Half the time I'm losing track of time these days.

NEGOTIATOR: Well, you know, when you're having fun, the time just gets away from you.

STEVE: Well, this is exactly it. I've never had such a great time.

When David was in a good mood, the negotiators tweaked him about his musical abilities.

DAVID: Well, some people have said that I'm one of the hottest guitar players in the nation.
NEGOTIATOR: You ought to get out more [laughter].

The comfortableness opened David right up. Sometimes, it was like he was talking to a therapist, getting deep.

DAVID: You know . . . I could be the Devil himself, you know what I mean?
NEGOTIATOR: That's true.
DAVID: Instead of being the Lamb, I could be the Devil here . . . getting ready to put people in Hell.
NEGOTIATOR: That's true.
DAVID: Seven Seals.
NEGOTIATOR: Probably some people have thought that, too.
DAVID: Oh, yeah. More so than the other way.

The negotiators felt statements like this showed that David didn't really believe he was the messiah. Another time, he told the FBI if he was really God, he was going to punish WhatABurger for their low-quality meat. The negotiators thought long and hard about that "if." But David had been doing this for years. Playing devil's advocate on himself, telling people to prove he was who he said he was.

It may have been that David had a lot of scam artist in him, as many in the FBI thought. But he did indeed have doubts about himself that were real and long-standing. The teenager who thought he was just a bucket of filth hadn't entirely disappeared.

Even the tactical guys joshed with the Davidians. One morning the guys in the Brads shouted good morning to the people in the compound. "Time to get up!" they announced, like Waco was a summer camp and they were the eager beaver counselors. Eggs and bacon are frying on the griddle, they called. Anyone hungry?

And then, mock-solicitous: What would you like to hear this morning as far as music? Any requests?

David answered back, "What about a little Joe Satriani?!" Someone else called, "How about something classical?" The kids yelled out for the sounds of barnyard animals, their favorite.

Good, wholesome fun.

Early in April, Marc Breault arrived in Waco. He quickly became a resource for journalists on the scene, as a decoder of David's theology.

David had announced that the world was in the middle of the Fifth Seal. If the End Times were approaching, as he claimed, certain things would soon be apparent to all. A darkening sun, a blood-red sun, stars falling from the sky. The Bible said, in Revelation 6:9–11, that the apocalypse would not occur until a fixed number of martyrs had died for Christ. Koresh believed that number to be two hundred million, which included everyone since the creation who had given their life for God.

As the days went on, and signs of the Apocalypse failed to appear, there could only be one explanation, in Marc's opinion: The figure of two hundred million had not yet been reached. More people had to die.

"He has to figure how to get out of the box he made for himself," Breault said. "The Fifth Seal is his worst nightmare at the moment."

On April 9, David sent a four-page letter out to the FBI. In it, he issued a warning about catastrophes to come. He signed it "Yahweh Koresh."

He specifically mentioned a dam close to Waco. There would be an earthquake soon and the dam would burst. Steve was really worried about that. "The thing about the Lake Waco area," he told the FBI, "Old Mount Carmel being shaken, about the dam being burst? Guaranteed, guaranteed, that is serious."

There were several dams nearby, and Waco did sit near the Balcones Fault, which ran from near Del Rio in the southwest up to the Dallas area. It had been dormant for millions of years. City officials ordered the structures examined for cracks or explosives. Maybe some Davidians or their sympathizers had planted dynamite up there. But the dam was pretty massive. If the Davidians were going to blow it up, it would take a hell of a lot of nitroglycerine.

Marc read the four-page document and wasn't impressed. "I'm pretty sure it's an old letter," he told journalists. "If he had written one now, it would probably be about the Seven Seals. I think he did this just to stall for time. Now the FBI will have to try to figure out where he's coming from. It's just throwaway theology."

Two things did stick out to Marc. The first was when David quoted a passage from Psalms that mentioned the words "it raised him up." He had talked about that years before. "Vernon used to teach that when it said it raised him up," Marc told reporters, using David's given name, "it meant he was resurrected."

The other was David quoting Revelations 6:11: *And white robes were given unto every one of them; and it was said unto them, that they should rest yet for a little season, until their fellow servants also and their brethren, that should be killed as they were, should be fulfilled.* "He's trying to tell the FBI that he's the one who is going to conquer them," Marc told the reporters. "He's talking tough. He's not thinking about coming out at this stage, not based on the Scriptures that he's giving out."

The FBI sent the letter off for analysis. Dr. Murray S. Miron, a Syracuse University professor and a psycholinguist, went through it line by line. The note bore "all the hallmarks of rampant, morbidly virulent paranoia," Miron wrote in his report. He believed that Koresh saw himself as God's agent on earth, and that this was causing him to disassociate. "This multiple personality–like condition provided him with a shield of imagined invulnerability and unmitigated power."

The professor believed that this unsettled state would cause David to fight. He saw no suicidal ideations in the letter and doubted that David would surrender. He even thought that the Davidian leader might launch a counterattack on the FBI. "In my judgment, we are facing a determined, hardened adversary who has no intention of delivering himself or his followers into the hands of his adversaries . . . His is not the language of those at Masada or Jonestown. He intends to fight."

Two other experts combed through David's letter. Dr. Joseph Krofcheck was a psychiatrist who'd provided threat assessments to the FBI before. Cliff Van Zandt was the head of the FBI's Behavioral Science unit. Their conclusions:

"Koresh is probably a functional, paranoid type psychotic. He appears in a superior mode to the people who he has gathered around him . . . He is not a multiple or split personality, but his own different external manifestations of the same personage."

David moved through various identities; when challenged or opposed, he seamlessly flowed into the next one. This was a protective measure; David saw the world as belonging to him. No one had the right to put him down. "Koresh is a user of others . . . He is willing to kill, to see his followers die, and to die himself. In his fluid identity mix, the delusional Messiah God is stronger than the human reality of his trial, television talk shows, and any book deal . . ."

The two experts presumably knew little of David's early relationships with older men, but they'd picked up on his childhood fears. He'd built barriers to the kind of psychological erasure that his stepdad and others had tried to enforce on him. David had protected himself as a boy by imagining various heroic roles to play: the track star, the rock star, the preacher. The analysis hearkened back to the poem he wrote as a teenager: "*To me there was, yet never was / one person for me to be.*"

The memo ended on a pessimistic note. David wasn't going to go down easily. "The government," the authors wrote, "is the hostage in this situation."

THE MANUSCRIPT

O N APRIL 10, another letter arrived.

Friends,

I offer to you My Wisdom. I offer to you My sealed secrets. How dare you turn away my invitations of mercy? I know your sins and your iniquities. None are hid from Me. When will you ever fear and be wise? Your only Savior is My Truth. My Truth is the "Seven Seals."

You're not rejecting a man by fighting against David My servant, no, for I have given and revealed My Name to Him. Read Isaiah 45. The Name Koresh is My surname and all men are My sons and the work of My hands . . .

Yahweh Koresh

Steve asked about another note. If David wrote to President Clinton, would the president read it? Because David had composed one. Was it worth sending out?

The negotiator said that Hillary might not let Bill see it. It wasn't clear if he was kidding or not, but the letter never arrived.

Still, the president. David was growing more grandiose, not less. The

April 10 letter was written as if David had merged with God. It didn't bode well.

Concertina wire arrived at the site, double-stacked in bright steel rolls six feet high that sparkled in the sunlight. The Hostage Rescue Team began enclosing the compound with the stuff. It was to keep anyone from going in or out.

Two days later, the FBI sent Janet Reno a plan for another tear gas assault on the compound. She responded by asking, "Why now? Why not wait?" The FBI replied that, among other factors, should the siege continue even a couple of weeks longer, the HRT would have to be withdrawn for training, possibly before the end of April. Reno wanted more information before she would make a decision.

On April 14, Brigadier General Peter Jan Schoomaker, assistant division commander at Fort Hood, and an Army colonel flew to Washington. Dick Rogers was on the FBI airplane with them and brought the two men up to date on the plan. It called for the gradual insertion of nonlethal tear gas over hours or days, to slowly force the Davidians from the compound. At one point, Rogers asked Schoomaker what he thought. "We can't grade your paper," Schoomaker replied. At the meeting, the military officers were just as tight-lipped. They were briefed on the operation but offered no significant thoughts or comments.

Reno met with a tear gas expert. He related the fact that no one had ever conducted laboratory tests with regard to the impact of tear gas on children. There were only anecdotal reports of kids having been exposed accidentally. They were generally positive in that no permanent injuries had been observed. One of the participants in the meeting, in trying to show the relative safety of the method, told Reno that American soldiers were exposed to tear gas "at least annually" during training.

Around this time, President Clinton called Bernard Nussbaum, his White House counsel. "What do we do about Waco?" he asked. Nussbaum replied that he'd consulted with Janet Reno and told her to get advice "from the professionals," then make her decision. "We should stay out of it," he told Clinton.

"No, I know a lot about this stuff, Bernie." Clinton mentioned a prison riot and some other law enforcement crises that had occurred when he was governor of Arkansas.

Nussbaum repeated his advice: Stay clear of it.

"I want to have some input into this," Clinton said.

"Mr. President, you're the president of the United States, you're not the governor of the United States." Nussbaum thought it was a good line.

Clinton finally relented. But he wanted Reno to consult with the military—specifically, with Chief of Staff of the Armed Forces Colin Powell—before she did anything.

"That's a good idea, Mr. President," Nussbaum said. He passed the message on to Reno.

Soon after, David told the negotiators he was going to compose a manuscript on the Seven Seals. He'd dictate it to Judy, who'd type it up. When it was finished, he and the others would leave Mount Carmel.

David was high on the prospect. He was going to write something world-altering.

DAVID: I'll be in custody in the jailhouse. You can come down and feed me bananas if you want. I'll be splitting out of this place. I'm so sick of MREs.

NEGOTIATOR: So, I'm gonna let you go so you can get back to work because, David, frankly, I'm eagerly awaiting this manuscript.

DAVID: And I'll tell you what, it's gonna blow your socks off.

But the more David thought about the manuscript, the more pessimistic he grew about its reception. When he emerged from Mount Carmel, people weren't going to be interested in the Seven Seals. "They're going to say, do you molest young ladies? Have you eaten babies? Do you sacrifice people? Do you make automatic weapons? . . .

"That's what they're going to be interested in. Sensationalism . . . You know as well as I do, that people in this world, they want something dramatic and sensational. No one's going to let me sit in front of the camera and read Psalms 40 to them to prove the first seal."

Steve was coming to the same conclusion. He couldn't understand why people weren't responding to David's message. "When it comes right down to it, people want to have their plastic Jesus or their plastic Gods or whatever in their imagination they think God is or isn't."

Despite the gloom, Judy Schneider continued to type David's manuscript. One of the negotiators asked when might this thing be done. Judy replied that at this rate maybe a year.

For Jeff Jamar and his team, that was unacceptable. It was a hard marker. They would go a different way. Jamar and the others began to press for approval to insert tear gas into the compound.

Reno dug into the details of the FBI's plan. David and Steve had made numerous references to flames, but Reno was more concerned with the possibility of an explosion inside Mount Carmel. The FBI believed Koresh had the materials to cause a large detonation.

On Thursday or Friday night, April 15–16, the attorney general was unable to sleep. "Oh my God, what if he blows the place up?" she thought. "What if he holds children up in the windows and threatens to shoot them?"

Webster Hubbell, the assistant attorney general, called Byron Sage. He asked how the negotiations were going. Was there hope? Byron told him they were at a "total impasse" with the Davidians.

Briefings on the proposed tear gas assault continued. During one, Reno recalled an FBI official saying that children were being abused inside the compound. "He's beating the babies," the official said, in her recollection. "Wait a minute, actually beating the babies?" Reno replied, obviously concerned.

Reno assumed the remark was prompted by the FBI's listening devices. That the FBI was hearing abuse or hearing about it through the bug tapes. Hubbell recalled hearing the same thing: Child abuse was happening inside Mount Carmel.

David had raped and beaten children before the siege, that was well-documented. But the FBI had no information that sexual abuse was currently happening inside Mount Carmel. Koresh was seriously wounded and likely physically unable to do much except rest. It was old information.

Reno peppered the FBI with questions. Could they insert some kind of gas into the compound that would put the Davidians to sleep? Could an airplane fly over and spray the gas? The FBI told her no on both counts.

FBI Assistant Director Danny Coulson spoke to the idea of building a fence around Mount Carmel and starving the Davidians out. There were several downsides to the plan: First, it was estimated that the group had a year's worth of food inside the compound. Then there was the hierarchy: David and his lieutenants would probably get most of the available food and water, leaving his followers to suffer. If supplies ran short and the rest of the Davidians were on the brink of starvation, Koresh would most likely negotiate new supplies in order to avoid deaths in the compound.

If they went ahead with an even longer siege, Reno thought about what the next year would look like. The Davidians would be filthy and increasingly malnourished. The sexual abuse, which she believed to be ongoing, would most likely continue. When the siege was finally over, HRT might enter the compound and find most or all of the residents dead.

Still, on Friday, April 16, Reno rejected the FBI's tear gas proposal. She didn't state her reasons. Hubbell relayed the decision to Deputy Assistant Attorney General Mark Richard. When Hubbell asked how the bureau would respond, Richard said they would be upset. Hubbell called FBI Director Sessions and asked him to come to his office. Furious at the news, Sessions requested a meeting with Reno to ask her to reconsider.

Hubbell left to grab Reno. He returned about ten minutes later with the attorney general. Reno and Hubbell hadn't discussed the matter at length, but something had changed in the director's mind. She ordered the FBI to prepare a statement and briefing book.

It was an indication she was going to approve the mission. The assembled officials were startled. There'd been no conversation with Sessions.

The next day, the FBI delivered a three-ring binder, which included all the relevant information given to Reno over the preceding weeks, along with a statement outlining the tactical operation to insert tear gas into the compound. Reno scanned the statement. She didn't read the supporting documents, she only wanted to know they were there. What Reno paid the most attention to was the chronology of events.

One of the sections, Tab B, number 11, stated that during one FBI meeting with the attorney general, there were references to Koresh physically abusing minors at the compound during the siege. FBI officials later said the dating of that information was a typo. The references were to the bureau's earlier interviews with ex-Davidians, which had resulted in allegations of child sexual abuse and physical beating of minors.

The proposed date for the tear gas assault was Monday, April 19. As with the initial ATF raid, the choice was intentional. Weekends were typically the busiest times for emergency rooms, so Saturday and Sunday were ruled out, in case Waco became a mass casualty event.

On the afternoon of Saturday, April 17, Reno gave the operation the green light, with conditions. If the Davidians did anything to risk the lives of the children during the assault, the agency was to withdraw. "Get the hell out of there" was Reno's summary of her directive.

The attorney general didn't reveal the basis for the reversal. Later, she commented: "I can't say there was one particular point that finally tipped it . . . As of Friday night, I didn't feel comfortable enough with proceeding. But I think it was the culmination of all the factors, that the situation in the compound was deteriorating, that we were concerned about people in the compound and the fact that he could do what he did at any time and we would be in the less favorable position to control it."

On Sunday, Reno went to the White House to brief the president. Her account of the meeting and Clinton's memory of it are somewhat different. In Reno's version, she emphasized that April 19 was not "D-day." Getting the Davidians to surrender might take time. The tear gas insertion was only the start of the endgame.

Clinton's account of the conversation was more expansive. He recalled that Reno told him that the FBI wanted to storm the compound and arrest Koresh and those who'd taken part in the killing of the ATF agents and other offenses. Reno said that she was concerned by reports that Koresh was molesting children and that he might initiate a mass suicide. Clinton also recalled Reno saying that the FBI believed that too many resources that were needed elsewhere were being utilized at Waco. She told him the FBI estimated that the tear gas would cause the followers to leave the compound within two hours. Reno asked for Clinton's okay for the plan.

The two accounts weren't necessarily in conflict. Reno and Clinton each came away from the meeting with different aspects of the operation front and center in their minds.

For his part, the president told Reno about a standoff that had occurred when he was governor of Arkansas. A right-wing group was burrowed into their mountain camp in the north of the state. They were spread out among several cabins and were heavily armed. The FBI proposed storming the site.

Clinton decided to consult a war veteran, "someone who'd fought in the jungles of Vietnam." The veteran flew above the site and came back and told the then-governor, "If those people can shoot at all, you'll lose fifty men in the assault." Clinton canceled the operation and ordered a blockade of the camp. The standoff later ended peacefully.

The president suggested something similar. But Reno responded with several points: the FBI didn't want to delay any longer; the reported child abuse could continue; the Davidians had food supplies that far outpaced what the right-wingers in Arkansas had; and the standoff was costing a million dollars a week.

"It is your decision," Clinton told the attorney general. The talk lasted fifteen minutes.

As the FBI finalized its plans, David's attorney, Dick DeGuerin, received a letter. It was signed by David and was in his voice:

> Hello Dick,
>   . . . I was shown that as soon as I am given over into the hands of man, I will be made a spectacle of, and people will not be concerned about the truth of God, but just the bizarrity of me – the flesh (person).
>   I want the people of this generation to be saved . . .
>   We are standing on the threshold of Great events! The Seven Seals, in written form, are the most sacred information ever!
>   David Koresh

On April 16, David told the FBI he'd finished the section on the First Seal. Judy was busy typing it out.

But the FBI seemed to have given up on the whole idea. "Mr. Koresh does not have any more than a ninth-grade education, so he does not write very well," a spokesman told the press. "So everything will have to be rewritten . . . We really have no idea how long it's going to take . . . They have refused to be pinned down on any time certain."

The next day, another letter was placed outside the compound, much in the same vein as the first two. "I begin to do My 'strange work,'" David wrote in it. It was a quotation from Isaiah 28.

A milk-carton bug caught the Davidians talking about keeping fire trucks off the compound. "Nobody comes in here," one said. "They couldn't even bring in the fire truck," Steve replied, "'cause they couldn't even get near us."

Steve talked with the FBI about the Bible being fulfilled. "If you look at the prophecies, it talks about a place in the last days that's plowed like a field. Do you think, perchance, it could be this place?" The Brads had left ruts and furrows all over the property, which, if you thought about it, resembled a field that had been plowed. "It seems like it's being fulfilled," Steve continued. "I would have never dreamed."

And if you went deeper, wasn't the compound, scarred and abused as it was, a place larger in its implications? "This has been America," Steve said. "It's come to the place where I think this all needs, everything needs to really end as far as I'm concerned . . ."

"The Constitution has been so ripped apart and run over its principles that, you know, do what you got to do, honestly? . . . They can burn the place down. Bring—like I said the other day—bring in your Abrams tanks and just run the whole place over and then stick a gravestone over the place."

Why leave the compound if the whole country was being disfigured and brought to heel by hidden Babylonians? Let it turn into a graveyard until David redeemed it.

LETTERS

I N WACO, FAMILY members of the Branch Davidians were gathered in motel rooms, hoping for the chance to see their loved ones. Some spoke to journalists. Others sent tapes into the compound or simply watched the live feed on TV.

Journalists tracked down Sandy, David's old girlfriend. In the years since she'd dated David, she'd moved more than once, trying to keep one step ahead of him. She felt like a fugitive—not just because of David, but other weird stuff that had happened in Texas. She seemed to draw the crazy energy of the world to her, like she was dragging this long tangled-up trail of bad experiences and wrecked things, clanking and clattering behind her. At least that's how it felt.

But before the ATF raid, David would find her once or twice a year and come see her, trying to win her back. He would show up at her house. "Come to Mount Carmel," he'd say. "Come sing with my band."

In her mind, she knew he wanted to control her, but the way he spoke, it was as if he cared about her so much that he didn't want her to make one false move, and that's why he was there.

Sandy refused to go. She'd tell him, "You're not who you see yourself as, David." But David wouldn't listen, as always. He'd get spun up into some long-winded speech, and there went a couple of hours out of her life.

Sandy believed that, if she went to Waco, he would use her as a sign from God. "I told you all about Sandy, who rejected me but has now repented! Here she is!" It would be proof of his prophecies. She would be part of whatever destruction David was headed toward. She couldn't do that.

What she really wanted was to go to David's followers and warn them that David was preaching false prophecy. But her parents told her it wasn't her place to do that. God would find someone else to play that role.

Still, it all stressed her out terribly.

The last time David found Sandy, he knew the name of the small town she was living in but not her address. He showed up in a long flowing robe, looking for all the world like Jesus Christ. It took him three days to locate Sandy, and each day he had a different-colored robe on—white, then red, then black. He walked the streets, preaching. He really turned people's heads around.

Sandy didn't know he was there until she drove home from work one day and there was David in the driveway preaching to her boyfriend at the time. This had been going on for two hours. He'd brought his son Cyrus. David got out his guitar and sang a few songs for them. Her boyfriend just sat there like the Martians had landed. What the hell was this?

Her boyfriend got sullen after David left. He was confused, wouldn't talk for days, and when he did talk it was just to argue with her. Just David sprinkling her life with rainbows and sunshine all over again.

Sandy was thankful it wasn't worse. She was so afraid of David, not only of what he might do to her: stuff her in a trunk and drive off. It was that he might bewitch one of her family or friends and carry them off to Mount Carmel.

Now the journalists wanted to speak to her because a rumor was going around saying that she might be "the cause" of what was happening at Waco. By breaking up with David just before he went to Mount Carmel, the theory went, she'd tipped him over into insanity. Reporters swarmed her house. Sandy had to make a run for it and ended up at her lawyer's place. She hid out for weeks. Everyone wanted a piece of her that they could fit into their puzzles of what happened and why.

A publisher offered her a lot of money to do a book. He had professional photos taken of her, to go along with the proposal. But her family told her if she wrote a book, she would no longer exist for them.

The supermarket tabloids claimed they'd interviewed her. It was a lie. They said David had introduced her to the "church partying scene," which didn't exist. David had never hung out with any other church people and he'd never tried to give her alcohol. They even got the Sabbath wrong, saying that the SDA had church on Sunday.

Eventually, the reporters got to Sandy's mother. They jumped over her fence and knocked on her door until she answered. She handed over pictures of Sandy playing the piano, told them what they wanted to know. Her mom lived in a world where newspapermen were honest fellows.

For Sandy, the Vernon Howell she'd known and this David Koresh person seemed like two different men. It was like he'd been body-snatched. How he treated those women, she'd never suspected it was in him.

Others in David's past felt the strangeness of their association, too. David's daughter by Linda was a teenager in high school as the siege wore on. One teacher knew her identity, though the other students were unaware.

One day, this teacher announced that David Koresh's daughter was in their class and it would be nice if they could all support her. The girl was mortified.

The principal wanted to call the local news station and do an interview about having Koresh's daughter at the school. The girl's guidance counselor told him it would be a terrible idea. He relented.

People followed her. It frightened her. Later, it turned out some of the men were FBI agents. The head of the FBI called her afterward and told her he was sorry.

More letters from the public came into the FBI headquarters in Washington. Most had ideas for ending the standoff. They included flooding the building with water, pumping the compound full of ether, which would put the Davidians to sleep, and spraying the perimeter of the building with tons of fire suppression foam—the kind used at airports during plane crashes—so that David couldn't see out of the windows.

Some wrote to protest what the FBI was doing, echoing Steve's assessment of the state of the Constitution. "Make no mistake about it," wrote one concerned citizen, "the people do not adhere to this Government because they feel justice is being carried out or that the system is equitable, it is merely because we know that the Government is too strong to beat . . .

"I . . . urge you to halt this inhuman terroristic attack upon the people of the Branch Davidian Sect and halt the Governments' infringement upon the Basic Human Rights of all its citizens before this Government shares the same fate as the British-Colonial Government of the United States Colonies."

The Davidians hung out more signs: "FBI GOD SEES YOUR LIES" one said; "RODNEY KING WE UNDERSTAND" read another. The Davidians were aligning themselves with a Black man savagely beaten by police two years before. It was certainly off-message for the far-right supporters that were gathered at the perimeter.

One of the HRT agents noticed a new message, written on a bedsheet, hanging from one of the windows. It was different from the others that had been put out before. He called it in to the command post. Written in Magic Marker, the sign read "THE FLAMES AWAIT. ISAIAH 13."

The biblical passage recounted something Amoz, Isaiah's son, had seen in a vision of Babylon.

> *Wail, for the day of the Lord is near;*
> *it will come like destruction from the Almighty.*
> *Because of this, all hands will go limp,*
> *every heart will melt with fear.*
> *Terror will seize them,*
> *pain and anguish will grip them;*
> *they will writhe like a woman in labor.*
> *They will look aghast at each other,*
> *their faces aflame.*

One of the Davidians had drawn flames around the words.

On April 18, Byron spoke to the HRT chief, Dick Rogers. He told Rogers the tear gas plan wouldn't work. The Davidians would refuse to come out and the assault would place the negotiators in a difficult position with

David and the others. The trust that they'd managed to build would be gone, and David's paranoia would ramp up even higher.

Despite his concerns, preparations for the tear gas plan continued. A number of David's classic cars were towed away; one was crushed by an FBI tracked vehicle when it became snagged during the towing. Other, less valuable cars were mashed by the armored machines. David watched from a compound window. "You're going to place this day in the history books as one of the saddest days in the world," he told a negotiator.

The bugs gave the FBI a glimpse into the Davidians' thoughts on what was coming. "It may be scary," Steve told the others. Another man said: "You always wanted to be a charcoal briquette." Then a third voice: "There's nothing like a good fire to bring us to the earth."

48

GAS

I T WAS SIX a.m. on April 19, still dark. Most of the Davidians were asleep. The phone rang and Steve picked up.

"Steve? This is Byron Sage. Can you hear me now? Okay. This is Byron Sage. I need to advise you of something that's very important. Can you understand me? Okay. We're in the process of placing tear gas into the building. This is not an assault. We are not entering the building. Do you understand that? This is not an assault on the building . . . Do not fire your weapons. If you fire, fire will be returned."

Steve hung up.

The loudspeakers outside buzzed and then came to life. Byron's voice over the cold fields. The negotiator was set up across the road from the compound, near the undercover house the ATF has used for their raid a month and a half earlier.

The Davidians snapped awake. They went looking for their gas masks. Someone inside the compound took the phone the FBI had been using to speak with Steve and David and threw it out the front door.

In Washington, Janet Reno awoke before dawn in her rented apartment and went to the FBI building to monitor the assault. She and her lieutenants watched the CNN live feed, but the audio came from the FBI's operations center, a specially equipped RV parked by the side of Route 7 outside Waco.

At 6:04 a.m., a specially modified armored vehicle with a hose attached to its turret advanced toward the front of the compound. It punched through the wall and began spraying the CS2 gas, actually a fine powder, into the rooms.

As Byron watched, the skins of the Abramses were covered in tiny sparks. It looked like someone had attached lit sparklers to the tanks. An unidentified voice came on the radio, saying the Davidians were shooting at the tanks. When Byron looked at the compound, he spotted muzzle flashes in the windows.

"These fucking idiots," Byron said.

The gas billowed through the rooms. The Davidians tried to find spaces where the acrid powder hadn't reached, but it was seemingly everywhere. Eyes streaming with tears, coughing and struggling to breathe, the Davidians fought back panic. The gas produced a burning sensation in the mouth and ears; some followers felt they were choking. Their vision blurred.

At 7:21 a.m., the bugs inside the compound recorded a conversation:

UNIDENTIFIED MALE: Is there a way to spread fuel there?

UNIDENTIFIED MALE: OK . . . what we do . . . You don't know.

UNIDENTIFIED MALE: I know that won't spread . . . get some more.

UNIDENTIFIED MALE: So we only light it first when they come in with the tank right . . . right as they're coming in?

UNIDENTIFIED MALE: Right.

UNIDENTIFIED MALE: That's secure . . . We should get more hay in here.

UNIDENTIFIED MALE: I know.

Two minutes later:

UNIDENTIFIED MALE: Is there any way to spread fuel in here? There.

UNIDENTIFIED MALE: I don't know. I know that one [unintelligible] . . .

UNIDENTIFIED MALE: So we only light them as they come in [unintelligible], right? Not if they don't come in.

The HRT guys inside the Brads could hear rounds ringing off the metal skin, and when they looked at the compound's tower, they spotted followers moving up the stairs with long guns in their hands. The Davidians were firing at them, violating the rules of engagement. "Compromise," an HRT operator called out on the radio. This was the signal to the grenadiers that the parameters of the mission had changed and they could now fire plastic ferrets containing the CS gas into the compound, in addition to what the tanks were putting into the building. When fired, the ferrets launched toward the building, their flight stabilized by wings at the bottom of the projectile. When the ferret slammed into a wall or a floor, the nose ruptured, releasing the powder into the air.

Now, instead of gradually inserting the tear gas into the building section by section, the strategy switched to flooding every room with as much as possible, fast. The agents took out their M79 grenade launchers, loaded with the plastic ferrets containing 40mm liquid CS gas, dropped the back hatch of the Brads and stepped out. They began firing, trying to arc the ferrets into the compound's windows. After a couple of tries, they were consistently putting them on target.

The agents quickly depleted their supplies. At 7:45 a.m., administrators began phoning FBI field offices, asking if they had any ferrets to spare. The Houston office found forty-eight and drove them to Waco.

A lot of gas was going into the rooms.

At no point during its discussions with Janet Reno had the FBI informed her or her associates that there was a possibility they would use pyrotechnic rounds in the planned assault. The leaders of HRT did believe it possible that one of their agents would be required to use the M0651 rounds, which was a pyrotechnic. But that fact wasn't included in any of the documents in the operations plan provided to Reno, nor was it mentioned in the briefings.

And in the beginning, the agents shot only nonpyrotechnic ferrets. Then, around eight a.m., a member of the Hostage Rescue Team, David Corderman, asked Dick Rogers for permission to fire M0651 rounds. He had noticed that the plastic ferrets were bouncing off the sheets of plywood covering the work pit outside the wooden building. He felt that the heavier M0651s had a better chance to penetrate.

Rogers radioed his okay. The agent shot three pyrotechnic rounds at the pit, which bounced off the plywood covering and fell next to the pit. No pyrotechnic rounds were fired at the building itself.

A bullet came across the road and pierced the garage door of the surveillance house, embedding itself in the wall beyond it. It had missed Byron by a few feet.

The tanks growled furiously. At around nine a.m., one moved toward the building again, punched another hole in the exterior and sprayed the CS powder. Another slammed into the corner of the building, partially collapsing it. The building began to shake as the tank drove through the walls. The floors buckled. There was a sound of wood crackling and snapping.

At the FBI center, the officials tuned in to CNN, watching the mission live, along with millions of Americans. The officials were startled by how much damage the tanks were doing.

"Holy shit," someone said.

"I hope that's a bad camera angle," said FBI Assistant Directory Danny Coulson.

It was bad optics for sure.

Inside, Clive Doyle was in the chapel. He could hear the crying of children from the concrete bunker that sat under the tower in the middle of the compound. The tear gas powder had gotten on their skin and they were scratching at their arms, whimpering with pain. When he took off his gas mask, Doyle felt a burning sensation on his skin from the powder.

At 9:20 a.m., David and Steve were recorded on the bug tapes.

DAVID: They got two cans of Coleman fuel down there? Huh?
STEVE: Empty.
DAVID: All of it?
STEVE: Think so.
DAVID: Did you check?
STEVE: Nothing left.
DAVID: Out of both cans?
STEVE: I got some mineral oil left.

At around 10:30 a.m., Reno called President Clinton. Based on reports she'd received from FBI officials, she told Clinton the operation was going well and she was encouraged by the progress. Some people were coming out. That information was incorrect. No one had yet emerged.

Soon after, she left the building and got into a dark blue Lincoln driven by an FBI agent. She was heading to a speech at a Baltimore conference. From the back of the car, she called and asked for an update. She was told that Koresh hadn't come out or communicated with the FBI.

Ten minutes later, the Davidians hung a sign out the window. "WE WANT OUR PHONE FIXED." At 9:35 a.m., negotiators began calling for a Davidian to exit the building and bring the telephone back inside. But they made it clear the connection would be reestablished only if the Davidians agreed to come out.

No one responded.

At 11:27 a.m., weakened by the ramming of the tanks, the building's roof partially caved in. In the next half hour, more walls and ceilings collapsed; agents in the field could now see directly into parts of the building.

At 11:31 a.m., a CEV-1 pushed into the building and sprayed gas toward a concrete vault where, unknown to the FBI agents, many of the Davidian mothers and their children were hiding. The spraying continued for twenty-four minutes.

Inside, unidentified Davidians continued talking about fuel. The bug tapes picked up their words.

"Need fuel," one said.
"Do you want it poured?"
"Have you poured it yet?"
"David said pour it, right?"
"David said we have to get the fuel on."
"I've already poured it."

Some of the fuel splashed onto the Davidians. This happened to Clive Doyle, whose clothes were saturated with kerosene, though he later denied helping set the fires.

And then:

"Real quickly you can order the fire yes."

"So we only light it first when they come in with the tank right . . .
    right as they're coming in."

"That's secure. We should get more hay in here."

From between 11:17 a.m. to 12:04 p.m., more talk about fire.

"Do you think I could light this soon?"

"I want a fire on the front . . . you two can go."

Graeme Craddock saw some of the other Davidians pouring fuel
around the chapel. There were prearranged locations in the compound
where the Davidians spilled the accelerant, including some of the hay
bales that lined the walls inside. A follower came down the stairs and
shouted: "Light the fire."

As his followers began setting fires, David cried, "Don't light it up!" He
saw that no FBI agents were emerging from the tanks or coming toward
the compound. David's strategy was clear: He believed FBI agents would
enter the building and he wanted them to die along with his followers.

But the tear gas wasn't the beginning of another tactical raid. The FBI
had no plans of coming in. If the fires were lit, no one but the Davidians
would burn.

By the time David called out, the hay bales were already alight.

An FBI agent was stationed at the sniper outpost about a hundred
eighty yards from the chapel. He was watching the building, using a pair
of binoculars and a spotting scope. He saw the outlines of two Davidians;
it looked like they were pouring fuel from canisters. He called it in.

A little later, an HRT operative was watching a white male Davidian
through field glasses. The man was on the second floor of the tower. The
man bent over, did something, then moved a little and bent over again.
The operative thought the man could be lighting a fire. A few seconds
later, he saw smoke.

HRT agent Jim McGee was inside one of the Brads when he saw a puff
of smoke in one corner of the main building's second story. He was like,
"Oh man, that doesn't look like tear gas." It was white, thick, and it was
pouring out one of the windows.

McGee got on the radio. "I think we got smoke coming out of the red-white corner," using the code for that part of the building. Before he could get off the radio, another HRT guy was calling in. "Yeah, I got smoke." McGee knew the voice, knew the agent was looking at a different part of the compound. "There's no way he can see smoke," he thought. "He must be seeing something else." Then he realized that there had to be multiple fires.

McGee had been a wildland firefighter for six years. He knew the compound was built of CDX plywood and two-by-four framing. With twenty-mile-an-hour winds, that was bad news. "Man, that's unbelievable," he told the guys in the Brad. "It's going to go up like kindling." He gave it twenty minutes before the whole thing was in flames.

A local man, J. J. Robertson, who'd been working at the Salvation Army truck parked outside the perimeter, was curious about what was happening. He walked through the woods toward the compound. As he got closer, smoke began seeping among the briar and scrub brush, a billowing, acrid fog. He could hear helicopters above him. It sounded like they were moving fast.

When he looked down at his feet, it seemed as if the ground cover was moving. It was rabbits and foxes and other small animals, running away from the fire.

Inside the compound, Ruth Riddle was on the second floor near a hole that had been punched in the exterior wall. She felt the air growing hotter. The floor beneath her feet was warming up. She could hear a rushing, crackling noise, as if the prairie winds had invaded the building.

Flashes of fire shot down the hallways. They got closer and closer, pushing a wall of heat in front of them. Riddle jumped through the hole.

Agent McGee saw the woman leap. She landed awkwardly in the debris in front of the building. It looked like she might have twisted her ankle.

Then the woman did the damndest thing. She turned and walked back into the first floor of the compound, close to the flames.

McGee called for the driver to get closer. When the Brad had maneuvered next to the building, he dropped the hatch. "Are you crazy?" one of the guys called after him. There were possible shooters in there. The woman herself might be a shooter. But McGee jumped out, leaned his rifle against the side of the Brad, and ran for the building.

Riddle was lying facedown on the ground, like she'd dropped there from the roof and died. Just the weirdest thing. McGee nudged her. She turned and looked at him.

"Who are you?" she said.

He shouted that he was with the FBI and they needed to get out of there. The fire was roaring behind him. He was worried less about it than the superheated air that would flow from it, crisping his lungs and drowning him in his own fluids. He'd seen it before.

"Where are the children?" he yelled.

She turned her face away from him, said nothing.

"Where are the kids? Tell me where the children are."

Nothing.

"Look, the ceiling is going to collapse on us. We've got to get out of here."

He grabbed her. She was deadweight, giving him no help. He dragged her out through the hole in the wall and got her to the Brad. She never said a word.

The snipers and observers near the compound began to hear gunshots. Some were random and sporadic, and the FBI agents assumed they were rounds cooking off in the fire. But there was a second sequence that sounded rhythmic. They believed that Davidians were being shot inside Mount Carmel.

Byron continued to talk on the loudspeaker. "Steve, David, we're attempting to contact you via the telephone . . . If you cannot do that, if the lines have been cut, indicate with a flag out the front door." Moments later, a flag appeared. But no one picked up the phone.

Byron saw the first whiffs of smoke soon after the others spotted them. He wasn't surprised; he thought the Davidians were burning evidence and destroying the crime scene in order to avoid prosecution later. Without any physical evidence, it would be the ATF's testimony against the Davidians' testimony, and it might go the Davidians' way, you never knew. But seconds ticked by, then minutes, and still nobody came out.

Janet Reno had finished her speech in Baltimore. She was at a local hotel having lunch when an FBI agent informed her about the fire. She got into the dark blue Lincoln and headed back toward Washington. She told the agent driving the car to hurry.

From the back of the car, Reno called FBI headquarters. She asked several times about the children. Had any been spotted? Had any children gotten out?

Byron turned his back to the monitor. He had to keep speaking, but the sight of the burning compound was disturbing to him.

"Bring your children and leave the building," he said. "Fire is plainly visible. We observed people lighting the fire. Leave the building. Leave your weapons behind and locked in the building." Silence.

"You will not be harmed. You will not be fired on. Put your weapons down and leave the building. Shit."

In Washington, FBI and Justice officials were watching on TV. "Oh, my God, they're committing suicide," somebody said. Another official replied, "That's not suicide, that's homicide."

President Clinton watched the CNN live feed. He felt sick.

He wanted to speak to the press and take responsibility for the operation. Two of his close advisers, Dee Myers and Bruce Lindsey, agreed. But the White House communications director, George Stephanopoulos, told him it was too early. Not all the Davidians were confirmed dead; Koresh might hear the president's words and kill his remaining followers. Clinton agreed to wait.

At 11:40 a.m., unidentified voices were heard on the bug tapes. "I want a fire around the back," said one. Then, "let's keep that fire going."

Clive Doyle was on the stage in the chapel, behind a wooden partition. About ten others had retreated there as the day progressed and the tanks inserted more and more gas into the building. Doyle had planned to die and be translated into the new life. His daughter Shari was deeper inside the building.

Wayne Martin, the lawyer, walked in, wearing a gas mask. He went over to the wall, turned, and leaned his back against it. He slid down until he was sitting on the floor.

Everyone was watching Martin, wondering if there were further instructions on what to do. Had David said anything? What was happening?

Martin pulled the gas mask off. "You'd better just pray," he said.

There were no gas masks for the kids—they didn't exist, one couldn't buy such a thing—so Davidian mothers and fathers in the concrete bunker grabbed towels and stuck them in buckets of water. Then they held the drenched cloths to their children's faces.

Heat began pressing into the small area on the stage where Doyle and the others were. It was above their heads and then all around their bodies. People began screaming. They dropped to the floor and rolled along it. Perhaps some of them had caught fire, Doyle couldn't see, but certainly the heat was rushing in waves. It was pitch black inside the narrow space, and claustrophobic.

David Thibodeau, the rock drummer, heard someone shouting about fire on the second floor. He ran upstairs, toward the chapel attic, to see what was happening. He had to step across some flooring laid across the rafters to get there.

When Thibodeau got close to the attic, he saw a wall of fire roaring down the hallway. The sound was louder than anything he'd heard in his life. He felt he was choking.

He turned around and ran back downstairs.

Doyle kept waiting for the change to happen, for his body to begin the translation. The heat was almost unbearable, and still nothing happened except the terrible pain he felt. He was confused. He was afraid, too, that if he went outside, the FBI would shoot him.

The fire seemed to fly through the air. The wall that Thibodeau was standing next to ignited. As he became aware of the flames, they were already leaping upward. He heard the hair on his head beginning to sizzle. He knew if he stayed there, he would burn to death. A hole had opened up in the wall in front of him and he stumbled through it.

He thought he would be the last to make it out, but he turned to glance at the building and saw Doyle coming out after him, his arms covered in flames. Doyle was patting his sleeves with his bare hands, trying to put out the fire.

"Hold your hands up," someone barked. Thibodeau did as he was told and staggered forward, stiff-legged. Something exploded behind him. An enormous wave of heat pressed against his back for a second, then swept past him.

When he looked back, the building's roof and upper floors were being consumed by roiling balls of fire eating their way upward into the sky. He thought, no one will survive that.

Doyle staggered forward. He rubbed his arms and watched the skin roll up in his hands. The jacket he was wearing was melting from the heat onto his skin. His arms smoked.

The loudspeakers were blaring, echoing. "David, don't do this to your people. David, don't do this to your people . . . Be a messiah, not a destroyer . . . Don't lead them to destruction. Bring them out."

Amid the roar of flames, Steve Schneider could be heard talking to himself. "What's taking them so long?" he said. Steve was waiting on the angels.

Ten minutes after the first puff of smoke from the compound, just after 12:30 p.m., the main tower collapsed in a plume of smoke and fire. Underneath it was the bunker where the Davidians' bus was buried. Byron stopped talking on the loudspeaker and turned to look at the compound. He reached down with his right hand and clicked the power switch on the PA system off.

A T-intersection about a mile from the compound had been designated a medical triage site. A Brad appeared on Double EE Ranch Road, moving fast. It reached the T and it hit the brakes and spun around. As it shook to a stop, the back gate started to lower.

You could see little wisps of smoke wafting out of the interior. When the door was fully lowered, it became clear there was someone in the back. It was Marjorie Thomas, one of the Davidians. Her flesh had been so terribly burned that she was cooking alive.

They put her on a chopper and flew her to a burn center at a nearby hospital.

Live shots of the compound going up in flames went around the world. Bonnie Haldeman was working an overnight shift as a nurse. She was in one of the patient rooms giving a woman her meds. The TV was on in the room, the volume low. She glanced at the screen and saw the tanks punching holes in the compound walls.

"Oh my God, what's going on?" she thought to herself.

She kept her eye on the facility's TVs as the morning passed. She saw the first puffs of smoke. "People are going to start coming out," she thought. When they didn't, she imagined they were down in the bunker and it was taking them a while to get out. One reason for the delay and then another flitted through her mind.

At one point, she was called to the phone. It was Connie Chung, one of the hosts of the TV show *A Current Affair*. "What are you feeling right now, Bonnie?" Chung said. Bonnie didn't know how to describe what she was feeling.

Maybe Vernon got out, she kept thinking. The cameras were far away, you couldn't pick up much detail. Maybe they weren't capable of catching the little figures of people escaping. The kids must have gotten out. Even as the building began to collapse, she kept that last thought in her mind.

Debbie Bunds was watching. She felt that people were dying right on television. People she'd known, people she'd seen born, grown up with. David was killing them. He was too much of a coward to come out and face the music.

She felt sick. But as she watched, she pleaded in her mind: "Please, let David be gone."

Kat Schroeder, watching at McLennan County Jail, felt the opposite. Dying was the right thing to do. She felt that her friends were being translated before her eyes. "I should have died, too," she thought.

In the same jail, Livingstone Fagan didn't think anything had been lost. His wife and mother weren't gone forever. He expected to see them again soon. He decided to delay telling his children that their mother was dead. Or was she?

Eddie Goins, one of David's rocker friends from Waco, had been waiting for the Davidians to come out. He wanted to testify on their behalf in court. When he realized David was dead, Goins got angry. "He's been done shitty," he told people. "This is supposed to be America."

In England, Sam Henry was leaving a job. It was teatime. He was headed home to pick up some tools. Then he would head to another thing he'd taken on.

When he pulled into his street, he saw TV crews gathered around his gate. He approached them and asked what was going on. "Let's go to the studio," said one of the reporters, "and you can see what's going on."

Gail Monbelly, whose sister Bernadette was inside the compound, walked into her house. The phone rang. Her mother, asking if she'd seen the news.

"No, Mum, I've just got home from work, what's wrong?"

"There's been a fire."

"A fire where?"

"At Waco . . . Just put the TV on. I can't speak." She put the phone down.

Gail switched on the TV. She collapsed to the floor.

"I'll never laugh and joke with her again," Gail thought. "The person closest to me in all my life. My secrets have died with her." When something big happened in her life, the first thing she would think was "I have to tell Bernadette." That was over.

Sandy was still hiding from the press. Her lawyer didn't want her to go anywhere. But that day she snuck out and went to a grocery store. While she was doing a little shopping, she looked up and saw a TV tuned to CNN.

She found a telephone booth and called Bonnie's house. Bonnie had people screening her calls. Sandy told the person who answered that she was David's ex-girlfriend.

Bonnie came to the phone. She said, "Sandy, I think Vernon is dead."

"Yes, I think so, too," Sandy said. They both began to cry.

Bernard Nussbaum, the White House chief counsel, was in Poland on a trip with the vice president to commemorate the anniversary of the Warsaw ghetto uprising. He walked into his hotel and saw Mount Carmel burning on the TV set.

He called the White House. "What's going on?" he asked one of the president's aides.

"What's going on is what you see on TV. What's going on is they broke in and fire started and a lot of people are dead. But we're handling it. We and George Stephanopoulos."

Nussbaum began to regret telling Reno to trust the FBI. His opinion of the bureau had been too high. Later, the FBI's role in Waco came to remind him of the CIA's advice on the Bay of Pigs.

As for Marc Breault, he was at home in Melbourne when the phone rang near midnight, Australian time. When he picked up the phone, a woman identified herself as a reporter for the *Times* in London. She asked for his reaction.

"My reaction to what?" he said.

She told him about the fire. He turned on the TV and watched. The reporter was waiting for a comment.

Strangely, he found it hard to feel anything at all. He thought of the children. But as for the others, Marc felt he'd lost them long ago.

That morning, Timothy McVeigh was at a friend's house in Michigan. He was planning on heading to Waco the following day, to bear witness and perhaps do something—to take some undefined action that would help free the Davidians, though McVeigh couldn't think of what that might be. He was splayed out underneath his Chevy Geo Spectrum changing the oil when someone shouted at him to come watch the TV.

McVeigh and his friends watched in silence as the tanks inserted the CS gas into the building. McVeigh had been soaked in the stuff during Army training at Fort Benning, and had watched his buddies vomit, their skin scorched by the gas. Watching, he was horrified to think of what it felt like to a child, feeling their throats beginning to close. He stayed silent as fire consumed the compound.

"What is this?" he said finally. "What has America become?" McVeigh felt an impotent rage crawl along his skin and nerve endings. He'd just watched human beings attacked, murdered, and then incinerated by the government he paid taxes to. He vowed to avenge the Davidians. "The blaze at the Waco compound," wrote his biographers, "more than any other event, was a turning point in his life."

Chuck Hustmyre, the ATF agent, was in Louisiana. Two Texas Rangers had come to the office to interview some of the agents who'd taken part in the February 28 raid. They were investigating the murder of the four agents. Hustmyre and some others met them at the little ATF office in Metairie, Louisiana. After the interview, they went down to the Sheraton Hotel and the bar there. They were having a few drinks and they looked up at the TV and saw fire.

Hustmyre hadn't followed the siege all that much. He'd been too busy with funerals and work. At Todd's funeral, they'd driven the rural Tennessee roads on the way to the graveyard and people stopped their cars and got out and the men took their hats off and held them to their chests. It surprised Chuck, he'd never seen anything like that.

So that day, he didn't know who was inside; he wasn't aware there were children still in the building. His general impression was that a bunch of people had left Mount Carmel, and the people still remaining inside were the real hardcore guys. The ones who'd shot his friends.

And what he thought was "Holy shit, this is great. All those assholes are gonna die."

Byron felt stupefied. He walked outside toward the compound. He could feel the heat from the fire on his face. The building was visible, the walls tumbling and the roof collapsing until what mostly remained was a layer of rubble about a foot and a half high. He could smell the fire, too, and the things it had consumed.

He felt that he had failed, and everyone else within a half-mile radius had failed, too.

Not quite steady on his feet, Byron crossed Double EE Ranch Road and walked up the driveway. The fire had mostly burned itself out, but there were patches of flame and a thick haze of smoke low on the wreckage. Ammo cooked off in bursts and cans of food exploded in the heat. Guys from the Hostage Rescue Team had gone down into the construction pit to reach the underground bunker, where the children were believed to be.

Byron didn't give a shit about the adults, frankly—they'd made their bed—but he wanted to see the kids come out.

To reach the bunker, the agents waded through filthy, sewage-tainted water that reached their waists. They made it to the door of the bus and pushed inside. There were no children here, nobody alive, just corpses. They found the trapdoor that led to the rooms above. Parts of the building had collapsed on top of it and they couldn't force it open.

The men in black tech gear went back through the dark water and climbed up the side of the construction pit. They were alone. Byron understood immediately that no one else was coming out.

Throughout the day, the agents combed through the broken drywall and wood looking for survivors. When cans of food or spare ammo exploded, they'd drop to the rubble, then stand again. There was a cutting stench of rotting vegetables and fruit, along with the smell of singed flesh. Swarms of flies and bees hovered over the wreckage, their droning and buzzing the only sounds to be heard.

President Clinton spoke to Janet Reno that afternoon. He asked her about possible survivors.

At five p.m., Reno approached a lectern at the Justice Department briefing room. She began to read a prepared statement. "These are the hardest decisions in the world to make. My heart goes out to the families of the agents killed and those injured, as well as to those children and the families of those who perished in the compound today. We must all reflect on how we, as a society, can in the future prevent such a senseless, horrible, tragic loss of human life." She, pointedly, did not express any remorse for the adult Davidians.

After reading her statement, Reno took questions. A journalist asked whether President Clinton had approved the operation. "I approved the plan," she said, "and I'm responsible for it."

Another reporter rephrased the question, asking if Reno was trying to absolve Clinton of any responsibility. Her temper flared. "I made the decision," she said. "The buck stops with me." It was a phrase, borrowed from President Harry Truman, that she would use throughout the day's media appearances.

As the press conference went on, Reno bristled. To her, the reporters arrayed in front of her were nothing more than a pack of jackals. Their questions were pointed and almost enraged.

As the minutes passed, however, she noticed, or thought she noticed, something odd. The expressions of those in front of her changed. She saw sensitivity and comprehension there. It was as if they had all come through an event that was horrible and beyond understanding. She would never forget that moment.

After Reno spoke, George Stephanopoulos released a short statement from the president. "The law enforcement agencies involved in the Waco siege recommended the course of action pursued today. The Attorney General informed me of their analysis and judgment and recommended that we proceed with today's action given the risks for maintaining the previous policy indefinitely. I told the Attorney General to do what she thought was right, and I stand by that decision."

To White House watchers versed in the arcane language of political messaging, it seemed that Clinton was starting to walk away from Reno.

Clinton later recalled the situation differently. "Reno was being praised," he wrote, and "I was being criticized for letting her take the fall."

Twice in the Waco crisis he'd gone against his gut instinct. He'd approved the raid despite misgivings, and he'd hesitated to take full public responsibility for it. "I was furious at myself," Clinton wrote.

Late that evening, Reno went on the news show *Nightline*. The host, Ted Koppel, asked her, gently, about the possibility of resigning. "If that be the case, if that's what the president wants, I'm happy to do so."

That night, around 12:30 a.m., Reno's media appearances were done. She went back to her apartment and told the FBI agent guarding her to go on home. She closed the door behind him. She felt as alone as she'd ever been in her life.

The phone rang. It was her sister. She tried to buck Reno up. After a few minutes, they hung up.

The phone rang again. It was Clinton. He'd told her she'd performed well under tough circumstances. "Get some sleep," he said.

After leaving the compound, Byron got in his car and drove to his motel. He stripped off his clothes, turned the shower on hot, and stood under the stream of water. Then he crawled into bed and collapsed.

Later, it was probably a couple of hours, there was a knock at the door. He thought it was a reporter; as he strode across the room, he was ready to choke them out. When he opened the door, however, it was his Sheryl, his wife. She'd driven hours to be with him. They got into the bed and Sheryl held him. Neither of them said anything.

BODIES

THE SHOCK OF the event was compounded by the mystery of what had preceded it. Americans had never come to a unified viewpoint on who the Davidians were or what the standoff represented. The mass deaths, which arrived suddenly, changed that. It now seemed imperative to determine who had done what. It was an effort that was hobbled from the start and one that never really came to an end.

The next day a telegram arrived at FBI headquarters, addressed to Director Sessions. It was from an ordinary citizen. "YOU HAVE BROUGHT THE FBI TO AN ALLTIME GLORY VANQUESHING THESE DESPICABLE STATE ENEMIES IN YOUR VERY OWN DESERT STORM," it read. "HOW GLORIOUS." The writer told Sessions to resign, stating that it wasn't Koresh that Americans should fear, but the FBI's "Rambo mentality."

Letters arrived, too. "Mr. Jamar . . . ," read one. "It is outright cowardly to attempt to project blame of the killings onto Koresh or anybody else. How naive do you think people are?" The FBI was getting paid to wait out the Davidians, but their egos had interfered. The writer expressed the wish that Jamar and his men suffer the same fate as David and the others.

The day after the fire, President Clinton talked about Waco in a Rose Garden press conference. "The Bureau's efforts were ultimately unavailing," he said, "because the individual with whom they were dealing, David Koresh, was dangerous, irrational, and probably insane."

Clinton defended his attorney general. The White House, apparently, had been impressed by Reno's full acceptance of responsibility. "I will say this . . . I was, frankly, surprised would be a mild word, to say that anyone would suggest that the Attorney General should resign because some religious fanatics murdered themselves." There was applause.

Reno made a statement on the fire. In it, she cited the child abuse concerns as part of the reasons for going ahead with the tear gas. Those reports came from the FBI. Director Sessions made his own statement, in which he said the FBI had never told Reno that they believed child abuse was happening during the siege.

Reno went back to the briefing book that the FBI had provided her and carefully read through the documents. There was nothing about ongoing child abuse. Privately, she told an official at the Department of Justice that she had heard someone at an April 12 meeting saying that "the babies were being beaten." But there was no record of it.

Publicly, she continued to state that the mistake was hers. In her view, the FBI had been fair and hadn't pushed the child abuse idea. She also said that the supposed abuse was only one myriad concern that factored into her decision.

Autopsies on the Davidians were performed. The reports began to appear in July.

Seventy-six Davidians died inside the compound, including at least twenty children under the age of fourteen. Twenty of the bodies had received gunshot wounds, including at least five children. Some of the children had been injured by shrapnel from grenades that detonated inside the bunker. One child was stabbed to death.

Most of the others had died of smoke inhalation and carbon monoxide. Others had died of thermal burns due to the fire or suffocation, when they were buried under the rubble of the collapsing building.

David Koresh had been shot in the center of his forehead. As to who had fired the bullet, the finding was inconclusive. From the round's trajectory, the coroner couldn't rule out suicide. But it was more likely that the bullet had been fired by someone else.

David was found lying next to Steve, who had been killed by a bullet in the back of the head, with the bullet trajectory upward through the skull. The coroner found that it was not a self-inflicted wound.

One Davidian was found wearing a gas mask, holding an ammunition clip in her hand. Guns were omnipresent in the building, often found beside the burned remains of the Davidians. But it was often hard to determine whether the person had died from suicide or had been shot by others.

One family huddled together, seven of them. They were bunched in close, touching each other. As they expired from the gases released by the fire, their bodies had fallen forward, until they were found in a clump of entangled limbs. On the second floor, just below the tower, a number of Davidians were found together. They were carrying handguns and bayonets. As the fumes overcame them, they dropped the weapons at their feet. When they were all dead and the flames licked at their clothes, their bodies appeared like spokes in a wheel.

Among the debris: Forty-eight fully automatic machine guns. Sawed-off shotguns, two .50 caliber Barrett sniper rifles, antitank rifles, more handguns and silencers, along with parts for making pipe bombs and hand grenades. And a metal lathe used for making silencers.

Books were discovered among the rubble, many of them related to weapons. The titles included *Homemade Semtex; Homemade C-4; Improvised Munitions, Black Book, Vols 1 and 2;* and *CIA Field Expedient Methods for Explosive Preparations.*

There were numerous hearings and studies of the Waco siege and the events that led up to it, the most significant of which were the 1993 Department of Justice probe and a 1999 investigation ordered by Janet Reno and led by Senator John Danforth, which explored possible government misconduct before and during the siege.

One of the findings that emerged during the probes concerned the five Davidians who died in the initial ATF raid on February 28. Three of them had been shot point-blank. Peter Hipsman had multiple wounds, but the fatal one was a bullet to the back of his head at close range. Hipsman may have been severely wounded in the initial shootout and then finished off by the Davidians. This was corroborated by a question overheard on one of the bug tapes. In it, a follower asked David for permission to put an injured member out of their misery.

Perry Jones died of a bullet wound in his mouth. The Davidians who'd left the compound told officials that Jones had been shot in the stomach by ATF agents while he was standing next to David. But the autopsy didn't find any such wound on the body.

Even more mysterious was Winston Blake, the British follower who'd told a friend he wanted to return to the UK for a funeral but never made it. He'd died from a bullet that entered just behind his right ear. There were gunpowder traces on the skin at the wound site, indicating he'd been shot at close range.

A relative back in England became obsessed with finding the truth of Winston's death. One theory was that Winston refused to take up arms on February 28. Years before, he'd hurt his knee playing soccer, and the injury hampered his movements. Perhaps he'd been unwilling to fight because he'd be unable to escape, the friend thought, and the Davidians had executed him because of it. The mystery was lost in the swirl of conspiracy theories and accusations that followed in the wake of the tragedy. What happened in Winston's final moments remain unclear.

Some believed that the government had engineered David's death. Jean Holub, David's grandmother, refused to believe that one of his followers had shot him. "There's no way those people would have killed themselves," she said. "The F.B.I. snipers shot him and then realized that they had to burn the place down to cover it up."

Others felt that David was not really dead at all. Don Bunds, the engineer from California and father to David Bunds, returned to Pomona after the fire. "They collected his bones, but he's not dead," he told David. "He's coming back to chop our heads off." He was terrified.

It was a popular theory around Waco, too. There had always been talk of secret passageways at the compound. "I think he'll show up in two or three years," one woman who sold Koresh T-shirts told a reporter. "I think he got out through one of those tunnels or something. Even if they had water in them, I bet he had scuba gear. He got out somehow."

Some of the surviving Davidians looked forward to David's return, and the return of their children and spouses. Clive Doyle and Sheila Martin, Wayne's wife, chose to stay in Waco for that reason. They often met for a weekly prayer session. When the End Times came, Clive Doyle believed he would see his daughter again. Sheila believed she and Wayne would meet in time. Her translation was delayed, but resurrection and glory would come.

Doyle considered David and the others to be martyrs. He remained faithful to David's teachings. Part of it was so that he would be reunited with his daughter. "I don't want her coming back and finding Dad went off and jumped off a cliff because he gave up everything," he told reporters. Martin agreed. "My peace of mind . . . is that God will eventually raise them up and they will be part of the group that will be in the Last Days bringing truth to others."

After the fire, Bonnie Haldeman visited Mount Carmel and walked among the ruins. "I have my faith in the resurrection," she said. "We'll see them all again."

Eventually, the rubble was cleared away and a fence put up around the site of Mount Carmel. "This is going to be like Graceland," said David Mevis, a T-shirt seller. Most of the land is now occupied by a private prep school, but a group of Branch Davidians maintain a memorial and church on the property as well.

The HRT returned to training at Quantico. After the fire, some pencil-necked dude from headquarters got up in front of the agents and said, "Now none of you guys have any emotional problems, right? Everybody's good to go?"

A lot of them were having emotional problems, in fact. Nightmares, PTSD, other things. But no one was going to say it in front of this dude. Everybody said, "Yeah. No problems. All good." And that was as far as the counseling went.

Eight Davidians were convicted of crimes related to the deaths of the four ATF agents, including firearms charges, possession of a hand grenade, and aiding and abetting voluntary manslaughter. They were given sentences of between five and forty years and fined between $1,000 and $50,000.

None of the defendants apologized in court for their parts in the deaths of Steve Willis, Robert Williams, Todd McKeehan, and Conway Charles LeBleu.

No federal agents were charged with any offenses regarding the deaths of the Branch Davidians.

Alternative theories about what had happened at Waco sprang up almost immediately after the fire. Skeptics leveled two main charges at the FBI: starting the fire on April 19 and shooting and killing Davidians during the inferno.

A great deal of evidence about the inferno emerged in its aftermath. The Coleman fuel cans mentioned in the bug tapes survived the fire, blackened and bent. Investigators submitted them to experts, who found they'd been punctured from outside, something that arsonists often do. Investigators also found a handmade torch in the kitchen area, one of the spots where the fire had begun. Arson dogs were brought in and detected traces of accelerants in the places that FLIR, or Forward Looking Infrared, cameras had identified as points of origins for the flames. These were confirmed by lab tests on the materials in those areas.

The evidence pointed overwhelmingly to the Davidians having started the fire. Nine Davidians had emerged from the building on April 19. All survived, some with severe burns. Seven of the nine survivors, including Clive Doyle, were found to have traces of fuel on their clothes. The body of one of the dead followers, Raymond Friesen, showed extremely high levels of benzene, an ingredient in petroleum-based fuel. He may have inhaled fumes containing the chemical.

The findings of arson experts, the traces of accelerants found on the followers' clothes, and the testimony of Graeme Craddock attesting that he'd seen Davidians lighting fires all pointed to the same conclusion. But it was the repeated references by the Davidians on the bug tapes to spreading fuel and lighting fires that was the strongest evidence that David Koresh had ordered the blaze started, and his followers had obeyed.

While researching a documentary on Waco, the gun activist and filmmaker Michael McNulty found a shell from an M0651 pyrochetechnic round in an evidence locker. The FBI had previously denied that any such rounds had been fired at the compound.

The agent who shot the rounds, David Corderman, testified that he fired two or three M0651 rounds during the early hours of April 19. He said he did so because the plastic ferrets were bouncing off the roof of the bunker. An FBI surveillance plane was taking photographs of the assault and in one of them a puff of white smoke can be seen on the outside of Mount Carmel. Corderman confirmed that was one of the M0651s he fired.

Corderman pointed out that the rounds were fired hours before the fire began, which made it highly unlikely, if not impossible, that they ignited the fire. The government's experts agreed.

Those who rejected the government's account pointed to footage recorded by the FBI's Nightstalker plane as it circled over the compound. It employed FLIR technology, which sensed infrared radiation—essentially, heat signatures—with a thermographic camera. The FLIR tapes showed repetitive flashes coming from positions near the tanks that were inserting gas and smashing into the structure at the back of the compound. Some researchers concluded that the flashes came from the muzzles of weapons fired by the FBI. The bureau consistently denied that any of its agents had fired their weapons on April 19.

One agent, Charles Riley, did tell his superior that, on the day of the FBI action, he'd heard shots fired from one of the bureau's sniper posts. The sniper occupying that post was Lon Horiuchi, the same sharpshooter who had shot and killed Vicki Weaver during the Ruby Ridge standoff. The agent later recanted his statement.

The FLIR evidence was studied by a number of experts in the field. It turned out that FLIR analysis was very much an art, and different technicians saw different things in the tapes. The *Washington Post* showed them to fourteen different experts. Seven said they showed gunfire; seven said they showed solar reflections.

Revelations about pyrotechnic rounds and the emergence of the FLIR tape gave fresh oxygen to conspiracy theories that continued to flourish around the Waco siege. Polls showed confidence in the government's story was weakening. Janet Reno ordered the 1999 Danforth investigation to get to the bottom of the new allegations. Danforth commissioned a study of the FLIR footage from Dr. Dan Frankel of Photon Research Associates. He submitted a thirty-four-page report on September 11, 2000, making three main points:

First, the flashes were not caused by weapons discharging. "Their duration is far too long and their spatial extent is far too great." Frankel concluded the glints were most likely caused by the sun's reflections or heat energy from FBI vehicles reflecting off debris or pools of water on the ground.

Second, the FLIR video technology wasn't designed to pick up muzzle flashes from small arms fire. The FLIR camera scanned any given point in the field of view once every 16.67 seconds, which meant that shorter duration events, like gunfire, might not be picked up by the device at all.

Third, there was strong evidence that the Davidians were firing at the federal agents during the insertion of the tear gas, "but none of their muzzle flashes are detectable on the videotape." This made it clear that the FLIR was not recording gunshots. "The absence of muzzle flash detection on the FLIR tape does not prove that weapons were not actually fired during the final assault," but the flashes found on the tape were not evidence that they were.

The finding was buttressed by the coroner, who found no evidence that bullets fired by the FBI or anyone outside the compound had wounded or killed any of the group members. (He also found that none of the Davidians had died as a result of the tear gas.)

Another charge leveled against the government concerned the original February 28 raid by the ATF. Many people—including some inside the ATF and FBI—believed that the raid was intended to gain a high-profile win for the bureau. In early 1993, before the raid, the ATF had suffered a spate of negative press. Former agents were suing the bureau for racial discrimination and sexual harassment. *60 Minutes* had aired a highly critical segment on the bureau, citing those lawsuits. And the ATF was scheduled for congressional budget hearings on March 10, only a week and a half after the Mount Carmel operation.

Mike Wallace, the *60 Minutes* correspondent, interviewed numerous ATF members after the raid and reported that "almost all the agents we talked to said they believe the initial attack on that cult in Waco was a publicity stunt—the main goal of which was to improve A.T.F.'s tarnished image." Chuck Hustmyre agreed. "Yeah, I mean, that was my impression," he said. "When Waco happened, there's no way that these guys weren't primarily looking at, 'Hey, man, we're going to get a news coverage. It's going to be a big operation, it's going to be a successful operation and, God, our budget's going to skyrocket next year.' That had to be what they were thinking about.

"But it's not like it's unique to ATF. Every agency is trying to make themselves look good. All the guys at headquarters level or even SAC level, all they ever worry about is the budget."

No evidence of the budget theory has emerged: no memos, no testimony by ATF administrators, no internal reports.

For their part, Bill Buford and the other planners of the mission vehemently deny they were ever pressured to stage a raid because of the congressional hearings or other concerns. The idea that they would send agents to face a .50 caliber sniper rifle in order to acquire more funds remains, to them, grotesque.

Three decades after the raid and the siege, many still question who was ultimately responsible for Waco. The standoff fueled the rise of a new generation of right-wing patriot groups and militias, who believed that the ATF, the FBI, and the US government had revealed their true nature during the crisis. At the congressional hearings on the tragedy, one of the spectators held up a sign: "ATF KILLS FAMILIES." For those who believe the Davidians were targeted and murdered by the government, the events of April 19 were the clearest example of the tyranny that Americans now lived under.

"Waco can happen at any given time," Mike Vanderboegh, a leader in the Patriot movement, which had emerged a decade before and brought together American populists, nationalists, far-right militia members, and tax resisters. "But the outcome will be different this time. Of that I can assure you."

In the years after Waco, Timothy McVeigh wrote the ATF two letters. "All you tyrannical mother fuckers," he said in one, "will swing in
the wind one day." McVeigh was dreaming of action by then. He and
his friend Terry Nichols went to work building a five-thousand-pound
bomb out of ammonium nitrate and nitromethane. When it was finished, they installed the bomb in the back of a Ryder rental truck and
parked it in front of the Alfred P. Murrah Building in Oklahoma City,
chosen because it hosted offices of the DEA, the Secret Service, and the
ATF. McVeigh wanted to kill federal employees, who he believed to be
fascist thugs in service of a tyrannical cabal. He also wanted to create a
tableau equivalent to the ruins of Mount Carmel: a federal building in
the middle of the American heartland smoking and in ruins. A photo
negative of Waco.

On the morning of April 19, 1995, the second anniversary of the Waco
inferno, McVeigh detonated the device, killing 168 people, including 19
children. Two dead for every Davidian.

With the mass murder at Oklahoma City, the chain that had started at
Ruby Ridge (three dead) and had continued through Waco (ninety-two
dead in total) reached a new casualty level. McVeigh became one of the
first archetypes of the far-right domestic terrorist, the clear-eyed white
loner who becomes a patriot and then a murderer, out of necessity, if you
ask them.

It's intriguing to think of what David would have thought of McVeigh
and the long line of political killers that followed him. David had embraced the "live free or die" credo late in life, but it was always part and
parcel of his religious visions. Steve Schneider was much more the resident conspiracy theorist at Mount Carmel, the "Don't Tread on Me" guy.

McVeigh and the others stripped David of his original meaning. In
their view, he was a free man who'd been burned alive by fascists, a somewhat different slant than David would have chosen. The fact that the
Davidians had never really been able to speak to the press after the first
day of the siege meant that their inner lives were a mystery. They could
be written over—and they have been, many times.

Before he was executed in 2001, McVeigh spoke about the tragedy:
"Waco started this war. Hopefully, Oklahoma would end it." But it didn't
end it. The far-right imagination is inspired by resentment, and it needs

to be constantly refreshed with proof of the crimes against it. Waco in flames remains the glimpse behind the curtain, hidden truth made visible. It still inspires.

The journalist Mark Potok, who'd spent the entire siege covering the siege for *USA Today*, went to see *Waco: The Rules of Engagement* at the Capri Theater in Montgomery, Alabama. It was one of two influential documentaries that came out in the years after the conflagration. The film was getting great reviews. Outlets like NPR had praised it.

The Capri was the only arts cinema in Montgomery, a home for indie and foreign films and a kind of oasis for hipsters and lefty types in conservative Montgomery. There were about fifty people in the audience. Potok knew many of them. Most, like him, were old-school liberals.

Potok had spent a lot of time researching Waco, reading the negotiation transcripts and studying the after-action reviews. He'd covered the trials of the Davidians after the fire. The conspiracy theories that had taken root troubled him.

When the movie started, Potok's spirits sank. The film accused the government of murdering the Davidians, and the FBI of firing into the compound during the inferno, things he knew were untrue. As he listened to the other viewers around him, he realized that many of them accepted the film's version of events. "Oh my God, oh my God," someone gasped, "the government murdered them!"

Potok felt he was watching a myth being cemented into place.

FBI agents who were at Waco struggled with this growing misperception of the feds' responsibility. One agent's father asked him if the bureau had set the fire, killed those kids. His father had always been a true-blue supporter of the FBI.

Byron Sage received a letter: "I hope you get everything that's coming to you. You know what the penalty is for first degree murder. Signed, A Patriot." One of the penalties for murder in Texas was death. Byron considered it a threat.

Others would be at parties and hear the most outlandish theories, tossed off as if they were banal truth. The White House aide Vince Foster, who participated in discussions about the FBI's tear gas plan, was killed because of what he knew about Waco. Koresh was running a CIA safe house. Clinton had ordered the raid to get rid of ATF agents who were privy to his personal secrets. But the main line of argument was this: The federal government didn't like people with strange ideologies and a fondness for guns, so they'd exterminated them.

It was often housewives, lawyers, chamber of commerce types saying these things. Ordinary Americans, not fringe groups. The controversy had slipped into the American mainstream.

Jim McGee, the HRT member who'd saved Ruth Riddle from the fire, later estimated that the Davidian children were sixty feet from where he was that day. He wondered if they were still alive while he shouted at Ruth Riddle. He wondered if he might have saved them.

McGee eventually got divorced, with stressors following Waco a contributing factor. He left the FBI and became a professor of criminal justice at William Carey University in Mississippi. There he found that his students, most of whom hadn't been born when Waco happened, believed all kinds of things about it: The FBI had used flamethrowers. The FBI had intentionally killed babies.

McGee had a sequence of photos from the scene blown up, eight or ten of them. They showed him coming out of the Brad and running toward Ruth Riddle, then dragging her out of the building. He asked the students: "So, do you really think that I would be doing that if we were on the other side of the compound shooting flamethrowers into the compound? You think that as the Davidians came out we were grabbing them and dragging them back in?"

50

SPECTERS

SANDY MOVED AGAIN and kept moving. It was like she was still running from David, even though he was dead.

After the fire, some people Sandy had known for forever started looking at her differently. It was like she was a witch who held the power of life and death over certain people. As they saw it, she'd jilted this cult guy and caused him to go off the deep end. What kind of magic did she possess? There were a few letters, even death threats.

Sometimes she wondered if they were right. Had she been the trigger that set off the disaster? Maybe if she'd let David put her in that car trunk, and married him, barefoot and pregnant, there would have been no Waco.

Or maybe you would have burned up along with everyone else, she said to herself.

Bonnie returned to her job. Every so often, she would receive letters from supporters of the Branch Davidians. Other notes arrived, too, condemning her for raising David. Once, someone sent her a Mother's Day card. It was signed, "Your Boy." She cried when she opened the envelope.

The curse of the family's mental illness returned. In 2009, Bonnie was taking care of her younger sister, Beverly, who was found to be schizophrenic decades before. One morning, Bonnie arrived at Beverly's house to take her to the doctor. Inside the home, Beverly stabbed her to death.

Kat Schroeder was charged with first-degree murder in the deaths of the four ATF agents. She testified against her fellow Davidians at trial, then accepted a plea bargain on the reduced charge of resisting arrest. She was sentenced to three years in prison. She was the only Davidian to plead out.

Her youngest son, Bryan, would tell those who asked where she was: "You know the war that killed my father? She's in jail because of the war."

The *Waco Tribune-Herald*'s "Sinful Messiah" series was named as a finalist for the 1994 Pulitzer Prize for investigative journalism. But members of the Waco media were often blamed, erroneously, for what happened. The *Trib* reporter Mark England left journalism in 2000 and rarely spoke about Waco afterward. One of his former editors talked to him one time about the events at Mount Carmel. "We'd started out to change the Davidians," England said, "but in the end we changed ourselves."

"I think he felt the blackness of it more than the rest of us," the editor said.

The KWTX cameraman Dan Mulloney was officially cleared by congressional investigations. But the fog of suspicion initiated by the ATF's cover-up was never dispelled. One law enforcement official compared it to a cancer that ate at Mulloney from inside. Mulloney spiraled, drinking on the way down. He eventually took a job at a Waco bar, Charlie's Corner, the only thing he could find. In 2001, he passed away from alcohol-related causes.

Jim Peeler, who had inadvertently alerted one of the Davidians to the impending ATF raid, continued working at KWTX but he felt his life had ended on February 28. "Have you ever seen the movie *The Sixth Sense*, where a man was completely dead but really didn't know that he's dead?" he told a journalist who looked him up years later. "Well, that's me, ya know. My body, physically, doesn't know that it's dead, but my heart, my heart really knows that it's over with."

George Roden escaped the Big Spring psychiatric hospital in 1993. Not long after, his lawyer received a call. It was George, asking for money for a plane ticket to Israel. He wanted to celebrate Yom Kippur there. He was captured soon after.

George filed several suits against the state of Texas demanding, among other things, that residents of the psychiatric facility be taught martial arts, "because as patients and convicts we are denied the use of guns to protect ourselves . . . when we are released into the free world society." He asked for $200 million in damages. The suit was dismissed.

Two years later, George went missing again. He traveled all the way to New York City, where he was recaptured outside the Israeli Consulate, where he'd gone to request a visa for travel to the country. Roden told consulate officials that he was Jewish and that assassins from the Palestine Liberation Organization were attempting to kill him.

In 1998, he escaped a third time, but was found on the grounds of the hospital. He had died of a heart attack.

The ATF agents who'd taken part in the February 28 raid suffered largely in silence. "We'd lost so much," one agent wounded in the raid told a journalist. "I live in constant pain. I lost a big chunk of my leg. I had friends who were killed."

The subject became taboo at the bureau. The byword was: "Don't talk about Waco."

Bill Buford, the agent who helped plan the raid, suffered from panic attacks for years afterward. He would have vivid dreams, too, in which he was back in that room in Waco, feeling himself getting shot. In this dream, the Davidian he fired at—the one who was waiting in ambush in the hallway—came back into the room and took aim at Buford.

The dreams were just dreams. Other things, he couldn't shake off. When he'd returned from Vietnam, Buford had been called a baby killer. After Waco, he was called it again.

Later, long after the raid, Buford was talking with some of the guys from the Houston office. They talked about going into Chuck Sarabyn's office after the February 28 operation and finding rolls of film that had been shot by the surveillance team at Waco. They had never been developed or been sent to Buford. In every operation he'd been on that required surveillance, film like that would have been processed and the photos sent to the planners. This time, nothing.

Then there was the pit. The guys told him that, out of the thirty-plus days they'd surveilled the compound, the Davidians were working in the pit maybe fourteen of them. "Our whole plan would have been different had we known that," Buford thought.

Why didn't he see the photographs? Why wasn't he told that the Davidians didn't go to the pit every day? He could never understand it.

After leaving the Branch Davidians, which he'd been part of since he was five years old, David Bunds became a regular Sunday-keeping evangelical in Glendale, California. One day he was at a retreat in the San Bernardino Mountains. It was a bunch of Christians getting together to do Christian things and talk about God and Jesus and have meetings and hang out and fellowship together.

David looked around at the others on the retreat. He noticed how average everybody was. Christians were always going on about Jesus or the spirit and "We've got this belief and we've got that belief and it's just so amazing." But to David, he couldn't get over how ordinary everyone looked. "It's just people," he said to himself. Ordinary people and all their ordinary daily things.

It was just so mundane. David was like, "Where's, where's it gone? Where's all this crap that we're talking about all the time?" A question occurred to him. He said, "What would it be like if Christianity really was just man-made? If it wasn't handed down from God. What if it was just a thing that people do?"

If Christians got together, what would it be like if God wasn't real? And he thought to himself, well, it would be just like this.

It was like an epiphany. Right then, Christianity just fell apart for him. A couple of months later he'd stopped going to church and become your average, secular American. He didn't believe in anything.

Years after the fire, Marc Breault returned to Mount Carmel with his wife, Elizabeth Baranyai Breault. As they approached the compound, they listened to one of David's Bible studies on the car's tape player. David's voice rose and fell, at times quiet and soothing, other times rasping with menace.

They drove the car onto Double EE Ranch Road and gazed at the site, which, apart from a memorial that had been set up there, looked like any other piece of Central Texas farmland. Marc felt spooked. It was as if the Davidians were still there, still praying and gathering for Bible studies as they waited for the End Times. He could see in his mind the place as it once was: the playground for children; the men and women as they ran the obstacle course; the tower; David's Camaro parked out front; and the hive of activity as they built the enormous building, which had now vanished.

It brought the past back to him. One moment in particular. He thought of David's visit to Australia in 1990, after Marc had left the group. He thought of the debate at the home of one of David's followers where David had caused such a scene, claiming he felt the same pain that Christ had felt on the cross.

A few months before that meeting, David's anguished voice as he cried out would have rooted Marc to the floor in terror. To be the cause of the messiah's pain was a serious offense against God. Marc's heartbeat would have accelerated, and waves of guilt would have swept over him.

But instead, Marc felt something new inside him. Watching David, he felt normal. His mind was as clear and untroubled as a cold night sky.

That night, Marc had looked down at himself in the room, with David gesturing silently, as if from a movie camera fixed high above them. He could see the other followers, the Australians he knew so well, their expressions touched by emotions that passed slowly over their faces. They were still in the message. They were filled with a fear that almost choked them, just as it had once choked him.

That weight had lifted away. Now Marc could see the people below were trapped in a delusion. They were experiencing things that weren't real. As he watched, he felt a deep compassion for the human figures below.

They were struggling with an enormous problem. How to live. David was, too.

That night, Marc had accepted that there was a great deal of work ahead of him. He was going to turn against David even more passionately, and they would fight, and it might end badly for either of them, or for others. Perhaps in death.

But the first part of his journey was over. I'm free, he thought to himself. I'm myself again.

EPILOGUE

FOUR MONTHS BEFORE the ATF's cattle trailers turned onto Double EE Ranch Road and sped toward the Branch Davidian compound, a meeting took place in a YMCA high up in the Colorado Rockies. It was a gathering of the faithful of the far right. A small number of Klansmen, neo-Nazis, Christian Identity followers, and gun-rights extremists sat in a cool, uncluttered conference room and spoke about the coming end of freedom and the arrival of the Antichrist in their beloved republic.

The meeting had been called to address the Ruby Ridge incident, where Randy Weaver's son and wife had been killed by government agents outside their Idaho home after Weaver failed to appear in court on firearms charges. The men talked about how Ruby Ridge was the opening shot in a long war. Louis Beam, a neo-Nazi and official of the Aryan Nation, gave the keynote. He warned of more terrors to come. All the people in the room, he said, all Americans, would soon be subjugated by soldiers who would burst into their homes and take control of their lives. Their guns would be taken. Their ideas would be outlawed. Many of them would be murdered where they stood, and the survivors would become subject to "the tender mercies of a government gone mad." That government was already planning an "open armed confrontation of some sort" to speed things up.

It was as if these men, sitting in a humble room at the YMCA, had seen Waco before it happened. David Koresh had been foretold twice, once by Lois Roden, the second time by Louis Beam and the others. But the scenes at Waco exceeded even the men's harshly lit imaginations: the hulking Army tanks; the fortress filled with praying people, soon to be dead; the bright yellow FBI logos on the backs of the agents' black jackets; the fire.

For the far right, Waco made a secret world visible; "Waco became a door," wrote Sharon Ponder, a frequent contributor to right-wing websites, "and a finger of God for the nation." The far right not only gained a set of martyrs, the legitimacy of its enemies—the ATF, the FBI—was publicly weakened.

In 1994, the first major militia sprang up in Michigan. Smaller, loosely organized groups had convened in other states before, but the Michigan militia attracted thousands of members and drilled them in antigovernment ideas. Many more such outfits followed. And they didn't merely lie in wait. In the early nineties, the FBI was opening about a hundred domestic terrorism cases a year. At the end of the decade, it was ten times that. By the mid-nineties, militias were operating in every state in the union, with as many as 250,000 total members. Waco had indeed been a door, and millions walked through it and into a world where conspiracies grew like wild bamboo. Ordinary people—your mailman, your doctor, your husband or daughter—learned that America was being corrupted and sold to evil ones.

Another watershed came just eleven days after Waco. On April 30, 1993, the computer scientist Tim Berners-Lee released the source code for the first-ever web browser, which he called Mesh. It allowed people to search the internet, for free. Simply typing in the words "Waco" or "David Koresh" linked people who'd felt unheard for most of their lives and invited them into a glorious movement that was going to right the many wrongs of the world.

The actual David Koresh and the actual Branch Davidians were barely acknowledged by the militia movement. David would have been mortified to learn that he'd become hugely famous and millions of people recognized his name, but almost none of them knew what he believed in, or cared. One of the reasons David gave to the FBI for not coming out of the compound was that Americans were vulgar: People weren't going to ask him about the Seven Seals, he feared, they were going to ask him about having sex with teenagers.

He was right, of course. Nobody remembered the letters he sent out from the compound; no one started the Church of David Koresh. The sex issue, too, dropped away almost immediately. What really mattered, what moved millions of people about his story, was that a tyrannical government, in their eyes, had murdered him in cold blood. David would never have wanted to be a victim—it was weak, and his purpose was to avenge the martyrs, not to become one—but that's what he ended up as.

Uncannily, though, this new movement did get something right about him. His narcissism, from an early age, guided him everywhere he went. David refused to accept the judgment of others; he refused to accept anything that didn't exalt him. The true facts of his life were intolerable to him. He needed a place where he could live with some degree of self-love. He created it, and it sustained him for years.

The men and women who took up his cause often do the same. They see portents and signs of the government's despotism in small, everyday things. They tend the narcissist within and seek out leaders who are egotists themselves, and who are capable of this same kind of fabulous world-building. They demote reality and make it serve them.

David told people that he was the Messiah and that God wanted him to sleep with young girls and own fully automatic rifles. If you're close to God, then everything you do is allowed. Those on the conspiratorial right have followed a similar pattern: if the cause is right, nothing in it can be wrong. Nothing inside you is corrupted; everything points toward future glory. Those who doubt and hate you serve only the devil.

As with David, the conspiratorial right sought a battle in which their world and the sordid world of Satanic power and decadence would collide, and a winner would be declared at last. David's came at Waco, the movement's came at the Capitol on January 6, 2021. The two events sprang from the same American soil, which has for centuries been crisscrossed by men and women who believe that violence cleanses the land for something infinitely more wonderful.

ACKNOWLEDGMENTS

Many thanks to Ivy Givens for her superb editing of a manuscript that had grown to alarming size. I'm also grateful to Mark Robinson for his wonderful cover, Chloe Foster for her interior design, and Sarajane Herman for her copyediting. My thanks to Susan Canavan and Ashley Lopez at the Waxman Agency for their creative advice and support. David Bunds was an invaluable source for Branch Davidian history and Deborah Bunds, Mark Potok, Jim McGee, Marc Breault, Chuck Hustmyre, Sharon Kidd, and Bill Johnston, among others, graciously contributed their narratives to the larger one. Many thanks to Sandy for telling me the story of her time with David Koresh.

Finally, a writing note: as some readers will realize, the book's technique was inspired by Norman Mailer's 1979 masterpiece, *The Executioner's Song*.

ENDNOTES

PROLOGUE

xv Agents had given him the finger: FBI negotiation transcript, tape #69, pg. 7. https://vault.fbi.gov.

xv "You boys are murderers": FBI negotiation transcript, tape #181, pg. 40.

xvi "Absolutely untrue": FBI negotiation transcript, tape #57, pg. 26.

xvii "Oh, I told you": FBI negotiation transcript, tape #90, pg. 43.

CHAPTER 1: BONNIE

3 "Let me see what's wrong": Bonnie Haldeman and Catherine Wessinger, *Memories of the Branch Davidians: The Autobiography of David Koresh's Mother* (Waco: Baylor University Press, 2007), pg. 6.

5 The Adventist leader John Harvey Kellogg even introduced his wildly successful corn flakes in an effort to cut down on sexual desire: Matt Soniak, "Corn Flakes Were Part of an Anti-Masturbation Crusade," mentalfloss.com, March 6, 2018. https://www.mentalfloss.com/article/32042/corn-flakes-were-invented-part-anti-masturbation-crusade.

5 He was eighteen: Kenneth R. Samples, Erwin M. de Castro, Richard Abanes, and Robert J. Lyle, *Prophets of the Apocalypse: David Koresh and Other American Messiahs* (Grand Rapids: Baker Books, 1994), pg. 18.

6 Later, Texas introduced: Interview with Kim Everett, editor, *Garland Texan*.

7 Bobby even had a girlfriend: Haldeman and Wessinger, *Memories of the Branch Davidians*, Kindle pg. 102.

7 one he would marry: Jim McGee and William Claiborne, "The Transformation of the Waco 'Messiah,'" *Washington Post*, May 9, 1993.

CHAPTER 2: VERNON

8 Later in life: Marc Breault and Martin King, *Inside the Cult* (New York: Signet, 1993), pg. 27.

8 From birth: Bonnie Haldeman and Catherine Wessinger, *Memories of the Branch Davidians* (Waco: Baylor University Press, 2007), pg. 8.

8 No one told Vernon: Kenneth R. Samples, Erwin M. de Castro, Richard Abanes, and Robert J. Lyle, *Prophets of the Apocalypse: David Koresh and Other American Messiahs* (Grand Rapids: Baker Books, 1994), pg. 20.

9 Maybe he felt: Pamela Colloff, "A Mother's Words," *Texas Monthly*, February 2009.

9 He was trying: Jim McGee and William Claiborne, "The Transformation of the Waco 'Messiah,'" *Washington Post*, May 9, 1993.

11 "I remember the room": Haldeman and Wessinger, *Memories of the Branch Davidians*, pg. 15.

11 Fishing offered an escape: Bill Minutaglio and Jeffrey Weiss, "Portrait of Koresh Full of Contradictions—Parents Try to Reconcile Memories as Ex-Followers Paint Other Image," *Seattle Times*, May 2, 1993.

11 He'd go out: FBI negotiation transcript, tape #182, pg. 6.

12 Joe grabbed Vernon: Video of various Branch Davidian interviews, www.youtube.com/watch?v=9LB6nvIqX2g.

12 Vernon had golden hair: Haldeman and Wessinger, *Memories of the Branch Davidians*, pg. 7.

12 The use of *yes, sir*: Interview with Vernon's childhood friend Bivins.

CHAPTER 3: DALLAS

14 "macho man": Jim McGee and William Claiborne, "The Transformation of the Waco 'Messiah,'" *Washington Post,* May 9, 1993.

14 Roy was thirty-four: Haldeman and Wessinger, pg. 11.

15 "Don't take me": Samples et al. pg. 20.

15 "It was the state's feverish headquarters": Stephan Harrigan, *Big Wonderful Thing: A History of Texas* (Austin: University of Texas Press, 2019), pg. 1192.

17 You would think: FBI negotiation transcript, tape #45, pg. 17.

17 "What kind of bird is that?": Ibid.

17 Sometimes, when Vernon was young: Marc Breault and Martin King, *Inside the Cult* (New York: Signet, 1993), pg. 29.

18 It was like his world: Dick J. Reavis, "Mr. Retardo," *Dallas Observer*, July 27, 1995.

18 "Four eyes": Breault and King, *Inside the Cult*, pg. 29.

18 "Mr. Retardo": Dick J. Reavis, "Mr. Retardo," *Dallas Observer,* July 27, 1995.

18 In his heart: FBI Negotiation tape #217, pg. 14.

20 "I just fell madly in love": Interview with Teresa Beem.

20 Bonnie finally gave in: FBI negotiation transcript, tape #45, pg. 11.

21 He went home: Ibid., pg. 12.

21 Vernon would get in bed: "The Branch Davidians: In Their Own Words," Uncontrolled Video, 2016, www.youtube.com/watch?v=UqhnMoKfrHg.

22 It was like he went: Reavis, "Mr. Retardo."

23 the Bible studies: Kenneth R. Samples, Erwin M. de Castro, Richard Abanes, and Robert J. Lyle, *Prophets of the Apocalypse: David Koresh and Other American Messiahs* (Grand Rapids: Baker Books, 1994), pg. 22.

CHAPTER 4: VERNON AND ROY

24 Sometimes Bonnie would get mad: Kenneth R. Samples, Erwin M. de Castro, Richard Abanes, and Robert J. Lyle, *Prophets of the Apocalypse: David Koresh and Other American Messiahs* (Grand Rapids: Baker Books, 1994), pg. 174.

24 "You'd argue with Jesus Christ!": FBI negotiation transcript, tape #46, pg. 25.

24 "I don't even know": FBI negotiation transcript, tape #137, pg. 36.

26 That was one: FBI negotiation transcript, tape #217, pg. 12.

26 "When earth is closest": FBI negotiation transcript, tape #45, pg. 26.

26 "Now Vernon": Ibid.

27 Bonnie got ticked off: David Thibodeau, *Waco: A Survivor's Story* (New York: PublicAffairs, 1999), pg. 76.

27 "It's terrible": Samples et al., *Prophets of the Apocalypse*, pg. 21.

27 Then a bunch of older boys: Jim McGee and William, "The Transformation of the Waco 'Messiah,'" *Washington Post,* May 9, 1993.

27 Vernon kicked: Marc Breault and Martin King, *Inside the Cult* (New York: Signet, 1993), pg. 29.

28 Roger was the favorite: Interview with Marc Breault.

28 An icebox in his chest: FBI negotiation transcript, tape #90, pg. 43.

28 When Roy got to drinking: Bonnie Haldeman and Catherine Wessinger, *Memories of the Branch Davidians* (Waco: Baylor University Press, 2007), pg. 31.

28 He would shout at Bonnie: Interview with Sharon Kidd.

28 "Dear God": FBI negotiation transcript, tape #45, pg. 25.

29 It said one word: FBI negotiation transcript, tape #45, pg. 27.

29 It happened to someone: J. J. Robertson, *Beyond the Flames* (San Diego: ProMotion Publishing, 1996), pg. 263.

CHAPTER 5: THE CLUBHOUSE

30 To bulk up: Chuck Lindell and Pamela Ward, "Howell said to have lived double life: Odd mix of kindness, arrogance charmed some, scared others," *Waco Tribune-Herald,* May 2, 1993.

31 By the finish line: Marc Breault and Martin King, *Inside the Cult* (New York: Signet, 1993), pg. 30.

31 He could run for hours: FBI negotiation transcript, tape #46, pg. 23.

32 "Get out there": Bonnie Haldeman and Catherine Wessinger, *Memories of the Branch Davidians* (Waco: Baylor University Press, 2007), pg. 18.

32 He and his friends talked: FBI negotiation transcript, tape #218, pg. 3

33 fork more of it: FBI negotiation transcript, tape #219, pp. 37–38.

33 But after a few minutes: Ibid., pg. 36.

33 In 1972, when he was thirteen: Haldeman and Wessinger, *Memories of the Branch Davidians,* pg. 17.

34 It got heated: Interview with Sharon Kidd.

34 To his parents: Haldeman and Wessinger, *Memories of the Branch Davidians,* pg. 20.

34 Finally, Bonnie told Vernon: Pamela Colloff, "A Mother's Words," *Texas Monthly,* February 2009.

35 By the time he finished: Jim McGee and William Claiborne, "The Transformation of the Waco 'Messiah,'" *Washington Post,* May 9, 1993.

35 They just wanted to smoke weed: Dick J. Reavis, "Mr. Retardo," *Dallas Observer,* July 27, 1995.

35 "What different reasons?": FBI negotiation transcript, tape #45, pp. 14–16.

35 His aunt Sharon let him know: McGee and Claiborne, "The Transformation of the Waco 'Messiah.'"

36 "I'm just not like these dudes": FBI negotiation transcript, tape #45, pg. 16.

36 He had small hands: FBI negotiation transcript, tape #182, pg. 17.

37 But the fact that his own kin didn't want him around: McGee and Claiborne, "The Transformation of the Waco 'Messiah.'"

38 Bobby said sure: Ibid.

CHAPTER 6: VERNON AND LINDA

39 for Bonnie to buy him: Bonnie Haldeman and Catherine Wessinger, *Memories of the Branch Davidians* (Waco: Baylor University Press, 2007), pg. 20.

39 Vernon was off work: Ibid., Kindle location 268.

40 he wanted the chord changes: Jim McGee and William Claiborne, "The Transformation of the Waco 'Messiah,'" *Washington Post*, May 9, 1993.

41 She'd been hanging out: FBI negotiation transcript, tape #45, pg. 30.

41 After they arrived at Linda's house: Ibid., pg. 31.

41 "My God, here I am": FBI negotiation transcript, tape #45, pp. 32-33.

42 "God, what's going on?": Ibid., pg. 38.

43 "she'd had an abortion": FBI negotiation transcript, tape #46, pg. 2.

44 "Your love is the best": FBI negotiation transcript, tape #46, pg. 8.

44 Linda would let Bonnie come by: Interview with David Bunds.

45 He couldn't eat: Marc Breault and Martin King, *Inside the Cult* (New York: Signet, 1993), pg. 34.

46 Vernon moved out of his car: FBI negotiation transcript, tape #48, pg. 41.

46 He'd cry for hours: Kenneth R. Samples, Erwin M. de Castro, Richard Abanes, and Robert J. Lyle, *Prophets of the Apocalypse: David Koresh and Other American Messiahs* (Grand Rapids: Baker Books, 1994), pg. 24.

46 One day, he set the car on fire: Haldeman and Wessinger, *Memories of the Branch Davidians*, pg. 21.

48 All the books of the Bible: Kenneth G. C. Newport, *The Branch Davidians of Waco: The History and Beliefs of an Apocalyptic Sect* (Oxford: Oxford University Press, 2006), pg. 215.

49 "You're really hurt, aren't you?" Dick J. Reavis, "Mr. Retardo," *Dallas Observer*, July 27, 1995.

CHAPTER 7: SANDY

50 Growing up in Tyler: Unless otherwise noted, the information in this and the next chapter comes from multiple interviews with Sandy.

CHAPTER 8: EVERY STORY TELLS A LIE

58 Months before: Interview with Stewart Waterhouse.

59 "I just love seeing two young people": The information in the rest of this chapter comes from multiple interviews with Sandy.

CHAPTER 9: WILD WINDS

62 He would take a piece of the Gospel: Interview with Sandy.

63 When he described his latest: Ibid.

63 As Vernon got more and more: Ibid.

63 During one of his "sermons": Ibid.

CHAPTER 10: LOIS

69 "strong, stubborn and persevering": Stuart A. Wright, *Armageddon in Waco: Critical Perspectives on the Branch Davidian Conflict* (Chicago: University of Chicago Press, 1995), pg. 36.

69 She went into the baptistery: Kenneth G. C. Newport, *The Branch Davidians of Waco: The History and Beliefs of an Apocalyptic Sect* (Oxford: Oxford University Press, 2006), pg. 118.

70 As they drove: Brad Bailey and Bob Darden, *Mad Man in Waco* (Waco, Texas: WRS Publishing, 1993), pg. 38.

71 "But what do you think": From 1977 tape of Lois Roden speaking to followers in Glendale, California, private collection.

72 God was showing Lois: Mary Lasovich, "Her crusade: To tell the world the Holy Spirit is feminine," *Whig-Standard* (Kingston, Ontario), February 28, 1981.

72 "My work is to bring forth": Bailey and Darden, *Mad Man in Waco*, pg. 65.

72 They hated the new teaching: No author, *Toronto Star*, February 4, 1981.

72 "Women preaching is like a dog walking": Bailey and Darden, *Mad Man in Waco*, pg. 67.

73 She even traveled: Marc Breault and Martin King, *Inside the Cult* (New York: Signet, 1993), pg. 34.

CHAPTER 11: THE DAVIDIANS

74 As Vernon pulled into Mount Carmel: Unless otherwise noted, the material in the rest of this chapter comes from multiple interviews with Deborah Bunds (neé Kendrick).

74 Debbie had always felt: Ibid.

76 When he got ready to leave: Kenneth G. C. Newport, *The Branch Davidians of Waco: The History and Beliefs of an Apocalyptic Sect* (Oxford: Oxford University Press, 2006), pg. 178.

76 You could actually see the bones: Kenneth R. Samples, Erwin M. de Castro, Richard Abanes, and Robert J. Lyle, *Prophets of the Apocalypse: David Koresh and Other American Messiahs* (Grand Rapids: Baker Books, 1994), pg. 32.

78 She moved him into a tiny room: Marc Breault and Martin King, *Inside the Cult* (New York: Signet, 1993), pg. 38.

79 A lot of the more scholarly types: Marc Breault, "The Psychology and Theology Behind David Koresh and the Branch Davidians," *Marc Breault Ramblings* (blog), April 30, 2018. blogspot.com/2018/04/the-psychology-and-theology-behind.html.

80 Anyone who wanted to pass: Newport, *The Branch Davidians of Waco*, pg. 166.

80 America would become Babylon: Ibid., pg. 229.

81 "within the lifetime of people": Ibid., pg. 163

81 "Vernon do this": Breault and King, *Inside the Cult*, pg. 38.

81 She wanted to build Vernon up: Interview with David Bunds.

81 He was humble: Breault and King, *Inside the Cult*, pg. 38.

82 "George had this wild idea": FBI negotiation transcript, tape #182, pg. 3.

83 He had a thirty-six-page pamphlet: J. J. Robertson, *Beyond the Flames* (San Diego: Pro-Motion Publishing, 1996), pg. 125.

83 "There is a new King": Ibid., pg. 124.

84 "if my wife had been away": George Roden pamphlet, *The Demise of the Antitypical Lucifer in the Branch Kingdom,* unpaginated, Texas State University.

84 The two would often chat: Robertson, *Beyond the Flames*, pg. 103.

84 Lois and the others were attacked: Breault and King, *Inside the Cult,* pg. 66.

84 You're the *last* son of a bitch: Jim McGee and William Claiborne, "The Transformation of the Waco 'Messiah,'" *Washington Post,* May 9, 1993.

85 It got so bad: Interview with Sandy.

CHAPTER 12: THE MEETINGS

86 Vernon believed that the body: Kenneth R. Samples, Erwin M. de Castro, Richard Abanes, and Robert J. Lyle, *Prophets of the Apocalypse: David Koresh and Other American Messiahs* (Grand Rapids: Baker Books, 1994), pg. 194.

87 "Give him a hearing": Ibid., pg. 35.

88 People fell to their knees: J. J. Robertson, *Beyond the Flames* (San Diego: ProMotion Publishing, 1996), pg. 202.

90 There could no longer be any doubt: Marc Breault and Martin King, *Inside the Cult* (New York: Signet, 1993), pg. 42.

91 Now he was quiet: Interview with Deborah Bunds.

92 The two didn't yet have a marriage license: Samples et al., *Prophets of the Apocalypse,* pg. 39.

92 "Why, with this message": Interview with David Bunds.

93 Lois's daughter thought that was strange: Brad Bailey and Bob Darden, *Mad Man in Waco* (WRS Publishing, 1993), pg. 74.

93 At one meeting: Robertson, *Beyond the Flames,* pg. 203.

93 "To begin with": Bailey and Darden, *Mad Man in Waco,* pg. 87.

93 "This V.W. Howell is a cult leader": Ibid., pg. 79.

CHAPTER 13: RACHEL

94 She'd disobeyed the Lord: Marc Breault and Martin King, *Inside the Cult* (New York: Signet, 1993), pg. 42.

94 He had a list of the names and addresses: Ibid.

96 When they saw her: Kenneth R. Samples, Erwin M. de Castro, Richard Abanes, and Robert J. Lyle, *Prophets of the Apocalypse: David Koresh and Other American Messiahs* (Grand Rapids: Baker Books, 1994), pg. 40.

96 In her pain: Interview with David Bunds.

96 But now she told her followers: Marc Breault letter to Sherri Jewell, December 11, 1990. Private collection.

97 She refused to return it: Interview with David Bunds.

97 The Davidians gossiped: Ibid.

98 As the flock gathered: Ibid.

98 "I am so sad for some": J. J. Robertson, *Beyond the Flames* (San Diego: ProMotion Publishing, 1996), pg. 108.

98 At the chapel: Samples et al., *Prophets of the Apocalypse,* pg. 42.

99 Only a few followers: Ibid., pg. 41.

100 "So there began": Brad Bailey and Bob Darden, *Mad Man in Waco* (WRS Publishing, 1993), pg. 74.

101 "It's basically a holy jihad": Breault and King, *Inside the Cult,* pg. 95.

101 Then and only then: Ibid., pg. 43.

101 One young woman: Bailey and Darden, *Mad Man in Waco,* pg. 72.

CHAPTER 14: DAVID BUNDS

105 There they revealed to him: Kenneth G. C. Newport, *The Branch Davidians of Waco: The History and Beliefs of an Apocalyptic Sect* (Oxford: Oxford University Press, 2006), pp. 181-82.

105 He was, therefore: Ibid., pg. 183.

105 I AM THE SON OF GOD: Koresh pamphlet, Texas State University, Ashes of Waco collection.

107 It was another blessing from above: FBI negotiation transcript, tape #13, pg. 11.

CHAPTER 15: PALESTINE

109 Vernon put down a deposit: Interview with David Bunds.

110 A few of the men: Marc Breault and Martin King, *Inside the Cult* (New York: Signet, 1993), pg. 44.

110 At night, the believers gathered: Interview with David Bunds.

110 "Faith," he told them: Ibid.

CHAPTER 16: THE GOLDEN STATE

114 "You know, the government is going to kill me": Interview with Sharon Kidd.

115 He felt he'd won: Interview with David Bunds.

117 In 1985, Clark entered a VA hospital: Interview with Sharon Kidd.

117 Sometimes, Vernon would give a job: J. J. Robertson, *Beyond the Flames* (San Diego: ProMotion Publishing, 1996), pg. 120.

119 When she first met David Bunds: Deborah Bund, untitled college essay, November 6, 1998. Courtesy of Deborah Bunds.

CHAPTER 17: MARC

121 In January 1986: Unless otherwise noted, the material in this chapter is from multiple interviews with Marc Breault.

122 He returned to Hawaii: Marc Breault, "The Psychology and Theology Behind David Koresh and the Branch Davidians," *Marc Breault Ramblings* (blog), April 30, 2018. blogspot.com/2018/04/the-psychology-and-theology-behind.html.

122 He quit his job: Ibid.

123 Other preachers and televangelists: Kenneth R. Samples, Erwin M. de Castro, Richard Abanes, and Robert J. Lyle, *Prophets of the Apocalypse: David Koresh and Other American Messiahs* (Grand Rapids: Baker Books, 1994), pg. 49.

124 "We all saw so much hate": Marc Breault and Martin King, *Inside the Cult* (New York: Signet, 1993), pg. 125.

125 Word began filtering: Samples et al., *Prophets of the Apocalypse*, pg. 46.

126 He spent a long time thinking: Ibid., pg. 47.

126 She nodded: Ibid., pg. 48.

126 Wayne Martin, a Harvard-trained Black lawyer: Ibid., pg. 46.

127 He raped her: Interview with David Bunds.

CHAPTER 18: STEVE

130 "God, geez": FBI negotiation transcript, tape #223, pp. 2–3.

130 "I don't go anywhere": FBI negotiation transcript, tape #62, pg. 37.

130 He was expecting someone impressive: FBI negotiation transcript, tape #222, pg. 40.

131 If you had a house: Michael Hirsley, "Adventists Kicked Out Cult Leader," *Chicago Tribune*, March 2, 1993.

132 Vernon didn't explain: Kenneth G. C. Newport, *The Branch Davidians of Waco: The History and Beliefs of an Apocalyptic Sect* (Oxford: Oxford University Press, 2006), pg. 204.

132 He told his followers: Ibid.

133 Marc, who knew his Scriptures: Ibid.

133 He said the guy: J. J. Robertson, *Beyond the Flames* (San Diego: ProMotion Publishing, 1996), pg. 210.

133 "I sell God": FBI negotiation transcript, tape #177, pg. 43.

133 "Hazel, you're gonna be a movie star!": Texas State University, Texas collection, Mark Swett Collection, Box 9, Schneider speeches, folder 1.

134 The Schroeders drove back: Video interview by Catherine Wessinger, "Kat Schroeder: Part 1," May 15, 1991. www.youtube.com/watch?v=gXzdPa2aJPE.

134 The shacks were built: Interview with David Bunds.

135 Marc found it annoying: Interview with Marc Breault.

135 "Just imagine": Marc Breault and Martin King, *Inside the Cult* (New York: Signet, 1993), pg. 21.

135 Vernon was at a loss: Interview with Marc Breault.

138 "I was in a desert": Ibid.

CHAPTER 19: THE RAID

143 Vernon wanted the bad guys: *Oral Memoirs of Gary J. Coker, Jr.: A Series of Interviews Conducted by Glenn Jonas and Daniel B. McGee*, November 20, 2003, Religion and Culture Project, Baylor University Institute for Oral History.

144 He stopped taking the medicine: FBI negotiation transcript, tape #29, pg. 15.

144 But the problems continued: Interview with David Bunds.

144 One time, Vernon told the Davidians: Ibid.

144 *It's painful to him*: Ibid.

145 a makeshift graveyard: Marc Breault and Martin King, *Inside the Cult* (New York: Signet, 1993), pp. 95–96.

145 "banging gongs": Interview with Bill Johnston.

145 "They're a bad bunch": Marc Breault and Martin King, *Inside the Cult* (New York: Signet, 1993), p. 97.

146 He'd gotten the sheriff: FBI negotiation transcript, tape #36, pg. 22.

146 The salespeople remembered: Breault and King, *Inside the Cult*, pp. 97–99.

146 On November 3, 1987: Unless otherwise noted, this account is drawn from various newspaper reports on the raid and FBI negotiation transcript, tape #182, pg. 10.

148 It was the McLennan County Sheriff's Department: Brad Bailey and Bob Darden, *Mad Man in Waco* (WRS Publishing, 1993), pg. 84.

148 "He was coming": FBI negotiation transcript, tape #37, pg. 3.

148 "Just go ahead": Ibid., pg. 9.

149 Dickerson walked by: FBI negotiation transcript, tape #182, pg. 16.

149 "Sir, excuse me?": FBI negotiation transcript, tape #37, pg. 13.

CHAPTER 20: COKER

150 The father of one of the guys: Interview with David Bunds.

150 Vernon pushed to get: Unless otherwise noted, this material in this chapter is drawn

from *Oral Memoirs of Gary J. Coker, Jr.: A Series of Interviews Conducted by Glenn Jonas and Daniel B. McGee*, November 20, 2003, Religion and Culture Project, Baylor University Institute for Oral History.

150 He made some forty-five records: Brad Bailey and Bob Darden, *Mad Man in Waco* (WRS Publishing, 1993), pg. 86.

153 All the Davidians sat down: *Oral Memoirs of Gary J. Coker, Jr.: A Series of Interviews Conducted by Glenn Jonas and Daniel B. McGee*, November 20, 2003, Religion and Culture Project, Baylor University Institute for Oral History.

153 "The evidence will show": Mark England, "Prosecution claims Roden target of assassination plan," *Waco Tribune-Herald*, April 13, 1988.

153 five Ruger: Adam Nossiter, "Warning of Violence Was Unheeded After Cult Leader's Gun Battle in '87," *New York Times*, March 10, 1993.

153 He could put a curse: *Oral Memoirs of Gary J. Coker, Jr.: A Series of Interviews Conducted by Glenn Jonas and Daniel B. McGee*, November 20, 2003, Religion and Culture Project, Baylor University Institute for Oral History.

154 "Today it's George Roden": Adam Nossiter, "Warning of Violence Was Unheeded After Cult Leader's Gun Battle in '87," *New York Times*, March 10, 1993.

154 He responded by inviting everyone: Ibid.

155 "A lot of jurors commented": Bailey and Darden, *Mad Man in Waco,* pg. 93.

155 "It was a Black man": Adam Nossiter, "Warning of Violence Was Unheeded After Cult Leader's Gun Battle in '87," *New York Times*, March 10, 1993.

155 Weeks later: FBI negotiation transcript, tape #182, pp. 20–22.

156 "weapons and ammunition": Adam Nossiter, "Warning of Violence Was Unheeded After Cult Leader's Gun Battle in '87," *New York Times*, March 10, 1993.

156 They stood and smiled: Jim McGee and William Claiborne, "The Transformation of the Waco 'Messiah,'" *Washington Post,* May 9, 1993.

157 He made it clear to Coker: FBI negotiation transcript, tape #182, pg. 23.

157 "I'll never be back": Lee Hancock, "How the 1993 Waco standoff began with a bloody gun battle that federal agents now regret," *Dallas Morning News*, February 25, 2018.

CHAPTER 21: MOUNT CARMEL

158 At a bakery: Darlene McCormick, "A prophet for profit? Branch Davidian leader took his followers for all they had, former cult members say," *Waco Tribune-Herald*, March 6, 1993.

158 Wayne Martin, who had a passion: Marc Breault and Martin King, *Inside the Cult* (New York: Signet, 1993), pg. 223.

159 When it came to the tax bill: Ibid., pg. 108.

159 They picked up garbage: Breault and King, *Inside the Cult,* pg. 116.

160 As the dog lay twitching: Interview with Marc Breault.

160 "Here are these Christians": Breault and King, *Inside the Cult,* pg. 128.

160 Everyone was required to do their shifts: Interview with David Bunds.

161 Later the Star-Tex propane company: Bailey and Darden, *Mad Man in Waco,* pg. 117.

161 "Look at the way": Breault and King, *Inside the Cult,* pg. 25.

162 One time, Wayne Martin: Interview with Marc Breault, and Marc Breault, "The Psychology and Theology Behind David Koresh and the Branch Davidians," *Marc Breault Ramblings* (blog), April 30, 2018. blogspot.com/2018/04/the-psychology-and-theology-behind.html.

CHAPTER 22: DAVID AND VERNON

164 Vernon was becoming crueler: Unless otherwise noted, the material in this section is drawn from multiple interviews with David Bunds.

165 "If you ever touch me again": Interview with Deborah Bunds.

CHAPTER 23: NEWBOLD

166 What he wanted: Marc Breault and Martin King, *Inside the Cult* (New York: Signet, 1993), pg. 118.

167 "Great! Next time": Ibid.

167 "The lectures . . . are OK": Albert A.C. White, "From Seventh-Day Adventism to David Koresh: The British Connection," *Andrews University Seminary Studies* 38, no.1 (spring 2000): pp. 107–26.

167 His firstborn: BBC Radio 5 Podcast, *End of Days*, 2018, "Episode One: A Prophet on Campus."

168 "I don't know that yet": BBC Radio 5 Podcast, *End of Days*, 2018, "Episode Two: Crowded House."

168 When she went to the meeting: BBC Radio 5 Podcast, *End of Days*, 2018, "Episode One: A Prophet on Campus."

169 Vernon's reasoning: Muriel Pearson, Spencer Wilking, and Lauren Effron, "Who was David Koresh: Ex-followers describe life inside apocalyptic religious sect involved in 1993 Waco siege," ABC News, January 2, 2018.

170 Or he'd tell one of his loyal followers: Breault and King, *Inside the Cult*, pg. 141.

170 "All of you are gluttons": Ibid., pg. 133.

170 On special occasions: Ibid., pg. 134.

170 "Yeah, the Mark of the Beast": Kenneth R. Samples, Erwin M. de Castro, Richard Abanes, and Robert J. Lyle, *Prophets of the Apocalypse: David Koresh and Other American Messiahs* (Grand Rapids: Baker Books, 1994), pg. 32.

CHAPTER 24: THE SCREAM TAPE

172 "In our study this afternoon": Kenneth R. Samples, Erwin M. de Castro, Richard Abanes, and Robert J. Lyle, *Prophets of the Apocalypse: David Koresh and Other American Messiahs* (Grand Rapids: Baker Books, 1994), pg. 45.

174 They crouched: Darlene McCormick, "Living in a cult's shadow: Children released from compound told of harrowing experiences," *Waco Tribune-Herald*, June 19, 1993.

174 "If I ever see you": Affidavit of Michelle Tom, February 23, 1992. Private collection.

174 There was even a "whipping room": Darlene McCormick, "Living in a cult's shadow: Children released from compound told of harrowing experiences," *Waco Tribune-Herald*, June 19, 1993.

174 The others were often called: Staff and Wire Reports, "Raised in fear: Life as cult kids," *Waco Tribune-Herald*, May 5, 1993, and Associated Press, "Children reveal abuse," *Waco Tribune-Herald*, May 4, 1993.

174 The screaming resumed: Affidavit of Bruce Gent, undated. Private collection.

175 Nicole must have reported: Interview with David Bunds.

175 On another occasion: Affidavit of James Tom, February 23, 1992. Private collection.

175 He could go to the local music bars: Mark England, "12 children killed in fire Howell's, ex-member says," *Waco Tribune-Herald*, September 5, 1993.

CHAPTER 25: UNREAL COLOSSAL SUPERMARKET

177 "I'm a real professional": Kenneth R. Samples, Erwin M. de Castro, Richard Abanes, and Robert J. Lyle, *Prophets of the Apocalypse: David Koresh and Other American Messiahs* (Grand Rapids: Baker Books, 1994), pg. 70.

177 "You know when an animal's scared": Mark England, "FBI list names of children: Howell refutes classifying teen-age girls with others," *Waco Tribune-Herald*, April 5, 1993.

177 The reason: Staff and Wire Reports, "Raised in fear: Life as cult kids," *Waco Tribune-Herald*, May 5, 1993.

178 he would have a thousand wives: Affidavit of Bruce Gent. Private collection.

178 Then his widows: Marc Breault and Martin King, *Inside the Cult* (New York: Signet, 1993), pg. 74.

178 "You know, you ever heard": Interview with David Bunds.

178 "I said, 'God, what is love?'": Interview with Marc Breault.

178 "I suffer": Ibid.

179 "We're going to the supermarket": Breault and King, *Inside the Cult*, pg. 146.

CHAPTER 26: THE NEW LIGHT

181 "Why did you marry": Marc Breault and Martin King, *Inside the Cult* (New York: Signet, 1993), pg. 161.

181 "So, Scott, how does it feel": Ibid., pg. 162.

181 By the end of the meeting: Kenneth R. Samples, Erwin M. de Castro, Richard Abanes, and Robert J. Lyle, *Prophets of the Apocalypse: David Koresh and Other American Messiahs* (Grand Rapids: Baker Books, 1994), pg. 71.

181 The only comfort: Breault and King, *Inside the Cult*, pg. 186.

182 Vernon screamed: Samples et al., *Prophets of the Apocalypse*, pg. 64.

182 "That's God's spaceship": Breault and King, *Inside the Cult*, pg. 186.

182 He became obsessed: Darlene McCormick, "Pair refutes reports of child abuse: Howell followers say young had normal upbringing at Branch Davidian compound," *Waco Tribune-Herald*, June 27, 1993.

183 "Sometimes, I just want to have a nice steak": Grace J. Adams and Poia Alpha, *Hearken, O Daughter: Three Sisters from New Zealand Travel to Waco* (Pennsauken Township: BookBaby, 2018), Kindle location 1041.

183 It went on for weeks: Mark England, "Follower 'integral' in negotiations: One Davidian emerging as sect's spokesman in standoff at Mount Carmel," *Waco Tribune-Herald*, March 8, 1993.

183 Steve went to Marc: Interview with Marc Breault.

184 "Okay, gotta go": Interview with David Bunds.

CHAPTER 27: MARC AGONISTES

185 When they entered the chapel: Marc Breault and Martin King, *Inside the Cult* (New York: Signet, 1993), pg. 22.

186 If a follower didn't strike: Sara Rimer with Sam Howe Verhovek, "Growing Up Under Koresh: Cult Children Tell of Abuses," *New York Times*, May 4, 1993.

186 *We're with Cyrus*: Breault and King, *Inside the Cult*, pg. 179.

190 "to the god of life": Grace J. Adams and Poia Alpha, *Hearken, O Daughter: Three Sisters*

from New Zealand Travel to Waco (Pennsauken Township: BookBaby, 2018), Kindle location 540–55.

CHAPTER 28: THE RIVAL

195 In Australia, Marc: Unless otherwise noted, the material in this chapter is from interviews with Marc Breault and from Marc Breault and Martin King, *Inside the Cult* (New York: Signet, 1993), pp. 226–40.

197 "You say that Vernon": Marc Breault letter to Steve Schneider, June 21, 1990. Private collection.

CHAPTER 29: DOREEN

199 Poia and the others braced: Unless otherwise noted, the material in this chapter is taken from Grace J. Adams and Poia Alpha, *Hearken, O Daughter: Three Sisters from New Zealand Travel to Waco* (Pennsauken Township: BookBaby, 2018), Kindle locations 1067–1200.

201 "If she gives you any trouble": Marc Breault and Martin King, *Inside the Cult* (New York: Signet, 1993), pg. 248.

202 "So you want to fuck me?": Kenneth R. Samples, Erwin M. de Castro, Richard Abanes, and Robert J. Lyle, *Prophets of the Apocalypse: David Koresh and Other American Messiahs* (Grand Rapids: Baker Books, 1994), pg. 73.

CHAPTER 30: JERUSALEM LOST

203 In Australia, more followers: Unless otherwise noted, the material in this section is drawn from interviews with Marc Breault and from Marc Breault and Martin King, *Inside the Cult* (New York: Signet, 1993), pp. 224–40.

207 "The countdown to Armageddon": Marc Breault, "The Psychology and Theology Behind David Koresh and the Branch Davidians," *Marc Breault Ramblings* (blog), April 30, 2018. blogspot.com/2018/04/the-psychology-and-theology-behind.html.

208 He also wanted to eliminate: No author, "Newspaper says Koresh had 'hit list,' Madonna obsession," UPI, June 8, 1993.

CHAPTER 31: WACO

210 The Davidians did over 90 percent: J. J. Robertson, *Beyond the Flames* (San Diego: Pro-Motion Publishing, 1996), pg. 199.

210 When asked why: Interview with David Bunds.

211 "When [William] Travis": Jan Jarboe Russell, "David Koresh and the Myth of the Alamo," *Texas Monthly*, June 1993.

212 War films were David's favorites: Kenneth G. C. Newport, *The Branch Davidians of Waco: The History and Beliefs of an Apocalyptic Sect* (Oxford: Oxford University Press, 2006), pg. 241.

212 "This is what it's going to be like": Marc Breault and Martin King, *Inside the Cult* (New York: Signet, 1993), pg. 184.

212 The Davidians acquired: Brad Bailey and Bob Darden, *Mad Man in Waco* (WRS Publishing, 1993), pg. 156.

212 They installed "hellfire switches": Kenneth R. Samples, Erwin M. de Castro, Richard Abanes, and Robert J. Lyle, *Prophets of the Apocalypse: David Koresh and Other American Messiahs* (Grand Rapids: Baker Books, 1994), pg. 14.

212 They even started a line: Dick J. Reavis, *The Ashes of Waco* (Syracuse: Syracuse University Press, 1998), pg. 27.

213 "Peter jumped the gun": Ibid., pg. 184.

213 "You just brought me": Cathleen Decker and Mike Ward, "Koresh, Bright and Dark," *Los Angeles Times*, March 2, 1993.

CHAPTER 32: THE TRIAL

214 And he knew that Steve: Interview with Marc Breault.

215 In January 1992: Unless otherwise noted, the rest of the chapter is drawn from Marc Breault and Martin King, *Inside the Cult* (New York: Signet, 1993), pp. 1–14.

218 The *Current Affair* piece aired: Martin King, "You're not leaving alive," 9news, Australia, January 31, 2018.

218 "There will be blood": Sue Ann Pressley, "Witnesses Say Waco Warnings Went Unheeded," *Washington Post*, July 22, 1995.

219 followers installed: Mark England, "Cult on alert for assault: Sources, government papers indicate group expected ATF raid," *Waco Tribune-Herald*, April 24, 1993.

219 David wanted him back: Dick J. Reavis, *The Ashes of Waco* (Syracuse: Syracuse University Press, 1998), pg. 184.

219 "I don't know when": "Letter to Mum," July 18, 1992, Texas State University, Texas collection, Mark Swett Collection, Box 1.

219 "Grandma, it's coming": Sam Howe Verhovek, "'Messiah' Fond of Bible, Rock and Women," *New York Times*, March 3, 1993.

219 "Bring your family": Mark England, "Cult on alert for assault: Sources, government papers indicate group expected ATF raid," *Waco Tribune-Herald*, April 24, 1993.

219 In England, the brother-in-law: Mark England, "'No one wants to help': Troubled brother-in-law wants to clear cult member's death," *Waco Tribune-Herald*, January 23, 1994.

220 Other Brits got in touch: Unless otherwise noted, the rest of the material in this chapter is drawn from BBC Radio 5 Podcast, *End Of Days*, 2018, Episodes Three and Four.

222 They would go up to David and say, "When is something going to happen?": Teresa Talerico, "Prophecy came true, cultist says: Defendant's FBI Negotiation tape says Koresh foretold apocalyptic attack; prosecution rests," *Waco Tribune-Herald*, February 16, 1994.

222 They weren't afraid: Reavis, *The Ashes of Waco*, pg. 185.

CHAPTER 33: THE INVESTIGATION

225 Larry Gilbreath was a driver: Emily Wichik, "An Untold Story of Waco," CBS News, December 29, 2017.

226 "The situation with respect to this cult": Marc Breault and Martin King, *Inside the Cult* (New York: Signet, 1993), pp. 290–93.

226 He began by looking: Lee Hancock, "How the 1993 Waco standoff began with a bloody gun battle that federal agents now regret," *Dallas Morning News*, February 25, 2018.

227 In total, Koresh had spent: Brad Bailey and Bob Darden, *Mad Man in Waco* (WRS Publishing, 1993), pg. 153.

227 That included 104 "upper receivers": Dick J. Reavis, *The Ashes of Waco* (Syracuse: Syracuse University Press, 1998), pg. 33.

227 Also on the list: Report of the Department of the Treasury on the Bureau of Alcohol, Tobacco, and Firearms Investigation of Vernon Wayne Howell, also known as David Koresh

(Washington, DC: U.S. Government Printing Office, 1993), to be referred to from here on in as "Treasury Report." Part One, Section One: The Probable Cause Investigation.

227 That November: Ibid.

228 "John Wayne lied": Interview with Bill Buford. The rest of the Buford material in this chapter is taken from this source.

229 Sarabyn didn't have extensive experience: Mark England, "Colonel: Raid based on old information—Delta Force commander in on ATF review says inexperience, system to blame," *Waco Tribune-Herald*, September 19, 1993.

229 And then there was the specter: Charles Hustmyre, "Waco, Ten Years Later: An Agent's Perspective," undated, unpublished manuscript, and Treasury Report: Part One, Section Two: The Decisionmaking Process Leading to Forceful Execution of Warrants.

229 Aguilera told Marc: Interview with Marc Breault.

230 How do I know: Breault and King, *Inside the Cult,* pg. 302.

230 When the time came: Interview with Marc Breault.

231 "They will get their guns": Sue Ann Pressley, "Witnesses Say Waco Warnings Went Unheeded," *Washington Post,* July 22, 1995.

231 One other thing: Treasury Report: Part One, Section Two: The Decisionmaking Process Leading to Forceful Execution of Warrant.

232 With his silver wire-rimmed glasses: Tommy Witherspoon and Mark R. Masferer, "Residents, businessmen say Howell not a recluse," *Waco Tribune-Herald,* March 4, 1993.

232 "Forget I asked": Darlene McCormick, "Agencies rebuffed ATF plan to lure Howell: Bureau unable to arrange meeting outside compound," *Waco Tribune-Herald,* October 3, 1993.

232 Or they could fake: Treasury Report: Part One, Section Two: The Decisionmaking Process Leading to Forceful Execution of Warrants.

232 In case they decided: Robert Bryce, "Waco's Drug Buster," *Austin Chronicle,* June 23, 2000; "The Tragedy at Waco: New Evidence Examined," Congressional report, December 28, 2000; Chuck Hustmyre, "Trojan Horse: Inside the ATF raid at Waco, Texas," undated manuscript. In addition, the 1996 congressional joint report later confirmed that the BATF misled the Defense Department as to the existence of a meth lab at Mount Carmel in order to obtain "non-reimbursable support in a prompt manner."

233 If you wanted your men: Treasury Report: Part One, Section Two: The Decisionmaking Process Leading to Forceful Execution of Warrants.

CHAPTER 34: SURVEILLANCE

234 They also had motorcycles: Ibid.

234 They looked older: Chuck Hustmyre, "ATF in Waco: An Agent's Perspective on Planning," undated manuscript. Courtesy of Chuck Hustmyre.

235 The pit was approximately: Treasury Report: Part One, Section One: The Probable Cause Investigation.

236 The agency was now effectively blind: Mark England, "Investigators blast ATF: Five top brass leave after giving go-ahead to raid gone 'tragically wrong,'" *Waco Tribune-Herald,* October 1, 1993.

237 David visited the town: Mark England, "Colonel: Raid based on old information—Delta Force commander in on ATF review says inexperience, system to blame," *Waco Tribune-Herald,* September 19, 1993.

237 The only person: Mark England, "Agents believed cultists wary at start, log shows," *Waco Tribune-Herald,* June 21, 1994.

237　The worst option: Treasury Report: Part One, Section Two: The Decisionmaking Process Leading to Forceful Execution of Warrants.

237　The planners eventually abandoned: Lee Hancock, "How the 1993 Waco standoff began with a bloody gun battle that federal agents now regret," *Dallas Morning News*, February 25, 2018.

237　On February 17: Chuck Hustmyre, "ATF in Waco: An Agent's Perspective on Planning."

238　"Come on, Robert": FBI negotiation transcript, tape #25, pg. 17.

239　He even talked: Treasury Report: Part One, Section One: The Probable Cause Investigation.

239　The bad guys had been arrested: Treasury Report: Part One, Section Two: The Decisionmaking Process Leading to Forceful Execution of Warrants.

239　the tactical teams didn't: Chuck Hustmyre, "ATF in Waco: An Agent's Perspective on Planning."

240　On February 22: Darlene McCormick, "Agencies rebuffed ATF plan to lure Howell: Bureau unable to arrange meeting outside compound," *Waco Tribune-Herald*, October 3, 1993.

240　The memo arrived: Interview with Michael Langan.

241　Simpson responded: Brad Bailey and Bob Darden, *Mad Man in Waco* (WRS Publishing, 1993), pg. 167; Michael Langan, "The Next Page: Waco, after 25 years," *Pittsburgh Post-Gazette*, March 24, 2018.

241　They gave Higgins: Interview with John Simpson.

242　"People are here for life": Marc England, "Davidians observe Passover," *Waco Tribune-Herald*, April 19, 1992.

242　By early February 1993: J. B. Smith, "Branch Davidian tragedy at 25: How the story overtook the storytellers," *Waco Tribune-Herald*, February 24, 2018.

242　"If the Bible is true": Chuck Lindell and Ward Pamela, "Howell said to have lived double life: Odd mix of kindness, arrogance charmed some, scared others," *Waco Tribune-Herald*, May 2, 1993.

243　The *Trib* scheduled: J. B. Smith, "Branch Davidian tragedy at 25: How the story overtook the storytellers," *Waco Tribune-Herald*, February 24, 2018.

243　"We've got to, Robert": *Inside Waco*, BBC4 documentary. https://www.youtube.com/watch?v=tojTEzyfıyc

244　"It's going to be soon": Teresa Talerico, "Prophecy came true, cultist says: Defendant's FBI Negotiation tape says Koresh foretold apocalyptic attack; prosecution rests," *Waco Tribune-Herald*, February 16, 1994.

244　"When we came downstairs": J. J. Robertson, *Beyond the Flames* (San Diego: ProMotion Publishing, 1996), pg. 9.

CHAPTER 35: HOOD

245　But his partner, Todd McKeehan: Interview with Chuck Hustmyre.

246　Some of the agents wondered: Ibid.

247　Once the entire property: Treasury Report: Part One, Section Two: The Decisionmaking Process Leading to Forceful Execution of Warrants.

248　The technique was designed: Mark Wilson, "How failures during the Waco siege changed everything for the FBI, ATF," *Austin American-Statesman*, April 19, 2018.

248　"We're going to have": Interview with Chuck Hustmyre.

248　A few of the agents: Mark Wilson, "How failures during the Waco siege changed everything for the FBI, ATF," *Austin American-Statesman*, April 19, 2018.

248 But the guys: Dick J. Reavis, *The Ashes of Waco* (Syracuse: Syracuse University Press, 1998), pg. 33.

249 They notified local hospitals: Ibid., pg. 31.

249 When he got back: Interview with Roland Ballesteros.

250 In Fort Hood: Ibid.

CHAPTER 36: THE ELEMENT OF SURPRISE

251 Some Army geek: Interview with Chuck Hustmyre.

252 A supervisor came hustling up: Treasury Report: Part One, Section Four: The Assault on the Compound.

252 He was worried: Ibid.

252 All the agents: Chuck Hustmyre, "ATF in Waco: An Agent's Perspective on Planning," undated manuscript. Courtesy of Chuck Hustmyre.

252 Jones turned back: Treasury Report: Part One, Section Four: The Assault on the Compound.

252 But the agents at the center: Mark England, "Investigators blast ATF: Five top brass leave after giving go-ahead to raid gone 'tragically wrong,'" *Waco Tribune-Herald*, October 1, 1993.

253 "I really have to go": Treasury Report: Part One, Section Four: The Assault on the Compound.

253 "This is it for me": *Inside Waco*, BBC4 documentary.

253 At least one Davidian: J. J. Robertson, *Beyond the Flames* (San Diego: ProMotion Publishing, 1996), pg. 10.

254 "Did you see any weapons?": Lee Hancock, "How the 1993 Waco standoff began with a bloody gun battle that federal agents now regret," *Dallas Morning News*, February 25, 2018; Treasury Report: Part One, Section Four: The Assault on the Compound.

254 "What are you going to do": Lee Hancock, "How the 1993 Waco standoff began with a bloody gun battle that federal agents now regret," *Dallas Morning News*, February 25, 2018.

254 Sarabyn jumped in a car: Treasury Report: Part One, Section Four: The Assault on the Compound.

254 ATF personnel filmed: Dick J. Reavis, *The Ashes of Waco* (Syracuse: Syracuse University Press, 1998), pg. 33.

255 He shouted "Why?": Treasury Report: Part One, Section Four: The Assault on the Compound.

256 Witherspoon walked quickly: J. B. Smith, "Branch Davidian tragedy at 25: How the story overtook the storytellers," *Waco Tribune-Herald*, February 24, 2018.

256 "This doesn't seem right": Pamela Colloff, "The Fire That Time," *Texas Monthly*, April 2008.

256 "covey of quail": Treasury Report: Part Two, Section Four: The Flawed Decision to Go Forward with the Raid.

256 The ATF didn't hear the conversation: Mark England, "Investigators blast ATF: Five top brass leave after giving go-ahead to raid gone 'tragically wrong,'" *Waco Tribune-Herald*, October 1, 1993.

257 A bullet just missed: Brad Bailey and Bob Darden, *Mad Man in Waco* (WRS Publishing, 1993), pg. 168.

257 The pilots turned: Chuck Hustmyre, "Trojan Horse: Inside the ATF raid at Waco, Texas," undated manuscript. Courtesy of Chuck Hustmyre.

257 Their job was to control: Mark England, "Investigators blast ATF: Five top brass leave after giving go-ahead to raid gone 'tragically wrong,'" *Waco Tribune-Herald*, October 1, 1993; Treasury Report: Section Four: The Assault on the Compound.

258 Roland was running: Unless otherwise noted, the material in this chapter relating to Ballesteros's experiences come from an interview with Ballesteros.

258 A bullet hit the Honda: J. B. Smith, "Branch Davidian tragedy at 25: How the story overtook the storytellers," *Waco Tribune-Herald*, February 24, 2018.

259 Someone in the surveillance house: Ibid.

259 "We're going to get blamed": Ibid.

259 We don't have any: Pamela Colloff, "The Fire That Time," *Texas Monthly*, April 2008.

260 "Oh my God": Interview with Chuck Hustmyre.

260 The agent and the kid: Lee Hancock, "How the 1993 Waco standoff began with a bloody gun battle that federal agents now regret," *Dallas Morning News*, February 25, 2018.

260 Darlene McCormick, the co-author: BBC Radio 5 Podcast, *End of Days*, 2018, "Episode Five: Under Siege."

261 He was turning the corner: Chuck Hustmyre, "Trojan Horse: Inside the ATF raid at Waco, Texas."

261 Sprague grabbed Willis: Teresa Talerico, "Death of agent detailed: Witnesses at cult trial describe 'eerie' entry into compound and firefight that followed," *Waco Tribune-Herald*, January 22, 1994.

262 Agent Kevin King was hit: Chuck Hustmyre, "Trojan Horse: Inside the ATF raid at Waco, Texas."

262 "If I'm gonna die": *Inside Waco*, BBC4 documentary.

263 "When I start firing": Agent Keith Constantino interview with Talk 107.3 radio, February 28, 2018.

263 After gathering his wits: Chuck Hustmyre, "Trojan Horse: Inside the ATF raid at Waco, Texas."

263 If he'd had the right gun: Constantino interview with Talk 107.3 radio, February 28, 2018.

265 He slumped to the ground: Chuck Hustmyre, "Trojan Horse: Inside the ATF raid at Waco, Texas."

265 The minute Williams was hit: Pamela Colloff, "The Fire That Time," *Texas Monthly*, April 2008.

265 Before he could get off a shot: Chuck Hustmyre, "Trojan Horse: Inside the ATF raid at Waco, Texas."

265 "It's a war zone": Pamela Colloff, "The Fire That Time," *Texas Monthly*, April 2008.

CHAPTER 37: BYRON

266 "What are you all doing here?": Lee Hancock, "How the 1993 Waco standoff began with a bloody gun battle that federal agents now regret," *Dallas Morning News*, February 25, 2018.

266 "Hunting and grunting": FBI negotiation transcript, tape #159, pg. 53.

266 He jumped back inside: FBI negotiation transcript, tape #137, pg. 41.

267 She'd helped build the compound: Video interview with Kat Schroeder, May 5, 2015, Part 3. www.youtube.com/watch?v=pnl4hgbEdxA

267 Bullets had cut holes: Susan Aschoff, "After the 'war' at Waco," *Tampa Bay Tribune*, February 28, 2000.

267 Her first thought: Pamela Colloff, "The Fire That Time," *Texas Monthly*, April 2008.

267 "He nearly got me": Teresa Talerico, "Davidian recalls pact for suicide: Cult member says Koresh made plans for mass death after raid," *Waco Tribune-Herald*, February 2, 1994.

268 They would keep fighting: Video interview with Kat Schroeder, May 5, 2015, Part 3.

269 "They're breaking more weapons": Mark England, "Lieutenant coaxed cult cease-fire: Officer a key player in talks between Davidians, ATF," *Waco Tribune-Herald*, June 12, 1993.

269 "If they attack us": Ibid.

270 The man never fired: Teresa Talerico, "ATF agent fingers 2nd cult gunman: Defense lawyers argue Branch Davidian never fired his weapon," *Waco Tribune-Herald*, January 27, 1994.

271 "Yeah, this is Lynch": Mark England, "9-1-1 records panic, horror," *Waco Tribune-Herald*, June 10, 1993.

271 The FBI negotiator Byron Sage: Unless otherwise noted, the material on Byron Sage in this chapter and later ones is drawn from multiple interviews with Sage.

272 A decade later: Eric Benson, "The FBI Agent Who Can't Stop Thinking About Waco," *Texas Monthly*, April 2018.

272 One of his supervisors: Interview with Gary Noesner.

273 He said no: Ashley Fantz, "18 years ago, David Koresh called CNN," April 19, 2011. https://news.blogs.cnn.com/2011/04/19/18-years-ago-david-koresh-called-cnn.

CHAPTER 38: AMBULANCES

275 Mulloney shoved his camera: Robert Bryce, "The Wounds of Waco," *Texas Observer*, December 21, 2001.

275 "You son of a bitch!": Pamela Colloff, "The Fire That Time," *Texas Monthly*, April 2008.

275 "I told them!": Ibid.

276 The Dallas-Fort Worth all-news station: No author, "Role of Media Raises Questions in Standoff," *Baltimore Sun*, March 2, 1993.

276 "I am going home": Kenneth G. C. Newport, *The Branch Davidians of Waco: The History and Beliefs of an Apocalyptic Sect* (Oxford: Oxford University Press, 2006), pg. 253.

277 "Two-year-old girl": Tape of KRLD interview, Texas State University, Texas Collection, Box 8, OVZ, Folder 38.

277 "I just want to say": Ibid.

277 "Hello, Momma": Pamela Colloff, "The Fire That Time," *Texas Monthly*, April 2008.

279 One had a wound: Wilson Mark, "How failures during the Waco siege changed everything for the FBI, ATF," *Austin American-Statesman*, April 19, 2018.

279 Lecour was scared: Interview with Lecour, "Nobody Knows Why I'm Here: The Waco Siege," 2018. www.youtube.com/watch?v=jjmosG2YouU.

279 They kept him there: "25 years later: In-depth look at the 51-day siege at Branch Davidian Compound," ABC13 Houston.

280 The children came up: Drew Parma, "Suicide prospect feared from 1st day of standoff," *Waco Tribune-Herald*, April 20, 1993.

280 "I love my rebellious ones": Interview with Kat Schroeder, May 5, 2019, Part 9.

280 He was thinking that: *Inside Waco*, BBC4 documentary.

280 The women sat: Newport, *The Branch Davidians of Waco*, pg. 266.

281 "Everyone wants to go to heaven": Interview with Kat Schroeder, Part 10.

282 She issued them the correct ammunition: Teresa Talerico, "Davidian: Holy war a cult intent—Schroeder says Koresh predicted they would lose," *Waco Tribune-Herald*, February 3, 1994.

282 The youngest was twelve: Teresa Talerico, "Cultist says deaths were 'biblical': Schroeder says she armed children as young as 12 for apocalyptic ending," *Waco Tribune-Herald*, February 4, 1994.

CHAPTER 39: WASHINGTON

285 "If I had done an operation": Michael Decorcy Hinds, "U.S. Pleads with Cult Leader to Let His Followers Go," *New York Times*, March 7, 1993.

286 There was talk: Shannon LaFraniere, "Sessions Assails Charges in Ethics Hearing," *Washington Post*, January 24, 1993.

287 Her pioneering work: Paul Anderson, *Janet Reno: Doing the Right Thing* (New York: John Wiley & Sons, 1994), pg. 114.

287 "They know more": Natalie Russell, "I'm in Poland, and Waco Is Burning," UVA Miller Center website, April 19, 2017; interview with Bernard Nussbaum.

287 The SAC ain't the Lord: Interview with Bill Johnston.

287 They sometimes felt: "The Waco Siege - BPR Interviews: Gary Noesner Part 1 - Brown Political Review."

288 One FBI agent remarked: Interview with Byron Sage.

289 Eventually, fifty-two negotiators: Interview with Byron Sage.

289 He took those: Interview with Gary Noesner.

290 "Just my feelings": FBI negotiation transcript, tape #1, pg. 5.

290 "Come on": Ibid.

291 "By the time": *Turning Point, Waco: The Untold Story*, ABC News special, 1994.

292 "In that cast of thousands": FBI negotiation transcript, tapes #4 and #5, pg. 80.

292 "You all are going to kill us": FBI negotiation transcript, tape #6, pg. 9.

293 "This is the way": FBI negotiation transcript, tape #90, pg. 47.

293 "Jim, I'm going to win": FBI negotiation transcript, tape #6, pg. 5.

294 "He's asking a question": FBI negotiation transcript, tape #68, pg. 29.

295 "God promises to wipe away": FBI negotiation transcript, tape #51, pg. 7.

295 The FBI's Jamar prepared: Special Counsel John C. Danforth, Final Report to the Deputy Attorney General (Washington: U.S. Government Printing Office, 2000), pg. 38. https://commons.wikimedia.org/wiki/File:Danforthreport-final.pdf.

295 Eventually, 668 federal agents: Malcolm Gladwell, "Sacred And Profane," *New Yorker*, March 31, 2014.

296 Ten soldiers: Special Counsel John C. Danforth, Final Report to the Deputy Attorney General Concerning the 1993 Confrontation at the Mt. Carmel Complex, pg. 37.

297 "What are we getting": Interview with Gary Noesner.

298 "Well, as far as I'm concerned": FBI negotiation transcript, tape #22, pg. 7.

CHAPTER 40: IRRECONCILABLE

301 "You are full of shit!": FBI negotiation transcript, tape #84, pg. 35.

301 "No, I do not": FBI negotiation transcript, tape #36, pg. 3.

301 Noesner would then walk: "The Waco Siege—BPR Interviews: Gary Noesner Part 1—Brown Political Review."

302 One issue: Interview with FBI HRT agent Jim McGee.

303 But word hadn't gotten down: Interview with Byron Sage.

303 But the HRT knew: Interview with Jim McGee.

CHAPTER 41: DOUBLE-MINDED

304 "I mean": FBI negotiation transcript, tape #48, pg. 11.

305 "It's against our religion": FBI negotiation transcript, tape #48, pg. 34.

306 "I'd like to have him": FBI negotiation transcript, tape #62, pg. 29.

306 HRT operators: David and Steve protested the alleged mooning several times in the negotiation tapes. The contention is also described in Eric Benson, "The FBI Agent Who Can't Stop Thinking About Waco," *Texas Monthly*, April, 2018.

306 "Let me explain something": FBI negotiation transcript, tape #57, pg. 26.

306 "Bringing these tanks": BBC Radio 5 Podcast, *End of Days*, 2018, "Episode Five: Under Siege."

307 "Let's respect this": FBI negotiation transcript, tape #57, pg. 38.

307 "You and I both know": FBI negotiation transcript, tape #53, pg. 13.

307 "Listen, listen": FBI negotiation transcript, tape #65, pg. 4.

308 "Well, because I believe": FBI negotiation transcript, tape #105, pg. 48.

308 "damn belligerent bullies": FBI negotiation transcript, tape #66, pg. 32.

308 "Every one of them": FBI negotiation transcript, tape #92, pg. 25.

309 "When the Davidians sensed": *Turning Point, Waco: The Untold Story,* ABC News special, 1994.

309 Smerick felt pressure: Lee Hancock, "FBI misled Reno to get tear-gas OK, ex-agent alleged," *Dallas Morning News*, March 6, 2000.

309 "We felt this was an individual": Sam Howe Verhovek, "Death in Waco; F.B.I. Saw the Ego in Koresh, But Not a Willingness to Die," *New York Times*, April 22, 1993.

310 One bureau official told reporters: Ibid.

311 "This plan was based": Dick J. Reavis, *The Ashes of Waco* (Syracuse: Syracuse University Press, 1998), pg. 179.

311 Everybody avoided him: Teresa Talerico, "ATF lied to cover failure, agent says: Superiors said they didn't know they lost the element of surprise," *Waco Tribune-Herald*, January 29, 1994.

311 ATF administrators ordered: Reavis, *The Ashes of Waco*, pg. 179.

311 "John, I want to thank you": Robert Bryce, "Life After Waco," *Austin Chronicle,* June 23, 2000.

312 "tipped off the sect": Case outline, "WFAA-TV, Inc vs. McLemore," June 25, 1998, Texas Court of Appeals.

312 His wife, who worked as a receptionist: J.B. Smith, "Branch Davidian tragedy at 25: How the story overtook the storytellers," *Waco Tribune-Herald*, February 24, 2018.

CHAPTER 42: THE TRILATERAL COMMISSION

313 "It's time": FBI negotiation transcript, tape #76, pp. 10-1.

313 Eventually, the bureau: Lee Hancock, "How the Branch Davidians Set the Fires for a Self-fulfilling Prophecy of their Doomsday," *Dallas Morning News*, April 18, 2018.

314 Maybe light up: FBI negotiation transcript, tape #219, pg. 4.

314 He also seemed to be making sure: Interview with Jim McGee.

314 The FBI recounted the story: "The Tragedy at Waco: New Evidence Examined," Congressional report, December 28, 2000, pg. 881. https://www.congress.gov/106/crpt/hrpt1037/CRPT-106hrpt1037.pdf.

314 The Davidians angrily disputed: "The Waco Siege—BPR Interviews: David Thibodeau Part 1—Brown Political Review."

315 They thought there was a real chance: "The Tragedy at Waco: New Evidence Examined," pg. 871.

315 skills were perishable: Interview with Jim McGee.

316 The same conversation: Interview with Michael Langan.

316 It was the first time: Interview with Byron Sage.

316 Someone came up: Interview with Jim Jamar, "Waco: The Inside Story," *Frontline*, PBS, August 7, 1995.

317 Around this time: Interview with Gary Noesner.

318 "Do you have someone": FBI negotiation transcript, tape #73, pg. 43.

319 "They're all extremely sentimental": FBI negotiation transcript, tape #95, pg. 33.

319 "It's never changed": FBI negotiation transcript, tape #95, pg. 36.

319 "There's got to be some men": FBI negotiation transcript, tape #102, pg. 28.

320 "All of us": FBI negotiation transcript, tape #104, pg. 31.

320 "sixteen or eighteen": FBI negotiation transcript, tape #107, pg. 25.

321 "confirmed his belief": No author, "What Religion Does Alex Jones Follow?" August 5, 2022. https://www.npr.com.ng/what-religion-does-alex-jones-follow-jewish-or-christian-details-about-the-media-personality/.

321 "It was warned": FBI negotiation transcript, tape #153, pg. 35.

321 "You've got this maniac organization": FBI negotiation transcript, tape #159, pg. 39.

322 Oates apparently suggested: David McLemore, "Officials flooded with tips, insights on Koresh, his message," *Dallas Morning News*, March 11, 1993.

322 When the Davidians tried to speak: "The Tragedy at Waco: New Evidence Examined," pg. 599.

322 The FBI proposed flying: Rowland Nethaway, "'Mind control' machine—FBI so desperate it considered using Russian device on Koresh," *Waco Tribune-Herald*, March 4, 1994.

CHAPTER 43: THE HILL

323 Packs of journalists from Chile: Brad Bailey and Bob Darden, *Mad Man in Waco* (WRS Publishing, 1993), pg. 179.

323 Crews from Southwestern Bell: Michael Decorcy Hinds, "U.S. Pleads with Cult Leader to Let His Followers Go," *New York Times*, March 7, 1993.

324 "What is wrong with these people?": Interview with Mark Potok.

324 It did cause some amusement: Bailey and Darden, *Mad Man in Waco*, pg. 211.

324 "There ain't been this much": Paul McKay, "Cult Standoff — Curious Gather on Hill to See, Be Seen," *Houston Chronicle*, March 8, 1993.

325 "That can be checked out": FBI negotiation transcript, tape #117, pg. 12.

325 If he should die: FBI negotiation transcript, tape #182, pg. 30.

326 Jeff H. Terrell, thirty-one: Bailey and Darden, *Mad Man in Waco*, pg. 183.

327 "Hey, if these people: "The Waco Siege—BPR Interviews: David Thibodeau, Part 2— Brown Political Review."

327 "Well, the New World Order": Bailey and Darden, *Mad Man in Waco*, pg. 185.

328 Marian intimidated people: Ibid., pg. 186.

328 "Brother Dave's Guns": Mark England, "Cult, federal officials take Easter vacation: Sightseers take advantage of holiday; hawkers take advantage of sightseers," *Waco Tribune-Herald*, April 12, 1993.

328 "is your church ATF approved?": Photo, Steven Reece, March 1, 1993. Getty Images.

328 One who frequented: "Timothy McVeigh at Waco," *American Experience*, PBS, 2017.

329 "It seems the ATF": Lou Michel and Dan Herbeck, *American Terrorist: Timothy McVeigh and the Oklahoma City Bombing* (Pennsauken Township: BookBaby, 2015), ebook, pg. 223.

329 "I really, really need": Pamela Colloff, "The Fire That Time," *Texas Monthly*, April 2008.

330 Four years before: *Oral Memoirs of Donnie Wayne Adair: A Series of Interviews Conducted by Glenn Jonas and Daniel B. McGee*, August 20, 1993, Religion and Culture Project, Baylor University Institute for Oral History.

330 "Johnston? This is George Roden": Interview with Bill Johnston.

CHAPTER 44: NEBULA

332 "You, you ready for this?": FBI negotiation transcript, tape #112, pg. 14.

333 They called up: "The Waco Siege—BPR Interviews: Gary Noesner Part 1— Brown Political Review."

333 "It's moving through our galaxy": FBI negotiation transcript, tape #112, pg. 25.

334 "Not even close": "The Waco Siege—BPR Interviews: Gary Noesner Part 1—Brown Political Review."

334 Their heart rates: Sara Rimer with Sam Howe Verhovek, "Growing Up Under Koresh: Cult Children Tell of Abuses," *New York Times*, May 4, 1993.

334 They had their first taste: Susan Aschoff, "After the 'war' at Waco," *Tampa Bay Tribune*, February 28, 2000.

334 "A permeating and pervasive fear": Sara Rimer and Sam Howe Verhovek, "Fear Ruled Lives of Cult Children," *Baltimore Sun*, May 4, 1993.

335 Some of the kids: Pamela Colloff, "The Fire That Time," *Texas Monthly*, April 2008.

335 "I'm the new kid": Paul Anderson, *Janet Reno: Doing the Right Thing* (New York: John Wiley & Sons, 1994), pg. 1.

336 "There are two documents": "Waco: The Inside Story," *Frontline*, PBS, transcript, October 17, 1995.

336 "Byron, I liked": Ibid.

337 The men went out: Kenneth G. C. Newport, *The Branch Davidians of Waco: The History and Beliefs of an Apocalyptic Sect* (Oxford: Oxford University Press, 2006), pg. 294.

337 "Oh really?": FBI negotiation transcript, tape #193, pg. 16.

337 "No, well, let me": FBI negotiation transcript, tape #184, pp. 28–29.

337 The FBI was all punk talk: FBI negotiation transcript, tape #193, pp. 24–25.

337 "You're all going to hell": Mark Smith, "Koresh urged disciples to 'kill for God,'" *Houston Chronicle*, February 3, 1994.

337 "He not only understood": Kat Schroeder video, YouTube, Part 11. https://www.youtube .com/watch?v=aQx9MzgNNio.

338 "reckless disregard": Susan Aschoff, "After the 'war' at Waco," *Tampa Bay Tribune*, February 28, 2000.

338 "Don't make me go": FBI negotiation transcript, tape #140, pg. 46.

338 "Of course, the prophets say": FBI negotiation transcript, tape #136, pp. 27.

338 "I guess they take your clothes": FBI negotiation transcript, tape #141, pp. 37–38.

339 "They're on their way?": FBI negotiation transcript, tape #144, pg. 59.

340 "Hey, we're going to sub you": Interview with Gary Noesner.

341 "I don't think anybody else": "The Waco Siege—BPR Interviews: Gary Noesner Part 1— Brown Political Review."

341 His gut told him: Interview with Jim Jamar for "Waco: The Inside Story," *Frontline*, PBS, August 7, 1995.

CHAPTER 45: ACCEPTANCE

342 the compound was getting rancid: Pamela Colloff, "The Fire That Time," *Texas Monthly*, April 2008.

342 Babies cried: Ibid.

342 "If they go Barry Manilow": Sam Howe Verhovek, "Decibels, Not Bullets, Bombard Texas Sect," *New York Times*, March 25, 1993.

343 told agents to pull the chants: "The Tragedy at Waco: New Evidence Examined," pg. 1011.

343 David read the letter: Sara Rimer, "From Hope to Ashes: F.B.I. Negotiator Looks Back," *New York Times*, April 19, 1993.

343 "Again, this is not a threat": FBI negotiation transcript, tape #162, pg. 4.

344 "I really am not anymore": FBI negotiation transcript, tape #162, pg. 16.

344 "A lot of people here": FBI negotiation transcript, tape #162, pg. 32.

344 "I know it": FBI negotiation transcript, tape #162, pg. 39.

344 He and Judy: FBI negotiation transcript, tape #175, pg. 27.

344 "All of a sudden": FBI negotiation transcript, tape #186, pg. 36.

344 "Tell me honestly": FBI negotiation transcript, tape #214, pp. 31–32.

345 He had wrinkles: FBI negotiation transcript, tape #174, pg. 10.

345 "I'm looking forward": FBI negotiation transcript, tape #173, pg. 53.

345 "We don't have much time": Kenneth R. Samples, Erwin M. de Castro, Richard Abanes, and Robert J. Lyle, *Prophets of the Apocalypse: David Koresh and Other American Messiahs* (Grand Rapids: Baker Books, 1994), pg. 181.

345 Put a match: FBI negotiation transcript, tape #175, pg. 52.

345 "Sometime when you have a chance": Ibid., pg. 55.

346 But Jamar stuck by his guns: Interview with Jim Jamar for "Waco: The Inside Story," *Frontline*, PBS, August 7, 1995.

346 On March 27: Interview with Byron Sage.

347 "You don't know": FBI negotiation transcript, tape #205, pg. 17.

347 "Yeah, my babies": FBI negotiation transcript, tape #184, pg. 23.

347 "Half the time": FBI negotiation transcript, tape #tape 212, pg. 3.

348 "Well, some people": FBI negotiation transcript, tape #217 pg. 36.

348 Even the tactical guys: FBI negotiation transcript, tape #239, pg. 25.

349 The figure of two hundred million: Marc Breault, "The Psychology and Theology Behind David Koresh and the Branch Davidians," *Marc Breault Ramblings* (blog), April 30, 2018. blogspot.com/2018/04/the-psychology-and-theology-behind.html.

349 "He has to figure": Mark England, "Crisis Point at Passover," *Waco Tribune-Herald*, April 4, 1993.

349 "The thing about the Lake Waco area": FBI negotiation transcript, tape #203, pg. 7.

349 City officials ordered: Darlene McCormick, "FBI will let lawyer have 1 last talk: Today's conversation with cult leader could be final allowed until standoff," *Waco Tribune-Herald*, April 14, 1993.

350 "Vernon used to teach": Tommy Witherspoon, "'Yahweh' contacts Howell: Letter allegedly written by God and delivered to Davidians called a sign by some, a decoy by others," *Waco Tribune-Herald*, April 11, 1993.

350 "He's trying to tell": Mark England, "2nd letter promises no peace: Messages warns FBI not to harm Howell, 'God's lamb,'" *Waco Tribune-Herald*, April 13, 1993.

350 "all the hallmarks": "The Tragedy at Waco: New Evidence Examined," pg. 380.

351 "Koresh is probably": Ibid., pg. 403.

CHAPTER 46: THE MANUSCRIPT

352 The negotiator said that Hillary: FBI negotiation transcript, tape #213, pg. 39.

353 Concertina wire: "The Tragedy at Waco: New Evidence Examined," pg. 18.

353 "We can't grade your paper": Chris Plante, "Army reportedly declined to review FBI approach to Waco siege," CNN News, August 31, 1999.

353 One of the participants: "The Tragedy at Waco: New Evidence Examined," pg. 988.

353 Around this time: Natalie Russell, "I'm in Poland, and Waco Is Burning," UVA Miller Center website, April 19, 2017; interview with Bernard Nussbaum.

354 "I'll be in custody": "Witness to Waco," MSNBC documentary, 2009. https://www.you tube.com/watch?v=gLKPNvyrM30.

354 "They're going to say": "The Branch Davidians—David Koresh," *Cults,* Stitcher podcast, Part 5.

354 "When it comes": FBI negotiation transcript, tape #233, pg. 10.

355 Jamar and the others: "Revelations of Waco: The Legacy of Waco," *Waco,* directed by Dwight Fisher, February 28, 2018, Paramount Network.

355 "Wait a minute": "The Tragedy at Waco: New Evidence Examined," pg. 990.

355 Hubbell recalled: Ibid., pg. 1027.

356 If supplies ran short: Ibid., pg. 873.

357 "I can't say": Ibid., pp. 39, 71.

357 Clinton's account of the conversation: Clinton's version of the story is contained in Bill Clinton, *My Life* (New York: Knopf, 2004), pg. 498.

358 "It is your decision": "The Tragedy at Waco: New Evidence Examined," pg. 995.

358 "Hello Dick": J. J. Robertson, *Beyond the Flames* (San Diego: ProMotion Publishing, 1996), pg. 269.

359 "If you look": FBI negotiation transcript, tape #242, pg. 12.

359 "The Constitution has been so ripped apart": Ibid., tape #242, pg. 16.

CHAPTER 47: LETTERS

360 Journalists tracked down Sandy: Unless otherwise noted, material in this section comes from multiple interviews with Sandy.

362 More letters from the public: FBI Records: The Vault—Waco Main File Part 01 of 10, March 7. https://vault.fbi.gov/waco-branch-davidian-compound.

363 One of the Davidians: Pamela Colloff, "The Fire That Time," *Texas Monthly,* April 2008.

CHAPTER 48: GAS

365 "Steve? This is Byron Sage": FBI negotiation transcript, tape #245, pg. 3.

365 the Davidians snapped awake: Pamela Colloff, "The Fire That Time," *Texas Monthly,* April 2008.

366 "These fucking idiots": FBI negotiation transcript, tape #245, pg. 7.

367 they spotted followers: Interview with Jim McGee.

367 A lot of gas: Ibid.

367 Rogers radioed his okay: "The Tragedy at Waco: New Evidence Examined," pg. 5.

367 three pyrotechnic rounds: Special Counsel John C. Danforth, Final Report to the Deputy Attorney General (Washington: U.S. Government Printing Office, 2000), pp. 29–30.

368 It had missed Byron: Pamela Colloff, "The Fire That Time," *Texas Monthly,* April 2008.

368 "Holy shit": "The Tragedy at Waco: New Evidence Examined," pg. 899.

368 Inside, Clive Doyle: "The Branch Davidians: In Their Own Words," Uncontrolled Video, 2016. www.youtube.com/watch?v=UqhnMoKfrHg.

369 At around 10:30 a.m.: Paul Anderson, *Janet Reno: Doing the Right Thing* (New York: John Wiley & Sons, 1994), pg. 193.

370 "I want a fire on the front": This excerpt and the ones to follow are drawn from various sources: Lee Hancock, "How the Branch Davidians Set the Fires for a Self-fulfilling Prophecy of their Doomsday," *Dallas Morning News*, April 18, 2018; Teresa Talerico, "Recordings May Reveal Fire's Origins," *Waco Tribune-Herald*, February 15, 1994; "The Tragedy at Waco: New Evidence Examined," pg. 1532.

370 Graeme Craddock saw: "Admissions of Branch Davidians," Interim Report to the Deputy Attorney General, July 21, 2000, pg. 8. https://www.hsdl.org/?view&did=731749.

370 The operative thought the man: Ibid., pg. 123.

371 "It's going to go up": Interview with Jim McGee.

371 A local man: J. J. Robertson, *Beyond the Flames* (San Diego: ProMotion Publishing, 1996), pg. 310.

371 Flashes of fire: "Turning Point, Waco: The Untold Story," ABC News special, 1994.

372 "Who are you?": Interview with Jim McGee.

372 "Steve, David, we're attempting": FBI negotiation transcript, tape #245, pp. 10–11.

373 Byron turned his back: Interview with Byron Sage.

373 "You will not be harmed": FBI negotiation transcript, tape #247, pg. 10.

373 "Oh, my God": "The Tragedy at Waco: New Evidence Examined," pg. 875.

373 About ten others: "The Branch Davidians: In their Own Words," Uncontrolled Video, 2016. https://www.youtube.com/watch?v=UqhnMoKfrHg.

374 There were no gas masks: Muriel Pearson, "Survivors of 1993 Waco siege describe what happened in fire that ended the 51-day standoff," ABC News, January 3, 2018. https://www.youtube.com/watch?v=9LB6nvIqX2g

374 Heat began pressing: "The Branch Davidians: In Their Own Words," Uncontrolled Video, 2016. www.youtube.com/watch?v=UqhnMoKfrHg.

374 He turned around: "The Tragedy at Waco: New Evidence Examined," pg. 660.

375 When he looked back: Katy Forrester, "Waco survivor says Netflix show finally exposes the FBI's 'horrifying crimes' and the real story is more disturbing," *Irish Sun*, May 29, 2020.

375 Doyle staggered forward: "Revelations of Waco: The Legacy of Waco," *Waco*, directed by Dwight Fisher, February 28, 2018, Paramount Network.

375 "David, don't do this": FBI negotiation transcript, tape #247, pg. 11.

375 Ten minutes after: Drew Parma, "Bunker last refuge for most in cult: Last remnant of compound has yielded more than half of bodies found," *Waco Tribune-Herald*, April 30, 1993.

375 Byron stopped talking: Eric Benson, "The FBI Agent Who Can't Stop Thinking About Waco," *Texas Monthly*, April 2018.

375 A T-intersection: Interview with Bill Johnston.

376 At one point: Pamela Colloff, "A Mother's Words," *Texas Monthly*, February 2009.

376 "Please, let David be gone: "Witness to Waco," MSNBC Documentary, 2009. https://www.youtube.com/watch?v=gLKPNvyrM3o.

376 Kat Schroeder, watching: Jeff Truesdell, "Waco Survivors Still Believe Cult's Teachings 25 Years After Siege," *People*, January 24, 2018.

376 "He's been done shitty": Darcey Steinke, "The Waco Siege," *Spin*, July 1993.

376 "Let's go to the studio": BBC Radio 5 Podcast, *End of Days*, 2018, "Episode Six: Blind Faith."

377 Gail Monbelly, whose sister: Ibid.

377 Sandy was still hiding: Interview with Sandy.

377 Bernard Nussbaum: Natalie Russell, "I'm in Poland, and Waco Is Burning," UVA Miller Center website, April 19, 2017; interview with Bernard Nussbaum.

378 "What is this?": Lou Michel and Dan Herbeck, *American Terrorist: Timothy McVeigh and the Oklahoma City Bombing* (Pennsauken Township: BookBaby, 2015), pg. 247.

379 To reach the bunker: Interim Report to the Deputy Attorney General, July 21, 2000, pg. 126.

379 Byron understood immediately: Eric Benson, "The FBI Agent Who Can't Stop Thinking About Waco," *Texas Monthly*, April 2018.

379 Throughout the day: Brad Bailey and Bob Darden, *Mad Man in Waco* (WRS Publishing, 1993), pg. 1.

380 She, pointedly: Paul Anderson, *Janet Reno: Doing the Right Thing* (New York: John Wiley & Sons, 1994), pg. 194.

381 "Reno was being praised": Bill Clinton, *My Life* (New York: Knopf, 2004), pg. 499.

381 Late that evening: Anderson, *Janet Reno*, pg. 196.

381 The phone rang again: Ibid., pg. 198.

381 After leaving the compound: Interview with Byron Sage.

CHAPTER 49: BODIES

382 "YOU HAVE BROUGHT": FBI Records: The Vault—Waco Main File Part 01. https://vault.fbi.gov.

382 "The Bureau's efforts": "The Tragedy at Waco: New Evidence Examined," pg. 575.

383 Publicly, she continued: Michael Isikoff and Thomas Pierre, "Reno says decision fully hers," *Waco Tribune-Herald*, April 20, 1993.

383 Most of the others: Interim Report to the Deputy Attorney General, July 21, 2000, pg. 132.

383 David Koresh had been shot: Darlene McCormick, "The Price of Loyalty," *Waco Tribune-Herald*, May 12, 1993.

384 David was found: Eric Benson, "The FBI Agent Who Can't Stop Thinking About Waco," *Texas Monthly*, April 2018.

384 One family huddled together: *Turning Point, Waco: The Untold Story*, ABC News special, 1994.

384 On the second floor: Ibid.

384 Among the debris: Darlene McCormick, "Remains show cult's dual life: Officials find evidence of group's aggressive and peaceful nature," *Waco Tribune-Herald*, May 30, 1993.

385 Even more mysterious: Mark England, "'No one wants to help': Troubled brother-in-law wants to clear cult member's death," *Waco Tribune-Herald*, January 23, 1994.

385 "There's no way": No author, "Waco Inferno Remembered By Davidians," *New York Times*, April 18, 1994.

385 "I think he'll show up": Sam Howe Verhovek, "Investigators Puzzle Over Last Moments of a Cult," *New York Times*, May 5, 1993.

386 "I have my faith": Pamela Colloff, "The Fire That Time," *Texas Monthly*, April 2008.

386 "This is going to be": Mark England, "Decimated compound draws crowds anyway: 'This is going to be like Graceland,' shirt merchant says," *Waco Tribune-Herald*, July 6, 1993.

386 "Yeah. No problems": Interview with Jim McGee.

387 Arson dogs were brought in: Interim Report to the Deputy Attorney General, July 21, 2000.

387 Seven of the nine survivors: "Revelations of Waco: The Legacy of Waco," *Waco*, directed by Dwight Fisher, February 28, 2018, Paramount Network.

387 The body of one: Interim Report to the Deputy Attorney General, Medical Analysis, July 21, 2000, pp. 10-11.

388 Corderman pointed out: "The Tragedy at Waco: New Evidence Examined," Congressional report, December 28, 2000, pg. 13.

388 One agent, Charles Riley: Jonathan Weisman, "Doubts raised on Waco cover-up; Documents found in House files refer to military tear gas," *Baltimore Sun*, September 14, 1999.

389 the flashes found: "The Tragedy at Waco: New Evidence Examined," pg. 21.

390 "almost all the agents": Gordon Mclean, "The Noisy Echoes of Waco," *Vice*, April 20, 2013.

390 "Yeah, I mean": Interview with Chuck Hustmyre.

390 ATF KILLS FAMILIES: "Revelations of Waco: The Legacy of Waco," *Waco*, directed by Dwight Fisher.

390 "Waco can happen": Tara Isabella Burton, "The Waco tragedy, explained," *Vox*, April 19, 2018.

391 "Waco started this war": Clyde Haberman, "Memories of Waco Siege Continue to Fuel Far-Right Groups," *New York Times*, July 20, 2015.

392 The journalist Mark Potok: Interview with Mark Potok.

392 "I hope you get": Interview with Byron Sage.

CHAPTER 50: SPECTERS

394 After the fire: Unless otherwise noted, the material in this section comes from multiple interviews with Sandy.

394 Once, someone sent her: Charles Saul and Kathy Fair, "David Koresh 'was a prophet,'" *Houston Chronicle*, June 27, 1993, Page 1.

395 "You know the war": Susan Aschoff, "After the 'war' at Waco," *Tampa Bay Tribune*, February 28, 2000.

395 "Sinful Messiah" series was named: J. B. Smith, "Branch Davidian tragedy at 25: How the story overtook the storytellers," *Waco Tribune-Herald*, February 24, 2018.

395 "I think he felt": Ibid.

395 One law enforcement official: Robert Bryce, "The Wounds of Waco," *Texas Observer*, December 21, 2001.

395 He eventually took a job: Ibid.

395 "Well, that's me": Robert Bryce, "Life After Waco," *Austin Chronicle*, June 23, 2000.

396 "We'd lost so much": Lee Hancock, "How the 1993 Waco standoff began with a bloody gun battle that federal agents now regret," *Dallas Morning News*, February 25, 2018.

396 "Don't talk about Waco": Spencer Wilking, "ATF agents at fatal 1993 Waco raid describe being under barrage of gunfire," ABC News, January 5, 2018.

397 Years after the fire: Interview with Marc Breault.

EPILOGUE

399 "the tender mercies": Michael Barkun, "Appropriated Martyrs: The Branch Davidians and the Radical Right," *Terrorism and Political Violence* 19, no. 1 (2007): 117–42.

399 David Koresh had been foretold: Ibid.

400 "Waco became a door": Ibid.

INDEX

Martin, Sheila
  aftermath, 386
  ATF raid, 257–58, 267, 280
Martin, Wayne, 158, 162
  ATF raid, 257, 266–70
  conspiracy theories, 320–21
  the siege and negotiations, 336–37
  tear gas attack and death, 373–74,
    386
  Vernon's sexual abuse, 126
Masada siege, 326
masturbation, 47–48
Meet the Press (TV show), 311
Merkabahs, 104–5
methamphetamine, 143, 155, 159–60,
    233
Methodist's Children's Home, 324
Mevis, David, 386
"Miami Method," 287
Mighty Men, 217–18
  guard duty, 160–61
  raid on Mount Carmel, 145–49, 154
militia movement, 399–401
milk, 306, 313
Miller, William, 10, 23, 70
Mills Peninsula Hospital, 202
Miron, Murray S., 309, 350
"mirror person," 181–82
Monbelly, Bernadette, 168, 220, 377
Monbelly, Gail, 168, 220, 377
Montkemp, Josh, 324
Moral Majority, 122
Mormons, 10, 109
Morrison, Melissa, 294–95
Mount Carmel
  ATF raid of February 28. *See* ATF
    raid of February 28
  banishments, 165, 180–81, 185
  children of. *See* children of Mount
    Carmel
  construction of new chapel,
    210–12
  diet and food. *See* dietary rules at
    Mount Carmel

escapes, 219–22
  of Marc, 186–90, 195
fears of followers, 162, 164–65
finances and money, 112, 113,
    158–59
flag of, 211
founding of, 69–70
guard duty, 160–61, 165
guns at. *See* guns at Mount Carmel
male followers and, 180–84
receivership of, 71
Rodens and New Mount Carmel,
    71–73
schism between Lois and Vernon,
    94–107, 124–25
siege at. *See* siege at Mount Carmel
Vernon' raid on, 145–49, 150–51
Vernon's arrival at, 74–85
Vernon's return to, 158–62
Mount Zion, 104–5, 207
MREs (meals ready to eat), 212, 229,
    237, 342, 354
Mulloney, Dan, 260, 275–76, 395
Myers, Dee, 373

Nahum, 300–301, 308
nebula, 332–34
Newbold College, 166–67
"New Light" revelations, 62, 180–84,
    186, 197, 207, 343
New Mount Carmel, 71–73
Nichols, Terry, 391
Nightline (TV show), 297, 312, 381
Nightstalkers, 295, 388
Noah and the Ark, 338
Noble, Ron, 240–41
Noesner, Gary
  negotiations, 289–90, 296–97,
    299–303, 339–41
  power cut-offs, 316, 317
Noriega, Manuel, 342
Nuestra Familia, 272
Nugent, Ted, 314
Nussbaum, Bernard, 287, 353–54, 377